The
BAROMETER
HANDBOOK

A Modern Look
at
Barometers and Applications
of
Barometric Pressure

By

David Burch

ISBN 9780914025733

Published by
Starpath Publications
3050 NW 63rd Street, Seattle, WA 98107
Manufactured in the United States of America
www.starpathpublications.com

Cover design and illustrations by Tobias Burch.

Cover Photo credits:
The mercury barometer is traditional FitzRoy Barometer in oak frame manufactured by Mason of Dublin in about 1880. Photo compliments of Patrick Marney (www.partick-marney.co.uk).

The 5-inch antique aneroid barometer was made by Short & Mason of London, and retailed by W. Senter & Co of Portland, Maine in about 1900. Photo compliments of John Forster (www.barometerfair.com).

The electronic barometer shown is a 2009 prototype for a new model II of the JDB-1 barometer from Conex Electro-Systems in Bellingham WA.

The background image is a seasonal pressure pattern reproduced from the *U.S. Navy Marine Climatic Atlas of the World*. The full pressure data from this publication are included in Chapter 10.

$\star\; \star\; \star\; \star\; \star$
STARPATH.

Preface

Since the first public appearance of barometers some three hundred years ago, the barometer has traveled through history along two separate, parallel paths.

There has been the lineage of instrument makers and engineering scientists who focus on how barometers work, how to make and repair them, how to calibrate them, and how to tell a good one from not so good; and along the other path is the lineage of barometer users whose focus is on the meaning of atmospheric pressure and how to use that information to analyze and forecast the weather.

More often than not, neither group has had a compelling interest in the activities of the other group. Those who know about the instruments care most about the instruments. They have confidence their instruments will be used well and properly if they make a good one, without a particular interest in what that use will be.

Barometer users, on the other hand, do not often care about the ingenuity or craftsmanship that might distinguish one instrument from another. They have confidence that the makers will provide quality instruments so they can do their job of weather analysis. Often they do not question the accuracy of the instrument, or even realize that this is a question that might be asked.

That is not to imply anything is wrong—at least so far. We have today phenomenally accurate barometers in science labs and weather stations on the one path, and on the other path our knowledge of the global atmosphere—which is ultimately dependent upon individual barometer measurements around the world—has also improved phenomenally, considering the immense complexity of the science.

Science labs and professional meteorology are well in tune barometrically, but the broader field of barometer users have not kept up as well. And there are changes on the near horizon that will be best met if we know as much as possible about the more common types of barometers now in use. In short, there is some virtue now in bringing these two paths closer together, which is one of the main goals of this book.

To give an important example, you will hear it said that the reason the typical mariner is not using a barometer so much these days is because they have so many wonderful new weather resources at their finger tips. With a satellite phone and a PC you can be in any ocean in the world and with the push of a button have all the winds and pressures immediately plotted out in front of you. Push another button and you see what they will look like tomorrow, and the next day, and so on.

This very convenient type of data, presented in what is called the GRIB format, are direct outputs from the super computers of the weather services. It is part of the data mentioned above that is getting better all the time. But it is not fully dependable yet. These are *not* the official forecasts. In fact, this type of computerized forecast has not been vetted at all by a professional meteorologist. Nevertheless, the use of this data grows very rapidly every year.

The idea that having that type of data means you do not need to use your barometer is as wrong as possible. It is one of the strongest reasons to use your barometer. With an accurate barometer, you have a way to test the weather map. Once you have tested the maps, then indeed these are wonderful new ways to do weather work at sea, or on land.

A key point in this comparison is having an accurate barometer. This is another new concept to mariners and others as well. Throughout maritime history, mariners relied almost exclusively on pressure trends: up or down, fast or slow. They did not concern themselves with the actual value of the pressure. This has been the teaching since the earliest days. Now we have a new reason to know accurate pressures, and to that end this book covers the process of barometer calibration using natural pressures, which we have access to through online resources. This Internet procedure itself was not possible five years ago, so there is much new to modern barometer usage. There are of course other ways to calibrate without the use of the Internet.

Once we know accurate pressure from our barometer, there are other applications, one of which is the forecasting of tropical storms using deviations from the known mean pressures. To facilitate that procedure and for other applications, we reproduce in Chapter 10 the monthly mean sea level pressures and their standard deviations worldwide. The more you use your barometer, the more interesting this data becomes, as does its applications.

Besides all of that, the crucial role of a barometer in weather forecasting has not diminished, but it is slipping out of the textbooks way before its time, and we hope, here, to belay that trend as best we can.

Finally, an important new development in the past ten years or so is the advent of inexpensive electronic barometers. These can be very accurate and easy to use, but like all others, they must be tested. It is another goal of this book to introduce these new devices to those who have not used them before, and to present ways to evaluate them.

As the book proceeds, we inevitably end up addressing the two most common issues that barometer repair departments ever receive: (1) My barometer does not read the same as the weather reports, and (2) My barometer does not change.

The typical short answers are: (1) Weather reports are for sea level, but your barometer is at a higher elevation, and (2) Watch more carefully, the changes are small and slow. But these answers do not really convey much information. If we want more productive use of our barometers, we need more in-depth answers to these questions—from each of the two paths mentioned earlier.

Examples and weather maps are from
the Northern Hemisphere,
unless
otherwise noted.

Acknowledgements

Of the several book projects I have worked on over the years, none has been more rewarding and filled with discoveries than this one. Helping me along this venture were a number of people who care about this science and were kind enough to share their knowledge, expert opinions, and insights with me.

There are quite a few who deserve specific mention, but I must start with Merrill Kennedy, "The Barometer Man" (www.barometerman.com), who has earned that title through 38 years of study and experience as repairman, restorer, and calibrator of high-quality aneroids. We have spent countless hours discussing these instruments, and with each talk I learned more. This would have been a much more difficult task, if doable at all, without his help. So I will say again, what I have said many times before. Thank you Merrill.

My full list is long, but each person here has made a significant contribution to this book and I am very grateful to each of you. Early conversations with Robert Luke, Program Manager of the NWS Voluntary Observing Ship program, were influential on my decision to take up this project, and his specific reminder to heed the importance of temperature in barometry was confirmed at each step of the work. Several subsequent discussions with Pat Brandow, Port Meteorological Officer for the Pacific Northwest area, were always enlightening, and gave me invaluable insights into the practical use of barometers in ship reports. He also confirmed our in-house barometer calibrations.

Vacuum technology expert Steve Hansen of DiverseArts, LLC, designed and built our excellent barometer test chamber. We had many long discussions on this technology and applications of precision microbarographs. David Hale of Airflo Instruments, manufacturer of precision aneroids, provided unique insights into barometer production and gave several useful comments on the book. Dr. Jay Hendricks of the National Institute of Standards and Technology provided valuable comments on a related section of the text, which were much appreciated. I am also grateful to Roger F. Allen, President of Alti-2 Inc., who informed me, from a first-hand account, of the history and practical application of altimeters in skydiving.

George Huxtable, FRIN, provided information about Hooke's unique first marine barometer directly from an original in the Oxford Museum of the History of Science. He also figured out how it worked, which was not obvious from other accounts. Navigation historian Bruce Stark shared his insights and resources on the history of marine weather, just as he has done so often on the history of navigation. It is a pleasure to thank both of these gentlemen for the education and support they have given me over many years, on many aspects of navigation science.

Graham Bartlett and Steve Jebson, Library Information Managers at the U.K. MetOffice, very kindly and efficiently provided several unique documents and datasets, and answered other questions as well. Their hospitality was exceptional. Nearer home, Elizabeth Walsh and her associates at the Magazine and Newspaper Desk and Interlibrary Loan program of the Seattle Public Library did an absolutely wonderful job of tracking down and providing dozens of rare papers and books over the past year. The Internet has revolutionized how we can research a topic, but it is still a distant competitor to educated and dedicated librarians and the resources a good library has available.

Discussions with international airline Captain (and sailor) Jay Towne on all matters of aviation were always useful and always enjoyable. Dr. Kenneth Mukamal, MD of Harvard University kindly reviewed the presentation of his research on headaches and barometric pressure and offered several useful suggestions. Dr. Richard Langley, Geodesy Department, University of New Brunswick, shared his insights on several matters relating to GPS and the elusive concept of sea level.

Regina Moore at NWS's National Data Buoy Center explained barometer procedures and instruments used in their measurements and also provided a copy of Gerald Gill's classic research paper on his original design of the Gill pressure port. Laura Cook at NWS's Office of Climate, Water, and Weather Services kindly provided information about the reduction to sea level process used in the ASOS program. And a special thanks to Christopher Hampel, Calibration Scientist in Barometry at Environment Canada for several discussions of the Plateau Correction as used in Canada, and for his review of the related section in this book. And thanks to Bob McDavitt ("The Weather Ambassador") of the New Zealand MetService for providing special NZ station data for our barometer calibration service and for giving us permission to reproduce his Southern Hemisphere barometer rules, and for his checking the Northern Hemisphere ones we presented here.

John Lewis read the entire manuscript and offered valuable suggestions at several points. His job was made much easier by the preceding detailed review by Larry Brandt, friend and Starpath instructor. Larry went though each section of the book, found most of our errors, and offered many good suggestions for improvements—not just in matters of expression, but also in content as well in some cases. Thank you Larry. Your work remains very much appreciated.

Toby Burch produced the illustrations for the book and did the cover design and page layout. There is not a single drawing in the book that he has not conceptually improved in the process of creating it. I am very fortunate to have his collaboration on this project and on others.

Table of Contents

He who watches his barometer, watches his ship. *

* This saying appears to have originated with Henry Piddington in one of his books on Indian Ocean storms from the 1840s, probably *The Horn-Book of Storms for the Indian and China Seas*, 1844. He is thus credited with it by Jane Taylor in her *Hand-Book to the Local Marine Board Examination* of 1853. By 1865, this saying is referred to as a "maxim" without authorship in *Chambers's Journal of Popular Literature, Science, and Art*. In 1881 it was used by S. T. S. Lecky in the first edition of his famous *Wrinkles in Practical Navigation* (also without reference to its origin), which continued in print as a standard reference until its final (23rd) edition in 1956.

A barometer is an instrument designed specifically to measure atmospheric pressure, but this one measurement has diverse applications. So diverse, in fact, that the name of this instrument has come to mean a way to measure anything. It was recently explained to seventy million TV viewers in the first sentence of a U.S. vice presidential debate that the "barometer of the economy" is a soccer mom. But despite exposure to such figures of speech, it is the very image of the instrument as dependable and durable over several hundred years that has led to this etymology.

1.1 Overview

The main goal of this book is to explain what a barometer is and how we might use one to our best advantage in several applications. It is not intended as just a description of the instruments and an outline of their history, which we do only briefly, but more of a working manual on the "nuts and bolts" of practical applications, with an emphasis on the latest technology of both the devices and their applications.

The application we consider in most detail is the use of a barometer for the analysis and forecast of weather, using specific examples from marine weather. Pilots, farmers, fire fighters, sportsmen, and many other landsmen count on knowledge of the weather, but the mariner isolated on a ship at sea, a thousand miles from land, has as close a tie as possible to the barometer and the insights it can offer on prospective weather. This has been true since its very inception and remains true today, as reflected in the history of the instrument and its applications.

The barometer is nearly as venerable an instrument as is the mariner's compass, and coincidentally pioneering research on both instruments was carried out on the same, first-ever, worldwide voyage dedicated to scientific study. Capt Edmond Halley in 1696 to 1698 sailed throughout the North and South At-

lantic mapping the earth's magnetic variation as well as recording daily barometric pressures, which he correlated with observed weather patterns. Both sets of data were keystone steps to the productive use of each instrument.

Throughout the three-hundred-year history of the barometer, there have been numerous well-circulated reference texts that appeared with each new stage of its development. The modern bible from a practical point of view is the *Manual of Barometry*, from the U.S. Weather Bureau in 1963. From a mariner's perspective, the most famous is the *Barometer Manual* published in 1866 by Robert FitzRoy, known as the father of marine weather. He invented the concept (and the name) of a "weather forecast," and was a champion of the use of barometers on both land and sea. He was also the sea captain of the *Beagle* who took Darwin around the world on his great voyage of discovery (1831 to 1836) that served as the foundation of his theory of evolution. FitzRoy was later appointed head of the newly established Bureau of Meteorology, which evolved into the modern British Met Office, counterpart of the U.S. National Weather Service. A severe storm during the Darwin voyage that nearly sank the *Beagle* was later recalled by FitzRoy as one he might have avoided had he paid more attention to his barometer—an incident that certainly contributed to his conversion to the cause and lifelong devotion to its promotion.

Another goal of this book is to "introduce" the modern electronic barometer to new users and to those who have used more traditional designs for many years. This transition is actually a big step, especially for maritime applications. It is suggesting a transition from instruments that have been used and tested for 100 years to a completely new style that has been on the market for only a dozen or so years, with effectively no discussions of their properties or function in the popular literature. Furthermore, traditional aneroid barometers in use for the past 150 years or so are easily identified at first sight as scientific instruments, not to mention that the appearance of these devices has not even changed during this period. (Can we think of any other instrument, of any kind, that has not changed appearance in 150 years?) Many aneroid barometers even have open front panels to expose the inside workings of the instrument. On the other hand, many of the new electronic barometers look more like a gadget than a scientific instrument. And the fact that we are surrounded in our daily lives by essentially disposable electronic clocks and calculators and cell phones, does not help build the image of another electronic device, made quite possibly in the same factories where these other devices are made.

So the task at hand is to try to help establish guidelines for evaluating these new instruments—and the older styles as well—so that prudent users can separate out what are in fact instruments from what are more like gadgets. The electronic devices, just like the traditional aneroid devices, are not all the same, but very rarely can you tell this difference by just looking at them. The fact that a traditional aneroid device might look quite venerable is no guarantee of its quality.

No matter what your application is, be it predicting the wind and weather, or fixing the elevation of your hike across a mountain, or tuning the fuel injectors of a race car on the starting line, all applications are better served by an understanding of how the instrument works, and most important, how you can test that it is working properly.

1.2 What is a Barometer?

By the early1700's, barometers were known to most educated people as instruments that measure something related to the weather—and perhaps, in some individuals, to some level of well being. It was also discovered very early on that they have great utility in determining the elevation of terrain, and thus they became as much a practical tool for explorers wishing to document their finds as to seamen and landsmen wishing to anticipate the weather. This level of public understanding of these devices remains pretty much the same today, three hundred years later.

The instruments themselves, on the other hand, have evolved through three completely different designs during this period: mercury, aneroid, and electronic. It started with the simple design of an inverted glass tube filled with mercury, invented in 1643 by Torricelli, an associate of Galileo. This concept quickly found its way across Europe and into England, and by 1700 became standardized to the point they could be readily manufactured. Thus they moved out of "science labs" and into private homes, public buildings, and ships of the sea. Designs for maritime use continued to improve until the late 1800s, but it was a losing race. By that time mercury barometers were replaced almost entirely by the new aneroid design. Aneroid means "without liquid," because the new design was purely mechanical, with no mercury or other liquids.

The "Torricellian Experiment"

Torricelli and Galileo had in essence set about to measure how long a straw could be that you could still suck water through, primarily in response to more practical questions of how high water could be pumped in various applications. We know from the soda fountain that a foot or so works just fine, but is there a limit to how tall it could be? They got all the way to 33 feet, but it would go no higher.

The long straw behaved just like a short one, namely as long as you kept suction on the top, the column of water did not fall. But no matter how hard you tried, you could not pull water up a glass tube higher than about 33 ft.

Torricelli reasoned that when he removed the air from the top of the straw by sucking on it (pumping it out to be more precise), it was the weight of the air pushing down on the water in the basin at the base that forced the water up the straw. The 33-foot limit was reached when the weight of the water in the straw balanced the weight of the air pressing down on the basin of water. And if that interpretation was right, he supposed—which Galileo, by the way, did not think was true—that if he changed the liquid to be mercury, some 13.7 times heavier than water, then the column would only reach to (33/13.7) feet, which is about 29 inches.

And sure enough that was right. Though many of his contemporaries remained more interested in pumping water into tall decorative fountains, or over the tops of hills for irrigation, he realized his device could measure the weight of the air. It was not long till he noticed that the column height changed from day to day, and he rightfully suspected (for slightly the wrong reasons) that the weight of the air was changing. As we would say it now, when the local atmospheric pressure was low, the column of mercury was low, and when high pressure passed by, the mercury column was taller.

Unfortunately he was not able to make any useful correlation between his mercury height and the weather, because the height of the mercury expanded and contracted with air temperature and he was not aware of that. Nor was he able to prove that the air weighed less at higher elevations, which is also something he believed to be true. These discoveries using his device emerged only slowly over the next 50 years or so.

Torricelli's experiment itself, however, fairly quickly evolved into a simple operation that could be carried out by anyone, using the most basic equipment. This remains until today the epitome of a scientist's ideal experiment—easy to do, with simple, inexpensive equipment, and with rigorously reproducible results.

Here is how his experiment is described, but this is not a recommendation that you do this. On the contrary, you should not do this. Mercury can be toxic if not handled properly, and the glass tubes, open bowls, etc, make this in fact a hazardous way to handle it. This is something early researchers were not aware of, to the detriment of many. Even as late as the 1990s, dangerous levels of mercury vapor were being discovered in old science laboratories in England. Mercury spilled onto the floor and through the floor boards had collected for many decades in some cases, contaminating both air and surfaces.

Think of starting with a bowl of mercury and a clear glass tube about a quarter of an inch in diameter and 36 inches long that is sealed at one end. Then

fill up that tube with mercury (Figure 1.2-1). Place your finger over the open end of the tube to seal it, and carefully turn in over, and place the finger covering the bottom of the tube into the bowl, under the surface of the mercury, and very slowly remove your finger keeping the tube held upright in the vertical position. The mercury in the tube will run out somewhat, adding to what is in the bowl, but it won't all run out. It will leave a vacuum at the top of the tube about 6 inches long, and a column of mercury standing about 30 inches high in the tube.

The weight of the air on the surface of the mercury in the basin is forcing it up the tube, telling us exactly what we want to know from such a device, the atmospheric pressure, in a unit of atmospheric pressure that has come to be called "inches of mercury." The worldwide, season-wide average pressure is 29.92" and it varies with the weather usually not more than about ±1".

If we wanted to know the actual weight of the air from this apparatus, we could figure the weight of

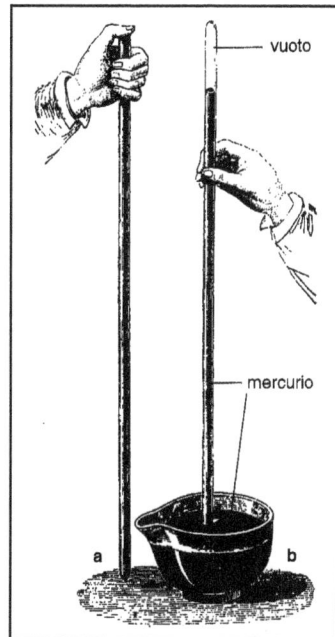

Figure 1.2-1 *Torricellian experiment that started it all... the science of barometers and atmospheric pressure, as well as the philosophical quest to understand the concept of a vacuum. Figure 1.2-2 illustrates the principle.*

the mercury column being supported. The quarter-inch-diameter tube has a cross-sectional area of πr^2 = $\pi(0.25/2)^2$ = 0.049 square inches. The weight of the mercury is the volume times its density (0.4889 lbs per cubic inch) and if the column balanced out at 30 inches, it would weigh (length x area x density) = 30 x 0.049 x 0.4889 = 0.72 lbs. This then would be the force exerted on the area of the tube at the base, so the actual pressure would be 0.72 lbs/0.049 square inches, which equals 14.7 lbs per square inch. This is illustrated in Figure 1.2-2, which shows a variation of the Torricellian tube called a mercury manometer. Notice that the actual diameter of the tube in use will always cancel out of this computation, so it is not crucial to the conclusion.

Many of the greatest scientists and philosophers of the time devoted some of their energy and intellect to the development, understanding, or application of this "Torricellian Experiment."

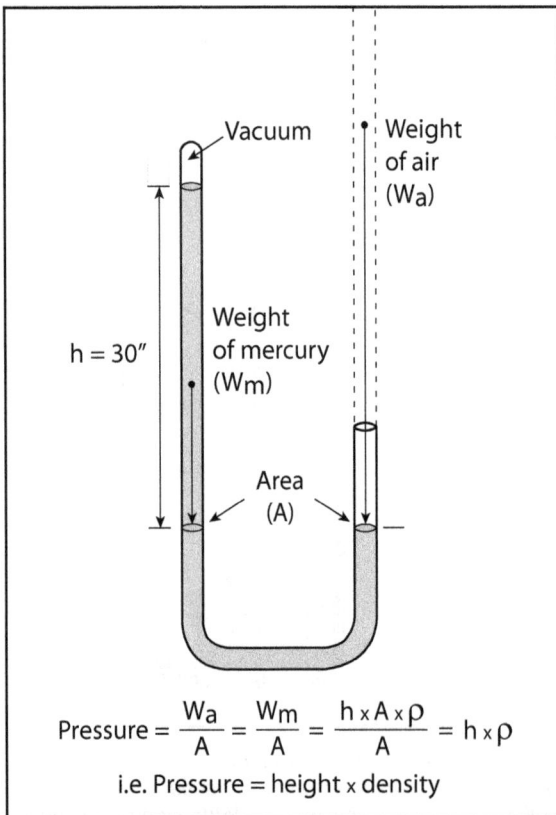

$$\text{Pressure} = \frac{W_a}{A} = \frac{W_m}{A} = \frac{h \times A \times \rho}{A} = h \times \rho$$

i.e. Pressure = height x density

Figure 1.2-2 *A mercury manometer.*

Galileo Galilei (1564-1642), Italian scientific giant, was the father of the scientific method. Among what are typically considered more profound discoveries, in the 1630s he confirmed the observations of others that water could not be pumped higher than 33 feet by suction and proposed a reason why, though it was not correct. Shortly before he died, he passed on this pump mystery to his new associate Torricelli, who made his mercury tube discoveries about a year later.

Evangelista Torricelli (1608–1647), Italian physicist and mathematician, is the central figure of this story. His main claim to fame is his work in 1643 on the original mercury tube. He has been forever honored with a unit of pressure called the Torr, equal to 1 mm of mercury as it stands in a mercury barometer. In 1644, he wrote: "We live submerged at the bottom of an ocean of air." He appreciated the fact that his device measured the weight of the air, but he was not able to fine tune the observations enough to associate actual weather changes with mercury heights. Though less known to the public, he made other important contributions to science and mathematics and succeeded Galileo as Professor of Mathematics and Science at Pisa.

Rene Descartes (1596–1650), French philosopher and scientist, was the first to put numerical scales on a "Torricelli tube," at which time he also sent a duplicate scale to an associate in 1647 so they could compare results. In this sense he deserves some credit for inventing "the barometer." There is even evidence that Descartes knew how they worked, having proposed a way to measure atmospheric pressure in 1631. On philosophical grounds, however, he would not accept the idea that there was a vacuum at the top of the mercury column, which could not help but lead him astray—which does not distract the slightest from his many profound contributions to mathematics and philosophy.

Blaise Pascal (1623-1662), French giant in science, mathematics, and philosophy, proposed that air became thinner as you ascend in the atmosphere and proved it in 1648 with a scaled mercury tube measured at two elevations, 3000 feet apart. Thus he established the use of barometers as altimeters, which spread rapidly around Europe and England.

He also defended his conclusion that it was indeed a vacuum over the top of the mercury, and in discussing this position and his barometer measurements he formulated a principle of scientific philosophy that remains today a cornerstone of modern science. "In order to show that a hypothesis is evident, it does not suffice that all the phenomena follow from it; instead, if it leads to something contrary to a single one of the phenomena, that suffices to establish its falsity." We can on some level thank the barometer for that insight.

He also derived Pascal's Principle, which states that pressure applied to an enclosed fluid is transmitted undiminished to every part of the fluid, as well as to the walls of the container. This is not only a key to the function of a barometer, but he could use it immediately to build the first hydraulic pump. He too has been rewarded with a unit of pressure called a Pascal, which is equal to 1 Newton of force per 1 square meter of area. It leads directly to the common unit of atmospheric pressure called a millibar, which is the same as a hecto Pascal.

Pascal was also a fountain of well-made aphorisms in his later writings. "Chance favors those who are best prepared" is a good one for ocean navigators and backgammon players to keep in mind.

Robert Boyle (1627-1691) was a wealthy Englishman, considered the founder of modern chemistry. He is most famous for Boyle's Law (1669), which states that the pressure of an enclosed gas is inversely proportional to its volume so long as the temperature remains the same. Thus if you have gas in a cylinder, its pressure will rise as the piston lowers to reduce the volume. Cut the volume in half and the pressure will increase by a factor of two. See Figure 1.2-3. Boyle described this process by thinking of a "spring in the air." When you compress the gas, the pressure builds, which acts like a spring resisting the compression. Recall these were days before the knowledge of atoms and molecules, so this was quite an abstract concept for the time.

He made this discovery while defending his belief that air pressure can in fact exert strong forces, which had come under attack in the ongoing arguments about the nature of air, and more importantly, the nature of a vacuum.

To carry out these experiments he and his assistant Robert Hooke also made significant contributions to air pump design and related technologies, and they were the first to use a mercury tube manometer as a pressure gauge for scientific studies of more basic matters, such as the proprieties of gases.

In a letter of 1665 and later in a published paper in 1666, Boyle was the first person to describe the mercury tube used to measure pressure as a *barometer*, thus establishing the name we still use today.

Robert Hooke (1635-1703), British, is often described as the single greatest experimental scientist of the seventeenth century. He has been called England's Leonardo. He made pioneering contributions in many areas of science and engineering, including the escapement and balance spring that ultimately led to accurate clocks, the discovery of plant cells (a word he invented for this use), as well as proposing a theory of evolution based on microscope work with fossils.

He also worked on astronomy and proposed a theory of gravity, which made him a rival of the great and powerful Newton, who shamefully succeeded in dampening the acclaim Hooke deserved at the time.

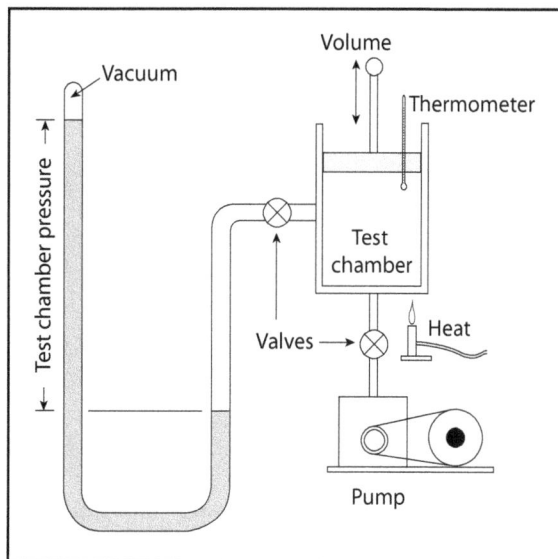

Figure 1.2-3 *A mercury manometer pressure gauge. Students around the world use this same type of apparatus that Boyle used to learn about the properties of gases. With such an arrangement, the temperature, volume, and pressure of the gas can all be varied to see how they are related.*

Hooke developed the theory of combustion, and he was a principal architect and surveyor in the rebuilding of London after the great fire. The list goes on into many fields, including the development of the first marine barometer used by Edmund Halley on the first-ever worldwide voyage of scientific discovery.

His namesake in the world of science these days, however, is Hooke's Law of Springs, which has a direct and lasting effect on the functioning of aneroid barometers, something he did not know about at the time.

Edmund Halley (1656-1742) was an English astronomer and sea captain. He is most famous for his prediction of what is now called Halley's Comet, but his contribution to the evolution of barometer usage is just as profound, though much less known. As mentioned earlier, he took a custom marine barometer (designed by Hooke) with him on his worldwide voyages of scientific discovery, during which he recorded pressures and correlated them with the weather observations in both hemispheres (1698-1700).

Other than noting the measurements, his actual logbooks do not include much detail about barometers, but the following year he published an article describing the Hooke barometer he used along with the declaration:

> "I had one of these Barometers with me in my late Southern Voyage, and it never failed to prognostick and give early notice of all bad weather we had, so that I depended thereon, and made provision accordingly; and from my own experience I conclude that a more useful contrivance hath not for this long time been offered for the benefit of Navigation."

John Locke (1632-1704), an English giant among philosophical thinkers, was also a weather buff, having known both Boyle and Hooke at Oxford. He measured and recorded what is considered the first systematic record of temperature, pressure, humidity, wind, and weather in England from 1666 to 1683. The data are cited in the article by Boyle where he first used the word barometer. So we can remember Locke not only for his profound influence on the thinking

of the American Founding Fathers and the subsequent Declaration of Independence, but also for the key role he played in associating barometric pressure with the weather we experience. Thomas Jefferson bought his first barometer in 1776, about 100 years later—and chances are the instruments were very similar.

An example of a modern mercury barometer of the type found in many laboratories even today is shown in Figure 1.2-4.

Aneroid Barometers

Gottfried Wilhelm Leibniz (1646-1716) was a German giant in philosophy and mathematics, inventor of the binary number system that modern computers are based upon, and inventor of a me-

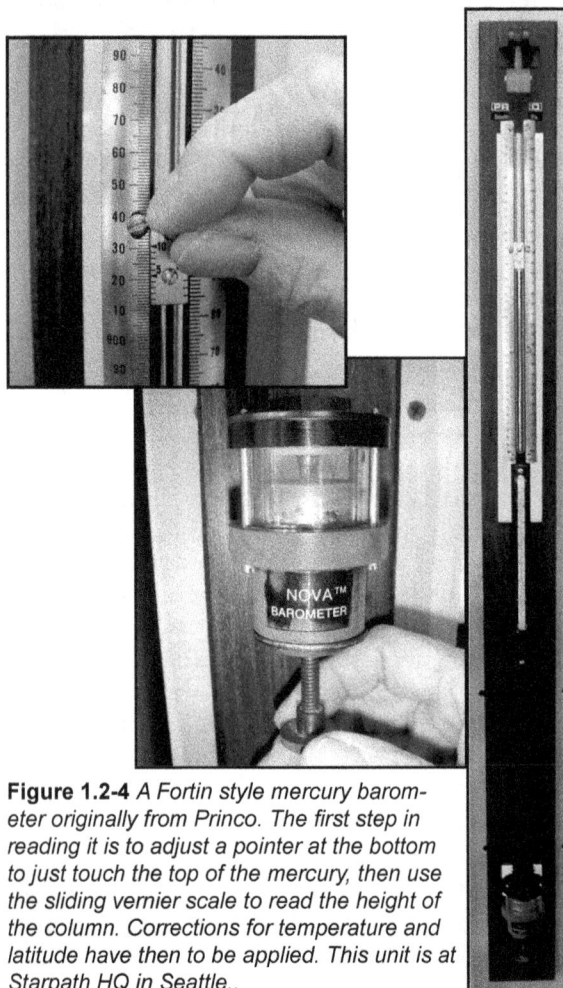

Figure 1.2-4 *A Fortin style mercury barometer originally from Princo. The first step in reading it is to adjust a pointer at the bottom to just touch the top of the mercury, then use the sliding vernier scale to read the height of the column. Corrections for temperature and latitude have then to be applied. This unit is at Starpath HQ in Seattle..*

chanical calculator, rival of Newton for the invention of calculus and other aspects of theoretical physics. Though not usually listed among his many brilliant achievements, he was the first person to propose the construction of a steel bellows aneroid barometer in several communications (with the famous Dutch scientist Daniel Bernoulli) from about 1700, but he did not have craftsmen available to build it. Thus the seeds of the future were at hand early in the history of barometers, but its realization had to wait for 140 years.

Nicolas Jacques Conte (1755-1805), French painter, engraver, and mechanical genius invented many practical devices and procedures and was a national leader in the birth of the French industrial revolution for which he received the first Legion of Honor award from Napoleon. He also created in essence the first aneroid barometer in 1798 to measure relative heights of hot-air balloons, but it was not pursued for use with atmospheric pressure measurements. He also was the inventor of what we now call the lead pencil.

Lucien Vidie (1805-1866), was a French engineer who designed, built, and patented the first successful aneroid barometer in 1844. He is described as a poor businessman who had legal troubles getting the instruments manufactured as well as defending his

Figure 1.2-5 *Aneroid barometer. They look much the same today as they did in 1850. Diameters vary from 2" to 8", but typically are 4" to 5". They are about 2 to 4" deep.*

patent, and was in and out of court for decades to follow. He apparently did not prosper greatly from the invention. Unlike others mentioned here who took part in the evolution of the barometer, he was not distinguished for other achievements.

Besides those mentioned, Pascal, Boyle, and Bernouilli had each considered the concept of an aneroid device but none succeeded in building one.

Aneroid means "without liquid," in that this is a barometer that does not use mercury as all precursors did. It relies on a vacuum sealed metal bellows (sometimes called a sylphon depending on how it is made) that expands and contracts in response to the atmospheric pressure outside of it. A clock-like mechanism then transfers this expansion and contraction into a dial setting that shows the pressure.

The generic aneroid barometer appearance is shown in Figure 1.2-5. Aneroids (shorthand for aneroid barometer) were introduced to the public shortly after their invention and many competing models were readily available worldwide by the 1860's. They became popular because they were smaller (about 5 inches or less in diameter) and more portable than the mercury devices. They were also more durable (no glass tubes or mercury to spill), they cost less, and they were easier to read.

Aneroid barometers were also considered more accurate at the time by some, but this was largely a misunderstanding tied to the fact that they were easier to read, and could be read to a higher precision. The challenge of distinguishing between "precision" and "accuracy" is with us still today, and it is a mantra that will come up in multiple settings as this book proceeds. For now we just note that proper questions on their inherent accuracy or limitations were raised in the scientific and maritime literature almost immediately when the instruments appeared across Europe and the UK in the mid 1800's. In any event, within 25 years or so, they had done away with their mercury-tube competitors as a popular barometer, though some mercury tubes remained on a few vessels till beyond 1900, and they remain in science laboratories even today.

It is only the fairly recent official declaration (in the U.S. and Common Market) that mercury can be toxic if mishandled, which has led to legal restrictions on the sale and transport of mercury (2007) that put mercury barometers to rest on still another level. A longtime popular source for laboratory grade mercury instruments in the U.S. (www.princoinstruments. com) discontinued selling them but keeps their earlier webpage and instruction manuals online. It's hard to give up something that has been such a good tool for so long, not to mention that there are likely hundreds in use around the world still. We have one in our classroom in Seattle.

There are still experienced antique dealers and barometer specialists that restore and sell antique mercury barometers. They have developed safe ways to transport them within the law. An Internet search on antique barometers will find many sources, worldwide. There are also companies such as Russell Sci-

entific (www.russell-scientific.co.uk) and Barometer World (www.barometerspareparts.co.uk) in the U.K. that sell classic mercury barometer kits and parts to be self assembled. They leave it to the customer to acquire locally the needed mercury and to fill it. The latter company also offers an extensive source of aneroid barometer parts as well.

Laboratory grade mercury barometers are available from the Dr. Alfred Müller Meteoroglogical Instruments Company in Berlin (www.rfuess-mueller. de) who have carried on with the production of the renown R-Fuess instruments that date from the 1800s. We have been told by those who have used the instruments that their mercury instruments No. 2k and 20k are unsurpassed in quality. This company also produces the R-Fuess precision aneroid barometers, which are among the best available today.

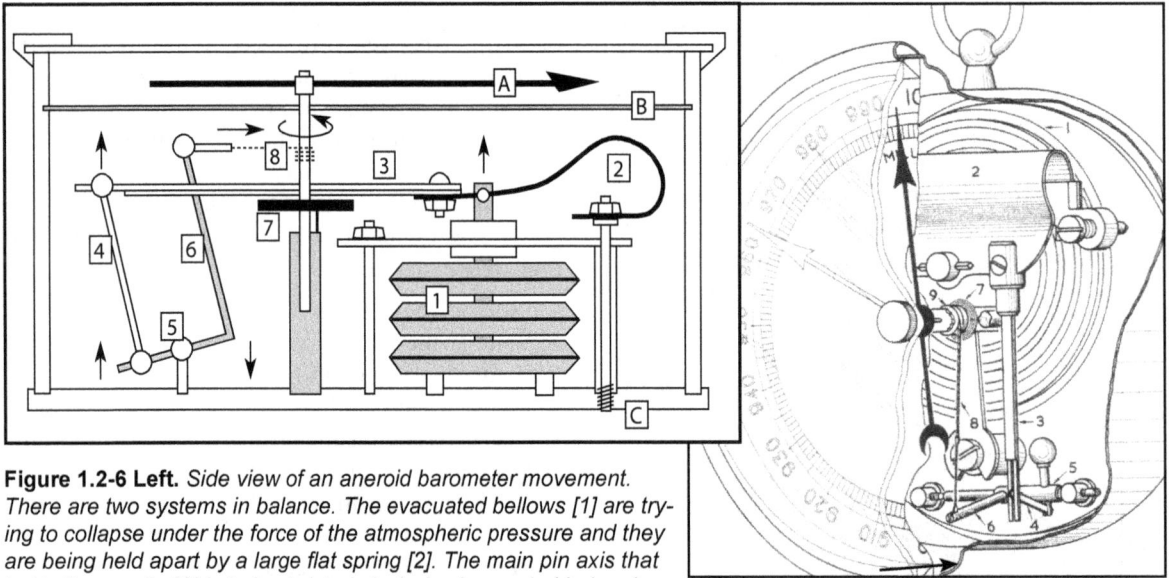

Figure 1.2-6 Left. *Side view of an aneroid barometer movement. There are two systems in balance. The evacuated bellows [1] are trying to collapse under the force of the atmospheric pressure and they are being held apart by a large flat spring [2]. The main pin axis that holds the needle [A] is being twisted clockwise by a spiral hairspring [7], which is being resisted by a counterclockwise twist from a thin chain [8] wrapped around it. When the pressure drops, the bellows have less force on them so the spring pulls them more apart, which in turn raises the arm [3] connected to rod [4]. As [4] is pulled up, the front side [6] rotates down on pivot [5]. This lets the thin chain [8] forward, so spring [7] wrap more chain on the pin, turning [A] counterclockwise showing a drop in pressure on the dial [B]. On the back of the device, there is a set screw [C] that makes small adjustments to the bellows height, so you can set the pressure right at a desired reading. Several adjustments are built into the movement so that the rotation of the needle can be made proportional to the change in pressure.*

Right. *A cutaway view of a similar movement. There are several movement designs in use today. Some aneroids have 1 bellows only, others have 2 to 5. The bellows are usually corrugated as shown, as this reduces distortion during expansion [hysteresis]. In better units, the bar [3] is usually a bimetal strip that bends with temperature to compensate for temperature changes in the bellows and main spring. Adapted from* Handbook of Meteorological Instruments, Vol. 1.

Aneroid barometers are the main type used at sea today. The heart of the instrument remains the partially evacuated, thin metal bellows, also called an aneroid capsule. As the external pressure varies, the bellows expand or contract, and this motion is used to indicate the pressure. Several bellows designs and movements have been invented over the years. One

Barographs

A "barograph" is usually thought to be an aneroid barometer with a strip chart that records the pressure as an ink trace on a drum, rotating in response to a wound spring (Figure 1.2-7). A sample barograph trace from a famous storm is shown in Figure 1.2-8.

Modern versions sometimes use battery-operated quartz clocks to rotate the drum. Barographs are very convenient on land or on large ships, but not practical on a small boat at sea. Often the trace you care about is in bad weather and then the trace ends up a broad smear as the instrument bounces around in the seas. Speaking from experience, it is difficult to avoid this. I have done an ocean passage on a 40-foot sailboat devoting half of a quarter berth to a conventional barograph, suspended into free space using bungee cords on four corners. The smear of the trace was still broad and erratic when the seas got rough. Larger deep-sea vessels, however, routinely use these at sea, especially those with extra dampening (Figure 1.2-7).

Barographs are a wonderful luxury, but if you record the pressure from a conventional barometer when you read it, you don't need the graph. Furthermore, we are likely to be more aware of what is going on with the pressure if we must read and record it, rather than having this all done for us.

It is true that if you record the pressure at each watch change, or simply routinely when on land, you get all the information the barograph provides (missing only the nice plot of the results), but that is not the whole story. When underway in the ocean we typically record the pressure all day *and* all night, but on coastal trips if we anchor out or tie up at night we typically do not have a watch on to record the pressure. A barograph feature can be quite nice in these circumstances to alert us to what took place over night.

The exceptions in ocean sailing are the single-handed and double-handed racing sailors who often have to keep irregular hours. They have discovered that a barograph trace is crucial because they do not always have time to keep systematic logbook records. A glance at the pressure trace over the past 2 hours or past 24 hours could alert them to something they might have missed otherwise. They often prefer an electronic trace (rather than conventional ink on paper) of the pressure, which brings up the next point.

To be more modern, we are better to think of the

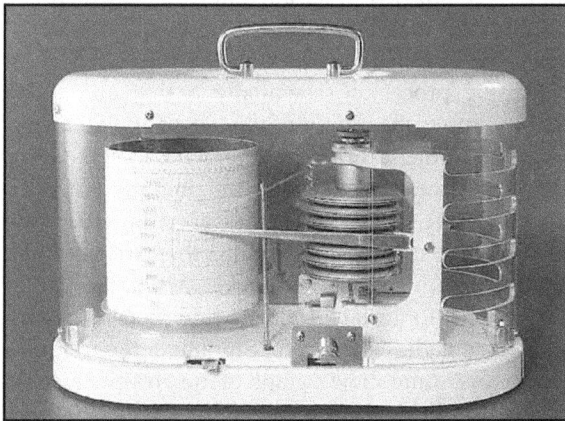

Figure 1.2-7 *A Fischer precision barograph with extra dampening for use at sea. They are also available in glass and wood frames. Drum rotation rates can be set to 26 hr or as high as 783 hr (32 days).*

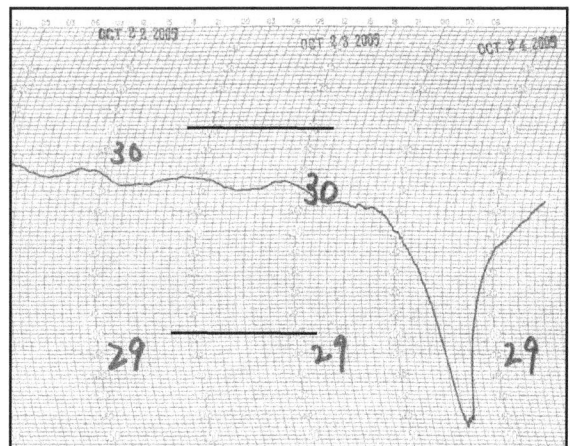

Figure 1.2-8 *A barograph trace of Hurricane Wilma as it crossed south Florida in October of 2005. The observed pressure dropped from about 29.60 to 28.54 (1002 to 966 mb) in 10 hours, but it had, 5 days earlier, set the Atlantic record Low of 882 mb (26.05") in the Caribbean.*

word "barograph" as meaning any barometer that records and displays past pressures. That makes many electronic barometers into electronic barographs, because these models store the data and display them graphically, or they allow users to push buttons to step back through past pressures. These offer nice histories underway without the smear of a printed record. Thus we might refer to "electronic barometers" as instruments that measure and display the pressure electronically, whereas "electronic barographs" are ones that can also display past pressures. One popular electronic barometer has a unique compromise of offering inkless printing onto heat sensitive paper so the user can get a smooth trace even underway in rough seas. On land, of course, all forms of barographs offer clean beautiful traces.

Typical aneroid barograph recording papers are for 7 days, but multiple traces can be recorded on one paper. Barographs are usually made with high quality aneroid movements. They are often works of art as well as dependable instruments. They are, however, often expensive instruments, varying from about eight hundred to several thousand dollars.

A "microbarograph" is a barograph with extra bellows and precision movements intended for more accurate measurements. The use of this name today is commonly intended to convey a quality instrument, though its origin can be traced to a significant expansion of the plotting scale that allowed for more accurate readings. Early Navy barographs had a 1-inch change in the pressure represented by a 1-inch range of the recording pen, but these were then updated to microbarographs that expanded this to 2.5 inches on the plot for each 1 inch of pressure change. Thus barographs can be characterized by the ratio of pressure change in inches to the corresponding sweep of the pen, as 1-1 barographs for the former and 2.5-1 microbarographs for the latter. This property can be used as a benchmark in comparing instruments.

Figure 1.2-9 shows samples of the electronic "barograph" display of a popular unit showing how you can change the scale to view the past 2 hours, or condense the scale to show the past 2 days.

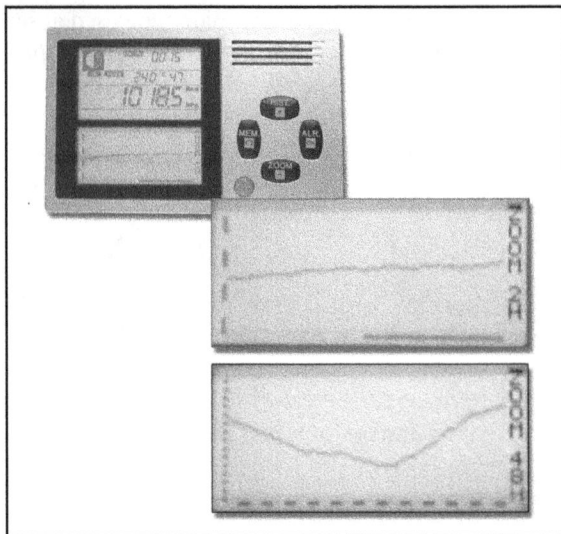

Figure 1.2-9 *An electronic barograph display from Vion model 4002, imported in the U.S. from France by Weems and Plath. The time range of the display can be varied to show the past 2 hr to the past 48 hr, as shown. Once a history display is selected, the user can step back through the data to view actual times and pressures recorded.*

Electronic Barometers

An "electronic barometer" (sometimes called "digital barometer") is a small electronic device with internal sensors and electronic circuits that measure atmospheric pressure and then display the value digitally—as opposed to an aneroid display, which is a pointer on a dial. The crucial components are a small electronic sensor that measures the pressure and an electronic processor (essentially a tiny computer) that interprets the output of the sensor and then controls the numerical display. There are several sensor designs, some of which are just tiny aneroid cells, and there are several designs of how the expansion of the cell is measured. The units themselves can be anything from a sleek modernistic design the size of a card deck to a plain 10-inch wide metal box with 2-inch tall digits. Some have computer interfaces, others do not. Some show a graph of the pressure history, others do not. Some are simply the component of a large wrist watch. Some are included in hand-held GPS units. Electronic barometers vary in price from $25 to $2,500. Samples are shown in Figures 1.2-10 and 1.2-11. Some are not as accurate as a common aneroid, others are the most accurate barometers in the world. Clearly there is more to say about these when it comes to choosing one.

The Future of Electronic Barometers

We still have primarily aneroid barometers on ships at sea—one of the most crucial barometer applications—but this will not be the case for long. Electronic barometers have in large part taken over popular applications on land (in weather stations, watches, GPSs, etc), and they will eventually do the same thing for navigation at sea. Just as the aneroids replaced the mercury tubes, technology marches on. It took the aneroids 50 years to replace the mercury barometers, but it won't take electronic barometers so long to replace the aneroids. It may take another 10 years or so for those actually using the devices, but to be conservative, give it 15 years, because most barometers on board are not used very much, and in these cases there is little motivation to change.

There is another factor, though, that will keep the aneroids on board some time longer, and that is electronic devices are often vulnerable to the environment and conditions at sea. The electronic solution will not be universally accepted until it has established some track record of dependability. There are obvious ways to make an instrument more dependable in the maritime environment, but to date not many electronic barometers advertise that feature.

On the other hand, almost every vessel of any size that goes to sea these days has a computer onboard, and very few of these are customized for the conditions at sea. So convenience and accuracy may win out over durability on the eventual selection of a barometer.

In the meantime, the prudent solution is to have both: an electronic barometer for accuracy and ease of use, and a good dependable aneroid as a backup. This is analogous to carrying a sextant on board, even though you do your primary, day to day navigation by GPS, the satellite Global Positioning System.

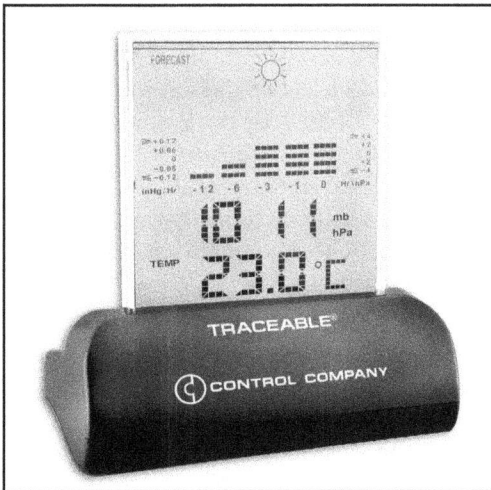

Figure 1.2-10 *Stylistic electronic barometer and thermometer, with graphic pressure trace (Traceable 4259). The retail price is $24 to $32. This device is unique among the low-priced units as it actually has a published guaranteed accuracy of ±12 mb from the manufacturer. Several retail outlets for the device, however, list its accuracy as ±6 mb and others have it at ±3 mb. Clearly the calibration procedures (presented in Chapter 4) are called for to resolve any uncertainty in the uncertainties.*

Figure 1.2-11 *Scientific electronic barometer (Vaisala PTB330), used as a pressure reference instrument around the world. The accuracy is ±0.1 mb; the retail price of the basic unit is about $2,300. Each is custom assembled in Finland. It is one of just a few premier instruments used by professional meteorologists, airports, and scientific laboratories. This instrument also includes a graphic display of past pressures. This one is more accurate than called for in routine work; the other is not accurate enough. Numerous compromises are available.*

I have to admit some sense of sorrow about an eventual phasing out of the aneroids, especially to the extent that my own writing—pointing out the virtues of electronic barometers—contributes to the process. I don't say that with any pride or pleasure. I have fond memories and ongoing pleasure working with aneroid barometers, and I have sailed many thousands of miles at sea depending on their measurements.

But I have also struggled in the past for long hours and days in the process of calibrating aneroids so they can best serve their purpose—I did not till recently have the good fortune to work with precision aneroids. Before the Internet, which now gives us instantaneous access to archived accurate pressures, the calibration of an aneroid device by an individual without scientific equipment was a tedious and time consuming process. It is much easier now, and a main purpose of this book is to explain how to do it. Most mariners still use these devices and there is good reason to continue doing so.

I mention the role of publications because it is not just the technology improvements themselves that fuel such transitions. Electronic barometers have been around more than a decade. At first they were all expensive, but now they are not. Nevertheless they have not caught on for general maritime application. But that was not due to their cost, high or low. It has been more—I am guessing—because of the way they look!

Maritime navigation is one of the most traditional of all occupations. Ship captains and yacht skippers are very conservative when it comes to running their vessels. At sea they must be self reliant and they want their equipment well tested and dependable. Every vessel master has seen an aneroid barometer on every ship and yacht they have ever been on since they were kids. No skipper rushes to replace that very symbol of maritime tradition with a little gray plastic box with an LCD read out—maybe even with little cloud icons that sometimes have rain coming from them, quite independent of what is actually going on in the sky.

I recall a brilliant biophysics professor in the 60's who had a love of music and guitars. He designed and built a revolutionary new guitar with remarkable sound quality. I was told he actually sent a model to Andrés Segovia, who played the instrument, and declared it to be the best sounding guitar he had ever played… but, he added, it was doomed to failure, because it did not look like a guitar. It was a trapezoid shape.

It is not technology that is going to expedite the transition, it is knowledge; knowledge that is gained from books and periodicals that describe the products and report on a user's experience with them. This is especially true with barometers because the fruitful use of them is not quite as simple as it might seem.

While it is indeed true that every ship and boat has an aneroid barometer on it, it is also fair to say that relatively very few actually use them, and even those that do use them, do not always use them to full potential.

This, of course, does not count professional merchant marine and navy vessels, run by expert crews familiar with all aspects of marine weather, including atmospheric pressure and barometers, and it especially does not count those professional ships taking part in NOAA's Voluntary Observing Ship Program. These ships work closely with the National Weather Service (NWS) Port Meteorological Officers (PMO), because the NWS relies on their accurate weather observations, four times a day throughout their voyages. The PMOs help with barometer calibration and in measuring techniques. Ships' officers also undergo required marine weather training as part of their licensing preparation. Those volunteering to take part even get extended training.

And it does not count some yacht navigators who have taken it on their own to learn these things as they recognize the fundamental value. Quite a few ocean racing navigators are in that category. Nevertheless, in the broader maritime and boating world, most navigators are not familiar with barometer usage, despite the fact that every vessel has one on board.

But this is not at all their fault. It is not even the fault of the schools where they studied, nor the books they used. The need and value of accurate pressure measurements and barometer understanding has simply not been presented in any of these modern texts we know of—barring, of course, our own efforts over the years, which, though I would like to think were influential on some level, have not changed the world!

Most popular books on marine weather over the past 30 years barely mention barometers at all—a very strong statement, but easily tested. And those that do mention watching the barometer, at most say that all that matters is whether or not the pressure is rising or falling, and is it doing this fast or slow. None ventures so far as to say the actual magnitude of pressure has any value—except possibly in quoting typical pressure drops one might see as they fall into the abyss of a typhoon. For some reason, that doomsday sequence is frequently reproduced. Ironically, if we use our barometer wisely, we can most likely avoid ever seeing that situation.

Furthermore, most texts do not venture even a hint of what might be a fast rate of pressure change versus a slow rate, expressed as, say, millibars per 3 hours, or any units you like. To be fair, there are many factors that go into that answer, any one of which might dominate the result, so it is not at all an easy subject to discuss. But no discussion at all, with or without qualifications, reflects some disconnect from practical barometer usage.

Modern books have typically omitted the role of knowing the absolute value of the pressure (as opposed to just trends and rates) for two understandable reasons. First, they were not aware of any use for that data. In other words, if I know from my accurate barometer and knowledge of elevation corrections that the true pressure where I am in the ocean is 1024.5 mb, what do I do with this? And second, for the most part they could not measure it to a useful accuracy if they wanted to.

One obvious application of accurate pressure is testing the weather maps we get at sea. We always stress that *there will always be a forecast, and they are not marked "good" or "bad."* It is up to us to decide, and the barometer is a key to doing so.

But this is not common procedure, because the typical vessel does not have a calibrated barometer. They cannot measure the pressure accurately enough to make this test. If they tried to confirm a weather map by comparing to their own observed pressure,

or carry out other tactical observations using target pressures, making the assumption that their barometers worked right (without calibration), they would soon find that they did not get useful information. If something does not work, a sensible navigator stops doing it.

The problem is even more insidious than that. When there is a total disregard for accurate values of pressure throughout the maritime culture, there is no motivation to check to see if it works right at all. Consequently mariners have no way to know if their barometer is even going up and down properly, which, in fact, very many do not. Thus by ignoring calibration we are not only losing the use of accurate pressures, we also diminish the value of observed trends and rates as well. Without a tested barometer, we cannot even judge accurately on inland waters (where we might not use weather maps at all) if a forecasted storm is earlier or later than predicted.

Two important things have changed in the past few years that call for a change in the way we look at barometers. First we have the Internet that gives us an easy way to calibrate an aneroid barometer, so it can now be used for accurate pressures, and second, we now have many options for dependable, affordable, and accurate electronic barometers. A quality electronic barometer has the notable advantage of being accurate over its full pressure range once it is set right at any one pressure. This is, unfortunately, not true with common aneroid barometers. Needless to say, we have to check the electronic barometers as well, at least once, to be sure they are behaving as advertised.

Another, rather indirect reason electronic barometers have not been adopted on some vessels is many of them display the pressure only to the nearest mb, ie 1024 mb instead of 1024.4 mb. The World Meteorological Organization (WMO) and NWS standard for recording and reporting pressures is a tenth of a mb, so instruments without this precision cannot be used in any official capacity.

Ironically, an electronic barometer that shows pressure to the nearest whole mb is actually rounded from the nearest 0.5 mb, so when we write 1024 we mean 1024.0 ±0.5. In contrast, essentially any aneroid barometer meets the tenth of a millibar reading requirement untested, because the user can always estimate the tenths. In most cases, however, the best a careful user can estimate the location of the needle between adjacent mb ticks is about ±0.3 mb. In other words, a typical digital pressure specified to the whole mb is probably as accurate as an aneroid dial estimated to the tenth, if not in fact more accurate.

But having the tenths displayed is still best. This tenth of a mb display is actually quite valuable for early detection of trends, even if the pressure itself is not accurate to that level of precision.

1.3 What does it Measure?

Like most topics of the mind and matter, either the problem or the solution starts with the Greek philosopher Aristotle (384 BC – 322 BC). He had enormous influence for many hundreds of years. Some of his thoughts on a wide variety of subjects have withstood the times, others were not even good approximations. His role in the evolution of knowledge about how a barometer works was profound—wrong, as it turns out, but nevertheless profound.

He had created an incorrect theory of motion, which he used to "prove" that a vacuum could not exist. According to his theory if a force were applied to an object inside a vacuum it could reach an infinite speed because there was nothing to resist it. And since he knew an infinite speed was impossible, he concluded, and convinced other leading philosophers well into the barometer days of the 1600's, that he had logically proven a vacuum could not exist.

A couple hundred years prior to the barometer, the Catholic Church had added real dogma to his conclusion by stating that it was also the opinion of the Church that a vacuum does not exist. This raised the theory to a whole new level as they controlled what everyone was supposed to believe. Historians puzzle over this decision of the Church, because they were adamantly opposed to many of his other theories.

Presumably the church argument was something along the lines that God is everywhere, so there cannot be a place without God, so a vacuum could not exist, because all agreed it was a place without anything in it. The fact that Aristotle had "logically proven" an outcome they desired must have been attractive.

Still well before the barometer days, however, the Church had a slight change of heart. Some insightful monks had been thinking on this for a hundred years or so, and they convinced the powers that be, that this was not the best position to take. They could not accept the concept of Aristotle *logically* proving something about nature. Their argument was that God was all powerful, therefore if He wanted to make a vacuum, he could—Aristotle was not going to prove away this power. So the new official Church position was a vacuum could exist if God chose to make one, but He chooses not to, and He prohibits any act of nature to make one. Any attempt by humans to make a vacuum was doomed to failure.

Thus we come to the famous edict that "nature abhors a vacuum," which was on the minds of all the philosophers and scientists of the barometer days. That is the setting that adds the real significance (at that time) to the work of Galileo and Torricelli. First, Galileo discovered the true laws of motion, which showed that Aristotle's theory of motion was completely wrong. That made his famous proof of the impossibility of a vacuum also totally wrong. The entire underpinning of the (human) argument against vacuums no longer existed.

Then Torricelli turned the tube of mercury upside down and showed everyone in the world how to make a vacuum. So in perspective, it is not difficult to see why so many of the leading thinkers of the day were more concerned with what was in the top of the tube than they were with ideas about the device measuring the weight of the air.

The idea of nature abhorring a vacuum had been accepted for 100 years. Even Galileo would not accept that it was pressure on the surface of the mercury forcing the mercury up the tube. He and others to follow believed that this thing called vacuum had some power of its own to suck the mercury up the tube in what would be a natural act of self-destruction—nature abhorring the vacuum.

Torricelli did not accept this, but rather had the right interpretation of the weight of the air forcing the mercury up. But he could not, and did not, prove this. It was not till about 50 years later that Boyle and Hooke made a large air pump and put the entire apparatus into a bell jar they could evacuate. Then, as illustrated very schematically in Figure 1.3-1, they could show directly that the height of the mercury column was a direct measure of the atmospheric pressure on the surface of the bowl. In short, they could artificially change the "atmospheric pressure" on the bowl and see what happened to the column. It is the same way we calibrate barometers today.

Furthermore, the concepts of *air with weight* and *atmospheric pressure* were still vague, and not well related in the early days. Long before Torricelli, for example, it was known that air was a fluid analogous to water, and it was known that the forces within fluid water increased with depth. The simple experiment shown in Figure 1.3-2 was well known at the time, but the message it was trying to relate about the atmosphere was not fully appreciated.

Or maybe it was to some. As mentioned earlier, Torricelli believed that air has weight, and he believed the weight decreased with increasing altitude, but we had to wait for Pascal to prove this some 50 years later. Significantly, from our present perspective in this book, Torricelli also believed that this weight

of the air changed from time to time, but he was unable to prove this beyond observing that the height of his mercury column did change when left alone. He could not correlate this with weather because he did not understand the effect of temperature on the height of the mercury column, which masked the effects he anticipated. He did not know the magnitude of the changes to expect with the weather. Descartes may have been the first to actually observe atmospheric changes and in that sense use the tube as what Boyle called a "barometer."

Once it was confirmed that the pressure did change from time to time, it was still not at all clear why. This question became one of the many stimulating questions of the scientific community of the late 1700's. Recall that this period witnessed many worldwide voyages with barometers on board and careful logs of wind and weather. So the world's pressure patterns were beginning to be known fairly well.

Barometer data was ahead of scientific theory to explain it for quite a while. Even the idea of a gas itself was not known at the time. Boyle was again in the forefront of this discovery by doing such things

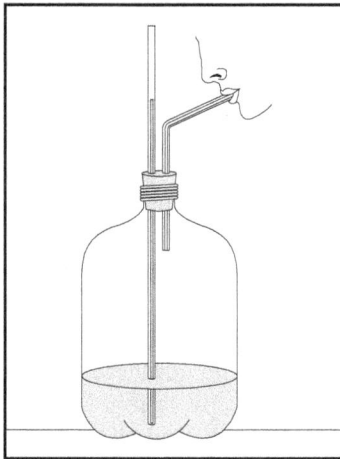

Figure 1.3-1 *The molasses experiment. Here is a simple way to picture how the liquid barometer works. Imagine molasses in a sealed jar as shown. Blow in to create higher pressure and the column rises. Suck out to reduce the pressure and the column height goes down. This is an analogy of the Boyle and Hooke experiment that first proved that the height of the mercury was indeed a measure of the pressure on the surface at the base.*

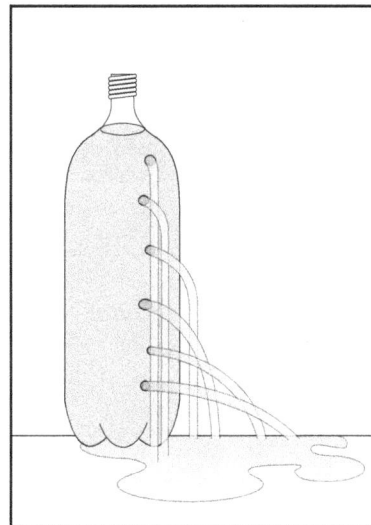

Figure 1.3-2 *Pressure as a function of water depth. This simple concept was well known long before Torricelli's barometer invention. It shows how the pressure in a fluid increases with depth, which in reverse shows why atmospheric pressure decreases with increasing elevation.*

as noting that a sealed bag with a piece of meat in it would expand with some "new kind of air" as the meat decomposed. This was one of the first discoveries of a gas other than air. Various other gases were soon discovered, but it was not till the 1770s that the composition of normal air was discovered.

Karl W. Scheele, a Swedish apothecary, and Joseph Priestley, an English clergyman, had independently discovered oxygen, but they did not know of its role in the atmosphere. They had also discovered nitrogen, though credit for that often goes to Daniel Rutherford (a Scottish student of Joseph Black), because Rutherford had the first publication in 1772. Joseph Black discovered carbon dioxide, among many pioneering contributions to understanding the nature of air.

Priestly later met and explained these discoveries to Antoine Lavoisier, a French lawyer and scientist who was studying the composition of air, and Lavoisier put the pieces together. He had already concluded that normal air was made up of two major components in the ratio of 3 to 1, and now he knew these had to be nitrogen and oxygen, the latter of which he then named—3.7 to 1 is the exact value, but these details were soon sorted out.

This much of the picture still did not explain the relationship between weather and the pressure of the atmosphere. The next lead actor in this play was **John Dalton (1766-1844)**, English chemist and meteorologist, who is famous for his theory of the atomic structure of matter and gases, as well as his pioneering work on the Aurora Borealis and on color blindness.

He was the one who finally explained what air really was, namely atoms (molecules) of individual gases—another blow to the diminishing number of Aristotelians who believed air was an element of its own. He went on to make the first classification of elements according to atomic weight.

But it is rather less well known that Dalton actually made this fundamental discovery of the nature of matter almost by accident while he was studying air, and in particular why the two primary gasses of the air did not settle out into layers of the individual gasses, but instead remained a uniform mixture. And it is also not so well known—at least in the physics books

I grew up with—that his actual primary goal was to understand weather.

We mentioned earlier the work of philosopher and weather buff, John Locke, but John Dalton was both weather buff and one of the leading scientific minds of the century. He made an even more detailed record and study of barometric pressure, temperature, humidity, precipitation, wind speed and direction, and cloud observations, 3 times a day, from 3 different cities over a five-year period. These data along with his compilation of worldwide knowledge to date formed the basis of his pioneering book called *Meteorological Observations and Essays*, first published in 1793. He then continued his observations and study for another 40 years and put out a second edition in 1834, but his primary discoveries were in the first edition, and he recognized that. The second edition was primarily a repeat of the first edition with addenda.

Thanks largely to the barometer, by the end of the 1700s, atmospheric pressure and the basic fundamentals of weather were already relatively mature subjects. It is hard to say they were "well understood," as some would say that weather is not well understood today—at least it remains a challenge compared to some other branches of science. Part of the problem is simply its overwhelming complexity—so many different interactions taking place and so many things that influence the results.

Another of the major contributions of John Dalton was his explanation of the role of water vapor in the air. Water vapor is the fuel of the atmosphere, and though the details were not all in place at the time, the seeds of understanding were sown and would be shortly revealed.

Dalton correlated low and high pressure with associated weather and advanced the correlation of winds with pressure. He confirmed that Lows bring rains and strong winds, and Highs bring clear skies and light airs. He put much of the puzzle together.

Though he does include some American data in his survey, he seems to have missed Benjamin Franklin's observation from the 1740's that a storm can move in a direction that is different from, even opposite to, the direction the storm winds are blowing.

This seminal observation was a first insight into how Lows move.

Much more understanding came from compilations and analysis of maritime logbooks throughout the 1800s and early 1900s. One of the most influential of these was the 1865 English translation of H.W. Dove's *Law of Storms* (first edition from 1844), which he dedicates to FitzRoy, thanking him for his support over the years. FitzRoy, in turn, makes an extended acknowledgement to Dove in his *Weather Book*, published the same year. Many of the barometer guidelines that FitzRoy made famous were adapted from Dove's early work, which is not to distract from Fitz-Roy's own observations and experience.

In fact, to some reasonable extent, we owe Fitz-Roy not only for his weather insights, but also for the Theory of Evolution, a circumstance that he recognized and was troubled by throughout his life. He like others felt his choice of religion threatened by these ideas, the background of which he himself facilitated. It was FitzRoy, after all, who sought out Darwin to provide intelligent company for himself on the long voyage of the Beagle, and it was FitzRoy's skill as a ship captain that got them safely through the storms and other tribulations of such a long voyage. A lesser seaman may not have succeeded, and the theories of evolution and natural selection may have been much delayed.

Edmund Halley had written the earliest paper (before 1700) addressing the issue of how winds are related to pressure. He proposed a first explanation of the trade winds, which was later improved upon by the Englishman George Hadley, and still further by the American William Ferrel. Halley presented the general distinction between Highs and Lows and their associated weather, and though his more general theories were off the mark in some cases, his scope was large and his ideas were the working model until Dalton codified the knowledge in 1792.

Knowledge as of the 1830s to 1840's was summarized and extended in the work of the German meteorologist Ludwig Friedrich Kaemtz titled *A Complete Course on Meteorology*, which was translated to English in 1845. It shows a high level of understanding for the time, with much on global barometric pressures and another extensive personal compilation of observations from Germany and several other European sites. Strangely, the book does not mention the work of Dalton.

Work of the American mathematician **William Ferrel (1817-1891)** was also much more pioneering than is often recognized. He not only clarified the global circulation (improving on Halley and Hadley), which earned him the namesake "Ferrel cell," which describes global wind flow poleward of the trades, but he also was the first to apply the Coriolis force formalism to wind flow, along with the major consequence we call the Buys-Ballot law for locating a surface Low from the surface wind direction, illustrated in Figure 1.3-3. His explanation of surface wind flow in 1856, was as clear and to the point as it ever had been before... *and after*. Ferrel was also the first to propose and define the "Plateau Correction" for reducing pressures measured at high elevations to their equivalent values at sea level (Appendix 3).

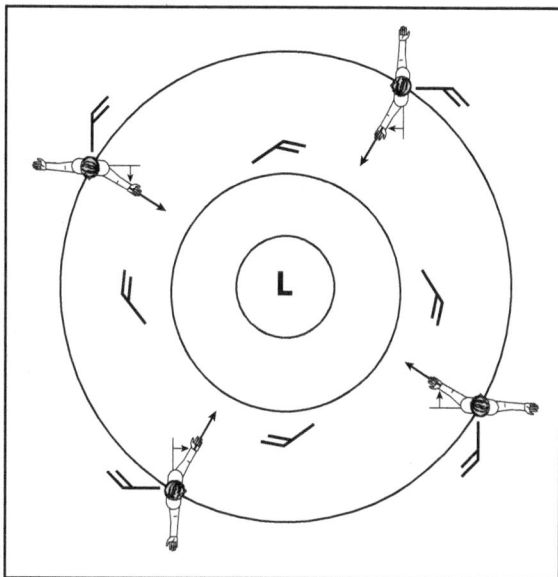

Figure 1.3-3 Buys Ballot Law in the Northern Hemisphere. Put your back to the surface wind and your left arm out to the side, then rotate it forward about 25°, and it will be pointing to the Low—or more precisely, toward the direction of the highest rate of pressure drop. The slight shift forward was not specified by Buys Ballot, but it is crucial to understanding all of weather. This shift converges wind into the Low, forcing it to rise.

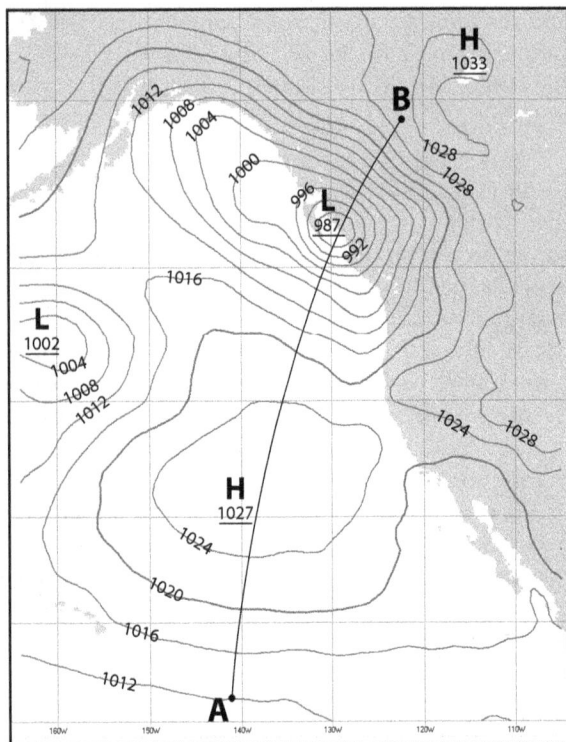

Figure 1.3-4 *Atmospheric pressure over the NE Pacific at 06 UTC, Dec 31, 2008. This map is an analysis from a NWS computer model downloaded from the Internet using the free weather service of saildocs.com.*

Each line is an isobar of constant pressure. The heavy line is 1020 mb. They are shown every 4 mb which is the U.S. standard. We see two areas of low pressure (Lows) marked L and two high pressure areas (Highs) marked H. The central values are shown in bold near the letters on this map. This map has been simplified by displaying only pressures.

To learn about this source of weather maps and the free software viewers to read them, send a blank email to info@saildocs.com.

A plot of the pressure cross section from Point A in the tropics to Point B in British Columbia, Canada is shown in Figure 1.3-5.

Average pressures worldwide by month are presented in Chapter 10.

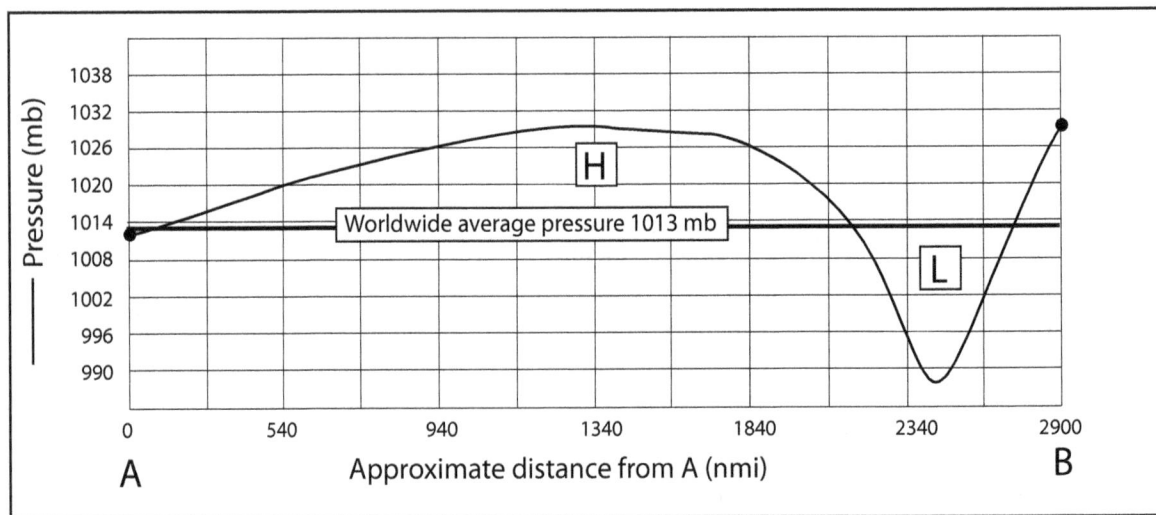

Figure 1.3-5. *Cross section from Point A to Point B on the map of in Figure 1.3-4 showing atmospheric pressures across the Pacific at this time. We see the deep Low off the coast of British Columbia and a broad High in the mid Pacific. Notice how the slope of the pressure curve is steep in the Low and gentle in the High. These are typical patterns as explained in the next Chapter.*

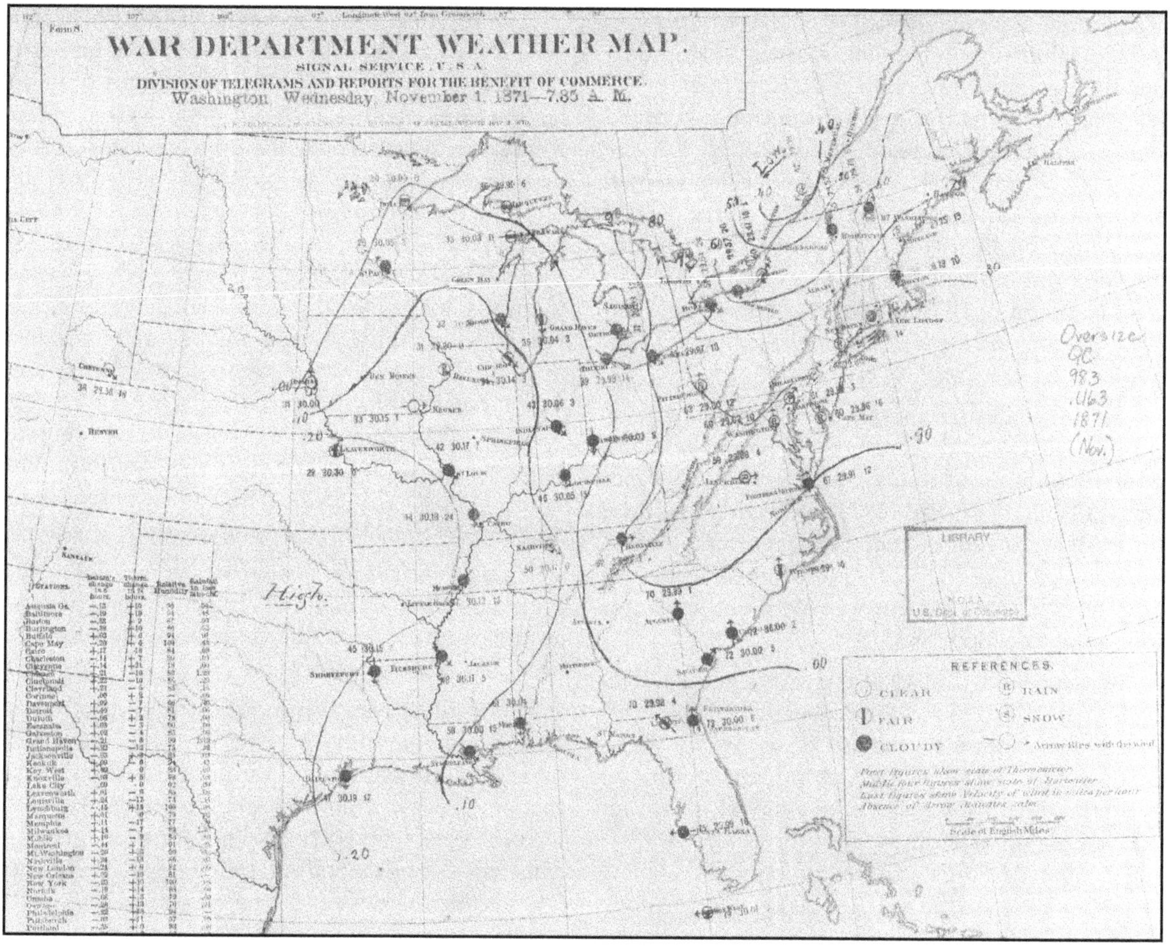

Figure 1.3-6. *Section of the first U.S. weather map with isobars and pressure labels from Nov 1, 1871. Maps for a few days before also had isobars, but Highs and Lows were not marked. In these early maps they labeled the isobars every tenth of an inch. The map is from the NOAA Central Library Data Imaging Project.*

Christophorus Henricus Diedericus Buys Ballot (1817-1890) was the Dutch counterpart and contemporary of Robert FitzRoy, and also an equally strong proponent of the barometer, with the same goal of predicting the weather for practical applications.

Buys Ballot published his law of wind directions actually a year after Ferrel did, but Buys Ballot probably gets the credit because he presented it with actual data and had used it practically for many years. Ferrel's work, in contrast, was more theoretical, though based on known global wind patterns—not to men-

tion that Ferrel published his pioneering paper on global winds in The Nashville Journal of Medicine and Surgery!

But it was probably the invention of the weather map that was the ultimate key to relating pressure not just to wind but to all of weather. "Weather map" can mean a lot of things, but usually it is a snapshot picture of the pressure pattern over a large area of the globe at a specific time. A modern sample is shown in Figure 1.3-4. A daily sequence of weather maps shows how Highs and Lows are moving across the globe.

Weather maps require gathering a lot of data over a large region at the same time, so their development had to wait for the invention and deployment of the telegraph in the mid 1800's. Maps including printed lines of constant pressure called isobars were just one of the many new developments in science presented at the World Fair at London in 1851. In another 20 years or so, maps based on telegraphic data—that do not look much different from maps we use today—were common place in the weather bureaus of England, Europe, and the U.S.. A sample is shown in Figure 1.3-6.

To further illustrate that scientists from many fields contributed to the development of barometers and understanding pressure, note that French astronomer **Urbain Le Verrier (1811-1877)** who rightly predicted the existence and location of the planet Neptune, was the first person to add isobars to weather maps, and also the first to use sequences of maps to trace storm motion and development.

By the period 1910-1920 there were enough data of this type collected that the Bergen School of Meteorology could formulate the first theory of how deep Low pressure systems are formed and how they move. It is called the Norwegian cyclone model, and it remained the primary theory until the 1980's when it was expanded by the Kaiser-Shapiro model.

These models have taught us that surface Lows are formed and directed by their interactions with the strong winds aloft, halfway up through the atmosphere. It is these winds that drag the Lows across the surface, and the fates of these surface Lows depend not only on the temperature and moisture content of the surface air but also on the shape and speed of the winds aloft.

The key to learning more about this interaction and weather in general is a careful study of barometric pressure. We can get immense amounts of information from satellites, including remarkably accurate wind speed and direction, and from these we can infer what the pressure must be, but ultimately we still rely on ships and airports and light houses, and countless numbers of dedicated weather observers worldwide—such as Dave Wheeler, MBE, whom I had the pleasure to meet at his home on remote Fair Isle in the North Sea. For thirty three years and going, he interrupted his farm work 15 times a day to don his boots and trudge out to his weather station, where he records the data, and then returns to his desk to type it up to send by Internet to the UK Met Office, which in turn shares the data worldwide. His human observations are still vital to mariners in this part of the world.

Ship's officers across the oceans are doing the same with their on-board observations, carefully taken and reported back to the Voluntary Observing Ship headquarters by satellite phone.

Granted there are more and more automated stations being put online, both on land and at sea, and there are more and more electronic barometers in use that are easier to read and care for, but there is still a crucial role, worldwide, for individual aneroid barometers—being tapped and stared at with flashlights and magnifying glasses to get accurate readings.

* * *

This has been just a cursory overview of barometers and atmospheric pressure. Please refer to the Further Reading for details and the fuller story. Much had to be left out and much was simplified. The goal was just to show how so much of fundamental science in diverse areas can be traced back to those who also worked on the barometer. Put another way, a good barometer of early scientific history is the history of the barometer itself.

There is some level of "chicken or the egg" when it comes to discussing pressure and units of pressure. To best understand the units, we need to know what we are measuring, but we can't discuss what we are measuring without giving it some units.

In Chapter One, pressure was the height of a mercury column and the units of pressure were inches. Now we wish to pursue the idea of pressure being the weight of the air above us, and that (same) pressure is best expressed in units of pounds per square inch. But when we turn to the weather maps to see what the weather services say the pressure should be, they tell us the pressure in units of millibars.

So please bear along here for a short while as we get this sorted out. We want to end up with a good working concept of what atmospheric pressure really is and the significance of the different units used to describe it.

A comparison of the world average atmospheric pressure in various units is shown in Table 2.1-1.

2.1 An Ocean of Air

Torricelli was the first to tell us that we live at the bottom of an ocean of air, with the full weight of it upon us, just as fish live on the bottom of the sea with even greater weight upon them. But we do not feel this pressure because it pushes on us from all sides. It effectively cancels out. We do not even know it is there—assuming we have enough to breathe—unless we feel it move. We can feel and see the effect of currents in this ocean of air in the form of wind. This wind can be a gentle, soothing breeze, a pleasure to behold, or it can be our worst nightmare of an uncontrollable demon destroying everything in its path.

If we think of the atmosphere as an ocean of air, these dramatic distinctions in the surface winds are the result of the waves in this ocean of air. If the sea of air is flat calm, there is no wind. If there are gentle rolling seas, we get light to moderate breezes, and when there are gigantic breaking waves plowing through the sea we get storms of wind on earth.

Air is a fluid, just like water but about a thousand times thinner. Unlike water, however, air is very compressible. Air is held to the earth by gravity; if the earth were not heavy enough to provide this attraction, the air would spin off into space from the outward centrifugal force caused by the earth's rotation. Because air is compressible and the holding power of gravity decreases with increasing elevation, most of the atmosphere is compressed into a relatively thin layer at the earth's surface, and this layer itself grows less dense with increasing altitude above the surface. Roughly 80 percent of the air is below 40,000 feet.

No matter how you picture the atmosphere, however, it is the uneven distribution of the air across the surface of the earth that creates global and local winds. Wind flows from regions that have more air toward regions that have less air.

There are several ways we can end up with more air in one place than another. First, it could just pile

| Table 2.1-1 The Standard Atmosphere* ||
Units	Pressure
mb	1013.25
inch	29.9213
Torr	760.000
kPa	101.325
hPa	1013.25
psi	14.6959

*This is the name of the average value of the atmospheric pressure, considering all latitudes and seasons. In most locations, the average pressure changes notably from month to month. Worldwide mean values are given in Chapter 10, along with their typical deviations.

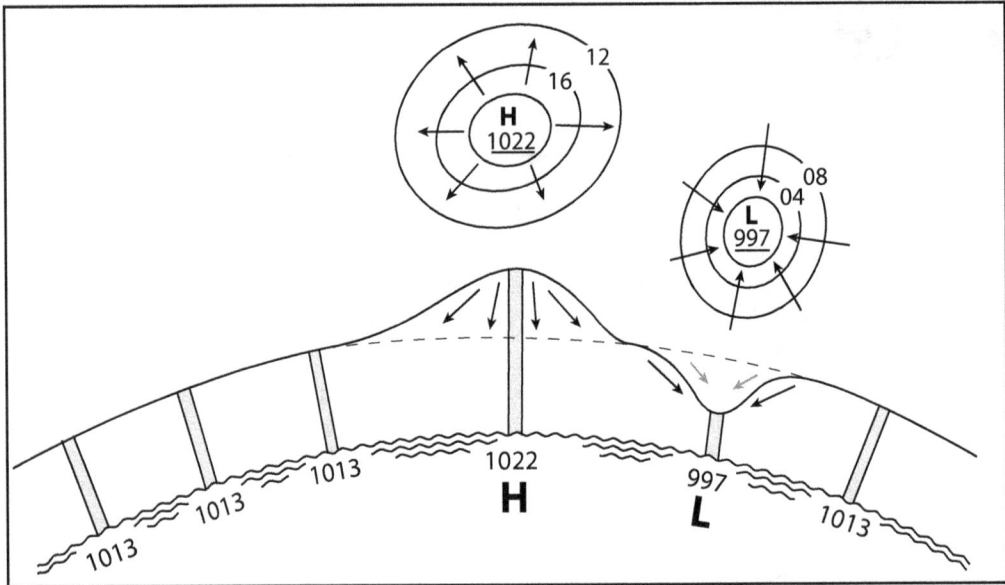

Figure 2.1-1 *Cross section (bottom) and plan view (top) of an idealized atmosphere showing air distribution over a span of some one or two thousand miles. The plan view is like a topographic map of the air, which is the basis of weather maps. Lines of constant pressure are called isobars. A "16" means the pressure is 1016 mb. The peak values are usually underlined. Gravity causes air to flow from higher to lower pressure, as marked by the arrows, diminishing the Highs and filling the Lows. The gray columns represent places where the weight of the air above is labeled. Compare this schematic pattern with the real one shown in Figure 1.3-4.*

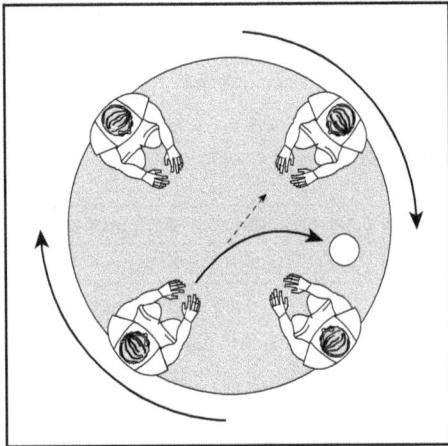

Figure 2.1-2 *Example of the Coriolis force in action on a local scale. When kids try to roll a ball to each other on opposite sides of a merry-go-round they miss because the reference plane is rotating under the ball. All objects that travel across the globe are affected, including winds, ocean currents, and ballistic missiles. The effect is the strongest at high latitudes and zero right at the equator.*

up, like waves on the ocean surface. When this takes place you can think of a topographic map of the surface of the ocean of air, as shown schematically in Figure 2.1-1. (Refer back to Figure 1.3-5 for a real sample of such a distribution.) You could map out this surface with a barometer to get the values shown. The average pressure would be 14.7 pounds per square inch, meaning a column of air with a cross section of one square inch extending from the surface to the top of the atmosphere would weigh 14.7 pounds. This is about the same as 1013 mb, which is the more common unit for atmospheric pressure. Where there is a lot of air, you would measure a high pressure (1022 mb in this example), and this region on the surface of the globe would be called a High. Likewise, areas where there is less pressure are called Lows. The Low in the figure is at 997 mb.

Piles of air, just like piles of water, have a natural tendency to fall back down and fill in the valleys. It is the force of gravity that is pulling the piles down into equilibrium, striving to leave the earth with a uniform thickness of air across the surface.

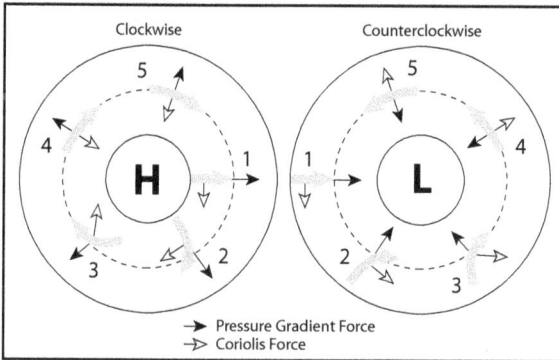

Figure 2.1-3 *Wind around Highs and Lows. The pressure gradient force (solid arrow), from gravity, pushes the air from High to Low, then the Coriolis force (open arrow) bends it to the right. In the absence of other forces, it keeps bending until the Coriolis force balances out the pressure gradient force, leaving the air circulating around the systems parallel to the isobars—clockwise around Highs and counterclockwise around Lows. In the Southern Hemisphere the directions are reversed.*

Thus all wind starts out flowing from regions of high pressure toward regions of low pressure. The mounds collapse, the holes fill in. But then (pardon the pun) there is a twist to the process. The Coriolis force turns the wind to the right. The turns come about because as the air moves across the surface, the surface rotates beneath it. Figure 2.1-2 shows a merry-go-round exercise that illustrates the Coriolis effect. In the Southern Hemisphere the wind turns to the left.

This basic rule for wind flow around Highs and Lows is shown in Figure 2.1-3. It starts flowing from high to low pressure, then the Coriolis force bends it to the right, and it keeps bending until the Coriolis force balances out the pressure driven force, and the wind is left circulating clockwise around the Highs and counterclockwise around the Lows. Notice that it is exactly the same forces causing the wind to flow opposite directions around these two pressure patterns.

That illustration refers to the driving force of the wind as the "pressure gradient force" rather than "gravity force," because that is a more general description of the process. Gravity acting on the weight of the air is certainly the initial cause of the pressure, but when it comes to describing forces on the wind we are better off thinking in terms of pressure rather

than gravity—in part because it is easier to picture pressure forcing the wind horizontally. Also, as we shall see shortly, the temperature of the air can also influence its pressure locally, and even though this too can be traced to gravity, it is ultimately the value of the pressure that we care about in describing wind and weather.

Figure 2.1-4 shows how you can imagine the pressure itself forcing the wind horizontally without reference to it being pulled down by gravity. This illustrates another fundamental concept in wind flow around Highs and Lows. When the isobars are close together the pressure gradient is said to be strong or steep, and the winds are strong. Storms and other strong wind systems will always appear on weather maps with very close isobars because the maps are always drawn with a constant separation between consecutive isobars. On U.S. maps, the standard separation is 4 mb.

Areas on the maps with light wind, on the other hand, have isobars that are farther apart. When the

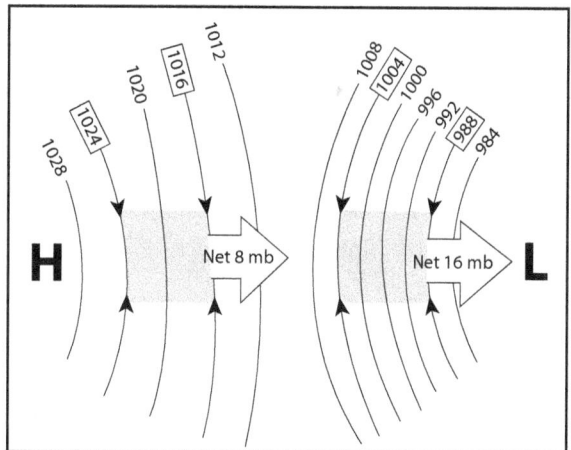

Figure 2.1-4 *Pressure gradient wind. The parcel of air in the High has an average of 1020 mb on each side, which cancel each other, but there is only 1016 on the leading edge compared to 1024 at the back. Thus the parcel is pushed from High to Low with a net pressure of 8 mb. This picture shows why the closer the isobars are the stronger the wind—the net pressure (force per unit area) is then higher. In the example here, the same region of air in the Low would be forced in the direction of low pressure with twice the gradient a similar parcel of air experiences in the High because the isobar spacing is smaller. Close isobars means a strong pressure gradient.*

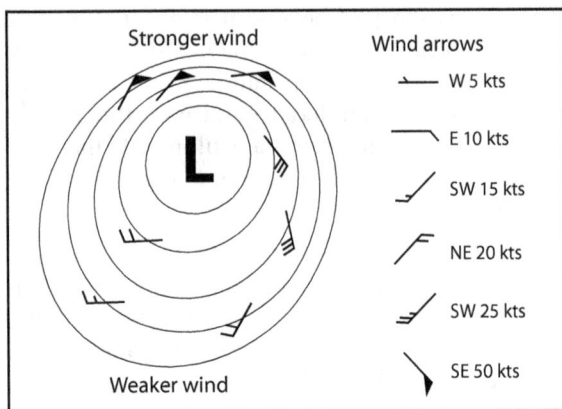

Figure 2.1-5 *When looking at a weather map, expect the strongest winds where the isobars are the closest. Wind arrows used on maps are shown on the right.*

isobars are far apart, the pressure gradient is weak, and the winds created from it are weak.

Figure 2.1-5 shows a Low from a weather map that has close isobars and strong wind on one side and separated isobars and lighter wind on the other side.

To illustrate why pressure is a better way to think of the driving force of the wind rather than gravity, consider that we can have "more air" in one place compared to another even though the height of the air is the same. We just need the air to be more dense. Since cold air is denser (heavier) than warm air, if we are in a region of cold air it will have a higher pressure than neighboring areas of warmer air.

Figure 2.1-6 shows how we can get regions of high and low pressure whenever the temperature distributions in the air are not uniform. Cold air is heavier than warm air, so when the heights of the air are about the same, cold air brings us high pressure and warm air low pressure.

There are many aspects to weather. Air temperature and precipitation are the two things we often care the most about on land, but at sea it is *always* the wind that is the key issue. Wind makes the waves, and the waves are usually the imminent threat to a vessel in a storm at sea.

On land or sea, however, the things we care about most are all tied to the atmospheric pressure. The pressure makes the winds as outlined above, but it is

also the pressure patterns that ultimately control the temperatures and precipitation we observe on land or at sea.

The air temperatures we experience are the result of the air mass we happen to be in, and these huge air masses (spanning hundreds of miles) move across the globe in direct response to the winds and pressure patterns present. A nice steady wind flowing from Hawaii up toward the Pacific Northwest, for example, can bring us unseasonable warm and balmy weather. It's called the *Pineapple Express*. But this express lane can also sometimes grab hold of a dying hurricane and nurse it back to fury on its journey north as well. Besides fair weather, this express lane has brought to the NW some of its worst storms in history.

Likewise, both on the west coast and on the east coast, a big High can park over the cold lands of a Canadian winter and the clockwise circulation around it brings down to the US extremely cold air for several days or more, called *Arctic Outbreaks*.

Thus Highs and Lows in the atmospheric pressure bring us our temperature changes, directly or indirectly, but they also create the precipitation we experience in a much more direct manner. In actual

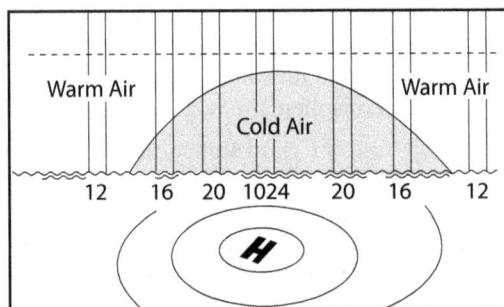

Figure 2.1-6 *High pressure area formed as a result of a cold air mass. The top shows a side view from the surface on up; the bottom is a sketch of the surface isobars.*

All across the top picture the temperature is decreasing with increasing altitude, but in the cold air it is doing so on a colder scale. The cold air weighs more than the warm air at all altitudes, and the temperatures are the same above the dotted line, so the total air column weighs more in the center of the High. Likewise a Low can be formed from a local warm air mass, which often takes place on a very local level such as over an isolated island as the sun rises.

conditions, wind does not flow exactly parallel to the isobars as shown in the idealized Figure 2.1-3. There is some friction on the surface that keeps the wind from bending all the way around in response to the Coriolis force. Thus the real wind on the surface tends to cross the isobars slightly, flowing out of the Highs and into the Lows, as shown in Figure 2.1-7.

Thus air coming into the Lows from all sides is forced to rise when it meets at the center, and as it rises it cools, eventually reaching the dew point where it condenses into clouds. The clouds in turn can become saturated and then it begins to rain—or snow if cold enough.

Air rising in Lows has to come down somewhere, and it does so in neighboring Highs. No matter how or where they are formed, Lows always have warm air rising inside them and Highs have heavier cool air descending inside them. Rising air is what makes clouds, so Highs are opposite to Lows in another big way. Lows have clouds and rain, Highs have clear skies and dry air.

The reason Highs are clear is again due to the temperature drop as you rise in the atmosphere. If it drops going up, it rises coming down. So any clouds that happen into the area of a High pressure start to descend, and as they descend they heat up and evapo-

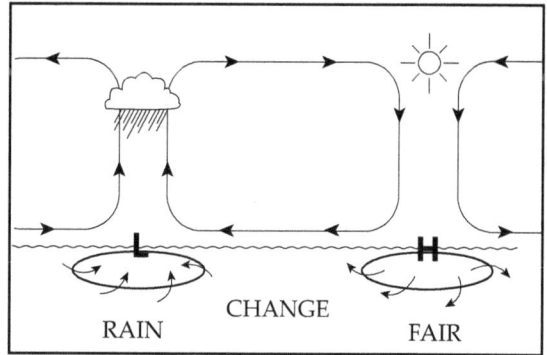

Figure 2.1-8 *Air rises in a Low and descends in a High giving rise to the typical descriptions of Lows as bad weather and Highs as good weather...and a first glimpse of why barometers are labeled as they are.*

rate, leaving clear, dry air. The circulation, horizontally and vertically, is illustrated in Figure 2.1-8, with a first look at why barometer dials are labeled the way they are. Properties of Highs and Lows are summarized in Table 2.1-2.

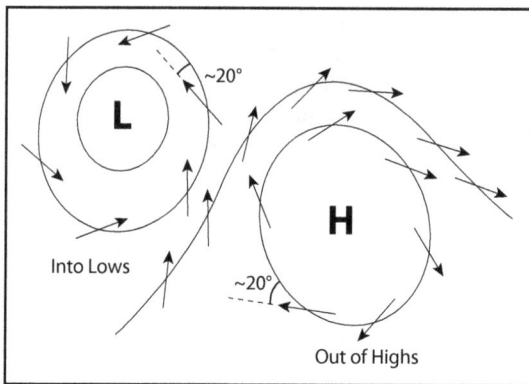

Figure 2.1-7 *Surface wind flow is slightly across the isobars, pointing some 15° to 30° into the Low or out of the High. At higher elevations where the effect of surface friction is no longer felt, wind flow follows the isobars without crossing them. In relatively calm seas 10° to 20° is a good approximation; in rough seas or on land, 20° to 40° would be a better guess.*

Table 2.1-2 Properties of Highs and Lows		
Alternative names	Highs, anticyclones	Lows, cyclones, depressions
Wind	Light and Variable	Strong and gusty
Circulation*	Clockwise* and slightly out	Counterclockwise* and slightly in
Sky	Clear, dry	Cloudy, rain
Vertical	Descending	Rising
Relative Temperature	Cool	Warm
Typical Pressures	1020 to 1040 mb	1000 to 970 mb
Centers of Action+	Pacific, Bermuda, Azores, Siberian	Aleutian, Asiatic, Icelandic
Elongated forms called	Ridges	Troughs
World surface Records	1084 mb Agata, Siberia December 31, 1968	870 mb Pacific Typhoon Tip October 12, 1979

* This is Northern Hemisphere (NH). In SH, reverse the directions. + These are regions where you are likely to find semi-permanent Highs or Lows. See Chapter 10

2.2 Units

The common units of atmospheric pressure are obscure at best. So far we learned that a 1-inch by 1-inch column of air extending from sea level to the top of the atmosphere weighs about 14.7 pounds. This is the typical value, averaged over all latitudes and seasons, called the standard atmosphere. Values in other units were shown in Table 2.2-1.

Pounds per square inch (psi) provides a natural unit for pressure as it tells us nicely what we are measuring. But that is not the unit of atmospheric pressure in common use, in part because the typical variations we experience with passing weather systems are small when expressed in psi. For example a typical low pressure (990 mb) would be 14.36 psi, and a typical high pressure (1020) would be 14.79 psi. The psi units are more than 100 times coarser than we want for careful weather work. It would be rather like measuring our body weight in tons. Pressure measurements other than atmospheric pressure, such as for car tires and scuba tanks, do use this practical unit of psi.

On land, the common unit of atmospheric pressure is "inches of mercury," which comes directly from the mercury tube barometer. Again, a very direct concept, the height of the mercury column that rises and falls as the pressure increases or decreases. In these units, the standard atmosphere air pressure is 29.92 inches of mercury, often just abbreviated to 29.92 "inches." Aviators and TV weathermen in the US use these units, but they are not the preferred units for use at sea.

The best pressure unit for marine use is the millibar (mb), which is the same as a hectopascal (hPa). On land or sea, once you leave the U.S., the hectopascal is universally the most common unit of atmospheric pressure. In these units, the standard atmosphere is 1013.25 mb.

To understand hectopascals, we need to convert the British units of pounds per square inch to the metric equivalent. The metric counterpart of a British pound-force is called a Newton. So after changing square inches to square meters, we get the metric unit of pressure called a Pascal.

1 Pascal = 1 Newton / square meter,

which then has several multiple forms:

1 kiloPascal = 1000 Pascals

1 hectoPascal = 100 Pascals

Another unit of pressure called a "bar" was proposed by the famous Norwegian meteorologist Bjerknes, whose research group gave us the Norwegian cyclone model to explain how storms are formed. One bar is roughly equal to the average atmospheric pressure on earth, but it was formally defined as

1 bar = 100,000 Pascals

1 millibar (mb) = one thousandth of a bar

= 100 Pascals

= 1 hectopascal (hPa).

Referring back to the size of the bar, we note that the standard atmospheric pressure 1013.25 mb would be 1.013 bars. So if someone wants to know roughly what the pressure is, you can tell them it's "about 1 bar"—or you could be fancier and say 1,000 mb. This is like saying the width of a fisherman's out-stretched arm span is "about 1 fathom," because that is where the unit came from.

If you are going to work with barometers and pressures, there is no way to avoid the conversion among these units, primarily between inches and mb. TV and commercial radio weather reports (almost always in inches) are very convenient, and some of the official reference pressures we can use for calibration are given in both units. And a prize barometer you find might be just as well marked in inches as in millibars, sometimes both.

The conversion factor between inches and mb can be traced back to the definition of the standard atmosphere. If you have a calculator at hand (or in your cell phone!), the official conversion factor from inches to mb is (1013.25/29.92) x inches = mb. Or vice versa, (29.92/1013.25) x mb = inches.

When you do not have a calculator, one way to make an approximate conversion in your head is to remember that:

30.00 inches = 1016 mb,

and

0.03 inches = 1 mb.

Take the difference between 30.00 and what you want to convert, round to the nearest 0.03, and apply the correction to 1016. For example, 29.80 is 0.20 different from 30.00, and 0.20 is about 0.21 which is 7 x 0.03, so 29.80 = 1016 - 7 = 1009 mb. (Exact is 1009.14.)

A crucial step to the study of pressure and barometers is to choose a unit to "think in." If you have spent a long time thinking in inches, then that will be your unit, and you should get a barometer that reads in inches, and stick with that.

But if you are starting from scratch, or do not have a total commitment to inches, then you will be far better off using mb (or hPa) as your unit of choice. If your main application is maritime, then you must switch to mb since this is the unit used worldwide in marine weather. All the maps, text and voice reports are in mb or hPa.

Table 2.2-1 Conversion Among Atmospheric Pressure Units		
mb	inches	Torr (mm)
100	2.95	74.9
10	0.295	7.49
1	0.0295	0.749
0.1	0.00295	0.0749
33.9	1	25.4
3.39	0.1	2.54
0.339	0.01	0.254
13.33	0.394	10
1.333	0.0394	1
0.013	0.0039	0.1
1 kPa = 1000 Pascals		
1 hPa = 100 Pascals		
0.1 hPa = 10 Pascals		
0.01 hPa = 1 Pascal		

Canada is a bit of an exception in that they give pressures in text reports in kilopascals, accurate to the tenth (which is equivalent to mb without the tenths), but they still label weather maps in hectopascals (mb). This does not change anything said, but you just see 101.6 kPa in Canada, where other countries would show this as 1016 hPa. The corresponding isobar on a weather map would still be labeled "16". Some few barometers are labeled in kilopascals.

By "thinking in the units" I mean we need to know if a reported pressure is a low pressure or a high pressure, and if the drop in pressure we observe is a fast one or a slow one. Trying to do this in several units is like thinking in two languages. It is harder to cover the nuances—really high, versus just high, etc.

Another unit you will see marked on some barometers is "millimeters of mercury," which is based on the same principle as inches of mercury, but expressed in metric units. An inch is exactly 2.54 centimeters, so a barometer reading of 30.0 inches is the same as 76.2 cm or 762 mm (Torr). This unit is used in scientific work, but not in land or sea weather reporting—except sometimes in Europe. Some barometers are marked in mm but they are relatively rare. Most aneroid barometers are marked in both inches and mb, and the choice boils down to which one do you want on the outer scale, because that is the one that can be read to the higher precision. Electronic barometers usually let you set the units to whatever you choose, which is another advantage they offer.

There is a convenient inches to millibar conversion table in Appendix 1, which is a quick solution when available. Sitting at a computer that is online, it is hard to beat Google for any conversion. In the search engine input field type "convert 30.06 inches of mercury to mb" and you instantly get "30.06 inches of mercury = 1 017.8316 millibars."

Remember, however, when doing such a conversion of units by computation, that you do not gain precision by the operation of changing units. Google has told us here a bit more than we want. We ask it to convert 30.06 inches, which means we have a pressure that is not 30.05 and not 30.07, meaning we know the pressure to within ±0.01 inch. From Table 2.1-2 we know that 0.01 inches = 0.3 mb. In other words, we do not know the pressure we are converting any better than ±0.3 mb, so everything Google told us beyond 1017.8 has no honest meaning.

It is hard to keep track of this type of reasoning for all units and values we might deal with and convert among, but for practical atmospheric pressures we can make some rules based on the WMO standard of specifying pressures accurate to 0.1 mb. We use mb or hPa in tenths, inches in hundredths, and mm in tenths. Thus we would write a pressure of 1017.8 mb as 30.06 inches or 763.4 mm. These are roughly equivalent levels of precision. The inches are a bit coarser (0.01 inch = 0.25 mb), but if we went to 0.001 we would exceed the WMO standard, and in fact be beyond the capability of all but the most expensive barometers.

For completeness there is one last note to make about these two most popular units of atmospheric pressure in the U.S. (millibars and inches of mercury) that might be of interest to some. The boldest way to state it would be: there is no rigorously correct way to convert between mb and inches of mercury because they are completely different units!

A millibar is an honest unit of pressure (force per unit area), whereas inches are a unit of length. Even if we agree we are measuring the height of a mercury column that is a direct measure of the atmospheric pressure, it is still a length. And that length itself depends not just on the actual pressure but also on several other factors. It depends on the temperature of the device, because the length of the mercury column expands and contracts with temperature, as do all metals, including liquid ones. The apparent pressure difference due to temperature correction alone going from 50° F to 90° F is about 0.11 inches of column length, corresponding to 3.7 mb.

And the length of the mercury column also depends on the latitude of the observation. Unlike temperature, the source of this dependence is not so obvious. It can be traced to the fact that the weight of the mercury column is balancing out the weight of the air holding it up. The weight of the mercury depends on the force of gravity (as does the weight of anything), which in turn depends on the distance between the center of mass of the mercury column and the center of mass of the earth.

If the earth were perfectly round and smooth, the force of gravity would not change with latitude, and the mercury height would not depend on latitude. But the earth is very slightly out of round, which makes a noticeable effect on the very sensitive measurements possible with a mercury barometer. The gravity correction to a mercury barometer pressure reading at the equator compared to latitude 45° is about 2.7 mb.

And we won't pursue the sticky point that all super-pure and super-clean mercury is not the same! The National Institutes of Standards and Technology (NIST) can even tell you what mine the mercury came from, because the isotopic composition is slightly different in various natural sources, which in turn has a slight effect on the density of the mercury. If the density is different, its weight is different, and the NIST measurements are sensitive enough to detect this.

So, the only way pressures measured in inches of mercury can be compared to each other is to normalize them to some standard values, which have been chosen to be 0°C and sea level at latitude 45°. So without some help here, we would have to consider that every pressure we hear of in inches of mercury assumes the temperature is 0°C and the location is at sea level at latitude is 45°. This makes converting to other units that do not depend on temperature and latitude very difficult, not to mention the fact that statements like "the barometer dropped 0.5 inches" do not specify a unique change in barometric pressure.

The way this fundamental quandary has been resolved is to invent an entirely new unit of atmospheric pressure called the "Standard Atmosphere" whose main job is to relate these two units. It simply states that 760 mm of mercury is exactly equal to the pressure of the U.S. and International Civil Aviation Organization (ICAO) Standard Atmospheres, which is 1013.25 mb. Thus when we convert 760 mm to inches, we get 29.9213 inches of mercury = 1013.25 mb, and this now constitutes the official, exact relationship between these two units. After that solution, we can simply carry on as if there were no fundamental problem, and think of this newly defined "inches of mercury" as a perfectly good unit of atmospheric pressure—which, of course, is what everyone does.

This type of solution to defining units that do not have a rigorous correspondence is not new to mariners. The nautical mile was considered 1' of latitude (or 1' of arc along any great circle on the surface of the earth) for a hundred years before we learned the earth was not round, and that in fact the length of 1' of latitude was not a constant. To resolve this, a nautical mile was simply officially redefined as 1852 meters, exactly. From then on, 1 nautical mile remains a good approximation to 1' of latitude, but it is not exact—as many mariners are learning as their GPS navigation becomes more accurate. The term "sea mile" has come to mean the traditional concept of 1' of latitude, though it is used more in the U.K. than in the U.S..

2.3 Pressure vs. Altitude

There are two key factors that affect the relationship between pressure and altitude. One is how does the pressure drop as we rise up in the atmosphere—the very question that puzzled Torricelli in the 1640's—and how do we define the zero point of altitude where we start counting from. The latter is usually called "sea level"—and immediately we come to a bit of a conflict.

Strictly speaking, "elevation" refers to the height of an object *on the surface of the earth* relative to some reference level, usually sea level. Whereas "altitude" refers to the height *above the surface of the earth*. Altitude in that sense is often referenced to the surface of the earth. When we are discussing atmospheric pressures, however, all elevations *and* altitudes are measured relative to sea level.

Sea level and elevation

The phrase "sea level" could stand for the level of the sea at any moment, but that is tricky because in many places around the world that level is going up and down several times each day with the tides. In some parts of the world the water depth changes just 1 ft or so, but in other parts there can be a 40-ft change during the day.

More often the phrase "sea level" implies the *mean sea level*, which is a reference level that averages out the effect of the tides. The mean sea level is the average water level at some specific place—it is the level that is

very slowly rising each year due to global warming. As the great masses of ice at the poles slowly melt, they add water to the oceans that causes this very slow but significant rise (about 3 mm/year).

Precise measurements of the mean sea levels around the world are complex because there are many factors that affect the sea level on a temporary basis. It is also difficult to get this data from tide gauges since the sun and moon go through a 19-year cycle of phase relationships that have to be accounted for in tide predictions. The most accurate sea level data come from ongoing satellite altimetry measurements, which can measure the height of the sea level to within an inch or so. The satellite positions (latitude, longitude, and altitude) can be computed and tracked very precisely relative to the center of the earth, and then radar onboard the satellites measures the distance from the satellite down to the sea surface below it with great precision. Sophisticated analysis, however, is still required to extract the desired sea level data.

With such precise measurements we learn much about our planet. First it is not exactly a sphere, but distorted very slightly to be shaped more like a doorknob, with the equatorial radius some 13 miles larger than the polar radius. This does not affect our surface navigation to any great extent, but it will turn out to be a significant factor when it comes to precise pressure measurements discussed later.

Also the sea level surface is not even smooth. Bumps and dips occur in response to underwater terrain. A giant deep-sea trench, for example, can gravitationally disturb the surface creating troughs some 250 miles wide and up to 50 feet deep in the surface of the ocean.

These surface level anomalies do not affect our use of atmospheric pressure—once we are clear on the terminology—but the prevailing atmospheric pressure itself does indeed have an effect on the measurement of the height of the sea level. The terminology we have to be careful about is "mean sea level pressure," often abbreviated MSLP.

The "mean" in this phrase refers to the pressure, not the sea level. It is true that you can say things like "The *mean sea level* is the average of all *sea levels*," or you could say "the *sea level* today in San Francisco Bay

is 4 inches below the *mean sea level* for that location."
So there are distinctions to these phrases, but when
it comes to discussions about pressure and elevation,
the terms "sea level" and "mean sea level" are the
same. Thus when we say "mean sea level pressure" for
San Francisco Bay in August we are referring to the average of all the sea-level pressures measured throughout the day for each day of August, over, say, the past
20 years. Mean pressures worldwide are presented in
Chapter 10.

You will also see SLP, for "sea-level pressure," but
this one is not too confusing. MSLP is the average

Where is Sea Level?

If you live on the coast or visit a tidal
shoreline, you can see the markings on
the beach or seawalls, or pilings in the
water, where the tide has marked the
various tidal water levels. If you want to
mark the place on a wall or piling where
the water would be exactly at the mean
sea level for that location, you would do
the following.

Go to a tide book or go online to find
the nearest tide station to that location.
Then for that location, look up the *mean
tide level*. That will be a permanent number for that location (let's call it 8.4 feet)—
permanent, that is, except for the very
slow increase over the years due to global
warming.

Then look up what the actual tide
height is at the present time, and suppose
that is 6.1 feet. So we are lucky. The tide is
lower than its mean value. Then go down
to the wall and make a permanent mark
2.3 ft above the water (8.4-6.1) and then
whenever the water reaches that mark, it
is exactly at mean sea level. If the present
tide happens to be higher than the mean
tide level, then you have to wait till it falls
below it to mark the height.

pressure at some location, whereas SLP is the pressure
there at some specific time. What is more challenging
to think about is the concept of sea-level pressure *at
your location* when you are on a high mountain plateau, a thousand miles from the sea!

If you are on a boat on the ocean, the pressure you
read is directly equal to sea-level pressure. But if you
are at home, say 300 feet above sea level, you will read
a lower pressure, because pressure always decreases as
you rise in the atmosphere. The pressure you read at
any elevation other than sea level is called your *station
pressure*.

For some applications, it is the station pressure
you care about most, such as when tuning the engine
of a race car just before a race. But if you want to know
about weather, you have to correct this station pressure to sea-level pressure, which will remove the elevation dependence of the data. If we did not do this,
we could be under a perfectly uniform, constant pressure over our part of the state, yet everyone in every
direction would read a different pressure depending
on their elevation.

Likewise, if we wish to find out what sort of actual weather pattern is passing over us at the moment
by checking with other station pressure observations
in various directions around us, this would be completely impossible, as it would be masked by elevation effects if we did not correct it. The effect is huge.
The change of pressure vertically is always way larger
than any changes horizontally.

A nice deep typhoon would be an example of
the steepest possible pressure drop horizontally, and
these might drop from 990 mb to 920 mb in 50 miles
approaching the center. That is a pressure gradient of
70 mb in 50 miles or 7 mb/5 mi. If you go up from
1013 mb on the surface to 5-miles elevation (26,400
ft), the pressure will have dropped to 354 mb, which
is 50 times greater rate of decrease than ever observed
horizontally in the deepest type of Low. But those are
the extremes. Just going up and down local hills of
300 feet (pressure change of 12 mb) will be much
more than the atmospheric pressure typically changes
in a day.

So the concept of elevation influence on pressure is fundamental to any application. The correc-

tion process is called "reducing station pressure to sea level pressure."

To illustrate the process, imagine you are at an elevation of 300 ft above sea level and you read a station pressure of 1016 mb, and right beside you there is a gigantic hole the size of a football field that is 300 feet deep. The question then is what is the pressure at the bottom of this hole? It will be higher than 1016, but we have to do some reckoning to figure how much.

We can make a good approximation using the standard atmosphere as a guide, because it tells us mathematically how in average conditions the pressure drops with altitude. When the conditions are not close to average at the moment, however, the reduction process for accurate values is more involved, and we postpone that description to Appendix 3. Generally making this conversion to sea level-pressure is not something we need to do, because the NWS does this for us at all of their reporting stations. *Essentially all pressures you ever read or hear announced from any official source are sea-level pressures, regardless of the elevation of the station reporting them.*

In fact, if you wanted to know the actual pressures being read on barometers in, say, Boise, ID (elevation about 2,300 ft) it would be very difficult to find it, unless you happened to have a friend in Boise with a barometer who you could call to ask. And the reason you can't find such station pressures reported anywhere is simply that they do not have any meaning, unless you know the precise elevation of the barometer. Call another friend there and you will get a different answer.

But we can go backwards, if we know the elevation of the barometer we care about. In other words, we can look up accurate sea-level pressure just about anywhere in the world on land (roughly every hour), and if we know the elevation of the barometer in question, we can figure out how much we need to deduct from the sea-level pressure to get the station pressure. The problem is knowing the elevation accurately. A 27-ft error in elevation is a 1-mb error in pressure.

In most circumstances, when you say your "elevation is 300 feet," it means your elevation is 300 feet above sea level. When you look at a topographic map—a common place to find your elevation—it will say that the contour lines are elevations above sea level.

If you want to learn more about the changes in sea level due to global warming, then sealevel.colorado.edu is a good place to start.

Pressure drop with elevation

As soon as anyone could climb a hill and come back down again, they knew the temperature got colder as they rose in the atmosphere, so that basic property was known and proven a long time ago. It was also suspected by many great thinkers of the 17th century and earlier that air was a fluid like water, and as such would exhibit increasing pressure with depth, or put the other way around, as Torricelli himself suspected, the pressure of air gets lighter as you rise in the atmosphere. This supposition, however, was not actually proven until Pascal arranged to have a barometer taken up a mountain and back down. This confirmed the concept, but there was still not enough data to quantify the behavior. The solution had to wait for another of the great thinkers of the past who contributed to our understanding of atmospheric pressure.

Pierre-Simone Laplace (1749-1827), French mathematician and astronomer, was one of the giants in the history of science. He is often called the French equivalent of Newton. Wishing to study atmospheric refraction to improve his astronomical observations, he needed to learn more of how the atmosphere changed with increasing altitude, and thus arranged for balloon measurements over Paris in 1804. From this data, along with his newly developed mathematical methods, he could derive, among other things, an accurate relationship between altitude and pressure, which is still the basis for how barometers serve as altimeters. It is called the *Hypsometric Equation*.

Torricelli anticipated it, Pascal first measured it, and Laplace finally understood it to the point he could write the correct equations for it.

2.4 The Standard Atmosphere

The phrase "standard atmosphere" has two distinct meanings. One is a unit of pressure, which we discussed in Section 2.2. The second is a generic description of an idealized average atmosphere that is used in science and engineering. The latter is often referred to as the International Standard Atmosphere, or just the "ISA."

As more information was gained about the vertical structure of the atmosphere, more applications became apparent. By the end of the first world war, two such applications were aircraft design criteria for the newly emerging aircraft industry and the construction of ballistics tables for long-range artillery, both of which depended upon the properties of air as a function of altitude. There was also the ongoing concern about creating accurate aneroid altimeters for these new aircraft.

So it was not so much atmospheric science itself, but rather practical issues of engineering that led to the creation of an average description of the atmosphere that came to be known as the Standard Atmosphere. This was meant to represent average conditions, worldwide, throughout the year. Its name and concept were first proposed by Willis Ray Gregg of the US Weather Bureau in 1920. It was clearly known that there would not be any one place or time that would ever have these exact properties of temperature, pressure and density as a function of elevation, and further that they would not even use the most exact data of the time, but rather they would favor a simple prescription. The sole purpose was to have some description of the atmosphere that would represent a reasonable average that could be easily incorporated into various applications.

Over the years the formulation has improved somewhat, but it remains essentially as originally defined. The latest version is referred to as the International Standard Atmosphere (ISA). The data and formulas are presented in Appendix A2. A summary is given in Table 2.4-1. Referring to that table, you see that as you go up in the atmosphere, on average the temperature drops at about 4.6 °F per 1,000 ft (called the *lapse rate*), but for our subject we care more about the pressure, which is dropping at a slower rate.

The temperature drop is linear; the pressure drop is exponential. In other words, if you go from the surface to 5,000 ft, the temperature drops 17.8°, from 59° to 41.2°, and if you go up another 5,000 ft to 10,000 ft the temperature drops again by 17.8°. The

pressure, on the other hand, drops 146.3 mb in the first 5,000 ft, but only drops 36.1 mb in the next 5,000 feet.

Meteorologists tend to remember this behavior relative to the 500-mb level, since that marks the point about halfway up through the atmosphere. That is, at the surface you have about 1,000 mb of pressure with all of the atmosphere above you, and at 18,000 feet you have on average about 500 mb, so that elevation marks the point where half of the air is above you.

If you go up another 18,000 ft to 36,000 feet the pressure is reduced by roughly half again to about 250 mb (227.3 to be exact), and go another 18,000 ft and it goes down by roughly half again to about 125 mb (95.7 to be exact). The 18,000-ft steps that cut the pressure by half are not exact, but still a good way to remember the behavior. Referring to the table, we see that some 78% of all of the atmosphere is below 36,000 feet.

Although the panorama of a giant storm on the horizon can seem immense at times, the atmosphere in which this is all taking place is actually very thin. Over three quarters of it is below 36,000 ft, an altitude where almost every one has been at one time or another during airplane travel. If the earth were the

Table 2.4-1 ISA*			
Feet	P (mb)	%	T (°F)
0	1013.25	0	59.0
12	1012.81		59.0
100	1009.6		58.6
500	995.1		57.2
1,000	977.2	4	55.4
5,000	843.1	17	41.2
10,000	696.8	31	23.4
18,000	506.0	50	-5.2
36,000	227.3	78	-69.4
54,000	95.7	91	-69.7

* ISA stands for International Standard Atmosphere. See Appendix A2 for more details. The % column shows how much of the total atmosphere is below that elevation, which is very roughly how much "thinner" the air is at that elevation.

size of an apple, the atmosphere would be much thinner than the skin on the apple. But we are smaller still, so it still looks big to us.

Most all of the air-mass distinctions and the frontal zones between them that we call "weather" are within the first half layer, below 18,000 feet. The exceptions are giant thunderstorms, which can reach well beyond that.

If you care to see the actual vertical profile of the atmosphere at a specific time and place, see weather.uwyo.edu/upperair/sounding.html. Here you can see actual balloon measurements (called soundings) of temperature, dew point, pressure, and density as a function of elevation. They are typically taken twice a day at many locations around the world. These can then be compared to the average values that make up the ISA. The fact that these two profiles are in fact different in practice is what makes the problem of accurately reducing a station pressure to sea-level pressure so difficult.

2.5 Pressure on Weather Maps

Barometers and weather maps are part and parcel of our understanding of atmospheric pressure. For example, in a later section we use weather maps to check the calibration of our barometers, and in a section after that we use our calibrated barometers to check weather maps from other sources.

The weather maps themselves are made on the basis of barometer observations taken worldwide four times a day at 6:00 and 12:00, AM and PM, Universal Coordinated Time (UTC), formerly called Greenwich Mean Time. The abbreviation 6z means 6 AM UTC; 18z means 6 PM UTC; etc. The times of 00z, 06z, 12z, and 18z are called the synoptic times. These are the times that weather maps are created, worldwide. If you want to compare your barometer reading with a weather map, then you have to know how to figure UTC, and you have to have a recorded observation of your barometer at that time. A good place to learn about time and time zones is www.time.gov.

To further pursue the relationship between barometers and weather maps, we take a quick look at how the maps are made. Official weather observers around

the world, as well as most airports, lighthouses, and automated buoys send the pressure readings (plus wind and other data) to their various national weather services at each synoptic time throughout the day and night. Various divisions of these weather services in turn use these data to update several mathematical computer models of the global atmosphere. The computer models then analyze what is taking place at the time, and they make predictions of what is going to take place in the future. There are five or six super computers around the world dedicated to an ongoing global model of the atmosphere.

Professional meteorologists around the world study the predictions of *all* the computer models available and then, relying on their own knowledge and experience, they make a consensus of the model outputs, and from that create the weather maps that they then publish on the Internet. They also distribute the maps to Coast Guards and other agencies that make them available by radiofacsimile or other means. They make a surface analysis map for the synoptic time that the data were gathered, and they also make a series of forecast maps. The Ocean Prediction Center (OPC) division of the NWS makes forecast maps for 24 hr, 48 hr, and 96 hr into the future.

We then, as end users of these forecast maps, can use our own barometers to monitor the progress of the weather systems forecasted on the map. That is one of the main reasons for having an accurate barometer. With it you can tell if a forecast is developing as predicted or not. On the other hand, if you do not have an official forecast, your barometer will be the key component to making your own forecast.

So the key steps in using weather maps are:

(1) Knowing what they are and how to get them,

(2) Finding your position on the map,

(3) Interpolating the pressure at your position, and finally,

(4) Being sure you are doing all this at the right time and that you are aware of the effect of your elevation on the pressure you read.

(1) Types of maps and where to get them

For now we care about just two types of maps. A *surface analysis map* is the one that explains what was taking place at the synoptic time it was valid for. The key word is *was* valid for—these maps will always be at least 3 hours old. They collect the data at precisely the synoptic times, then it takes a couple hours to analyze it and distribute the results.

The *forecast maps* are the predictions of what will take place later on. Generally they make a set of forecast maps each time they make a surface analysis. Each forecast map will, therefore, tell you both when it was made, and when it is valid for.

There are many sources of weather maps online these days, but a good place to start is the Ocean Prediction Center. This is a natural starting place for mariners because of their marine focus, but they include links to maps over land as well, including maps from other countries. These sources are listed in Table 2.5-1. We call the sources Ref. A, B, and C. Symbols used for the mapped station reports are explained in Figure 2.5-1.

A sample marine oriented map from Ref. A (OPC) is shown in Figure 2.5-2. Figure 2.5-3 shows the corresponding Unified Surface analysis map which is intended to incorporate the work of several NWS departments. The two maps are very similar, but not identical. The latter can be downloaded for any section of the U.S. and they show all the reports that were used. You can also compare to these the Canadian counterparts (Ref. C) and again, the maps will be very similar, but not identical. When an area you care about the most does show some discrepancy, your own barometer and wind observations could determine which map is the best.

(2) Finding your position on the map

To find your position on the map you have to either scale the latitude longitude lines or scale some geographic feature. If you do not know your latitude and longitude, then you can find it on Google Earth, or there are numerous sources online that convert addresses to lat-lon coordinates. This one does it several different ways: stevemorse.org/jcal/latlon.php.

When you use just sections of the Unified maps you do not get many coordinates, so this is harder. In Figure 2.5-3 we see only the 30 N latitude line and the 80 W longitude line (dotted lines). But you can always scale the land. If you live in Daytona Beach, FL for example, you know from a map that shows your city that you are on the beach, south of Georgia by a distance about equal to the width of Florida, and that is plenty enough information to find your location on a map to well within a fraction of a mb.

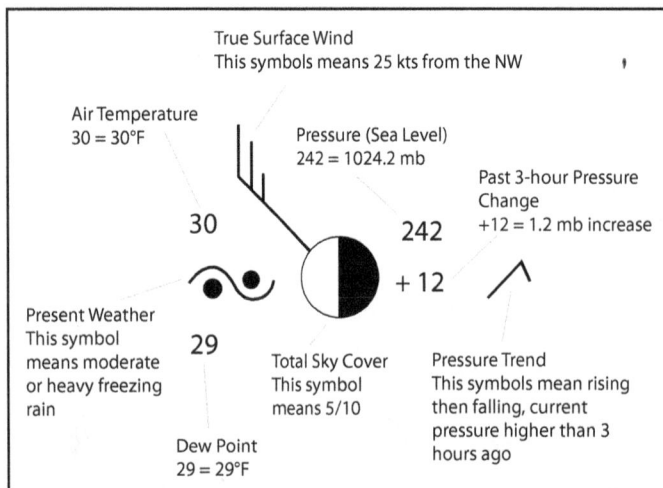

True Surface Wind
This symbols means 25 kts from the NW

Air Temperature
30 = 30°F

Pressure (Sea Level)
242 = 1024.2 mb

30

Past 3-hour Pressure Change
+12 = 1.2 mb increase

242

+ 12

Present Weather
This symbol means moderate or heavy freezing rain

29

Total Sky Cover
This symbol means 5/10

Pressure Trend
This symbols mean rising then falling, current pressure higher than 3 hours ago

Dew Point
29 = 29°F

Figure 2.5-1 *Station report symbols. Surface analysis maps often show the reports that went into their production using this symbol structure. Trends are discussed later in Section 5.5. Marine maps tend to use a more abbreviated report than those on land. Weather symbols can be found online or in textbooks.*

Recall that wind directions are defined as the direction they come from. A "north" wind blows from the north toward the south. A wind direction of 045°, means you face due north (000°), then turn 45° to the right, and you will have the wind in your face. A "sea breeze" blows from the sea toward the land.

(3) Interpolating the pressure

Once you find your location, the next step is interpolating the isobars to see what pressure you should have. If you happen to be right on an isobar you don't have to do this, and if you are exactly halfway between two of them, the task is simple. Your pressure is half way between the two isobars. But generally you will be some arbitrary fraction between the two, and usually even a crude measurement is better than a guess. One way to do this using just a straight edge marked off in tenths is shown in Figure 2.5-4. The example is for a vessel at sea, but the method can be applied to any map location.

(4) Time and elevation corrections

Finally we must remember that we can only compare our own barometer to a weather map 4 times a day and these are very specific times, the synoptic times. Thus to prepare for this, we should make a point of recording the barometer reading at these times. If we miss the exact time, we can always interpolate, but if the pressure is changing rapidly and we want to do the best we can, we should strive to record at the proper times.

And we must of course be aware of the elevation effect. We may be doing this comparison to calibrate our barometer, in which case we expect it to be off, and we would be in the process of finding out just how much it is off.

Or we could be using a calibrated barometer, which could mean we have a graph or table of corrections that we have to apply to our reading in order to get the proper sea-level values. Weather map pressures are always corrected to sea level, even when they draw them over places with very high terrain such as Colorado and other states in the SW U.S..

The main point is this, it is never a simple matter of just looking at your barometer and then looking at the weather map, or vice versa. We have to think about valid times and elevations, and calibration curves.

Figures 2.5-6 and 2.5-7 show how the motion of Highs and Lows are shown on both surface analysis maps and on forecast maps. Remember it is only the valid map time peaks that are written out in full such as 1025. Past and future values show just the last two digits, underlined. Figure 2.5-8 shows the definition of wind shifts that are crucial to forecasting with wind and barometer.

Table 2.5-1 Internet Sources of U.S. Surface Analysis Maps		
Coverage	*Source*	*Ref.*
Coastal lands and adjacent waters	www.opc.ncep.noaa.gov	A
Inland and adjacent waters	www.opc.ncep.noaa.gov/UA.shtml	B
Canada and much of the U.S.	www.weatheroffice.gc.ca/analysis/index_e.html	C

Figure 2.5-2 *Surface analysis map from Ref A. of Table 2.5-1. The lines of constant pressure are called Iso-bars. They are labeled with the last two digits of the pressure. A 24 on a line means that is the line where the pressure is 1024 mb. The locations of peak Highs and Lows are marked with a bold H or L, and peak values of the pressure are shown in full near it and underlined. Sometimes the symbols are overlapped and harder to read, such as near the tight 1028 isobar just SW of Lake Michigan. The peak pressure inside that isobar is 1030, though it is marked some distance off. The X to the SE of that High, marks the location of a Low, whose peak value is 1021 mb. Notice that this is a pretty high Low! The High farther on to the SW of it has a peak of 1026 mb. The only isobar around it is the 1024. There is a station report to the NE of the peak with wind of 15 kts from the N-NW with a pressure of 1023.8 mb. Notice the report just west of the south tip of FL. It shows winds of NE 15, with a pressure of 1022.5 mb. Compare this to the same report in the map below.*

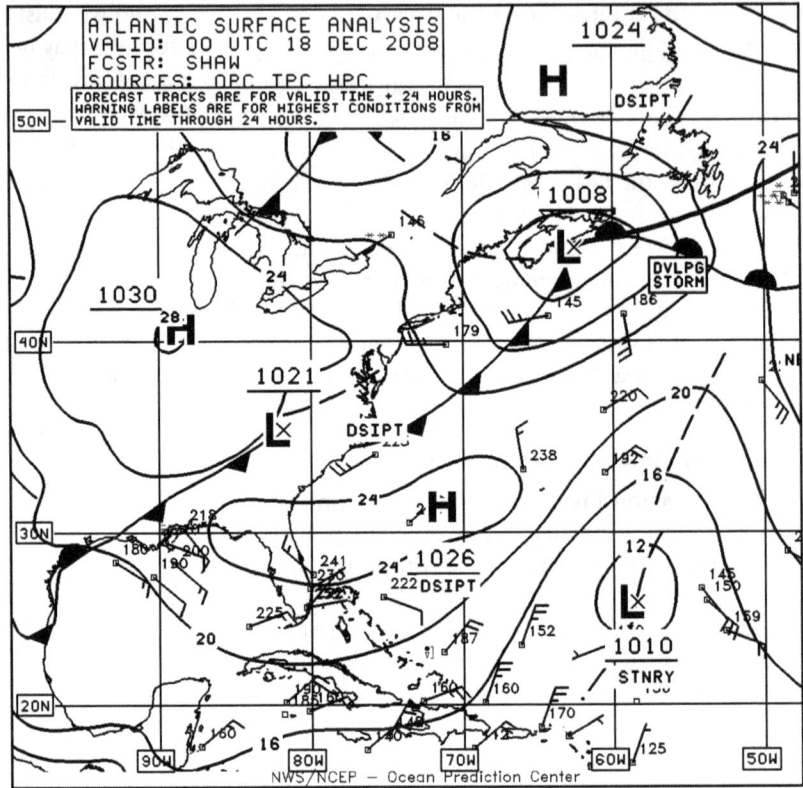

Figure 2.5-3 *Section of a Unified Surface analysis map, from Ref B of Table 2.5-1. These are available for any section of the U.S. It shows the isobars as well as many station reports that went into the analysis. If you lived near the south tip of the Florida Keys, you would expect a pressure of about 1022 mb at the time of this map, because that is halfway between the 1024 and 1020 isobars. Notice that the several reports around there are 1022-decimal-something, which is not a surprise, because it is these measurements that helped create the isobar locations as shown. Periodically you will see a report that does not agree with the isobars, which means a mistake was made somewhere.*

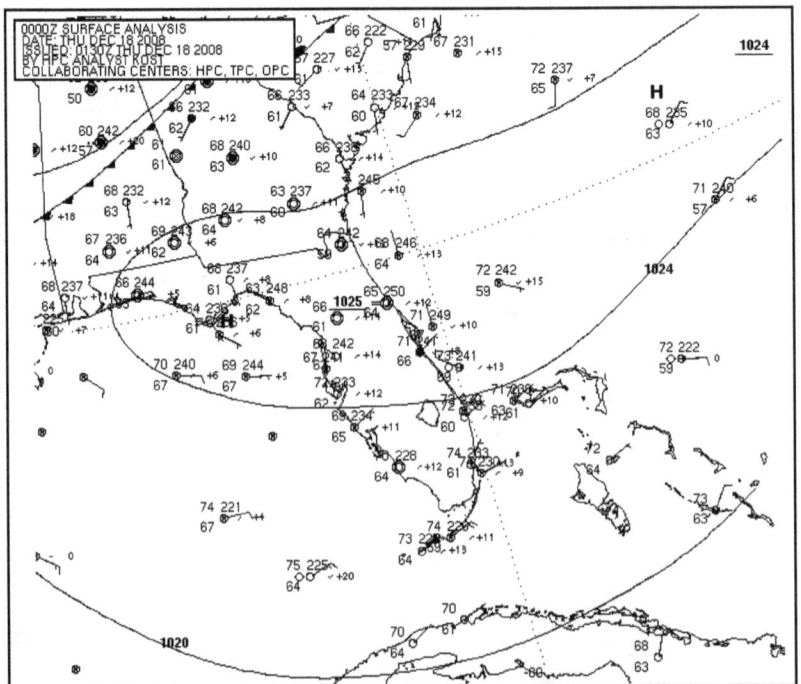

Figure 2.5-4. *Reading a pressure from a known location. At the time of this map, your vessel was located at 23° 00' N, 32° 30' W. Your well calibrated barometer read 1023.6 mb. Are the isobars correct on this map at your location? The answer is no. The map pressure at your location is 1021.0, which is a significant difference. The High is broader than the computer models know at the moment in this region. Notice there are not any ship reports in this region, which is always a sign that the isobars may be less precise.*

Procedure: plot your position carefully on the map using the lat-lon scales provided, which can be interpolated as indicated. Then sketch in isobars proportionally or interpolate their spacing in a similar manner. The point is that even a crude interpolation is usually better than just a guess, and we want the best possible reading.

This figure is from the book Modern Marine Weather.

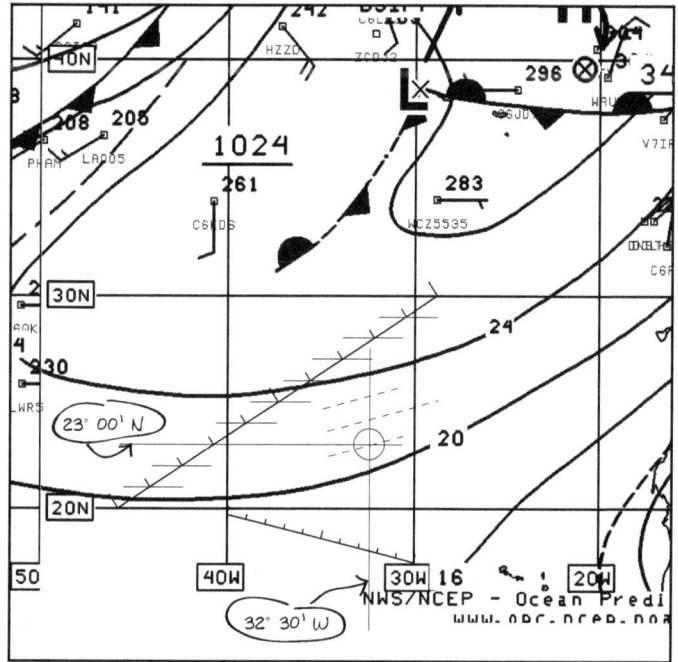

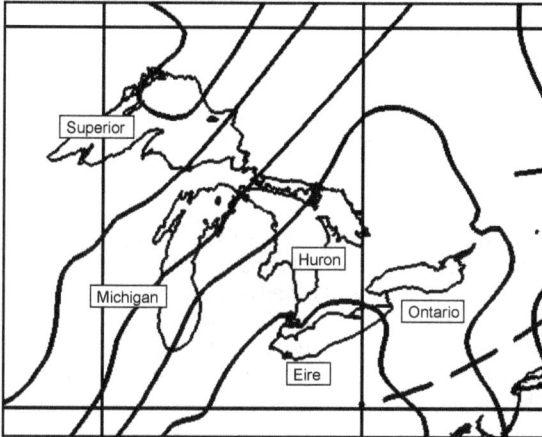

Figure 2.5-5. *A comparison of weather map isobars over the Great Lakes. The left is from a marine map (Ref A) and on the bottom is the map at the same time from a land based map (Ref B). The greatest pressure change across Lakes Huron, Michigan, and Superior is along the NW-SE direction. Lake Erie has about constant pressure across it, and*

Ontario has about a 4-mb drop in the E-W direction. Looking at the spacing of the isobars, we would find the most wind in Lake Michigan and eastern Lake Superior. Actual pressures, temperatures and wind observations can be read from the station reports shown on the map at the right. The maritime maps only show ship and coastal reports.

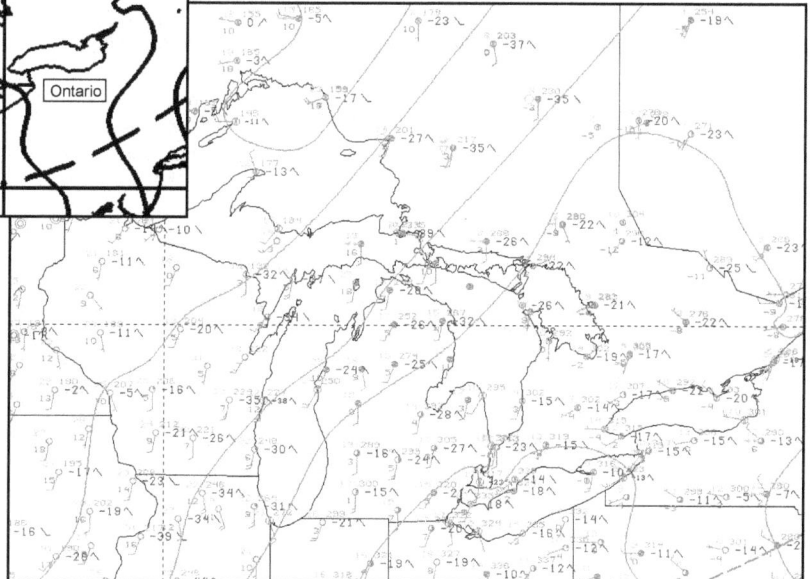

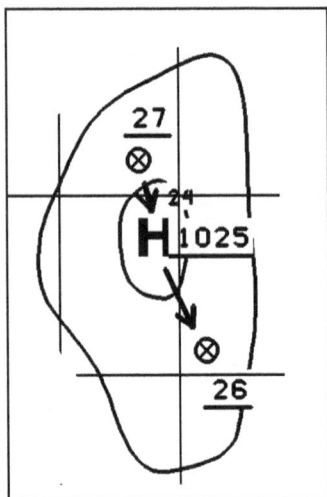

Figure 2.5-6. *Motion of a High. The location of a High 24 hr earlier than the valid map time is sometimes shown with a circled X. More often, the future location 24 hr later will be shown as well this way. The past and future values of the Highs are shown underlined with only last two digits used. This one was 1025 mb at the map valid time; it was 1027 a day before; and it will be 1026 tomorrow at this time. The peak value at the valid map time is always written out with all digits.*

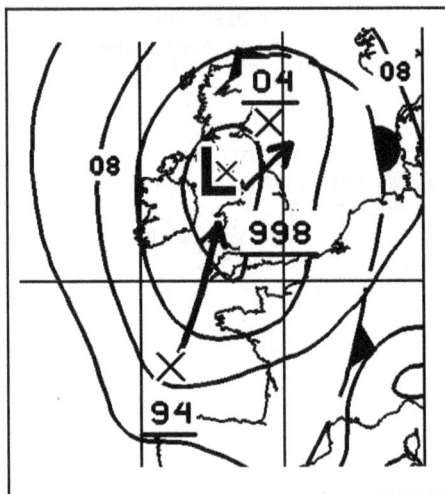

Figure 2.5-7. *Motion of a Low. Low positions are marked with open Xs. This one was 994 mb 24 hr ago; it is now at the valid map time 998 mb; and tomorrow at this time it will be 1004 mb. It is filling with time, as it moves across the British Isles. Isobars are only shown for the valid map time. The convention of using 2 digits underlined for ±24 hr and all digits at map time is the same for Lows and Highs.*

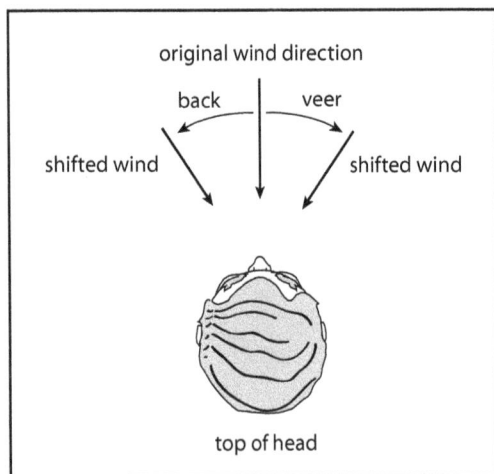

Figure 2.5-8. *Definition of wind shifts. When you face the wind and it shifts to your right, that shift is called a veer. If it shifts to your left, it is called a backing shift. These terms are independent of wind direction and they apply to both hemispheres. The figure shows a North wind backs when it shifts to the Northwest, but it veers when it shifts to the Northeast.*

Winds are named by the direction they come from. A North wind comes from the North and flows toward the South.

These wind shift terms are crucial to forecasting with wind and barometer. A backing wind with a falling barometer is a strong sign of approaching bad weather, just as a rising barometer with a veering wind is a sign of improving weather.

As we have seen in Chapter 1, there are three basic types of barometers, which all measure the same thing, but do it in completely different ways. The mercury tube barometer is how it all began, and we reviewed the key role it played in the history of the device. At this point, however, we move away from that device and concentrate the rest of the book on aneroids and electronic units, as they are the types now in practical application. There are many fine resources available on mercury instruments and quite a few skilled craftsmen in the US, UK, and Europe that work on these. References are in the Further Reading section. Thus we are left with the reading and care of an aneroid barometer or an electronic one in this chapter, and then the calibration and setting of these two types in the next.

3.1 Aneroid Barometers

To get the most from your barometer you must watch it and read it carefully. Small changes can mean a lot in some cases. It should be mounted somewhere at eye level, with a handy flashlight available for nighttime reading. And the instrument should be in view, up close, from a comfortable position, since it must be tapped lightly to get an accurate reading—there is a small chain wrapped around a pivot in the mechanism along with other contact points in the movement and tapping frees this so the needle can assume the proper reading. Don't tap it any harder than you would tap your nose. Tap it about 10 times, watching the dial as you do so.

Barometer tapping has become quite a ritual in aneroid usage over the years. It is described in the very earliest discussions, as well as the very latest. In some aneroids you find that tapping on the front of the dial brings you to an equilibrium value of the reading, but then if you tap on the side of the instrument it will find another value. The front tap released friction at one point; the side tap released another. Going back to a front tap will typically not change it.

This is something to be checked on your instrument. Some do not change with a side tap. Some are best with just a side tap. Get to know your instrument and you will get better results.

Despite this widespread tradition and in fact usual requirement, the need to tap an aneroid barometer to get a reading is not a particularly good sign. In fact, the very best of the instruments do not need to be tapped at all. They move up and down smoothly in response to pressure changes, and do not stick. If you tap one of these very good instruments, you may see the needle move, but it will come right back to where it was. And for any aneroid at all, it is likely best to discover the minimum tapping needed to get your answer, and not do more.

And while on this topic, we should dispel one piece of folklore that I have run across on several occasions—enough to imply it must be written somewhere. That is the idea that barometers are purposefully made to stick, and then to be tapped as a means of seeing which way the pressure has changed. This is completely untrue. The sticking is a defect, not an asset, and the way it actually moves when you loosen it with a tap, may or may not reflect how the pressure has been changing most recently.

Barometers on board should be located near the navigation station where the logbook is usually filled in, ideally in a place where it is seen frequently when passing. In many cruising sailboats I have seen them on a forward bulkhead (usually with a matching clock), facing aft over the settee. To read these you have to kneel onto the settee then twist forward, usually after moving sail bags and other items stowed on the settee. This is not a good arrangement. If you are the least bit uncomfortable reading it you will not get the best reading. At night it is even worse.

If you can't look straight onto it, you may read the wrong numbers—precision barometers have an arc of a mirror below the scale, so you can adjust your viewing angle until there is no reflection of the needle, which insures that you are looking straight at it. Other precision instruments use a unique double needle design to insure alignment.

An error from not looking straight on is called a parallax error (Figure 3.1-1). You may find that a magnifying glass will help you interpolate the location of the needle. It is important to always move your head from side to side to see the effect of parallax before settling in on the proper reading. Even the size of the needle can make a difference as shown in Figure 3.1-2.

At night or in low light during the day, a flashlight might be called for to help with the reading. This will usually cast a shadow of the needle onto the dial. There is a temptation to line up that shadow with the needle to minimize parallax, but this can be misleading when your source of light is not precisely over the dial. This can be especially a problem when using a magnifying glass to help read the dial because the magnifying glass is right where the light should be, and with the light off to the side a bit, the shadow is off to the side. In any event, a magnifying glass can be helpful for interpolating the needle position.

A 4- or 5-inch diameter dial is much easier to read than a smaller one, but with any dial, reading an aneroid barometer scale is rarely a trivial matter. Care and patience are called for. A main problem is the scale between, say, 1010 and 1020 is almost always marked with identical spacing and tick marks. No larger and smaller, alternating ticks, no half-way ticks, etc. So you must count each tick from 1010 to see if you are at 1014.4 or 1015.4. Also be sure you are starting right. In other words, it could be 1004, not 1014, etc. In this sense, reading the dial of a barometer is very much like reading the dial of a sextant. In principle it is very straightforward, but the numbers and ticks are small, and it is easy to make a mistake. As with sextant reading, don't just walk up to it, read it, write it down, and go on, but take a moment to double check your reading.

We want to do the best we can when recording the pressure. If the dial is small, meaning less than 3 inches or so across, it is much more difficult to read accurately than it is with larger dials. But with all dials, we need to interpolate the reading in most cases. Often we can develop a personal system using the width of the needle as a guide to estimating the pressure to a fraction of a mb.

When the needle is right on a mb line it is easy, and the needle exactly halfway between two lines also is easy for the 0.5 fraction—the human eye is remarkably accurate in detecting equal space on each side of the needle. The bigger challenge is everything else. Just a hair (maybe a half a needle width) either side of the middle could be a 0.4 or a 0.6, and likewise a 0.1 or 0.9 at the ends could be estimated depending on needle size.

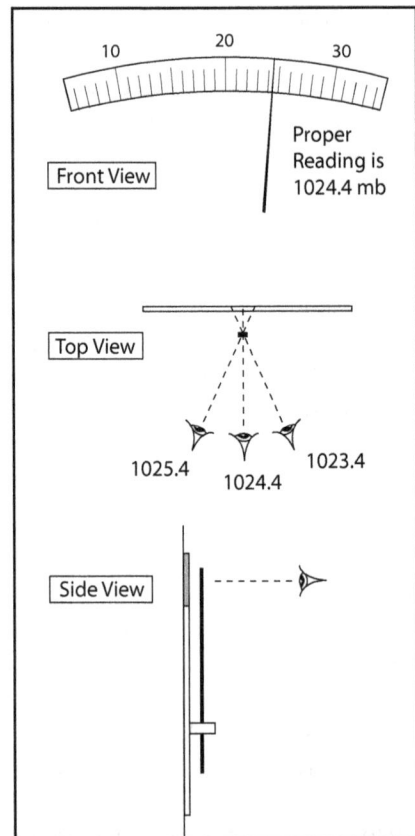

Figure 3.1-1 *Parallax error. If you do not look straight unto the dial you can have a large reading error.*

Figure 3.1-3 shows the more difficult estimates when the needle is about halfway between the middle and either side. The key to good data is to develop some system and use it consistently. Obviously the results will not be accurate to this precision, but that is not a reason to discard this care. With little practice it becomes automatic, and in the end your data will be better for it. Furthermore, if you take this care in the reading and have a decent instrument, you will actually notice the reading change as you record it if someone opens the door or companionway on a windy day!

There is typically a set screw on the back of most aneroid units that is used to set it as needed to the right pressure during calibration. Access to that screw might be a consideration when designing the barometer mount. You do have to get to it periodically.

There are typically two needles on the front of the dial. One is showing the present pressure and that is the one that changes when you adjust the screw on the back. That needle is usually black, and it usually has a tail section on the opposite side of the center pivot. You cannot change the location of that needle from the front.

The other needle is often gold or silver color and it does not have any "tail" on the opposite side of the pivot. We call this the *marker needle*, although it is often called the *set needle* in many books. The word *set* can be misleading in this application, since there are ways to "set a barometer" and this needle has nothing to do with that. Hence we take the liberty to use a new name.

The marker needle can be moved using a knob in the center of the dial on the front of the instrument. The marker needle has two purposes. You can use it to mark the present pressure by adjusting the gold needle to overlap the black one. Then when the actual pressure changes, the black needle will move away from the gold needle and you can see immediately how much the pressure has changed since you put them together.

The two needles have a different color for the obvious reason that it should help you remember which one is the one you read when recording the pressure. If there is any doubt, give the middle knob a turn to see which is just the marker and not the real needle. I have seen units where these two needles are nearly identical in shape and color (unforgivable!), and sure enough in one case during testing I recorded the reading from the wrong one. With the vast array of com-

Figure 3.1-2 *Needle size. Here we have two barometers with the same dial scale, each marked off in 0.02" units, but because the top needle is thinner, we can read it to 0.01" (29.13) much more easily than we can the bottom one (29.24).*

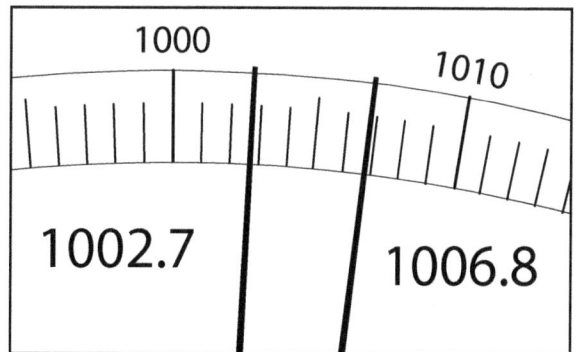

Figure 3.1-3 *Splitting hairs! After tapping the dial till the needle finds a consistent location, we want to do the best we can when recording the pressure. Here is an example of what you might use as a way to decide if you record a 0.7 or 0.8 for a dial like this one. Or if on the right side you cannot see any space between needle and reference line, but it is not quite centered exactly on the next line you might call it 0.9.*

mon barometer designs on the market you will more than once wonder why some feature was made the way it was. Examples come up below.

The gold marker needle can also be used to mark a specific *target pressure* you expect in the future, such as the peak depth of a trough you expect to pass over you. The tactical use of target pressures is discussed in Chapter 6.

It might be of interest to note that the highest quality (and most expensive) of the aneroid barometers often do not include a marker needle. The logic of this is not clear, but it could be simply the assumption that these will be reference units and not working units that would need one. On the other hand, some of the least expensive barometers do not include this marker needle either. Nevertheless, it is very valuable to have one.

Another practical application of the marker needle is to use it to count mb spacings. In poor light or with tired eyes on smaller dials, it is sometimes difficult to count the spaces, since they are not individually labeled. They are typically just 10 identical spaces between the tens labels. To facilitate reading, you can rotate marker needle to count them off as you move it across the dial to the reader needle.

Temperature can affect aneroid barometers and some are clearly marked with their compensated temperature range. Thus it is important to keep that in mind. Specific examples of temperature errors are given in the next section. Almost all barometers are indoor instruments, so this is not often a factor, but in some vessels it can get very hot below decks in the tropics. (As we shall see in Chapter 6, having accurate pressure is especially valuable in tropics.)

By the way, the pressure indoors should be the same as outdoors in most cases without having to leave a window open. A typical "air-tight" dwelling is still open enough for pressure equilibrium. With a good barometer, however, you could test this.

Some condominiums and apartment buildings attempt to pressurize the hallways to some extent with an intake fan to keep cooking smells within the units. With a good barometer you may be able to detect this effect. It has also been noted that air conditioning can have slight effects on the pressure reading in some cases.

Pursuing this issue of mounting location at home and underway, the best location would be a place with uniform temperature, meaning not in direct sunlight nor near a heater. A stout, vibration free wall or bulkhead is also best, so that door slams, engine noise, etc would not be felt. It is also best to avoid a location next to a door, open window, or companionway where the unit might be exposed to environmental changes in heat or wind. Strong wind blowing over a barometer can affect its reading (sometimes an issue when reading one in a cave), and even a strong wind blowing *outside* past your windows (at home or in the pilothouse) can also create changes of a mb or two. We have witnessed 0.5 mb changes in our office in the presence of strong winds outside—strong enough to notably tug at a heavy unlatched door slightly open in the gusts.

Aneroid barometers should always be read and kept in the orientation they had when calibrated, which is normally hanging vertically or lying flat horizontally. The instruments may even read slightly differently if they are rotated sideways. The top of the dial is generally 29.5 inches (about 1000 mb), and almost always, this is the symmetric center of the pressure dial.

For mariners underway, seemingly unrelated things like sea-sickness medication can also affect the reading. Some navigators find that Scopolamine patches (used to prevent seasickness), for example, blur their vision to the point that it is difficult or impossible to read the individual mb divisions on an aneroid dial. This is something that is easy to test on land and should be done, not just for the barometer reading alone, but to be sure you learn how you react to the sea sickness medication you intend to use at sea. Even more serious, if you happen to fidget with the patch and then actually rub your eyes, it will be a total blur out and you will not be able to read details for quite a few hours.

As a general rule, when watching the barometer for weather changes it is best to record the pressure every hour to the nearest tenth of a mb—or hundredth of an inch, using inches. You don't have to do this very long before the instrument becomes a valuable aid to your forecasting and general awareness of what is going on with the weather.

There is not much to the general care of these rugged instruments, but for a few exceptions to consider if you have a quality instrument. When traveling by car with your barometer, you should open the windows of your car when you close the doors, so you don't blast its bellows with the sudden increase of pressure created as you squeeze all the air into the car. This could cause a sudden compression of the bellows beyond its normal limit. I have not carried out the "destructive testing" to know for sure that this causes permanent damage, but if you ever happen to watch the dial of an aneroid barometer inside a car as you slam the door, you will understand the issue. You can almost hear the thing cry out in pain as its needle slams against one side.

Or what about the long slow torture of riding across the country in the pressurized cargo hold of a plane with pressure set to just 8,000 feet, about 753 mb (22.22 inches). This is way below the dial on any instrument, so it will be riding for some hours pegged against one side. The aneroid capsules are basically sealed metal springs, which must have some level of memory to work properly.

Recall Dr. Hooke, from Chapter 1. Besides his innovative work on barometer design, he is actually more famous today for what is called Hooke's Law of springs. It says that if you expand or compress a spring by an amount x, the restoring force resisting that displacement is –kx, where k is some constant. Springs working properly are perfectly linear. Pull it twice as much and you get twice the force pulling back. This is how we want the bellows in the barometer to work. But Hooke's law only applies so long as you do not exceed the elastic limit of the spring. Pull it too far and it won't come back at all, and some time before that happens, it stops being linear, and the restoring force is no longer predictable. If the spring is in a weight-scale and you put too much weight on it, you break the scale by exceeding the elastic limit.

Thus the question: what happens to the elasticity of an aneroid barometer's bellows when they are puffed up to way beyond their design value, usually

pegged against a safety stop for 6 hours? Most barometer sales departments are not going to be able to answer that. Some might say they don't think there is any problem, because they receive and ship the units by air all the time. Most manufacturers of common barometers will tell you the same thing.

An expert barometer repairman will tell you that if this is done very gently then it is probably OK, and in fact within limits, having the bellows fully extended for a while, once in a while, is good for them. (Keep in mind too, that the aneroid cells are pumped out and sealed at about 70 mb inside pressure when manufactured. So when the outside pressure drops, the bellows expand, but this expansion is still a relaxation for all outside pressures above 70 mb.)

The enhanced expansion at very low pressures rejuvenates the crystalline structure of the metal—sort of like stretching after sitting in the same position a long time. The problem is, when the bellows over expanded and pegged against a safety stop inside the unit, and then the aircraft runs into some common air turbulence, the unit gets a jolt at the worst possible time, and that can potentially damage them. Consequently, some high quality aneroids are vacuum tight units with a threaded tube that can be plugged completely for transportation by air. Reference manuals on the use of high-quality barometers always warn users to check them after air travel if they do not have that protective feature—better still, wait for one full day, and then check them.

As for the status of your own unit after it has been shipped by air, you have to determine it yourself with the calibration procedures of Chapter 4. Chances are it will be fine, but it is best to ship by surface when you can.

Another more subtle factor to keep in mind is what happens if you pull a spring apart a good amount, x, and hold it there for awhile, but do not exceed the elastic limit. After holding it there expanded for a long time with some force F, then reduce the force to F/2. Does the spring then contract to exactly x/2? The answer depends on the spring. Some springs behave very nicely, others have a memory of the extension and thus do not contract exactly as they expanded. When a spring shows some evidence of this memory it is said to have elastic hysteresis. A large post office rubber band is a good example of something that follows Hooke's law very well, provided you do not over extend it. If you let even a modest weight hang on it for some time, however, it stretches and no longer behaves properly.

Here is the key point. Most aneroid barometers show some level of hysteresis; even the highest quality models show some very small signs of it. This means, if the pressure goes up rather quickly and then sits there, you would see—if you had a way to measure it—that the instrument pressure continued to rise somewhat after the actual pressure had leveled off. Then when the pressure did go back down after such a sudden rise, it would not go down exactly as it went up, and when you got down to the same low pressure you started with, it would be slightly different. Tapping would not change it, but in a day or two it would drift back to what you had before, as the hysteresis settled out of the system. In a quality instrument this is a small effect, but one we should be aware of for all instruments that might undergo sudden or rapid pressure changes.

Hysteresis is always more pronounced when the stretch is put on rapidly, rather than when experienced in a slow gentle increase of pressure or spring extension. Shutting a car door on a barometer is obviously not slow, and if you do that, and then ask it to measure something accurately it may still be recovering from the blast and not be able to do it! If that should happen to your barometer, then you are more or less obligated to check its calibration. It is like when lightening strikes your boat. You are then obligated to check the compass. It just got blasted with an electromagnetic pulse like it never dreamed of, and we cannot be surprised that it is not its same old self.

So here is something to consider: when you buy a new barometer and carry it out of the store and into your car, give it a break and open a window before closing the door. Otherwise it is like getting a brand new pet and the first thing you do it whack it in the head! You can't expect nice behavior out of either one of them after that.

Notes on Barometer Travel by Air

As you go up in the atmosphere, the pressure drops at about the rate shown for the International Standard Atmosphere (ISA) in Appendix 2. At 18,000 ft you are down to half an atmosphere; in another 18,000 ft (at 36,000 ft) you are down half again, to one quarter of an atmosphere. Therefore high-flying cargo and passenger aircraft must be pressure-tight containers to maintain the safety and comfort of passengers and cargo. Ideally, the pressure tight fuselage would support a full atmosphere of pressure change, and then you could go clear to outer space and still not notice it inside. Unfortunately, this much pressure support is impractical, so some compromise is called for.

A typical pressure-protected aircraft may be certified for a pressure difference between inside and outside of 9.25 psi, but they more generally operate at an operational pressure differential of 8.6 psi, which is 0.6 atmospheres or 593 mb. In other words, they operate at a lower pressure differential than certified for so they put less stress on the fuselage.

As a plane rises off the ground, the inside pressure could (in principle) be kept at one atmosphere (1013 mb) until it reached an altitude where the pressure outside has dropped to 420 mb, because at this point the pressure differential (1013 - 420) is 593 mb. But it should not go higher without some compensation, because then the stress on the fuselage would exceed 593 mb.

To allow for higher altitudes, an automated pressure control system (operated by the co-pilot in some aircraft) lowers the internal cabin pressure so that the differential does not exceed 593 mb. It is not done at a single elevation as described schematically above, but rather in a uniform, programmed manner designed to match the take off, cruising, and landing pressures expected. As for specific cabin pressures, when flying at 37,000 feet (outside pressure 217 mb), for example, the cabin pressure of our typical airplane should not be higher than 217 + 593 = 810 mb. This cabin pressure corresponds to a "cabin altitude" of about 6,000 ft.

Airlines state that in practice the cabin pressures of high-flying aircraft are generally maintained between 5,000 and 7,000 ft, although at times it can be somewhat lower or higher depending on the aircraft and cruising altitude. Knowing the operational standard differential of 593 mb and the pressure versus elevation given by the ISA, you can estimate what the cabin pressure will be at any elevation. When co-pilots do these adjustments manually going up and coming back down, they describe the process as "the pilot flying the airplane and the co-pilot flying the cabin."

Recall that the world's record sea-level low pressure was 870 mb inside Typhoon Tip in 1979. This pressure corresponds to an elevation of 4,200 ft, but we are used to rather lower pressures than that routinely. Residents of Denver, CO, the "mile high city" (elevation 5,280 ft), live everyday at just 834 mb, way lower than the world record at sea level. So it is no surprise that most people do not experience any discomfort at 800 mb (cabin altitude of 6,000 ft). This, however, is a pressure of 23.6 inches, whereas the lowest reading on typical aneroid barometers is 28 inches, sometimes 27.5. In short, the standard aneroid barometer needle is solidly pegged against the low-pressure end when flying.

For those who want a barometer at home who live at high altitudes, there are custom units available with much lower setting that are designed for this purpose.

Most flights above 10,000 feet are in pressurized aircraft, but below that altitude many are not. Cargo and passenger flights on these aircraft at just 8,000 feet (752 mb) would expose barometers to more stress than those flying at 37,000 feet that do have pressure control.

It is difficult to predict what these effects might be. I do not know of any studies, and such details are not part of the specifications of aneroid barometers, other than noting the pressures are way below the minimum dial settings. A first guess is the main factor would be an enhanced likelihood of hysteresis for some period of time (24 to 48 hours), without necessarily causing permanent damage. But it seems there is no way to know for sure without doing a calibration as discussed in Chapter 4.

Again, we have to note another advantage for electronic barometers. Airplane travel is not likely to be a factor for electronic barometers, regardless of whether they are turned on or off when traveling. Quality models always specify the working pressure ranges, and most of the sensors in use are suitable to pressures way lower than one would experience in any high altitude flight. On the other hand, prudence still calls for a calibration to confirm this.

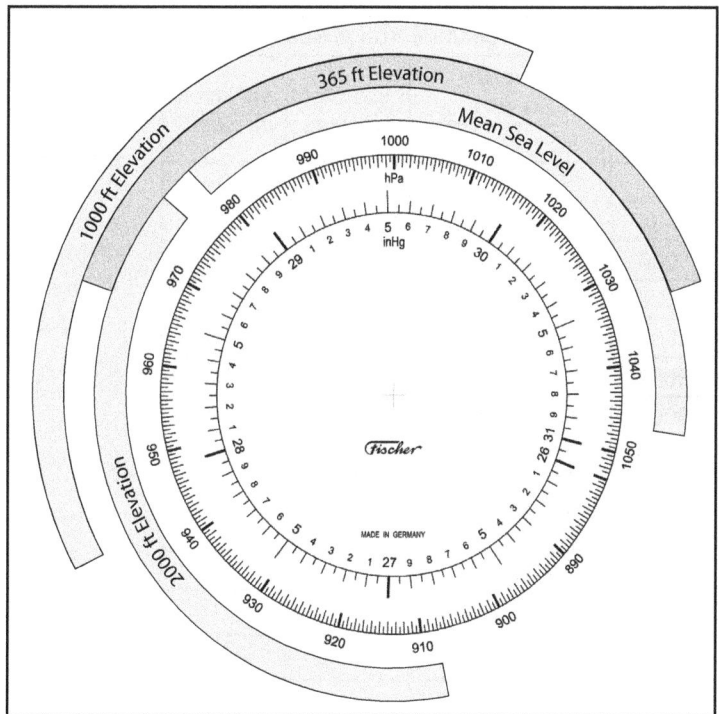

Figure 3.1-4 *A barometer dial showing the range of typical atmospheric pressures as a function of elevation. At sea level most pressures are observed to the right of center. At increasing elevation the pressures are on the left of the dial. This particular dial is designed to be used at elevations up to 800 meters (2,625 ft). With the set screw on a barometer you can usually compensate for about 900 feet of elevation, but more might compromise the accuracy depending on the quality of the instrument.*

Barometer Scales and Setting at Higher Elevations

Almost without exception, the top of the dial on every aneroid barometer is 1000 mb, whereas the average sea level pressure worldwide across the seasons is 1013 mb. The pressure of 1000 mb (29.5 inches) is actually the worldwide mean pressure at an elevation of about 365 ft elevation. Thus in a remote sense, the typical barometer is intended for people living at an average elevation of about 365 feet—which may not be too surprising since that is roughly the average elevation of England where much of the development took place.

We get some support for this idea from a note in *A Treatise on Meteorological Instruments* by Negretti and Zamba (1864), the leading British barometer manufactures of the 19th century, whose factory set world

Table 3.1-1 Barometers Above Sea Level				
Eleva-tion	Minimum low-end*		Ideal set pressure	Set screw mb shift**
feet	mb	inches		
0	979	28.91	1013	0
500	961	28.38	1013	18
1000	943	27.85	1013	36
1500	926	27.34	960	53
2000	908	26.81	942	71
2500	891	26.31	925	88
3000	874	25.81		105
3500	857	25.31		122
4000	841	24.83		...
4500	822	24.27		...
5000	809	23.89		...
5500	793	23.42		...
6000	778	22.97		...
6500	763	22.53		...

* This is how low the barometer must read to see typical low pressure events at various elevations.

** This tells how much you must adjust with the set screw to read sea level pressures on the dial. Even turning more than recommended, you cannot adjust for more than about 1500 feet.

standards for some time and essentially locked in the way the dials look until today. Referring to the word "Change" that labels the top position of 29.5 inches they say: "All that can be said in favor of these words is, that *within a few hundred feet of the sea level*, when the column rises or falls gradually during two or three days towards "Fair" or "Rain," (these are on opposite sides of "change") the indications they afford of the coming weather are generally extremely probable." Italics added to emphasise that they were at least thinking on how the elevation of the observer affects what we see on the dial and specifically how this particular elevation range relates to this central position on all dials.

Even more compelling evidence comes from Fitz-Roy's *The Weather Book—A Manual of Practical Meteorology* (1863), page 12, where he states during a discussion of the dial with 29.50 at the top "...on such scales: which seem to have been calculated for an average elevation of about 400 feet above the sea, to suit inland localities."

To the extent this interpretation is true, the zero point on a barometer scale is uniquely British, just as the zero point is on the longitude scale. The only barometers I have seen that have 1013 at the top instead of 1000 are from France, which in a way supports the theory!

In any event, when we use a barometer we must be aware of our elevation and how it might affect what we see. Besides the mean values, we need to know the typical range seen on the dial, which is about ±1 inch (34 mb). Thus at sea level we expect to see pressures from 1013 - 34 to 1013 + 34, or 979 mb to 1047 mb. This range as a function of elevation is shown in Figure 3.1-4. You will see that most barometers can be used up to 1,000 ft or so, and many, such as the one shown, can be used even higher.

If you plan to use a barometer at elevations of 2,000 ft or more, then it is crucial to check the range of the dial. Table 3.1-1 shows what the low-end pressure must be for various elevations if you want to see the typical span of pressures seen in nature—not the extremes, but the typical full range. Barometer use at elevations above about 3,000 feet call for special "high-altitude" barometer designs.

Set screw adjustment

The set screw at the back of the barometer can compensate for the elevation within some limits. This screw is on the bottom of some models, and in these cases it is often behind a larger plug that unscrews. When you turn the set screw it changes the pressure reading on the dial by actually adjusting the tension on the aneroid capsule. Some manuals say do not turn that screw more than one full turn (360°). Some barometers do not have manuals, or the manual does not specify limits on the set screw. In either case, it is best (initially at least) to restrict the turn of that screw to one half a full turn (180°), rather than a full turn.

One problem is you do not know where it is starting. I have never seen one with the zero position marked. So if someone in the past turned it, you do not know where you are starting. So step one is to start with your own reference line. Draw a line with pen or pencil on the case in line with the slot in the screw head, as shown in Figure 3.1-5. This might not be as easy as you would guess until you look. Some of the set screws are as deep as 2 inches inside the housing, so it is difficult to see it, let alone get a screw driver in to adjust it. In these cases, you may want to make a mark along the top edge of your screw driver so you can stay oriented as you turn the screw.

Figure 3.1-5 *A recessed set screw on the back of an aneroid barometer. A half turn (180°) is some 25 to 40 mb depending on the instrument. A hand drawn line is helpful to mark a reference location of the setting.*

You can find the approximate neutral orientation of the screw by noting the reading, then turning a quarter turn to the right, read again, then back to neutral (and hopefully the same reading you began with), and then quarter turn to the left and read—gently tapping as called for. If the dial change is about the same turning right and turning left, then do the same thing for one-half turns each way. A half turn from a neutral position will be a change on the dial of some 25 to 40 mb, with generally the higher quality units have the larger response.

If upon turning a half turn each way the dial adjustment is about the same but just in opposite directions, then your line marks the neutral position. But if the right turn brings the needle down, say, 36 mb, but the left turn brings it up only 14 mb, then your range (36+14) is 50, and half of that is 25. Your reference mark was not in the center. So turn the screw left to bring the pressure down by 9 mb (36-25), and make a new mark to show the neutral position. If you check from there it should go up and down 25 mb with a half a turn to the left and to the right.

Another reason for using only half a turn rather than a full turn is you run the risk of compromising the accuracy if this adjustment is on in full. As with many properties of aneroids, this will depend on the quality of the barometer. Higher quality barometers allow for a larger adjustment, the adjustment is smoother, and there is much less risk of degrading the performance. For any instrument whose pedigree is uncertain, a reasonable goal is to not use this set screw more than half a turn.

The set screw has two possible roles to play, depending on our elevation. If we are at sea level, the role is obvious. When we learn the correct pressure from an official source, we can use the set screw to make our barometer read properly at the pressure we set it to. At sea level it is best to wait until the known pressure is between 1010 and 1016, ideally 1013, (the typical midrange of pressure variations at sea level) before you set it. This will usually give the widest range of accurate readings.

Alternatively, if you are at a higher elevation, where pressures always read lower than at sea level, but you would prefer to read sea level pressure from your barometer if you could, then you might be able to use the set screw to set it to the correct sea level pressure. But there are limits to this approach. Referring to Table 3.3-1 you see how much you have to shift the setting as a function of elevation. At 500 feet you only have to shift it 18 mb to read sea level pressure. At 1,000 ft elevation you need to raise it 36 mb. From the recent discussion of how the dial responds to the set screw turns, you see that at 1,000 ft one half turn on some units would raise it safely to sea level readings. On good instruments you may be able to go a bit higher in elevation, and still turn it up enough to read sea level pressures, but that is about the limit.

So the set screw summary is: if you live below about 900 ft elevation, then you can and should adjust the set screw so that your barometer reads the proper sea level pressure. But if you live above 900 feet or so, you are best off figuring what the station pressure should be at your elevation (we cover this as we proceed) and then set your barometer to that pressure. For example, at 1,234 feet elevation, your pressure will read 44.5 mb lower than at sea level. Once your barometer is calibrated (Chapter 4), you can read your instrument, add 44.5 mb to it, and that will be the proper sea-level pressure.

3.2 Errors in Aneroid Barometers

Aneroid barometers are in principle simple devices. A sealed bellows expands as the pressure drops, and the extent of the expansion is a measure of the pressure. The mechanical arrangement used to measure the expansion is less complex than a simple watch. The problem is we want to measure something that does not change very much, so the system must be very sensitive to small changes, and as such there are unwanted effects that can also cause small changes that will appear as a pressure change if we are not aware of them.

Setting (Index Error, Long-term Drift)

Without any proof other than my own observations over the years, my guess is the largest source of error in the typical aneroid barometer is simply an improper setting. There is a screw inset on back of most devices (on the bottom of some) that lets you

adjust the pressure displayed on the dial. This must be set to the proper pressure periodically. When you visit a dealer with multiple instruments on display, it is not uncommon to see variations of 5 to 10 mb reflecting the fact that they have not all been set.

It is best to set the instrument at a pressure within the mid range (1010 to 1015) of the dial, which means waiting for the pressure to reach a value in that range, and then setting it to match it. Setting the barometer to be right at a high or low pressure can be a large source of error at the other end of the dial. It is important to set in the middle when you can, and then record the pressure and date when it was set.

Once the instrument has been set, it should be checked periodically and set again as needed. They will drift with time. Even the very high quality instrument used by the NWS are required to be checked and reset at least once a year.

The error caused by not being set properly is sometimes referred to as the "index error," which is a carryover term from the mercury barometer days, applied

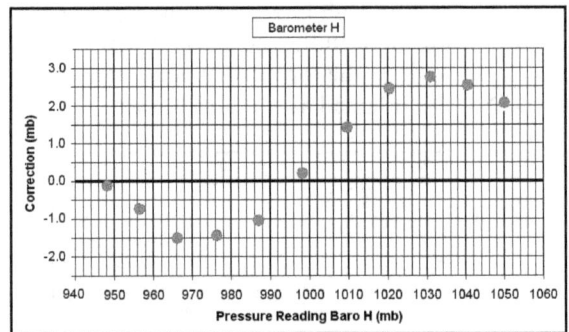

Figure 3.2-1 *A sample aneroid barometer calibration curve. This one is valid at 70° F, and this barometer was set to be correct at 1000 mb. These curves are not provided by the manufacturer; they must be determined by the user as explained in Chapter 4. In this example, if this barometer read 1020 mb, you would see from the curve that the correction is +2.5 mb, so the correct pressure is 1022.5 mb. If the instrument read 987 mb, the correction is -1 mb and the real pressure is 986 mb. This barometer sells for about $450; it comes in a heavy brass housing. The stated accuracy for this movement is ±3 mb, which does cover the errors shown. However, with this type of calibration curve the instrument now can give pressures accurate to within 1 mb, which is our goal for practical work.*

to aneroids as well. It is an unspecified combination of errors that are corrected for by setting the device to a known standard. Usually, the equally unspecified set of circumstances that cause this error to change over time is called "long term drift." It is mostly the crystalline structure of the aneroid capsule changing slightly over time.

Calibration curve

Setting the barometer is not the same as calibrating the barometer. You can set it in a minute or two to be right at a specific pressure, but that does not guarantee it will be right at other pressures. To test other pressures you have to make a comparison at some time between the reading of your instrument and the true pressure obtained from an official source or from another barometer that is known to be accurate. Procedures for doing this are presented in Chapter 4.

Figure 3.2-1 shows a sample calibration curve for a common aneroid barometer. This one was set to be right at 1000 mb, which left corrections of +2.5 mb at about 1030 mb and -1.5 mb at 975 mb. Had this instrument been set to be right at 1030 mb, it would have had an error of 4 mb at 975 mb.

It is important to keep in mind the role of such a calibration curve. This instrument had a predicted accuracy of ±3 mb. When set to be right in the middle of the dial, this barometer does in fact provide the promised accuracy without any calibration curve corrections. The calibration curve, however, provides two important services. First it shows the predicted level of accuracy was correct, but more important it shows how you can now improve on this fairly poor accuracy standard to get pressure accuracy down to much closer to ±1 mb, which is desirable for careful work.

Temperature Effects

Aneroids are made of metal, in fact several different metals, with varying shapes and functions in the measurement. When metal heats, it expands, and this changes the dimensions of the instrument, which can in turn distort the pressure readings. This was known from the inception of these devices, and since the mid 1800's there have been various designs to compensate for these temperature effects.

What was not known till a bit later, however, is that temperature variation changes the elastic properties of the bellows and that this has an even larger temperature effect on the barometer than the dimensional changes from expansion. As the spring weakens with increasing temperature, the pressure indicated by the instrument is too high. Thus as you go up in temperature you have to increase a negative correction, or decrease a positive one to account for it.

It was known from early times that the device could be corrected for temperature *at one specific pressure* with the judicious use of a bimetal strip that bends with temperature. This can be inserted into the deflection measurement system and configured to offset the zero point in a way that cancels out the unwanted temperature dependence. This could be achieved fairly well at one pressure, but not so effectively at neighboring pressures.

The second improvement was the inclusion of some residual gas (Po) in the bellows rather than completely evacuating them. Then at some outside pressure P, when the temperature changes, the inside pressure Po changes, and by choosing the right ratio of Po/P the effect of temperature on the bellows expansion can be canceled. With steel bellows, to compensate for temperature at 1000 mb requires a Po of about 77 mb. This, along with the bimetal strip, allows for temperature compensation at a second pressure, with relatively good correction in between them.

Table 3.2-1 shows how successful this approach could be, even before 1900. The tests were made with

Table 3.2-1 Barometer Corrections in mb as a Function of Temperature*					
Barom-eter	55°F	72°F	78°F	88°F	100°F
#2	-3.6	-4.6	-4.7	-4.9	-4.9
#3	-1.9	-3.0	-3.2	-3.2	-3.4
#4	-3.2	-3.2	-3.2	-2.7	-2.0
#5	-3.6	-3.6	-3.8	-3.8	-3.8
#6	-3.4	-3.8	-3.8	-3.6	-3.6
#7	-2.1	-2.1	-2.1	-2.1	-1.0

* From Kew Observatory studies, 1868 to 1898. These instruments were temperature compensated in much the same way they are today in common aneroids.

six different temperature-compensated instruments, from two different manufacturers. These tests were done at constant pressures, described as "normal." Even at the extremes, the compensation is good, within ±1.5mb. These data do not tell us about possible effects at varying pressure.

In the early 1900's a major improvement came with the development of Nickle alloys (Ni-span-C) for the bellows whose elastic properties do not change with temperature. These are the types in use now by the best professional barometers.

Nevertheless, even with the best temperature compensation and best materials, there is some level of temperature dependence to the calibration curve, which can only be learned from experimentation. Sample data are given in Figure 3.2-2.

Without further data, we are speculating that common instruments without any numeric specification other than "temperature compensated" could have errors of about this magnitude. Similar data from the early Weather Bureau Model ML-102-E, essentially a state of the art aneroid, show barely a 0.4 mb effect from 40° to 80° F, over the full working range of 800 to 1060 mb.

A modern state of the art aneroid such as the Belfort (Ni-span-C) Model 6079 has temperature compensation specified as accurate to ±0.015 mb x T, where T = temp - 70°. At 40°F, this is 30 x 0.015 = 0.45 mb. The Fischer precision aneroid barometer promises ±0.7 mb over 22°F to 104°F.

More generally for this class of instrument, *WMO No.8—Guide to Meteorological Instruments* describes the temperature compensation of a "good aneroid

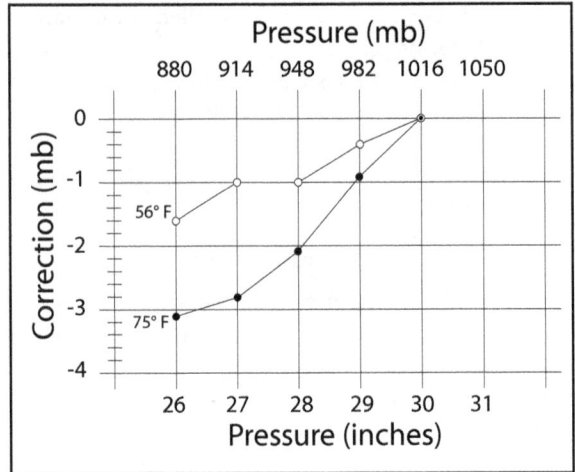

Figure 3.2-2 *Effect of temperature on an aneroid calibration curve. This data is from an 1898 study from the Kew Observatory in London, using the best aneroids available at the time. These units are not as good as the best of modern times, but they are comparable to "good quality" units today, according to antique barometer repairmen. And they are far better than the lower quality common units available today. The data shown are the averages of many measurements over a long period of time in temperature controlled rooms. In each case the aneroids were set to match a high precision mercury barometer at 1016 mb, and then the errors were recorded relative to the mercury as the pressure was lowered.*

We rely on this older data as these are not easy measurements to get accurately (i.e. to isolate temperature from hysteresis effects), and modern data could not be located. The purpose is to show the general trend and magnitude and these data do that well. They were studying aneroids for use as altimeters, so they did not cover the higher pressures, but the curves would presumably rise at about the same rate above 1016 mb.

barometer" as being one with a reading variation of less then 0.3 mb over a 54°F temperature change, for all pressures. This is rather wishful thinking for nonprofessional units, as they shortly after that admit that most "ordinary" aneroids achieve this only at one specific pressure. Also, when they say "good," they mean "best," as they refer to barometers intended for use in meteorological stations.

Some mid-line instruments describe their temperature compensation as adding ±2 mb uncertainty for each 10°C (19°F) difference from 20°C (68°F). Table

Table 3.2-2 Guessing Temperature Corrections*				
		970	1010	1050
10°C	50° F	A+x	B	C+x
20°C	68° F	A	B	C
30°C	86° F	A-x	B	C-x

* If you have a barometer that says it has an additional error of 2 mb (x=2) for every 10° C it is away from 20C, then this could be a first guess of how you could apply a correction that might compensate for some of the error until you knew more. For intermediate pressures, you can interpolate the correction, ie at 1030 and 990 use x/2.

3.2-2 shows a first guess way to apply such information that might improve your results.

Unfortunately, without printed specifications, there is no simple way to know what these corrections will be for an aneroid unit you have. If it is a high quality unit, marked "temperature compensated," then we might anticipate that it meets its accuracy claims within the specified temperature range, but in the end this is something we need to test. For modest quality modern units, it is unlikely the errors would be larger than 1 or 2 mb at 50°F or 90°F, for an instrument calibrated at 70°F.

Until you know more, you can use Table 3.2-2 as a guide to how the errors might come into play. We are relying on the concept that above calibration temperatures tend to soften the bellows, which makes them overreact, whereas colder than calibrated leads to stiffer bellows that do not react quite enough, hence the generic form of the corrections. This behavior is borne out in the data for the British Precision Aneroid Barometer (Mk2) presented in the *Handbook of Meteorological Instruments, Vol 1*, but it is still a guess for common aneroids.

Hysteresis

All aneroid barometers show some level of hysteresis, which is effectively a memory in the elasticity of the bellows. In high quality instruments this is a very small effect, and in any instrument it is difficult to isolate this potential source of error from a myriad of other small effects that might combine to mask it. We can, however, attempt a generic description of the process to shed some light on how the effect might show up, and how the size of the errors might be scaled if evidence of the effect can be identified at a particular pressure.

We must first go back to the basics. At the time of their construction, the capsules are evacuated, filled to about 70 mb of pressure, and then sealed. Thus, even the lowest atmospheric pressure on land or in the air, is still higher than inside the bellows, so the bellows are compressed. At an average outside pressure they are compressed more, and at still higher pressures they are compressed still more.

Thus we are back to having a spring under compression and we need to investigate how much it moves as the force changes that is compressing it. Figure 3.2-3 shows the ideal result. A perfectly linear relationship. Hooke's Law is obeyed, and we could call the vertical scales either bellows compression in some unit or outside atmospheric pressure in some unit. The practical problem the instrument maker must solve is the total distance the bellows compresses is very small, so they need to incorporate gearing to enhance the sensitivity, but still maintain a smooth and positive response to the expansion distance.

When you look carefully at a real instrument, however, you do not see this ideal behavior. With the best materials used and the best mechanisms employed, there will still be a slight difference in the pressures read when the pressure is decreasing compared to when it is increasing over a wide, steady pressure change.

> *The dial reading at any given true pressure is higher when the pressure is decreasing than when the pressure is increasing.*

You might think of the effect this way: when the pressure goes down, the bellows relax, but it takes them some time to relax completely. So until they relax completely, their expansion lags the immediate pressure outside, so the instrument reads too high. When the pressure is going up, the lag is in the other direction, so it reads lower than it should.

We can be more specific for an instrument set to read the correct pressure at midrange, when we consider changes across a large central span of the

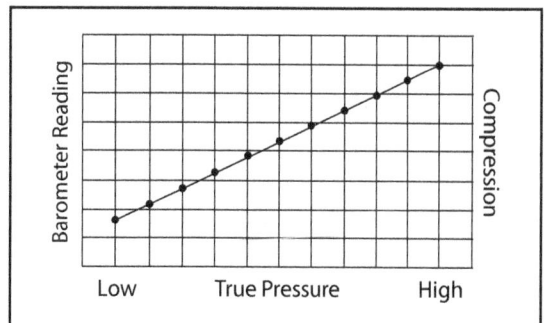

Figure 3.2-3 *An ideal linear response of an aneroid capsule to a changing pressure, for pressure going up or down, fast or slow.*

dial. Namely, the barometer will read somewhat too high when decreasing and somewhat too low when increasing. The extent of the difference depends on the full range being changed and how fast it is changing. It also depends on the recent history of pressure changes on that instrument. The effect is the biggest in the middle of the pressure range.

Since atmospheric pressures normally do not change very fast—at least we hope they do not—this effect on the barometer is not easy to see in typical weather patterns, but we can describe the behavior by imagining the barometer going up and down a hill. Early studies of hysteresis were in fact carried out in barometers intended for use as altimeters, since they routinely experience relatively fast changes in pressure.

Imagine ourselves at the base of an 1100-ft hill with a steady atmospheric pressure of 1040 mb (Figure 3.2-4). This we call the high end of our barometric range. At the top of this hill at this moment the pressure would be 980 mb, which is a reasonable low end of the barometric scale. We start our study by going halfway up this hill to 550 ft, where the true pressure is right in the middle of its full range at 1010 mb. We let the barometer sit here for half a day or so and then we set our barometer to be exactly right at 1010 mb. Then we slowly take it back down to the base of the hill and wait there for another half day or so for the instrument to come to equilibrium at precisely 1040.

(Notice we already know we have a good instrument that is well adjusted internally, because we set it right at 1010 and it is still right at 1040, over these slow pressure changes. We can assume we also took it slowly to the top of the hill and waited to confirm again that it read 980 mb as it should. We see shortly, however, that this nicely accurate barometer has very high hysteresis... which we exaggerate for this illustration.)

Now at the bottom of the hill with the barometer reading 1040, we start up the hill at a steady pace corresponding to a pressure drop of 2 mb per min, which is of course a very fast rate pressure drop. We record the barometer reading every 5 minutes. In 15 min we are passing the midpoint where we know the pressure is 1010 mb, but when we look at the dial we read 1012.5 mb. (*Pressure is decreasing, so it reads too high.*) We record that and keep going up. When we get to the top, where the true pressure is 980 mb, we read 981.5 mb, which again we record. Then we wait and watch the dial.

Over the next hour or so, we notice that the barometer is still slowly decreasing, even though the outside pressure has not changed and we have not moved. Eventually it reaches equilibrium at 980 mb.

The difference between the true pressure and the indicated pressure after a large pressure drop is called the *drift*. In this case the drift was 1.5 mb, after a pressure drop of 60 mb in 30 minutes. This behavior is illustrated in the top part of Figure 3.2-5.

Now with the instrument back in equilibrium at 980 mb, we start back down the hill, again recording our pressure relative to what it should be as we proceed. This time when we pass the midway point where the true pressure is 1010 mb, we now read 1007.5 mb, which we record, and proceed on down the hill. With decreasing pressure we were 2.5 mb high; with increasing pressure we were 2.5 mb low in the midrange. Then when we get back to the bottom where the true pressure is 1040 mb, we read 1037 mb.

The difference between the barometer's pressure reading at the high end after a cycle from high to low and back to high again is called the *after effect*. In this case, after a pressure cycle of up and down 60 mb the after effect was 3 mb (Figure 3.2-5).

The numerical value of the hysteresis of an instrument in some particular conditions can be thought of as the largest difference between rising and falling pressures, which will typically take place in the mid-

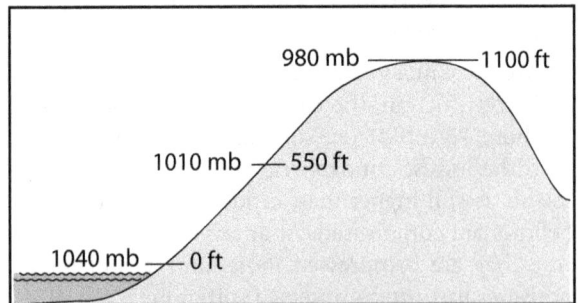

Figure 3.2-4 *Nature's barometer laboratory. A hill with known elevation markers.*

dle of the range being changed. In this example we would say the instrument had a hysteresis of 5 mb. This is an exaggerated value (5 mb/60 mb = 8%) for the sake of demonstration, and something like half of this is still large, and only found in a low quality instrument. In a high quality modern aneroid, the hysteresis is reduced to some couple of tenths of a percent of the pressure change, i.e. in this example a top of the line instrument would have only one or two tenths of a mb hysteresis over this range.

If you have doubts about your instrument, you can drive it up a hill and then park to see what the drift might be. A trip up a tall skyscraper might do the job as well. Record the pressure several times going up and again going back down, and repeat several times. If you have notable hysteresis, the effect will be largest about half way up—the building or the hill.

One of the Kew Observatory studies proposed an interesting way to compare hysteresis in various instruments. They first figure the hysteresis at each of about 10 steps from lowest pressure to highest pressure, then they average these. Then they figure the relative hysteresis at each point, defined as the actual hysteresis divided by the average value. And then they plot these individual relative hysteresis values versus their relative location along the pressure range, as shown in the bottom section of Figure 3.2-5. This way you can compare values from instruments that have large hysteresis with those that have very small hysteresis, and you can compare changes over various pressure ranges. Both scales are normalized.

The bottom figure shows two sets of data, one is the original Kew data (which had large hysteresis) and the other is from measurements made 65 years later with much better instruments—it was presented in the *Manual of Barometry*. This data had extremely small hysteresis. Both sets of data were averages of

many instruments. It was gratifying to see how well these two sets of data agreed when presented in this form. It seems to imply that we learn something about hysteresis from this presentation.

Namely, it looks like the maximum value (Hm) occurs near midrange of the pressure change, and that the maximum is about 1.4 times the average value (Ha). Put the other way, Ha = Hm/1.4. Then we can estimate that the drift is about 0.35 Ha and the after effect is about 0.65 Ha. Thus until we locate or measure evidence to the contrary, this provides a way to generically quantify the behavior of hysteresis. In other words, if we start with some estimation that Hm might be say 0.5% of the full range of the change,

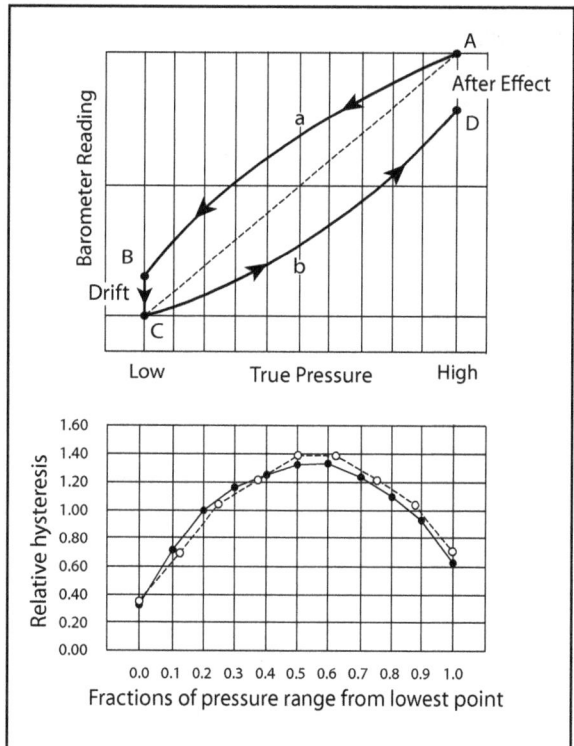

Figure 3.2-5 Top picture. *An actual calibration curve for a real aneroid, greatly zoomed in to show the small difference between rising and falling pressures, called hysteresis. The difference between the top curve and the bottom curve is the numerical value of the hysteresis at each pressure. The maximum value (a-b) is less than 1 mb in high-quality instruments but could be as high as several mb in lesser instruments. **Bottom picture**. A unique way to describe aneroid hysteresis that shows common behavior between the very best barometers and ones that are not as good. The open circles are the averages of data from 11 high quality barometers presented in the WBAN Manual of Barometry. The maximum hysteresis in these units (a-b) was about 0.2 mb. The solid circles are averages of many instruments taken from a Kew Observatory study in 1894. They had on average a maximum hysteresis of about 2 to 3 mb. The relative hysteresis is the value at any one pressure divided by the average of the values at all other pressures.*

then we could go on to estimate how the instrument would behave at any point along this change.

This would apply to only the first or second cycle through the large range, and further this would be the maximum effect, in that both these data sets used here were rapid pressure changes (WBAN 135 mb/ 6h and Kew 33 mb/ 5m)—far faster than we would ever see in nature. It is known, too, that if you cycle a barometer that shows hysteresis through several cycles, the hysteresis diminishes with each cycle. After about 5 cycles it is gone and stays gone for several days or more. After a month or so, however, it will return and be as it was originally.

Again, a good instrument should not display this behavior at all, but if you suspect it, there should be enough guidelines here to identify the effect. For practical usage there are not many cases where it will interfere with your analysis, but it could. Lows do sometimes approach fast enough that the timing of the minimum and subsequent rise—your analysis of the storm's behavior—could be distorted by the drift and hysteresis if large.

Scale error and Friction

Temperature errors and hysteresis errors are in a sense inherent limitations of the aneroid design. Luckily they have both been very much reduced or eliminated in high-quality aneroids, primarily by improvements in metal alloys. What is left is described by barometer engineers as "friction" and "scale error."

Friction is a combination of any residual hysteresis along with any resistance that might occur in any part of the movement. Referring back to Figure 1.2-6, you see there are many moving parts. To minimize friction some of the top line barometers use jeweled pivot points. Others use sharp connections that minimize the contact area and reduce friction. But the finer the contact the more delicate the instrument, so some compromise must be made. The best units are the durable ones with the least friction in the movements. The needle moves smoothly and they require very little if any tapping as the movement does not stick very much.

Scale error, on the other hand, could be thought of as including the residual temperature effects, but it is primarily the sum of slight errors in the internal adjustments that are made to convert the expansion of the bellows into the rotation of the dial in the proper ratio. Each instrument has several points were adjustments must be made to keep this relationship correct. If the movement is inherently of good quality, then it is these adjustments that affect what we see in the calibration curve. If all are set just right, then the dial reads the right pressure as is for any pressure. But if one or more of these scale adjustments are off, then we end up having to make that correction to the reading ourself.

We learn this by doing a calibration of the instrument. Once we find the list of corrections we need to make at each pressure, we can remove these errors of scale after we read the instrument. A good move-

Figure 3.3-1 *Jacob Jensen BXB112 a stylish design from Denmark. 5.5" x 2.4" x 0.9" Range 795 to 1050 mb, published accuracy ±5 mb, setting in elevation steps of 10m. Price $130 - $150.*

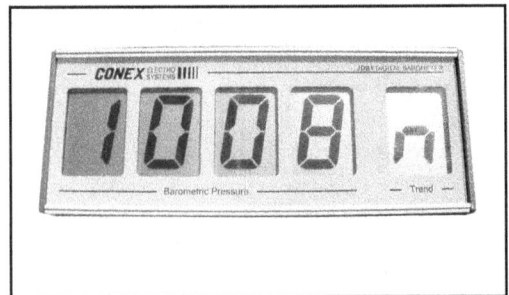

Figure 3.3-2 *Conex Electro JDB1. 9" x 2.8" (digits are 1.5" tall) x 1.5" Range 677 to 1050 mb, Accuracy ±1 mb after setting. Price about $190. Linearity < 0.5 mb. Shows inches or mb. Setting continuous at the push of a button. JDB2 in development displays tenths of a mb.*

ment that was simply not adjusted properly can be brought back up to high quality with a good calibration curve.

3.3 Electronic Barometers

The first thing to note about electronic units is even though they may appear an integral solid-state electronic device, there is at the heart of the system a delicate pressure sensor that has sensitivities similar to those of an aneroid device. Some of them in fact are tiny cells that measure the pressure much the same way as aneroid capsules except they do not transmit expansion and contraction mechanically but electrically. So step one is check the working temperature and pressure range of the device to be sure all is within specifications.

Chances are good that this is not an issue as they have typically broad ranges of use. But they do require all the cautions about mounting location as described for aneroid devices. No direct sun or wind, stable platform, and so on. And they still have to be mounted where they can be easily seen. On board it would be near the navigation station, and again it is valuable to keep a flashlight stored nearby for nighttime reading. With both aneroid and electronic barometers, it is always valuable to record the pressure at the synoptic times of 00, 06, 12, and 18z. These are the times the pressures are reported from the weather services and plotted on weather maps. If you are using land based maps, there are also accurate maps published at the intermediate hours of 09 and 15z.

Be sure to check the manual to learn how often the displayed pressures are updated. Unlike aneroid devices which are continuously responding to pressure changes (though you have to tap it to get the latest value), electronic devices do this in discrete steps. At specific time intervals they read the pressure and change the display. Some popular commercial units update every 6 seconds, whereas others update only every 15 minutes. Some units let the user set this sampling rate. When this option is there, the sampling rate usually affects the battery life. A first guess might be that making the sampling rate twice as fast would lower the life of the batteries by a factor of 2, though

with battery lives up to a year or two, this is not often a problem.

Some electronic barometers store past pressures that you can review in a graphic display or step back through and read for specific times. In some units, what you get in the history depends on what you select for the sampling rate. For example, if you have a unit that will store only 256 data points, then at 15-minute readings you have about 2.7 days of history that can be stored, but at 1-minute readings you have only 4 hours of data that can be stored.

Aneroid barometers have a wide range in quality when it comes to reading accurate pressures, but they do not look much different. And they have the same "controls," namely one set screw on the back and one marker dial on the front. Electronic barometers, on the other hand, typically look very different from one brand to another.

Electronic barometers have their own wide range of accuracies, but they also have a very wide range of appearances, options they offer, and how you interact with these options. Two samples are shown in Figures 3.3-1 and 3.3-2. Common among some of the inexpensive ones is the difficult combination of only being able to change the reading by changing the input elevation and at the same time the unit only updates every 15 minutes. For these, even if you know how much you need to change it, it is difficult and time consuming to do. So the main message is know how to set the device before purchasing it if possible. This is equivalent to using the set screw on the back of an aneroid. In contrast, some electronic models are trivial to set accurately. Press a button down and the pressure starts to slowly decrease. Let it up, press again, and it starts to slowly rise.

The choice of units in electronic barometers is usually not a factor at all, because most let you select between inches, mm, mb or hPa. High-end calibration standards have even more options. One subtlety to keep in mind is the precision of the display as discussed in Chapter 2. If you have a unit that shows mb only to the whole mb such as 1021 mb, then this same unit will almost certainly show this same pressure as 30.15 inches when you switch to those units. The displayed 1021 is actually 1021 ±0.5 mb because it would round to 1020 or 1022 outside of this range. The 30.15 shown is 30.15 ±0.005″ as it would also otherwise round to 30.14 or 30.16. The point is that 0.005″ = 0.17 mb, which is more than twice as precise as the mb display.

Put another way, suppose the pressure has been stationary at 1020.0 mb and then starts to rise at a steady rate of 1.8 mb per 3 hr, which is 0.01 mb/minute. On the mb scale, the stationary pressure reading of 1020 would not change till you got to 1020.5, which would take about 50 minutes. Then the next indication on the dial that would confirm that rise would be when it reached 1021.5, which would be 100 minutes later. So it took 150 minutes to get an indication of a rise and one confirmation of it.

On the inches display, the 30.15 would change to 30.16 in (0.17/0.01) = 17 minutes, with a confirmation in 34 minutes. So on the inches dial we get detection and confirmation 3 times faster than we would with a mb scale showing only whole mb. This only confirms the value of having a barometer that displays the pressure in tenths of a mb, which is the NWS and WMO standard. In this case the 1020.0 would go to 1021.1 in 5 minutes and the confirmation comes 10 minutes later, which is now twice as fast as when viewing the pressure in inches.

Tenths of a mb is the proven best choice for practical weather work. Our experience shows that even on instruments where the actual pressure is not accurate to the tenth of a mb, the linearity of the instruments is good enough that warnings of pressure trends can be detected very early with the tenths display. In an ocean yacht race, the potential of getting reliable warning of increasing pressure 2 or 3 hours earlier than your competitor could be a surprisingly important factor in the outcome of the race.

One important factor in the care and reading of mid-line and lower electronic barometers is often overlooked by users and rarely pointed out in the user's manuals or printed specifications. Namely, the displayed pressure can be very sensitive to the input battery voltage. Some units have a low battery warning, others do not. Some have a warning, but it may not come on early enough. The brightness or contrast of a liquid crystal display tends to dim when the bat-

teries get low, but you could lose accuracy before that happens.

One way to check this effect is to use a volt meter to read the voltage across the batteries while they are in place inside the operating barometer. When you approach the published lifetime of the batteries start a systematic study of voltage versus pressure. Record the voltage and pressure, then insert new batteries (or plug in an AC adapter) to see if the pressure changes, then go back to the old batteries and carry on with the tests. This way you will learn how the device behaves with varying levels of battery power.

The higher end units do not have this issue and they have a dependable low battery warning. But there are many styles of electronic barometers on the market and this is one factor to keep in mind when using the one you have. It is always good policy with any electronic equipment to write the date on the batteries when they are replaced. Then maybe write on the device itself, the sequence of dates that you changed the batteries.

As with aneroids, it can be instructive to record the ambient temperature when recording the pressure to be sure you stay within its working range. Otherwise the use of an electronic barometer is very simple.

There is no tapping required when reading an electronic barometer, though years of experience with aneroids might lead to such a compulsion—I have caught myself reaching toward one several times, and then enjoyed the joke to myself when I realized what I was doing. On the other hand, if you do see changes when you tap it, or rotate it, or gently shake it a bit, that is not a good sign, and you should ask the manufacturer about it.

3.4 Errors in Electronic Barometers

We have made the analogy several times between navigating by a GPS electronic system, backed up with the traditional mechanical sextant and the use of an electronic barometer backed up by a traditional mechanical aneroid. The analogy carries on into the realm of errors. We had a long discussion of potential errors and precautions when reading aneroid barometers, and there is a corresponding long list of concerns with using a sextant. When it comes to the use of GPS, however, or the use of electronic barometers, there is not much to do in the reading process but to record what the dial says.

There are no special user adjustments other than the a setting or adjustment function that lets you change the displayed pressure. If the setting requires an elevation, then it is important to learn what the minimum steps are and how that affects the reading.

The main errors inherent in the instruments are often related to the temperature compensation systems. Generally they have a broad range of working temperatures because they monitor the temperature and then regulate the pressure sensor output as needed. Nevertheless, recording the temperature with the pressure is valuable, especially in very cold or very hot environments, and to be alert to a possible source of error in these extremes.

All electronic barometers, from the very best to the bottom of the list, will also undergo some level of long term drift. One that is set properly now, could need adjusting in about one year. Good practice would call for checking this more frequently, however. They may drift more when new than when older. Naturally, the amount of the drift will be less on the high quality instruments than on the lesser ones. On the very best, for example, a drift of 0.2 mb in 6 months or so would be considered a very large drift (defective , in fact), whereas lesser instruments are not even stable to that degree at any time.

All electronic barometer sensors self-adjust for temperature changes as mentioned, but even with this adjustment they are sensitive to fast changes in temperature or to long periods of temperature extremes. A vessel left unheated for a long period may find that the barometer does not work to its specifications when it is first heated back up.

The temperature errors can come from colder or hotter temperatures than the calibration. If you calibrate the instrument at 60°F and then sail off to the tropics where the average temperature at the instrument is 85°, then this is a wide difference and you may find that this new operating environment has shifted your setting. In other words, when the manufacturer of common electronic barometers specifies a working temperature range of say 30°F to 100°F, they do not say you won't have to set it again. They are just promising that once you set it to meet the new ambient temperature it will be linear and accurate as the pressure changes. (Scientific instruments, on the other hand, do offer temperature ranges over which their absolute accuracies apply, without adjustment.)

One source of barometer error that is unique to electronic units is a dependency on the input voltage. When running on batteries, if the voltage drops below some threshold the accuracy of the reading can suffer. Even on units with a low battery warning, it can be that accuracy suffers by as much as 0.5 mb before the warning comes on. This point is discussed further in Chapter 8, on selecting an instrument. With an external power supply you can sometimes locate the threshold of critical battery voltage and be sure to avoid it.

Reading errors can also enter exactly as with aneroids when there is strong gusty wind outside. This effect will be more apparent with electronic units as they read to a higher precision. Thus in gusty conditions or sustained strong winds, watch the readings carefully before recording the pressure. The wind could cause pulses of up to several mb in some configurations. The appearance of this depends on how often the pressure is sampled and what type of averaging if any is taking place.

William Ferrel (1817-1891) American practical mathematician whose contributions to meteorology were as great or greater than his more famous contemporaries FitzRoy, Buys Ballot, and Maury. In 1856, he was the first to correctly explain global air circulation of the doldrums, trade winds, prevailing westerlies, and polar easterlies, creating his namesake Ferrel cell, correcting or replacing existing theories of the day. In the process he was the first to apply what we now call the Coriolis effect to global air flow, which was a crucial step to the future evolution of meteorology.

He also was also the first to present what we call the Buys Ballot Law for wind flow around a pressure pattern. His explanation of surface wind flow in 1856, was as clear and to the point as it ever had been before... and after!

(Buys Ballot published his law of wind directions a year after Ferrel did, but Buys Ballot probably gets the credit because he presented it with actual data and had used it practically for many years. Ferrel's work, in contrast, was more theoretical, though based on known global wind patterns, compiled by Maury—not to mention that Ferrel published his pioneering paper on global winds in *The Nashville Journal of Medicine and Surgery*!)

Ferrel taught himself mathematics and astrophysics as a youth in Pennsylvania and Virginia, enough to become a teacher of the subjects, but then went on to the newly established Bethany College. He then worked for Nautical Almanac Office and later for the U.S. Army Signal Corps, which evolved into the Weather Bureau in 1891.

He made numerous other important contributions to meteorology, astrophysics, and hydrography, and especially in the areas where these fields overlap. He was, for example, the first to prove that the action of the moon on the tides tended to slow the earth's rotation. It appears he was a man with great physical insight into the mathematics he used, without being constrained by a rigorous formalism.

In keeping with his custom of publishing pioneering work in obscure places, he was also the first to define and compute the crucial *Plateau Correction* needed to convert high-elevation station pressures to their equivalent sea-level values. This was first presented in Appendix 23 of the Army Signal Corps Annual Report from 1886. While his work in the back of this book was breaking new ground in meteorology, parts of the front of this book dealt with strange new "heliographic signals" being sent across the hilltops by Geronimo's warriors who had not yet surrendered... and thus a peek into the research environment of the early days of the Weather Bureau.

We cover in this chapter what we must do to our barometer, or to the numbers we get out of it, to be sure they are the correct pressure readings. A barometer is just like any other instrument. Just because the device might look very professional and the numbers are clear and easy to read, does not mean the numbers are right. Just think of stepping onto various weight scales to weigh yourself. Some we like better than others! All barometers are not equal, and unlike some other instruments, the price of a barometer is not always a measure of its quality. Now we learn how to evaluate a barometer.

4.1 What is calibration?

Let's review the basics. When we buy a car, we assume the speedometer and odometer are right. They don't come with adjustments, because this technology is pretty good. They generally are right. Periodically we pass mile markers on the highway and we can easily test the odometer. To do so, note the last few digits of the odometer as you pass a mile marker (say it reads 45.2), then if all is working right it should roll over to 46.2 when you pass the next marker. If it does that, you are done. You have checked the odometer and it is doing what it is supposed to do, get bigger by exactly 1 mile for each mile you travel.

If it does not increase by exactly 1.0 mile between these two markers, then at least one of three things is wrong. Either the odometer is not working right, or the markers were not 1.0 miles apart—or you made some mistake on your own, such as recording one of the numbers incorrectly, or misidentifying the markers. Thus, as with what we are going to do with the barometers, we have to be careful with our observations and record keeping. Then the only uncertainties we are left with are the reference data we use.

If the odometer had said this pair of markers was 1.2 mile apart, then we have to do this several more

times to decide if it is the markers that are wrong or the odometer that is wrong. It is not fair to do this just once and make a conclusion. As soon as we get into the business of checking instruments, we are better served by a systematic approach. You can call this the scientific method, or you can simply ask how much you are willing to bet that the speedometer is exactly right after just one measurement. If a lot were at stake, you may want to measure it again. Carpenters have good insight into these matters when they say, "Measure twice and cut once."

For comparison, odometers on boats (called "logs") are not nearly as dependable as those on cars. It is a much bigger task to measure a boat's motion though the water than it is to measure a wheel rolling on the ground. Consequently all vessel odometers come with a "calibration adjustment" for the user. The way you test the boat's odometer is the same way you test your car. Start by finding a measured mile along the waterway. They are shown on nautical charts periodically, or you can just measure one off from landmarks on the chart. Then you sail up and down the 1-mile route parallel to the markers, checking the log at each marker as done in the car. Then after 3 or 4 passes, average the results. Suppose the average of multiple runs shows your boat's log claims the known mile is 1.3 miles long. You have learned that your log is reading too high by about 30%.

When you read the instructions that come with these logs, they might tell you a sequence of buttons to push on the knotmeter to show you the value of K, the calibration factor. As an example, let's say the factory default value is K= 1.00. Then the instructions might explain how to run the measured mile, just as we did, and then instruct us to find a new value of K = (actual distance)/(log reading). In our case this would be K = 1.0/1.3 = 0.77. Next we just change K from 1.00 to 0.77 by pushing a few more buttons on the device, and then we have to run the mile again.

If we now get 1.0 from the log, we are done. If not exactly 1.0, we have to decide how accurate we want this, and either make more measurements to try and improve K, or let it go and live with the small residual offset we found—which instead of a 30% error we had and did not know it, we may now be down to say a 2% error, but more important we know what it is. In the terminology we are developing, we have "checked" the instrument and then "set" it accordingly so it reads right.

In this process what we have done is first checked an electronic device to see how much it is off, and then we have done what you might call "calibrate" it. Most manuals covering this type of operation would call this process "calibration," but when it comes to barometers and some other instruments as well, we have to be careful what we mean by this.

For example, the knotmeter and log of a boat are essentially the same as the speedometer and odometer of a car. In a car, something is measuring a quantity that is proportional to wheel rotation, and thus to distance covered; in a boat something is counting a small propeller rotating underwater. Some constant factor times the number of turns is equal to the miles traveled, and some constant factor times the rate of turns is the speed. In both cases it is generally true that if the odometer is right, then the speedometer is right. In boat talk, if the log is right, then the knotmeter is right. Also in both cases the operator's calibration factor K adjusts both speedometer and odometer at the same time—but as mentioned, users do not have access to "K" in cars.

Here is the rub. If we are to use just one value of K to "calibrate" this odometer, then we have to assume that this does not depend on the speed. In other words, if I did the mile marker test at 20 mph I assume I would get the same result at 60 mph. This is probably true in most cars (thus we do not really care that we cannot access K), but it is rather less likely true in boats. In boats the interaction of the water flowing past the small propeller can depend on where it is located on the hull and can depend on how fast the boat is moving. Thus it is not unheard of to have a boat knotmeter that works well from say 2 to 10 mph but then reads progressively less accurate as the speed gets much higher. This is not to say that the installa-tion and equipment cannot be made to work right (K= constant), but just that it could end up this way.

We are approaching the issue at hand. Part of the reason the concept of barometer calibration is not well understood these days is simply that the very word "calibration" does not have a unique meaning, even in the scientific laboratory. In individual cases it can be very clear, but the concept or definition in one application is not the same as in others.

A mercury thermometer is a simple example. If you have one with no scales on it at all, you could put it into a bowl of ice and water (which has a known temperature of $0°C$) and place a mark at the height of the mercury. Then put it into boiling water (known temperature $100°C$) and put another mark at the new height of the mercury. Then when you divided up the space between those two marks with 100 equally spaced marks, everyone in the world would agree that you have "calibrated" a thermometer. Some, however, would be quick to point out that the boiling point depends on your elevation (it is a pressure effect, not a temperature effect) and thus you need to look up the boiling point at your elevation for the second mark, and use it. But then you tell them you did it on your boat (sea level), so all is OK.

By "all is OK," I mean we know that the expansion of the mercury in the thermometer is "linear." That means if we have it right at 0° and at 100°, then we know for sure it is right at 20° or 50°, etc. Thus a "calibration" process depends on whether or not the output of the device is linear. The output of a speedometer is linear in that a car going 40 mph has wheels turning twice as fast as those going 20 mph and half as fast as those going 80 mph.

A high quality electronic barometer is a "linear" device. This means the voltage output (in, say, millivolts, mV) from the pressure sensor that gets converted to a digital value of the pressure on the instrument screen is directly proportional to the pressure it feels. If, hypothetically, 970 mb of atmospheric pressure created an output of 970 mV, then 1050 mb of pressure would create an output of 1050 mV. The significant implication of this definition and behavior is that once we know the device is "linear" we just have to set it once, at one pressure, to be confident it will be right at all other pressures.

And now the key point to be made. Most aneroid barometers in use today are not linear on the level of accuracy we need for high quality practical weather work. Some good ones are linear over the midrange of the dials (±1 or 2 mb), but even these tend to deviate at higher and lower pressures. For instruments like that, there is no one adjustment that you can make so that they read the right pressure over the full atmospheric pressure range.

If I may use another maritime analogy, a good electronic barometer behaves like a magnetic compass with no deviation error but just an offset lubber's line. After you make a single onetime correction for the lubber's line, all the other readings of the compass are correct.

On the other hand, a lesser quality aneroid barometer behaves more like a compass with a distinct curve of deviation errors. Such a compass will have not just an error when you are headed north, but a completely different error when headed east, or west, or northeast, or southwest, etc. The only way to use such a compass for careful navigation is to have a table of corrections. Then for each heading you sail, you check the table of corrections to see how much you have to shift the compass reading to get your proper magnetic heading. A lesser aneroid barometer requires such a curve of corrections such as shown in Figure 4.1-1. A good quality barometer does not require such a curve, which if measured might look like Figure 4.1-2.

The examples just cited were the best of one type of barometer and the worst of the other type of barometer. Our job with an actual barometer in hand is to decide where we are along that long spectrum, and what to do about it, so we can end up with accurate pressure readings. The point I want to emphasize at this stage is the phrase "calibrate your barometer" is not a simple idea like "weigh your barometer" and it is not the same as "setting your barometer."

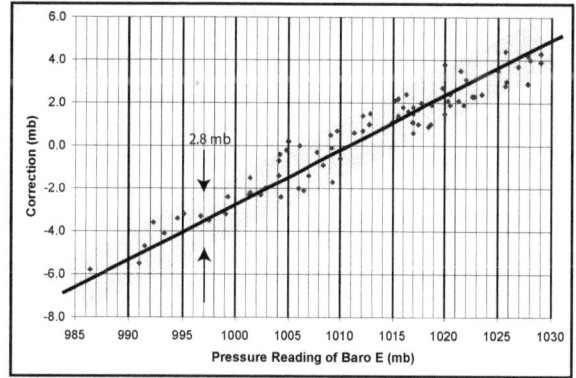

Figure 4.1-1 *A sample calibration curve for a low end aneroid barometer made by comparing its reading with NWS reports for its location. The process took several months during the winter in Seattle, where there is a relatively large range in pressures. (The barometer price was $250 due to a nice looking case and mounting.) This barometer was set to be right at 1012 mb. With that setting, all pressures from the instrument would be correct to within ±6 mb without any further corrections, but that is not accurate enough for practical use. With this calibration curve in hand, however, that large uncertainty could be reduced to about ±1.4 mb by applying the indicated corrections to the pressures observed. We could do better with a high-quality aneroid, but this is good enough to make the instrument useful for weather analysis. Without these corrections, even the apparent rate of change is very much distorted.*

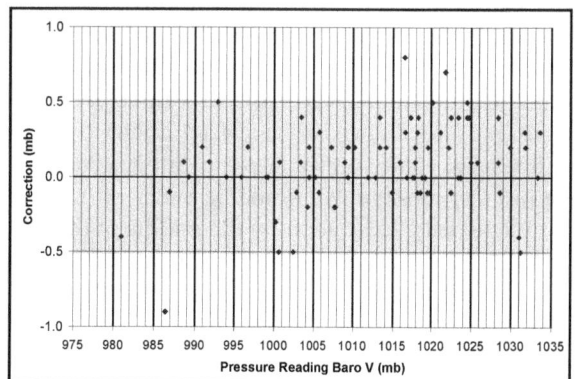

Figure 4.1-2 *A sample calibration curve for an electronic barometer that sells for about $190. In this case, the calibration process showed us that no calibration curve is needed for this instrument. We can simply state that the pressure it gives is accurate to ±0.5 mb once set properly, without further corrections. This shows the value of a good economical electronic barometer in that this is the best accuracy we could hope for from the very best aneroid barometer, which costs about $500, though the latter is likely to be more durable at sea over the long run.*

4.2 Setting versus Calibrating

Even if your barometer is very accurate at all pressures, you will usually not read from it the same pressures reported on the radio or TV, or on a weather map of your location until you set the instrument correctly. This is done with the set screw on the back of most aneroids or by digital control on electronic barometers.

If you are sure your instrument is equally accurate at all pressures (such as the one shown in Figure 4.1-2), then you can set the barometer to be right at any pressure and it will then be right at all others. But "right" is up to you to decide. If you are at sea level, there is no question. Just set it to read the reported pressure for your location (these reports are always sea level) and you are done. The next time you get an accurate pressure report from a map or the radio, you can glance at your barometer and it will read the same thing.

If you want to be able to make the same type of comparison between your barometer and the official reports, but your barometer is located at some elevation above sea level, then what you do is exactly the same thing! Just set your barometer to read what they say the pressure is at your location, and it will be right the next time as well. For aneroid barometers, setting directly to sea level is limited to elevations below about 1,000 ft, as explained in Section 3.1.

Again, to make this comparison by just setting the barometer and then getting correct values, we had to assume it behaved like the one described in Figure 4.1-2. If our barometer actually has a curve of corrections like those shown in Figure 4.1-1, then we would still set it at some specific pressure, but it would not be just any pressure. We would be better off waiting for the pressure to be about in the middle of the dial at say 1012 mb. Then if this instrument reads 1020 mb, you can refer to the curve to see that at that pressure you need to add 2 mb to the reading, which gives 1022 mb. That is the sea level pressure you will hear on the radio or see on weather maps.

Remember, though, we still have to keep in mind the timing. All the reports you get will be for some time in the past. If it is the radio, it is likely to be the value at the last whole hour, which means if the time is now 1050, chances are they are telling you the pressure back at 1000. Or worse, at 1110 they may not yet have updated the data to 1100 and it is still the value from 1000. That is why the Internet is usually the best source of pressure for comparison because they always tell you the valid times. Also when listening to a weather radio channel from NOAA, they sometimes give the pressure reports in sections and they might not be at the same times, so listen carefully.

So "setting" is something that is done after you have completed your calibration. Setting is an adjustment of your barometer to optimize your calibration. The calibration itself is a series or measurements at different pressures wherein at each pressure you compare what your barometer reads with what is known to be the correct pressure—or at least you are comparing with another barometer that you are confident is much more accurate than your own. The set of all differences for these measurements is called your calibration curve or calibration table.

You could in fact calibrate your barometer with your neighbor's barometer if you are confident his is accurate enough to cover your needs.

In practice you make some rough setting before the calibration process, but it is not crucial. Just set it to be about right, and then leave it till you get a good calibration curve, then you will know where you want to set it precisely.

The Calibration Chain of Command

One way to imagine the hierarchy of calibration is to consider having access to a custom mercury barometer of precise internal dimensions; super pure and super clean mercury; with scales machined to scrupulous precision, with accurate temperature measurement, in a pollution free environment, located at a known latitude. Then we devise a super precise way to measure the height of the mercury column by reflecting ultrasonic waves back and forth within the mercury column itself. Then we simply call the reading from this instrument, after properly correcting for temperature and gravity, the absolute true pressure. Whatever it says is right. We lock it up for safe keeping and hire people to take care of it, and we call this the "Primary Standard." That, in short, is a *very crude* description of one of the barometers at the U.S.

National Institutes of Standards and Technologies (NIST) in Gaithersburg, MD, shown in Figure 4.2-1. Put another way, it is the most accurate barometer in the world!

Once we have this Primary Standard established, if you want a calibrated barometer, you bring your barometer to this one and set yours to match it. Or more precisely, you compare it at various pressures and temperatures and then set it at the pressure that optimizes its calibration curve. If your barometer is high quality—which you will know when you start your careful comparison, along with having appropriate construction standards and long-term stability—you can then think of your barometer as a "Secondary Standard," and you can then set up shop somewhere else to offer calibrations to other traveling barometers.

In this terminology, the precision and accuracy of a "secondary standard" and a "primary standard" could be the same, but they still have important distinctions. The primary standard is based on fundamental measurements in units other than pressure. With the primary, we measure *length* of a mercury column to get *pressure*. With a primary standard we are obligated to understand and account for all the physics of the corrections and the theory that relates that length measurement to a pressure. With the secondary standard we are dealing all in pressure units.

We measure pressure with the primary and compare that to pressure measured with the secondary. The secondary standard could be as good a reference as the primary (meaning just as precise and just as stable or even more stable), but it does not use a fundamental measurement to get the pressure, which is required of a primary standard.

But that is not the full story. A Primary Standard also has to be one that the governing agency of the country (NIST in the US, or NPL in the UK) has decided is a Primary Standard, meaning it is indeed the best there is. No stones un-turned, no compromise on quality. For example, you could have a glass blower bend a tube of glass into a U-shape, seal off one end, then fill it with mercury. You will then have a fundamental, direct means of measuring pressure, but this is nowhere near a Primary Standard—but with a few easy corrections it could be better than many barometers on the market!

When the NWS calibrates a barometer they will use one of the standards defined in Table 4.2-1, which is described as "traceable" back to the NIST. The word "traceable" is used frequently when describing barometer calibrations. In its most elementary sense used by some in the barometer business, it simply means that someone has compared your barometer to one of theirs that has a certificate stating that it was

Figure 4.2-1 *NIST's 160-kPa Ultrasonic Interferometer Manometer (UIM) provides the nation with best-in-the-world capabilities for measuring absolute and differential pressure in the range of 1 Pa (0.01 mb) to 160 kPa (1600 mb), with an expanded uncertainty (k=2) of $[(6 \times 10^{-3} Pa)^2 + (5.2 \times 10^{-6} P)^2]^{1/2}$, where P is the pressure being measured. At P = 100 kPa (1000 mb) this is an uncertainty of 0.0052 mb. The UIM is only used for calibration of high-precision scientific instruments that are in turn used to calibrate other instruments as secondary standards.*

If you ask which of these pieces is the actual barometer, the answer is they are all necessary components of the system that measures these super precise pressures.

For more information about the NIST's barometer calibration program, see www.cstl. nist.gov/div836/836.06/index.htm, which is the source of this photo and others.

Table 4.3-1 WMO Classification of Barometers*		
Classification	Name	Definition
Category A	Primary or Secondary Standard	A barometer capable of independent determination of pressure to an uncertainty of at least 0.05 mb.
	The ultrasonic interferometer manometer at the NIST in Gaithersburg, MD accurate to 0.005 mb (5.2 ppm) is a primary standard. Precision commercial units with high stability and linearity serve as Secondary standards traceable to tests with a primary unit. The secondaries may have absolute accuracy of just 0.1 mb (still obviously quite remarkable) but with linearity of at least 0.05 mb they can meet the requirements of a Class A barometer. Several of these latter models are easily portable. Primary standards, almost by definition are not portable. They have entire laboratories and staffs built around them.	
Category B	Working standard	A barometer of a design suitable for routine pressure comparisons and with known errors, which have been established by comparison with a primary or secondary standard.
	High precision commercial units electronic or aneroid can serve these purposes. These are non-traveling units, as in regional NWS HQ. These units must be checked periodically with a Class A unit. This could be achieved with a secondary standard brought to the location of the working standard or vice versa.	
Category C	Reference standard	A barometer used for comparisons of traveling standards (N, Q) and station barometers (S) at field supervising stations of a National Meteorological Service.
	The crucial factor on these units is stability and linearity over the pressure region covered and the time period between comparison with the working standard and the station or portable units. The WMO standard for this is stated in terms of "index error," meaning if the pressure has not changed it should read the same within ±0.1 mb after transporting. This would be the class of barometer a Port Meteorological Officer would carry from his HQ to the ship's barometers he is checking. In practice many PMOs actually use high-quality barometers for this task, either a Class B in itself or capable of being one if checked when the working standard is checked. Since NWS and WMO standards require recording pressures to the tenth of a millibar, these units must be readable to that level.	
	In principle the accuracy of the setting they are displaying is the same as that of the working standard they refer to. If the reference standard is already a class B barometer, then their own reading is in principle as good as the one at their HQ.	
Above are the calibration units, below are the field barometers providing daily data for analysis and forecasting		
Category S	Station barometer	A barometer (aneroid or electronic) located at an ordinary meteorological station.
Category N	Portable aneroid	A portable precision aneroid barometer of first quality
Category Q	Portable digital	A portable precision digital barometer of first quality, to be used as a traveling standard

* *This classification of barometers was developed by the US Weather Bureau and presented in the* Manual of Barometry *in 1963. It was adopted by the WMO in the 1980s. In Chapter 8, we make a further classification of common barometers as "Decorative," Quality", and "Precision." All of the barometers in the table above are precision instruments.*

tested by a NIST secondary standard, and that it is still within the valid time of that certificate.

Others strongly argue that for a calibration to be considered "traceable to the NIST" takes far more than just using a traceable barometer for a reference. They would argue that more than one traceable references are needed, and that the procedures, overall equipment, and training of the testers all are crucial to the claim. The NIST website has many documents that discuss the process and terminology of calibration. Several are listed under Metrology in Further Reading.

In the next section we describe how you can calibrate your barometer using the pressures that nature gives you at home. In this case, we are assuming the pressures we get over the Internet for our location and time are accurate since they have been measured by a NWS barometer.

If you had a friend with a an accurate barometer then you could use his barometer as a reference to calibrate your own. His could be more accurate than yours under several circumstances. It could be a high quality instrument that comes from the manufacturer with a certificate of accuracy for that specific instrument—as opposed to just being a brand name of one that is supposed to be accurate, but has never been tested. Or it could be one he tested himself using the procedures of the next section, or one he sent off to a commercial calibration service and paid to have it calibrated.

With an accurate barometer and a test barometer in hand, you then have several options, depending on where you live. In Seattle, much of which is near sea level, we are lucky in that we could just wait till the outside pressure is about 1030 or 1035, which would be our high end comparison point. Then we could drive over to Snoqualmie Pass about an hour away at 3,000 feet. That will drop the 1035 down to 930 mb and we have our low end point. Then we should stop every 20 mb or so on the way up and back to get the intermediate points.

So if we assume the friend's barometer is correct, then we now have a curve for our corrections (just the difference between each of the readings when we stopped) and now your barometer and calibration

curve combination is as good as his, at least as far as accurate pressures are concerned at the temperature you used. Needless to say you have to do this inside the car with the heater on to regulate the temperature, otherwise it will definitely cool off as you go up, which could affect the results. You can call that table or graph your calibration curve, and you should note what the temperature was.

Another way to get your barometer calibrated is to send if off to a company that does such things listed in Section 4.8. They will not drive it up the mountain, but rather they put it into a test chamber with their own accurate standard and then simulate the trip up the mountain by pumping out the test chamber.

These methods and services are usually very good, but it is difficult to beat the simple method described below for doing this yourself using nature's pressures. It will take longer—unless you get lucky and a deep low passes by at the right time—but you will learn more and end up with a much more valuable instrument.

4.3 Sources of Accurate Pressure

To check your barometer or to carry out an actual calibration you will need some consistent source of accurate pressure reading for the area you are in. If you have access to the Internet, then this is the best way by far to do it. We will discuss Internet first and outline other methods after that. Remember the local libraries have Internet access and they will help you find what you need.

We start with the easiest way to obtain reference pressures, as it was designed specifically for that purpose. The calibration site is:

www.starpath.com/barometers.

At that site you can enter your latitude and longitude to view the nearest 10 sources of accurate pressure. You can also compute your elevation correction in units of your choice. Each reference station found is marked with the distance and direction to the station. Links to each of the stations are provided so you can get the data. There is also an option to select several stations to plot on a graph relative to your location so you can better picture where they are relative to you. There is an instruction sheet and work form provided, similar to the ones we discuss here.

The Starpath calibration site makes available US data from 3 primary sources; one is the list of all METARs, which are airport weather reports from around the world. US METARS are coordinated by the National Weather Service. The second is the list of lighthouses and buoys used by the National Data Buoy Center. The third set of reports is from the Center for Operational Oceanographic Products and Services (CO-OPS), which collects and reports meteorological data to help them analyze tide heights and other water levels. Data from New Zealand, Australia, Canada, and the United Kingdom have been added to the Starpath calibration site from contributions from these respective weather services. Others internationally are from master lists at the WMO.

Each of these sources has different conventions on how the data are presented, and how far they go back in time. Some have multiple formats. The free service at starpath.com/barometers has selected the ones most convenient for pressures.

Many of the airport stations have two pressures, one called "altimeter" or "altimeter setting" (usually in inches but often with the mb equivalent) and the other called sea level pressure. If only altimeter is given, then you can use that one. If there are two, they will be very close, usually within a mb or so. But when there is both, chose the sea level pressure. The abbreviation you see in METARS is SLP125, which means a sea level pressure of 1012.5 mb. Most stations give times in UTC which is the new name for GMT. To learn about time zones go to www.time.gov.

Most stations update the pressure every hour. Some are on the whole hour, others are not. Some stations give a pressure trend, usually in hPa (mb) change over the past 3 hr.

There are three things that can make the sea level pressure at your location different from the sea level pressure at the nearest reference stations. One is the time of the observation, another is the distance to the station, and another is the orientation of the isobars. Let's look at each of these individually.

Corrections for Time of Observation

It will soon become clear that you save time if you can record the pressures from your barometer at the times you know the source pressures will be available. The official pressures are usually recorded at the whole hour, so that is best, 08:00 for example, and not 08:21, which is often abbreviated to 0821.

But if you do not have the luxury of recording at the whole hour, then it is easy to correct for the time. If the station reports are, for example, 1020.0 mb 0800 and 1022.0 mb at 0900, but you only have a reading at 0821, then you can just interpolate the station value since we know the pressure rose by 2 mb in 60 minutes. The pressure at 0821 would be: $1020 + (21/60) \times 2 = 1020.7$.

Corrections for Station Distance

When relying on Mother Nature to provide the pressures, we have to take what we get. We also have to live with the closest pressure reporting stations. If we are lucky, a reference station is close by, and we can just use that one as our reference without any corrections.

How close is "close" is relative. In typical pressure patterns away from deep storms, the pressure change across a whole state in the US is some 4 to 8 mb. If you have some wind, then the isobars could be spaced at some 4 mb per 200 miles or so—closer for more wind, wider for less. So that is some 50 miles per 1 mb as a *very crude* average. So as a very crude guideline you might guess that if the wind is less than 10 kts or so, then any station within 50 miles might be a reasonable measure of your present pressure without any corrections.

In other words, if we can get reference pressures accurate to within 1mb we are doing well. That is our goal in the long run, but we cannot expect this approach to provide every single reading accurate to that level. Too many things can affect it. Our experience from doing this for many years shows that you can in fact get a good barometer calibration with this approach to getting reference pressures. We just need to get enough data to average out these uncertainties, which can generally be done within a month or so, unless you get lucky and a nice sequence of Highs and Lows comes by when you want it.

We can do better than using just one station if you happen to have two stations located approximately symmetrically about you, say one to the northeast and one to the southwest. If you are halfway between these two, then chances are your pressure is about halfway between the two values. For other distances you can interpolate as shown in Figure 4.3-1. Since you will be using the same stations each time, you just have to figure the scale factor, D1/(D1+D2), once and then it is a quick correction.

When you have 3 stations evenly spread around your location, you can interpolate among all of them as shown in Figure 4.3-2. This is not a mathematically rigorous solution to this type of interpolation, but it is easy to do, and accurate enough considering the uncertainties. And it will always be better than using just the closest station.

Corrections for Isobar Orientation

When you have two stations on either side of you that are opposite each other, then the interpolation of Figure 4.3-1 does not depend on the orientation of the isobars. You will always be scaling the distance between them in the right way. The isobars could be running parallel to the line between the two stations, or perpendicular to it, or any angle in between. So long as the stations are opposite, the interpolation is good.

But if you are not close to the line between the nearest two stations, then the orientation of the isobars makes a difference. If the isobars are roughly perpendicular to the line between the stations, then the interpolation is OK, but if the isobars are parallel to the line between them, we do not really know how much the pressure is off other than a good guess. In other words, if the isobars are parallel to the line,

then the two reference stations will have about the same pressure. Then the "good guess" means if you are not more than about 50 miles or so from that line and there is little wind, then that value will be good enough for this one data point.

The other solution is just to use 3 stations as shown in Figure 4.3-2. This procedure will remove much of the effect of the isobar orientation. You can find the orientation of the isobars from a quick look at the latest weather map for your region, given at www.hpc.ncep.noaa.gov/html/sfc2.shtml.

What to do without the Internet

The above methods all assume access to the Internet. But there are still many who prefer not to deal with computers and who have the good fortune of not having to. For them there are still numerous ways to get accurate pressure to carry on these calibrations. Here are some examples.

(1) The TV. One easy way to sneak up on your barometer calibration without using the Internet is to use the TV weather reports. Look for a couple reports from the closest towns and use these. Just put your barometer next to the TV along with a notebook to keep records in. Then record the time and your pressure reading along with a couple nearby reports. And just do it as often as you can. Or whenever you note that something has changed.

Whenever a storm is forecasted, pay special attention, so you can get data at low pressures. The same when a High or ridge is over the region. You can check

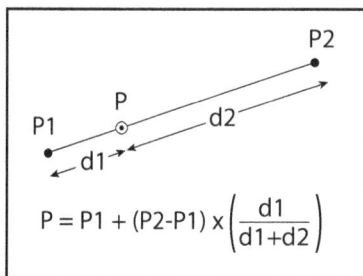

Figure 4.3-1 *Interpolating between two pressure reports. Example: D1 = 28 nmi; D2 = 59 nmi, P1 = 1023.4, P2 = 1021.7. Then D1+D2= 87, and P = 1023.4 + (1021.7 - 1023.4) x 28/87 = 1023.4 + (-1.7) x 28 /87 = 1023.4 - 0.5 = 1022.9 mb*

$$P = P1 + (P2\text{-}P1) \times \left(\frac{d1}{d1+d2}\right)$$

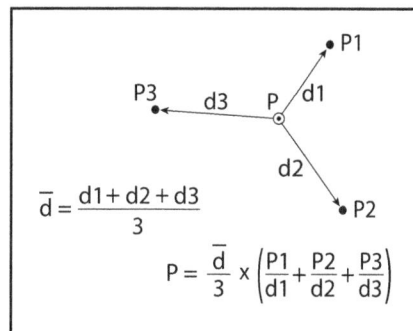

$$\overline{d} = \frac{d1+d2+d3}{3}$$

$$P = \frac{\overline{d}}{3} \times \left(\frac{P1}{d1} + \frac{P2}{d2} + \frac{P3}{d3}\right)$$

Figure 4.3-2 *Interpolating between three pressure reports.*

Appendix 1 to learn what the normal sea level pressure is for your location and month.

(2) NOAA Weather Radio. If you have a VHF weather radio receiver (hand held or a weather radio), then you can get the pressure every 3 hours on the regular NOAA Weather Radio broadcasts. But, again, you must be careful that you get the right pressure when doing this. In some areas the pressure from a nearby airport is included in the marine report which is updated every hour. Listen carefully to where the reports are from. It also helps to make a form for copying the data, since they will always give the observations in the same order. These are continuous broadcasts so you can listen any time, but they are only updated every 3 hours, though this may be changing since many of the reports are now automated.

If you want to know what times they are updated you can download your local Marine Weather Services Chart from www.starpath.com/navpubs. This map also shows specifically where the reporting stations are located. Printed versions can be purchased at www.starpath.com.

(3) Local Airports. A convenient source of pressure information for barometer calibrations in most metropolitan areas is the local airport. Their barometers are checked frequently by the NWS since these are used for altimeter settings. Most will have a flight information recording available by telephone. Phone numbers are available at:

www.faa.gov/airports_airtraffic/weather/asos.

The altimeter setting given in the phone recordings is given in inches of mercury, such as "altimeter 3007," which we can think of as their station pressure corrected to sea level. This one would be 30.07. After converting this to mb, you can use this for a sea level pressure calibration. Airport data by phone are updated every couple minutes, compared to the online reports which are updated typically every hour. (Temperature and dew point data, however, are only to the nearest whole degree by phone, but to the tenth online, which can make a difference in some applications.) If you live near a coast, you can use the NDBC service called "Dial a buoy" to get pressure, updated hourly. Call 888-701-8992 for instructions.

4.4 How to Find your Elevation

As mentioned in Chapter 2, you can find your elevation on a topographic map available from hiking suppliers and map stores, as well as from several sources online. Topo maps online do not always show the legends that define the elevation contours. Some are in meters with 5-m intervals; others are in feet with 40 ft or 20 ft intervals. The elevation you get that way will be relative to sea level and they state that clearly.

On the other hand, if you read your elevation from the adjacent land along the waterways of a nautical chart, the elevations there use a different reference. Elevations on a nautical chart are given as heights above the mean high water (MHW) level for that part of the chart. The MHW data are given in tables on the chart itself; they are not part of the data included in *Tide Tables*. Thus if you find the height of Hiker's Peak on a chart printed as 200 ft (above MHW) and you find from the chart that MHW is 20 ft, then the height of the peak above sea level is 220 ft. If you found this same peak on a topographic chart it would be listed directly as 220 ft.

Besides topo maps and nautical charts, you can also find your elevation online from sites like Google Earth or Microsoft's Virtual Earth. Just find your location there and put the cursor over it and read its elevation from the bottom of the screen. You have to zoom way in to get it accurately.

For even more accurate elevations you can use a custom website set up for this operation at www.starpath.com/barometers. With this site you enter your latitude and longitude (lat-lon) and then click "Find elevation" and the service logs into the US Geological Survey (USGS) National Elevation Dataset and gives you your elevation to within a fraction of a foot.

To get the best results, be sure your lat-lon are accurate. A GPS reading from your location would be best. Recall that in a position like 47° 34.245' N, 122° 20.567' W, the 0.200' of lat is about 600 ft; the 0.040' of lat is about 60 ft; and the 0.005' of lat is about 6 feet. The USGS dataset should be able to tell you the difference in elevation from one side of a street to the other, but you have to have the right lat-lon coordinates to get the answer right. This website should work worldwide.

Elevation data from each of these sources are compared in Table 4.4-1. To test the ideas mentioned above we took a test region where we had both topo map data and nautical chart data. Then we used the online sources as best we could to identify the locations, which brings up a key issue when trying to learn accurate elevation. In many cases it is difficult to locate your position on the map as precisely as you would like. Also it appears that the two most popular commercial applications of the NED do not overlay the data in precisely the same manner. We have tested in this in several cases using well defined locations, that are easy to pinpoint in the aerial photos used in these two programs, and elevations do not always agree. They do agree very well on reporting your latitude and longitude.

There are GIS (Geospatial Information Service) resources and software that are super precise, but their functionality and complexity are way more than we need for this application. The digital lat-lon input to the database as provided at www.starpath.com/barometers is an easy way to access accurate data.

You can also in principle get elevation from a GPS (set to 3D mode) but you will have to average what you see, and be sure you have a good view of the sky with satellites in all directions. Then monitor your fix precision. It must be good to get a usable elevation.

At Starpath HQ we get variations from 140 ft to 180 ft if just seeing 3 satellites through one window to the west, but the unit homes in on 160 or so when outside and a good fix from around the sky. If your GPS is stationary, then monitor SOG (speed over ground) to see that you are not moving—if SOG is bouncing around 0.1 or 0.2 kts when you are not moving, then you do not have a good fix.

The best way to use a GPS for elevation is to have contact with a WAAS (Wide Area Augmentation System) satellite for extra precision, or better still use a model designed for aircraft use that will also monitor the accuracy of the altitude. Land based navigation models monitor the accuracy of the horizontal position but not that of the vertical data.

To summarize this section, remember we are still in a bit of a circle here—of the chicken or egg variety. We need our elevation to calibrate our barometer (if we are not at sea level), but once we have a barometer well calibrated, it will end up being the best way to measure elevations at other locations. The question is how well can we do it? Recall the trick of defining a floor of a building as 12 feet, so we have the jingle of "point four four, per floor." Twelve feet of elevation causes a change in pressure of 0.44 mb. So if we want to use the barometer to get elevation accurate to 12 feet, we need our barometer to be accurate to at least 0.44 mb.

Table 4.4-1 Elevations near Budd Inlet, south end of Puget Sound*								
Latitude	Longitude	NED	Google Earth	Virtual Earth	Topo	Nautical Chart	Topo – Nautical chart	Topo - (GE+VE)/2
47 05.009 N 47.08348	122 53.975 W -122.89958	117.8	99	101	110	90	20	10
47 05.3 N 47.08833	122 53.9 W -122.89833	109.7	104	104	108	100	8	4
47 07.140 N 47.11900	122 53.586 W -122.89310	72.4	75	73	65-70	60	5-10	-9 to -4
47 04.3 N 47.07167	122 55.5 W -122.92500	151.6	161	162	160	140	20	-2
47 04.5 N 47.07500	122 56.7 W -122.94500	176.6	173	171	169	160	9	-2
Averages =							12.9	~0 ±1

* **Table Notes.** *In Budd Inlet the mean range of the tide is 10.5 feet and the mean high water is 13.4 feet. The NED data were found from www.starpath.com/barometers. NED = USGS's National Elevation Dataset. GE = google Earth, VE = Virtual Earth.*

4.5 Calibration Procedure

A reminder of what we are doing. We have a barometer in hand. It could be a brand new one or it could be one we have had for years—for decades even. We have been told throughout this book that more likely than not the pressures we read from this barometer *as it is now* will not be accurate. But we do not have to give up on this instrument. It could be all we need to do is set it right with the screw on the back to get it reading properly, but for the typical aneroid barometer that alone will not do the job.

To get accurate pressures from the barometer we need to construct a calibration curve, which is a list of the corrections that must be applied at each specific pressure we read across the full range on the dial. Then to get accurate pressure from the instrument, we read the dial, refer to the correction table, and make the correction.

The calibration process will also tell us the quality of the instrument. If the corrections are large and unpredictable, the device is not usable, and should be discarded. With large erratic errors, the device is not even dependable for indicating trends. On the other hand, if the curve of corrections is smooth and predicable, then chances are we have doubled or tripled the value of our instrument with the calibration.

For example, there are some barometers on the market for $300 or less that have very good accuracy specifications, but they do not often meet them. Whereas there are barometers for $600 that always meet their specifications. A good calibration curve may make the $300 unit's actual shipboard utility nearly equivalent to that of a $700 unit. In other words, the movement inside the $300 unit was a basically good one, it was simply not adjusted properly. The calibration curve tells you how to numerically remove the discrepancies that could probably have been removed mechanically with better quality control.

Step-by-step Barometer Calibration

(1) Station the barometer.

This means decide where you are going to do the calibration and keep the instrument at that location and elevation throughout the process. Changing the elevation or even moving it around the room is not good. This should be a place where it is easy to read and tap without moving it, and located so it is easy to record the pressures—a table top next to it or a clip board nearby, etc. It is best to have the logbook right next to the barometer, in a conspicuous place so you stay aware of the project and so it will be easy to pause and make another recording.

It is also valuable to make an initial estimate of the elevation of the barometer as stationed. For this you need two numbers: the elevation of the ground level at your location on earth, and then the "removal" correction, which is how high the barometer is above the local ground level. You can get the former for a known latitude and longitude from www.starpath.com/barometers (Section 4.4). Measure or estimate the removal as best you can. The elevation of the barometer is the sum of the ground elevation and the removal.

(2) Make an initial setting.

There are two choices here depending on your elevation and type of barometer, but they both start out with finding the sea level pressure for your location at the moment. For aneroid barometers at elevations less than 900 feet or so, you have the option of setting your barometer directly to sea level pressure using the adjustment set screw, as discussed in Section 3.1. If you are above 900 feet, then it is best to set your aneroid barometer to the correct pressure for your elevation. For example, if the reported sea level pressure were 1016.5 and the elevation of the barometer is 1,234 ft, then from Appendix 2 we see that the correction is -44.4 mb, and we should set the barometer to 1016.5-44.4 = 972.1. Appendix 2 only has elevation data for 1200 ft and 1250ft, so the value used here is interpolated, but you can also use www.starpath.com/barometers to get the correction for 1,234 ft directly.

Once you have made this adjustment, do not change or move the barometer till you decide the calibration is over. At that point, you may want to set it again, but for now it is crucial to not change anything.

If you are using an electronic barometer you can often set to sea-level pressure from higher elevations because the safe working range of typical electronic barometers is often much wider than for typical aneroids. Check the working range and then refer to Table 3.1-1 to find the lower limit. Many electronic units could be set to sea level pressure from the highest locations in the U.S.

Some electronic barometers let you set the pressure directly, just as done on an aneroid, but others require an input elevation and then they correct for you. In the example given above at 1,234 ft elevation, if your pressure read 972.2 mb and you then just entered that elevation into the barometer, the dial would change to 1016.5 mb. Usually when this display is in effect, there will be some electronic notice on the dial to let you know you are reading an adjusted pressure and not the unmodified station pressure.

(3) Start a logbook of pressure readings

It helps to make a form such as shown in Table 4.5-1 for recording the data. Ultimately you may want more columns, but this is the raw data needed for each entry.

Start by filling in the date and time and the reading of your barometer. You do not have to go online immediately to get the True Pressure, you can do that later if you are using that source. In this mode, you just record the pressure and time every time you walk by it and notice the pressure has changed some several mb or more from the last recording. Once you get a list of pressures, you can then go to fill in the true pressures.

If your schedule allows, it is definitely easier in the long run to record the pressures at a whole hour and then within the next 24h latest, go online to get the true pressure. That will be the quickest solution. Otherwise you have to track down archived data and then interpolate for times that are not whole hours.

On the other hand, if you are not using the Internet for the reference pressures, then the best approach will be to make a record whenever you obtain a true pressure. Using the radio, for example, you tune in the weather, get the pressure, then record it and then read your barometer and record it.

As soon as you cover a reasonable span of pressures you can plot out your data as shown in Figure 4.5-1. We have a good start, but still a long way to go. But

Table 4.5-1 Calibration Data*				
Local Date	Local Time	Baro Reading	True Pressure	Cor- rection
11/28/08	1400	1015.0	1015.0	Set
11/29/08	1100	1018.5	1019.5	-1.0
11/30/08	1400	1017.0	1017.6	-0.6
12/01/08	1000	1008.4	1007.7	+0.7
12/01/08	1700	1007.0	1005.7	+1.3
12/02/08	1000	1010.0	1009.4	+0.6
12/02/08	1200	1008.2	1007.0	+1.2
12/02/08	1700	1005.3	1004.1	+1.2

The correction is the difference between your barometer reading and the true pressure obtained from an official source.

having a graph as soon as possible helps keep progress in perspective. It shows the regions where more data are needed and starts to hint at the uncertainties involved. We don't know yet what the full curve will look like, but so far the instrument is accurate within ±1.5 mb from 1005 mb to 1020 mb, and we can be optimistic that as we get more data we will define the curve well enough to be able to get pressures accurate to within 1 mb with this instrument.

Appendix 4 explains one way to get plotted charts from data typed into a PC spreadsheet program, which is a convenient way to analyze the data. Free versions of the software called Open Office Calc will do just as well, and we can of course just write the notes on a pad of paper and graph them by hand on cross-hatch paper. No matter how you do it, the graph is a valuable way to evaluate the quality of your calibration.

When you plot your graph it is important that you plot the correction for each value of the barometer reading, not the true pressure reading. This will be apparent when you think through how you will use the curve. Namely, when the barometer reads 1006 mb, then we go to the curve to see the correction is + 1.4 mb, for a correct pressure of 1007.4 mb.

(4) Waiting for Mother Nature

If possible, it is best to use the same source of true pressures throughout the calibration. This entire process may take just a few weeks in a time and place with volatile weather, but it could take much longer if things don't change much. Note that once you have the procedure down and have done this a while, it will be obvious how to carry on with this process if you move the barometer onto a vessel. You can even do it underway with weather maps when cruising or racing, or driving a deep sea vessel across the globe. The weather map approach when underway is definitely less-accurate. It is better to do the calibration near suitable reference stations before departure.

But you can indeed get the ship's barometer on track in just a few days. I have used this procedure at various marinas when held up for some time using the VHF reports for that region.

As you accumulate data into your calibration, do not worry if you do not get the same results on your instrument each time the true pressure is at some particular value. It may be that you read 1022.5 one day when the report is 1025.0 and a few days later you might read 1024.0 when the report is again at 1025. This discrepancy can come from several sources as discussed earlier. In any event, this is precisely the sort of thing we are checking for. At this stage, don't worry about it, just gather as much data as you can.

Getting multiple readings for the same pressure tells about the variability, but you learn that quickly, and then multiple values are just taking up time without helping the calibration. Table 4.5-2 shows one way to make an easy table that lets you know what pressures you have and what you need to fill in the calibration. With such a table, you can glance at the pressure, then at the table to tell whether you are at a needed pressure or can skip this observation.

(5) Learning about your barometer

After you have gathered data over a significant pressure range, your plot of the corrections versus the pressure reading will tell the story of your barometer. It could be a happy story, or a sad story.

If all the data points are within ±0.5 mb, then you are done. The types of instruments most of us can afford are not going to be any better than that. In fact, some good instruments will not have any noticeable curve from low to high pressure, just a scatter of

Table 4.5-2 *Calibration progress table. When you start a calibration, make a list like this, and then place a dot next to the pressures you record as you get them. Then you have a quick overview of what you need to fill in the calibration. This calibration started out with a nice low pressure at 986, but we missed its rise back to normal values. Now we must wait for the next Low to come by.*

points all within 1 mb of zero point. If the instrument is consistently accurate to within 1 mb you will be able to use it for essentially all practical goals in weather analysis and forecasting.

A sample calibration from the late 19th century is shown in Figure 4.5-2. The best of modern barometers are now better than those from that era, but the common barometer of

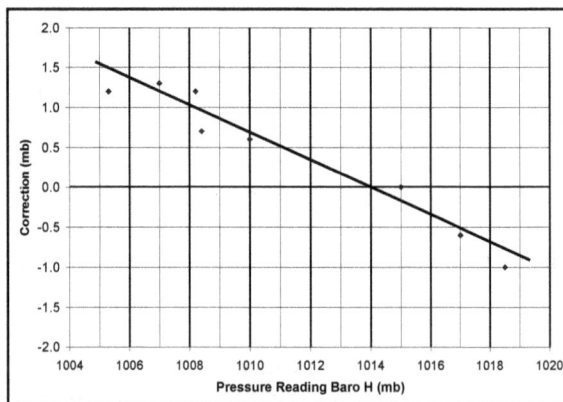

Figure 4.5-1 *Plot of calibration data from Table 4.5-1. It is just getting started but looks promising. There is a wide range of pressures where the instrument is correct to within ±1.5 mb, and we can likely do much better with more data. The straight line is just a first approximation of the curve, which in fact could be a curve or a line. With the line drawn in we can guess, for example, that the correction at barometer reading 1011.0 is +0.5 mb, for a true pressure of 1011.5 mb.*

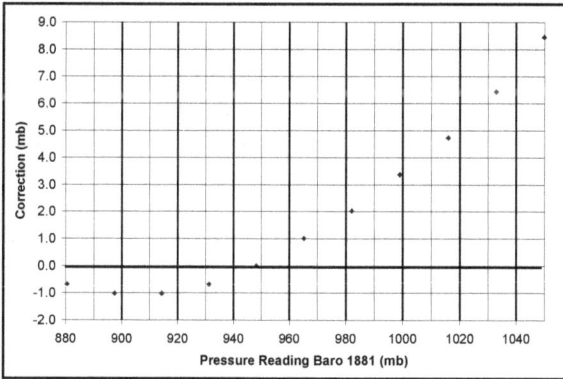

Figure 4.5-2 *Calibration curve from the late 19th century, made in comparison with a mercury barometer, from* The Aneroid Barometer, its Construction and Use, *by George. W. Plympton, 3rd edtion, 1890.*

today is typically not as good. Though the corrections shown are large, they are consistent and dependable, so that accurate pressures could be obtained using a calibration curve like this one. There are numerous curves like this one published in the Kew Observatory study of aneroids in 1898. See Further Reading.

The curve you get for the typical aneroid barometer taken off the wall or bulkhead, however, may not be so nice. Figure 4.5-3 shows just one of 6 that were published by the American Meteorological Society in 1992. All six they tested yielded about the same results. They were pointing out to teachers that they have to be careful when setting up a weather station for students. The authors concluded:

> "The selection of an accurate, economical barometer appears to be a difficult undertaking. No apparent physical feature of the tested barometers seemed to contribute to the accuracy of the instrument."

The instruments they tested cost less than $50 each in 1986—about $100 to $150 in today's dollars. They stated that somewhat better models could be selected and calibrated, and then would be usable for a weather station. Exactly the point we are making here.

The shape of the graph you get when you plot the corrections versus pressure cannot be guessed ahead of time. It could go up with pressure, or down with

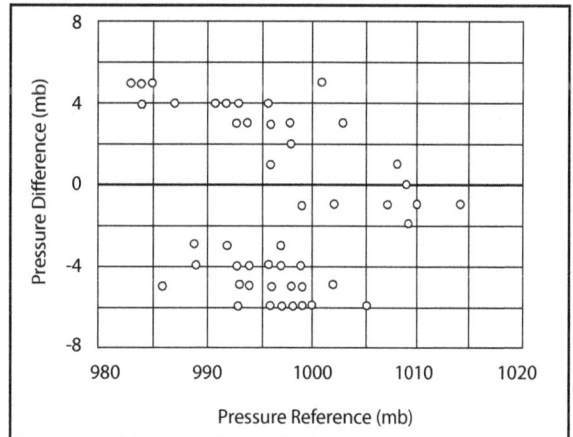

Figure 4.5-3 *Sample of a "calibration curve" that demonstrates that this barometer is not useful for practical weather work, nor almost any other application. At a pressure of 1000 mb, for example, this instrument might read 1005 on one day or 995 on another day. This sample was published along with 5 other brands, each with similar sad results. From* Basic Meteorological Observations for Schools: Atmospheric Pressure, *by John T. Snow, Michelle E. Akridge, and Shawn B. Harley,* Bulletin American Meteorological Society, *Vol. 73, No. 6, June, 1992, pp 781-794. Graphs from the other instruments look much like this one.*

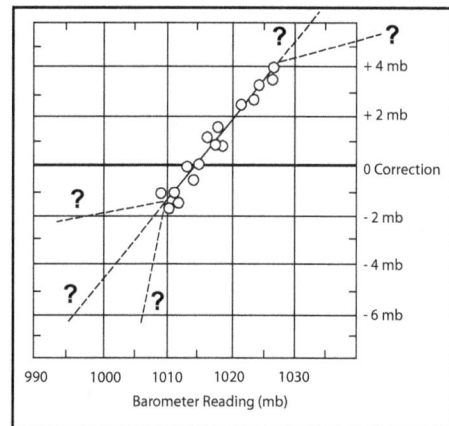

Figure 4.5-4 *A good start. More data are needed to learn how the instrument behaves at higher and lower pressures. The plot could be a line or a curve; it could go up with pressure or go down. From the Starpath Weather Trainer software (1990), which includes two other calibrations whose corrections of about the same magnitude go down with increasing pressure. These barometers were in the $200 price range at the time.*

pressure, or it could curve up and down (Figure 3.2-1). Figure 4.5-4 shows that when you have the middle part done you still don't know what the ends will look like. Remember, the ideal is a simple straight line at any constant correction. Then we just make that one offset and we have an accurate instrument.

Figure 4.5-4 was obtained "artificially" by putting the test barometer into a tank together with a calibration standard barometer and then slowly pumping out the air to reduce the pressure. The correction curve is then just the difference between the test barometer reading and that of the standard. That is the usual way it is done in calibration laboratories, several of which are listed in Section 4.8. That is certainly a faster way to do it, and some of professional calibrators use reference standards that might actually be more accurate than the NWS station barometers we are relying on when using Mother Nature to provide the test pressures. But in the long run, the use of natural pressures over a natural time span as we outline here is bound to give information more directly pertinent to what we want. This is an observation that has been made since the earliest writings on aneroids.

It might be especially true for the barometers whose quality and adjustment are marginal. The top of the line aneroids will show the same good behavior when being artificially tested or naturally tested, but lesser models might not respond well at all to the rapid pressure changes experienced in a test tank, but they might still be useful instruments if you collect their corrections over a longer, more natural sequence of pressure changes. I do not know this for a fact. It is just a guess, maybe even wishful thinking. Hopefully this book encourages more barometer calibrations using natural pressures and eventually we will learn the answer to this.

Though the data are not yet conclusive, there is some evidence that with more study the barometer in Figure 4.5-4 could be usable. The barometers represented in Figure 4.5-3, on the other hand, are all basically useless. The scatter in the data is so bad, that these instruments would not even be reliable ways to tell if the pressure is dropping rapidly or slowly. In some sequences of true pressure change, these instruments could even show the barometer going the wrong direction.

Figures 4.5-5 to 4.5-9 show several calibrations made with natural pressures. We see the full spectrum from an excellent barometer to a poor one. Notice that the barometer in Figure 4.5-6 would not be useful at all without the calibration, but with it, you could likely get pressures to ±2 mb, which could be tactically useful. In Figure 4.5-7 we see that the utility of instruments that advertise ±3 mb could be pushed to more like ±1.5 mb with the use of a calibration. Remember that the isobars on a weather map are 4 mb apart. Knowing our pressure to within ±1.5 mb is much more valuable than ±3 mb when it comes to coordinating the forecasts with our observations.

(6) Finessing the curves

After you have gathered data over a significant pressure range and have the data plotted out, the next step is to interpret the data and try to draw some form of curve through the results. The process is part art work and part science. Use your best judgment to draw a smooth curve through the data points that you would guess best represents the true behavior of the instrument.

The general guideline to "fitting the best curve to the data" is to draw the curve or line through as many points as possible that leaves about the same number of points above the curve as below it. The other guideline is if you see a point or two that are rather far off the curve of the others, then do not give these outliers much weight, or just ignore them, when drawing the curve. Figure 4.5-9 calls for special effort.

If the barometer is at all useful, this will be some smooth line or curve with a few straggling points that lie a bit off to one side or the other. The first guess should be that the behavior of the instrument is a smooth curve, and the deviations we see just reflect the uncertainties in our measurements.

Once we have a smooth curve drawn through our data, we can assume that the value on the curve is what the correct value would have been had we measured the correction at that pressure without any errors. At this stage, you can use your curve to look up corrections at each reading, or you may find it more convenient to go back to a table format.

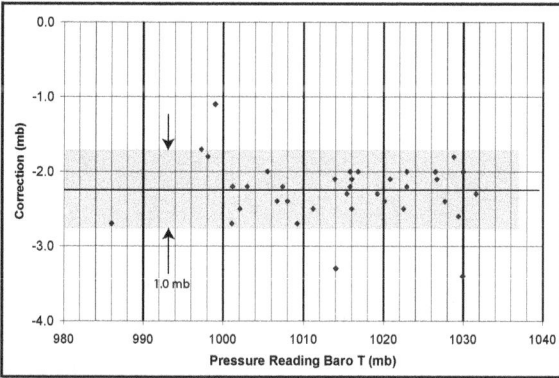

Figure 4.5-5 *Beginning of a calibration by nature of a Taylor aneroid from the 1960s, which had been tank tested to be accurate to ±0.5 mb from 900 to 1040. This barometer needs to be reset about 2.2 mb lower. The outliers here are likely due to uncertainties in the reference pressure.*

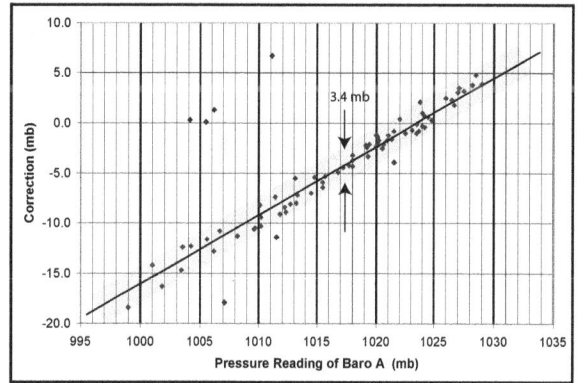

Figure 4.5-6 *Calibration of a popular barometer that sells for $140. The 4 higher outliers here are likely due to a common type of dial reading error (i.e. identifying the needle position as 2 mb past 1000, instead of 2 mb past 1010). In this example, the calibration process improves this instrument's utility from ±15 mb to about ±1.7 mb. If this is the only instrument you had, the calibration would make it significantly more useful.*

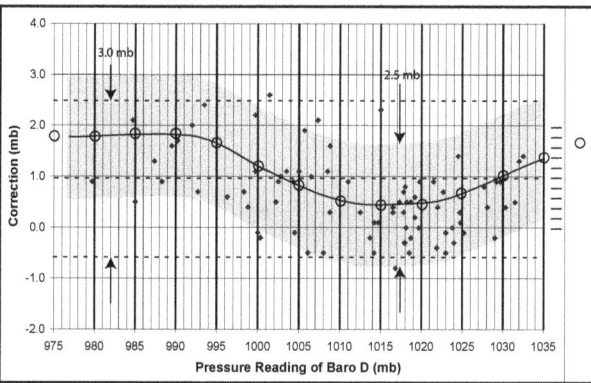

Figure 4.5-7 *Calibration of a popular barometer that sells for $280. It has a 3.5 inch dial and a heavy brass housing. Its accuracy is not presented in advertising, but the manufacturer states that it is ±3 mb across the dial. The calibration by nature shows that this sample is actually better than that. Even without using the curve the values were within ±1.5 mb after resetting to read 1 mb higher.*

The calibration curve always shows the best pressure to use when setting the barometer, but in cases like this it is best to just use this curve or a table made from it rather than trying to adjust the set screw by just 1 mb. The curve shown was just a best guess centroid to the many data points. The open circles are selected points for a table of corrections (Table 4.5-1). The value at 1040 mb was projected.

Table 4.5-1 Corrections	
Reading	*Correction*
987	+1.8
980	+1.8
985	+1.9
990	+1.9
995	+1.7
1000	+1.2
1005	+0.8
1010	+0.5
1015	+0.4
1020	+0.5
1025	+0.7
1030	+1.1
1035	+1.4
1040	+1.7

Table Notes. *The data here are taken from the open circles in Figure 4.5-7, which were selected equally spaced along the centroid of the calibration curve. After making these corrections to the reading, you could be confident that your pressure was correct to within about ±1.3 mb.*

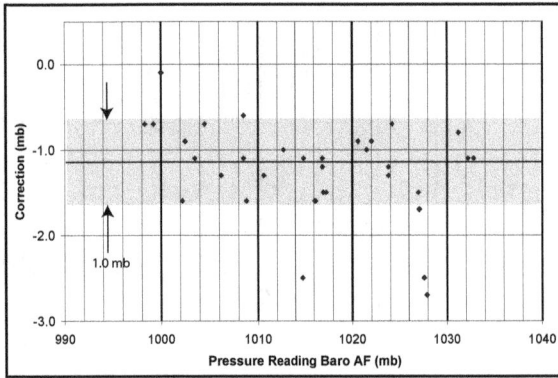

Figure 4.5-8 *Beginning of a calibration by nature of an Air Flo aneroid dated 1972, which had been tank tested to be accurate to ±1.0 mb from 920 to 1040. The simple rule "Subtract 1.2 mb from its reading" would provide accurate pressures over its range.*

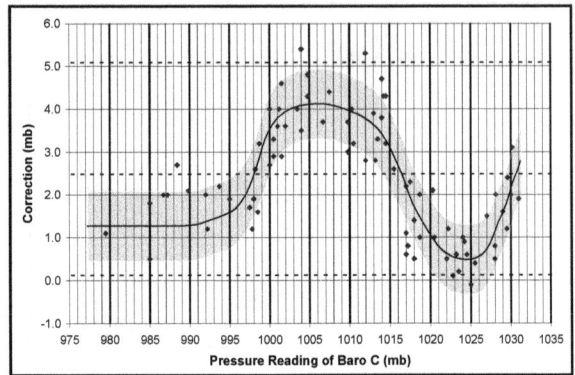

Figure 4.5-9 *A troublesome result. You could say "Add 2.5 mb to whatever you read and the answer will be right to within ±2.5 mb." In principal you could improve on this using the curve shown, and maybe achieve below 2.0 mb uncertainty, but it is not very reassuring. We at least found that 1025 mb was not a good place to set this instrument.*

To make a table, just make a list of even steps along the full pressure range, and for each of these read off from the curve what the corrections should be. Then you can post the correction table right next to the instrument and easily apply the corrections each time you record a pressure. A sample is shown in Figure 4.5-7 and Table 4.5-1.

If on the other hand, you can't draw a line through the results and there is no rhyme nor reason to the data, which are scattered all over the place as in Figure 4.5-3, then you have proven the instrument is not useful for weather analysis or forecasting. It is time to pitch it out and get a new barometer.

(7) Improving the calibration.

The job is well started at this point, but not done. Continue working on the comparisons whenever you can and record the corrections. As time goes by you get to know your barometer better and better. Careful monitoring will also let you know if the setting has drifted, which it inevitably will. Look for a drift if your average air temperature changes a lot, or for sure after you ship the instrument by air for any reason. Most aneroids will drift to some extent even without special cause, especially when brand new, so it is important to keep an eye on the calibration.

If your setting does drift off at some point, your calibration is most likely still valid, but just shifted in full by the amount of the drift. In other words, your calibration curve has reproduced all the accurate pressures you checked periodically, but then one day you notice that your barometer is 2 mb low at some specific pressure. That is the sign to keep an eye on it, and look for another check point. More likely than not, when you apply your old correction to another pressure it too will be too low by 2 mb. Your instrument has drifted. The first guess correction, which is probably right, is all corrections on your curve or table are now 2 mb too low. So just change the correction table and keep an eye on it. Make a log book entry of what has taken place since the last calibration, so you can monitor its behavior in the future. The careful use of barometers is a dynamic process.

It is best to not change the set screw to make it match the first calibration. Once you do that, you have to watch it again for a long time to be sure you have it set where you wish it to be, not to mention that it can be difficult on some instruments to make small adjustments to the setting.

The achievement and maintenance of a good barometer calibration takes some level of dedication, but the rewards can be high. An accurate barometer is your most valuable tool for analyzing and forecasting the weather. Any professional weather router or successful racing navigator will confirm this. But any navigator can benefit from its use, not just the professionals. Likewise, most would agree that an inaccurate barometer can be your biggest hindrance to these tasks.

If you have already invested in your barometer and maybe even be underway with it already, then the calibration as outlined (using wireless services for the pressure data) is the only option to testing its usefulness. But if you are still in the market for a barometer, then it definitely pays to look carefully into the accuracy specifications of the instrument. When choosing an aneroid, an actual calibration curve provided with the instrument would save you this initial testing, but even that should be checked periodically. The value of knowing accurate pressure is becoming more apparent each day (Chapters 5 and 6) and as such more dealers are providing this information. There are good electronic barometers under $200 and excellent, tested aneroid barometers under $500. Remember too if you already have a barometer and need a calibration sooner than Mother Nature can do it for you, there are commercial services that do this, as explained in Section 4.8.

Regardless of how you achieve it, based on my own sailing experience and that of many others I have discussed this with, accurate pressure will eventually contribute to an important routing decision underway, and you will be grateful for it.

4.6 Test your Barometer in a Skyscraper

Now that we know how barometers are supposed to work with changes in elevation, we come to the logical step of testing this. Maybe like Pascal, you can talk your brother in law into taking your barometer up a mountain or tall building, but if not, it is an interesting way to spend a few hours yourself to inevitably learn more about pressure and your barometer.

Before, during, or after a full calibration you might find it valuable to get a quick look at the instrument by making a notable change to its elevation. One way is to take it up a tall building. Recall that the typical height of each story of a building is 12 feet, and this elevation corresponds to a pressure change of

0.44 mb. This leads to our jingle "Point four four per floor," as an easy way to remember it.

In Seattle the tallest building is the Columbia Tower (Figure 4.6-1). It is 76 floors with a height of 937 feet. Note that 937/76 = 12.3 feet per floor, so our approximation is not far off. Thus from the ground level to the top floor of this building should be about 76*0.44 = 33.4 mb pressure drop. If you look this up in Appendix 2, you will see that the exact correction is 33.8 mb, but our estimate is close enough. When you make the test you need to ask someone in the observation level what the actual elevation above ground level is, or someway obtain convincing information.

Figure 4.6-1 *Columbia Tower building in Seattle, as an example of a barometer test lab.*

Then if your barometer reads 1016.0 on the ground level, you would expect it to read 1016.0 -33.4 = 982.6 at the top. If it does read this, or very close to this, then that is a good sign. Either you have no significant correction over these 33 mb, or the correction happens to be the same at each pressure but still possibly different in the middle. A stop on the 38th floor for a pressure reading would resolve that—meaning halfway up the building you actually use.

The other option is take your barometer for a Sunday ride up the nearest tall hill. Use a GPS to record the Lat-Lon of each location where you recorded the pressure. Then you can go to the National Elevation Dataset (www.starpath.com/barometers) to get accurate elevations for each location.

A nice example in Seattle (much of which is near sea level) would be the hour or so ride up to Snoqualmie Pass (elevation 3,000 ft). This type of trip would give you a span of 105 mb, which is essentially a complete calibration in a few hours (ie 1020 to 915), up and back with stops along the way every 15 mb or so. For this test it would be important to take a thermometer with you and do all the measurements inside the car kept at the same temperature. Three thousand feet would typically correspond to 11F° temperature drop, which could influence some barometers.

A trip up a mountain and back is an ideal way to check for hysteresis in your barometer (Section 3.2), since this exercise provides a relatively rapid change in pressure over a large range. Next time you go skiing or hiking in the mountains, take your barometer along for the car ride and check it out, both going up and coming back down. Remember to unfold from your observations any changes in the actual sea level pressure during the measurements.

4.7 Using a Weather Map to Check your Barometer

Here we discuss using a map to check the barometer as part of a calibration process, and then with our calibrated barometer, we turn right around in Section 6.3 and use the barometer to check other types of weather maps. Practice here helps us master the latter, which is one of the main values of an accurate barometer in marine weather.

As discussed in Section 2.5, the best source on U.S. surface analysis maps is

www.hpc.ncep.noaa.gov/html/sfc2.shtml.

They give full maps of the U.S. every 3 hours which you can download by region. The maps show the station reports that went into the computation of the isobars, but the lay of the isobars is easier to interpolate in this exercise. The isobars are 4 mb apart. An example of interpolation is shown for Galveston, TX in Figure 4.7-1.

The key to using these maps as your calibration source is to record the pressure from your barometer at the proper times, which are every three hours at UTC times divisible by 3, ie 03, 06, 09, etc. There is no good way to interpolate the maps for time if you

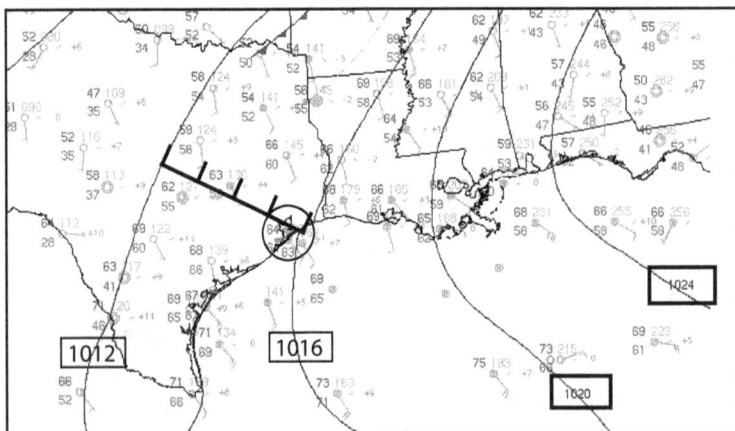

Figure 4.7-1 *Weather map of South Central U.S. valid at 03z, Feb 10, 2009. Galveston, TX is shown circled. The 1024 and 1020 isobars are labeled but the others are not. We can infer them as indicated. Then interpolating, we see that this map tells the pressure at Galveston at this time was about 1016.5 mb. Notice that a 2-mb error on a map like this is huge, which is why we try to get our calibrations accurate to ±1 mb. These maps are very useful for checking barometers every 3 hour throughout the day, on UTC hours divisible by 3.*

do not have data recorded at the exact time. When the pressure is changing rapidly, even 5 or 10 minutes can make a difference. The times are UTC (formerly Greenwich Mean Time), which is the same year round. There is no daylight saving on the Universal Time system. You can look up your local time conversion to UTC at www.time.gov.

4.8 Commercial calibration services

We have explained how you can calibrate your barometer on your own using the pressures nature gives you. Many of the samples shown here were done that way. It is an instructive process that gets you more involved with your instrument and ultimately leads to better barometer work. But it takes some time and certainly some luck, as you must experience a range of pressures to test the instrument. Also it can depend on where you live. If you live in the tropics, your pressure does not change much until a tropical storm wanders by. Then you get to see the low end, but it will be very rare that you ever get to see the high end. Or you may have a deadline that cannot wait for nature, such as the starting time of a yacht race, or the departure time for a ship's voyage with a new barometer. Taking your barometer up a tall building or high hill is another way to test its response, but this too requires some good luck on where you are at the time.

An alternative is to turn to one of the several commercial calibration services around the world. Another advantage of this approach is they typically have NIST traceable standards for reference pressures, which will likely be more accurate than you can do on your own with broadcasted or published pressure reports that you have to interpolate for location and time. In the U.K., Germany, and France they each have their own national standards that are similar to the NIST in the U.S.

The professional services will place your instrument into a chamber that can be evacuated and pressurized to test it over the full atmospheric pressure range relative to a high-accuracy pressure standard gauge, usually one of the types we have mentioned here in the text. Usually they do these tests at one specific temperature and make careful records of it. Sample test chambers are shown in Figure 4.8-1 to 4.8-3.

Figure 4.8-1 *A ready made high-quality test chamber available from www.th-friedrichs.com in Germany. This unit shows an aneroid barometer being calibrated relative to a reference mercury barometer. A second mercury barometer outside the chamber monitors ambient pressure. Typically the pumps, valve systems, and pressure standards are sold separately.*

Table 4.8-1 lists several companies that offer calibration services. Their procedures and the final products they provide to you as documentation of their work varies with each. One variable, for example, is the number of test points that make up the calibration. You can contact them individually to learn the details, schedules and so on. Fees for a basic calibration range from $75 to $200, depending on the calibration requirements.

When requesting a calibration it could be valuable to have information on how fast the procedure

Table 4.8-1 Barometer Calibration Services*		
Company	Internet	Phone
The Barometer Man (U.S.)	barometerman.com	970-640-0689
InnoCal (U.S.)	innocalsolutions.com	866-466-6225
Fisher (Germany)	fischer-barometer.de	+49 (0) 37341 487
Russel Scientific (U.K.)	russell-scientific.co.uk	+44 (0) 1362-693481
Starpath (U.S.)	starpath.com	206-783-1414

***Notes.** Several companies offer a service to calibrate or re-calibrate instruments that they manufacture, but not others. The companies in this table calibrate all barometers, aneroid or electronic. Arrangements and prices vary with the instrument and calibration needs.*

was carried out and how long the pressure remained at the individual test pressures before moving to the next. Generally though, the people offering these services are experienced in the calibration process and the calibration data they provide is dependable.

Figure 4.8-2 Left. *The Ideal Arrowsmith test chamber and standards gauges used by Merrill Kennedy (barometerman.com) for calibration using both a Vaisala PTB 220 and a Druck DPI 740 as standards. He offers aneroid repair services as well as calibrations, and sells a wide variety of new and used high quality instruments.*

Figure 4.8-3 *Test chamber used at Starpath HQ. The standard shown in an NIST traceable GE Druck DPI 142 (±0.10 mb); a DPI 740 is also used. A Davis Perception II is used to monitor ambient conditions during the test. A small diaphragm pump both evacuates and pressurizes, with adjustable regulators that limit the pressure range to >900 mb and <1050 mb. The chamber pressure can be set in seconds to a chosen pressure accurate to 0.1 mb. The controls are Fast Up or Fast Down (about 10 seconds to cover full atmospheric range), and Slow Up or Slow Down, which changes pressure at just less than 0.1 mb/sec. The chamber pressure port is connected to the standards instrument and to a Vernier BAR-BTA sensor connected to the PC (using Vernier Logger Pro software), which records and plots the chamber pressure vs. time. The chamber temperature is also recorded (Vernier GoTemp sensor) vs. time, as are photographs or video of the barometer face at each test pressure. A momentary switch on the panel activates a vibrator that "taps" the test instrument as needed.*

This system was designed and built by Steve Hansen of DiverseArts, LLC, in Owl's Head, ME. For further information (excluding pressure standards) see www.belljar.net/barometer.

Barometers have been used to forecast weather since their inception, three hundred years ago. Forecasts then, like forecasts now, however, are not always right, especially when based on just one piece of information such as barometric pressure. Books and articles that focus on barometers tend to overestimate their value in this process, whereas books on general weather tend to underestimate their importance.

I tried to overcome this tendency in *Modern Marine Weather*, which strives to present a balanced approach to using your own observations to analyze present conditions and forecast what might happen next. Even taking everything into account, you will not always be right, but you will be doing the best you can, short of having an official weather forecast in hand. Even with an official forecast in hand, your own practiced observations are crucial to evaluating the timing and specifics of the forecasts.

Modern Marine Weather serves as background for this chapter and a source for further study. Much of what follows in this chapter is adapted from that book.

Weather forecasting is best done using all possible observations. Crucial observations along with barometric pressure are clouds, winds, precipitation, and sometimes temperature. At sea, the sea state is another important observation. And in all cases, it is not just the present values that matter, it is the sequence of how each one has been changing. Trends are always crucial to detecting what is taking place.

But this is a book on barometers, so we are back to emphasizing what you can learn from the barometric pressure. At sea, the main concern is almost always wind, and the pressure is the key factor to predicting wind. Temperature and precipitation are only secondary concerns at sea.

On land, however, many barometer users care about temperature and precipitation more than wind

—unless they live on the coast in a hurricane zone, where wind is again a key issue. One of the problems we face in this context is almost all common barometers have the word "Rain" written on the dial. There is an obvious implication here that the barometer can forecast rain. As we shall see, there is only an indirect correlation between pressure and rain, and an even weaker correlation between pressure and temperature.

5.1 Significance of the Actual Pressure Value

As discussed in Chapter 2, Highs and Lows in pressure patterns are always relative. A pressure marked "H" on today's map could be marked "L" on tomorrow's map of the same general location—especially when in the range of about 1000 to 1010 mb. But this does not mean we have to disregard the actual magnitudes of the pressures completely, especially having at hand the worldwide mean pressure values given in Chapter 10. With that information, you can choose any location in the world, and any month of the year, and learn what mean sea-level pressure has been established. Furthermore, with the standard deviations also given there, you can determine the probability of the actual pressure you experience.

For example, as I write this I check the Internet to learn that the pressure in Santa Monica, CA (34.2N, 119.8W) on Dec 15, 2008 was 1012 mb, whereas the average December pressure there is 1020 mb. The present pressure is 8 mb below the average, which has only a 7% chance of occurring. In other words, this is uncommonly low for this month and so it merits a careful watch. Santa Monica did in fact have winds approaching 20 kts at the time, which is well above average, so there is some correlation in this example. But that was an absolutely random check. This is a more significant line of reasoning in the Tropics.

Outside of the Tropics, this type of reasoning is only a very broad application of statistics. Santa Monica could have the same pressure with much wind or with little wind, with rain or with clear skies, depending on the rest of the pressure pattern around them and how it is changing. We need to know more to be more specific. I just want to illustrate that with the right data, the actual value of the pressure is not meaningless.

The pressure you read on a barometer depends on the weather and on your elevation. It also, of course, depends on the accuracy and setting of your barometer, but if we assume the barometer is working correctly and is accurate, then what it reads depends only on your present weather and your present elevation.

Usually when we speak of "weather," we refer to more things than the atmospheric pressure—in fact some meteorologists do not even consider barometric pressure as an element of weather. They concentrate on the sensible elements such as the temperature and humidity, clouds, wind, precipitation, and so on. But when it comes to barometers, the only part of the "weather" it measures is atmospheric pressure. You may find barometers that include thermometers and hygrometers (for humidity), but we are not considering such "weather stations." We are talking here about just plain barometers that measure atmospheric pressure alone.

But with that said, it is important to immediately recall that what barometers read is far more affected by the barometer's elevation than it is by the local weather. So step one in considering the role of the actual pressure itself is to correct your reading to sea level. If you don't do that, then places like Denver are always in the middle of a hurricane!

Barometer Labels

Most books (including my own) usually say we should neglect the labels on a barometer, Rain, Change, Fair, etc, for the very reasons stated above. Namely, the actual weather we get depends on the overall shape of the pressure pattern and how it is changing and not on the specific value of the pressure. We were even warned of this in the 1800's by the very folks who made up the labels—as they were,

nevertheless, on the way to Patent Office to protect the use of them.

But let's be a little more forgiving for the moment. These labels have been on barometers since the mid 1800's and have essentially not changed since then. Can they be so totally useless and survive this long? There has got to be some element of truth in them—on some level.

Figure 5.1-1 shows common label patterns, and Tables 5.1-L, M, S summarize the labeled pressures.

Let's start with the easy parts in the long label pattern, marked L. The word "Stormy" is usually centered around 28″ (948 mb). It does not matter how the needle got there or when, or where you are. That is bad weather, just as labeled. No problem with that one.

Likewise, if you are anywhere near the "Very Dry" zone, centered at 1050, then indeed that is the case. There is no way to get there rapidly, so the air will indeed be dry, and the skies clear—though it might be very cold! Or it could be very hot, if you are in the center of a mid-ocean High in the summer. That label is also perfectly OK. In other words, we know from general principles what a High means and what a Low means, and these are just the extremes.

Elsewhere on the dial, life is not so simple and we must definitely consider trends, direction, and rates of change if the words are to offer any guidelines. Certainly there are no forces in nature that would call for anything unique happening at half inch intervals on a mercury barometer. Nor are their words in any language that uniquely describe what happens at these particular pressures. So they are in large part meant to adorn the dials with some "talking points," and hence the standard was established.

If we interpret "Fair" as "average," then that is about right on this long-pattern label, in that the average pressures of the world fall into that range. In other words, even though "Change" is centered at the top of the dial on essentially all instruments, you are more likely to see the dial at sea level in the "Fair" range of a long pattern dial. (To shift the average reading down to the Change zone at the top you need to be at an elevation of about 300 or 400 feet, which we

Figure 5.1-1 *Standard label patterns. L is the long description, M is a medium pattern, and S is a short one. These labels also appeared on mercury barometers as well. Example L is from a banjo style mercury manometer that converted the mercury height to a dial via a float on the second tube (invented by Hooke). The same pattern was and still is used on aneroids. Pictures L and M are compliments of barometerfair.com. The Taylor unit in S is compliments of barometerman.com. Other forms and slightly different alignments are seen on some units, but these are common patterns.*

Table 5.1-L Long Barometer Labels			
Inches	*mb*	*Label*	*~ Range*
28	948	Stormy	< 957
28.5	965	Much Rain	957 - 974
29	982	Rain	974 - 990
29.5	999	Change	990 - 1008
30	1016	Fair	1008 - 1025
30.5	1033	Settled Fair	1025 - 1042
31	1050	Very Dry	> 1042

Table 5.1-S Short Barometer Labels		
Inches	*mb*	*Label*
< 29	< 992	Rain
29 - 30	982 - 1016	Change
> 30	> 1016	Fair

Table 5.1-M Medium Barometer Labels		
Inches	*mb*	*Label*
< 28.5	< 965	Stormy
28.5 - 29.1	965 - 985	Rain
29.1 - 29.9	985 - 1013	Change
29.9 - 30.5	1013 - 1033	Fair
> 30.5	> 1033	Very Dry

speculated in Chapter 2 might have been the original source of this offset.)

And even though we can indeed get rain anywhere to the left of "Settled Fair," you are definitely not going to get to "Much Rain," without passing through "Rain." And you are not going to ever get to "Stormy" without in fact having "Much Rain." So the actual *sequence of labels* across the long-pattern dial is not unreasonable, regardless of which direction you consider.

The other two patterns (M and S) are similar, but grow progressively even more vague. For any of these labels to have much more meaning you have to watch how the needle changes.

Another way to look at the labels is to overlay any of the styles with a pattern of your own, similar to that shown in Figure 5.1-2. This is more generic for a possible meaning of a specific pressure, but any analysis or forecasting goal still depends on trends and rates, not just the needle location on the dial.

"Definitely Bad" and "Definitely Good" are still unique zones in most parts of the world. No matter how the needle got there, in the former you will most likely have strong winds, cloudy skies and precipitation. In the latter you will have light air, clear skies and no precipitation. There are exceptions that can come about when Lows and Highs pack up against each other, but the above will be right far more often than wrong.

Most observations of the dial will find it in this "Average" zone. And sure enough, the weather you

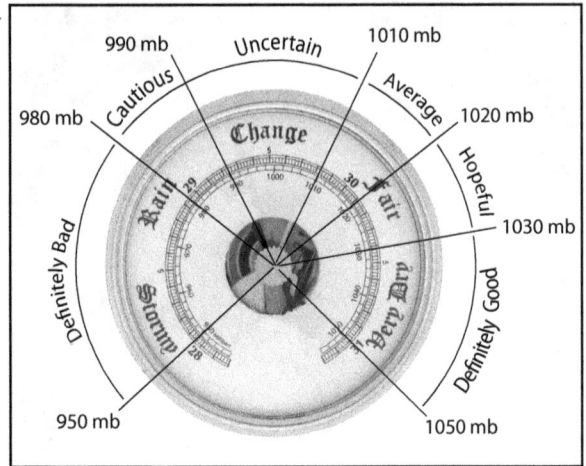

Figure 5.1-2 *Another way to look at the dial and labels of a barometer <u>at sea level</u>. Average pressures are typically between 1010 and 1020 worldwide, away from the several Action Centers (Table 2.1-2). Below 980 is always bad weather, and above 1030 is also almost always good weather. Other values depend on longer term trends, rates, and directions. But if you just look at the dial, and do not already know what is going on, these labels are reasonable guides. Below 950 is likely to be in a hurricane; above 1050 and you are approaching some national records.*

experience when the needle is there will more often than not be whatever your average weather is for that time of year. Likewise, it is more likely than not that if you have exceptional weather for the season, the dial will be outside of the Average zone.

But these are statistical averages. You could have exceptional weather with an Average reading, and you could have a reading rather outside the average without exceptional weather. The location of the needle is not gospel.

We do better by noting its history. If you are in the Average zone and the needle raises to the "Hopeful" zone, then you are at least on the way to "Definitely Good." But it is just "Hopeful"; it could turn around and go back without getting particularly good. But it is fair to call it Hopeful, because 1020 is already relatively high, so you are typically just getting better. Thus a slow steady rise in the barometer is a long standing sign of improving weather, just as a steady, slow fall of the barometer is a sign of unsettled weather with good chance of rain.

Strong Winds with Highs!

Usually high pressure brings light winds, but this is not always the case. When Highs interact with Lows the isobars can get compressed, leading to strong winds in regions where the pressure is still quite high. This is well known in the English Channel; it occurs even more often along the California coast in the summertime. Gale force winds with pressures in the 1020's, or exceptionally touching the 1030's, have been recorded.

The zone on the low side of "Average," called here "Uncertain" is just that. The needle can wander around in this zone with very little correlation at all with the present weather. Could be good and could be bad. It could move quite a ways one way here and then turn around and go right back. This is the zone on the borders of potentially deeper Lows.

Once you see the needle down in the "Cautious" zone, you have to be alert. It could in fact already be a gale outside, or it could be headed for one. Or this pressure could start back up without a serious storm. In any event, you are getting closer to "Definitely Bad," so if it is not bad already, this is your warning.

In this section we have just looked at possible meanings of the present pressure reading itself—giving it every benefit of the doubt that this might be useful. Later we look at the recent history of the readings to work toward a more realistic use of the barometer in forecasting.

Temperature and pressure

Another common barometer label that dates from the FitzRoy era is shown in Figure 5.1-3. It says

Barometer
Falls for Warm, Wet, or More Wind

—

Rises for Cold, Dry, or Less Wind

We have discussed the wet or dry, and the wind we come back to. For now we look for elements of truth in the temperature predictions. The correlation implied is that a falling barometer is associated with warmer air, and a rising one with colder air. The situation that shows that this is generically the case, or at least true on the very broad average, is shown in Figure 5.1-4.

Outside of the Tropics, Lows move from west to east in both hemispheres. An approaching Low brings a falling barometer and the counterclockwise flow around the Low in the Northern Hemisphere brings air up from the south. Since air from the south is generally warmer than air from the north, the prediction is likely true, at least on the long term average. The barometer can of course drop without the system being large enough or oriented adequately to bring in much

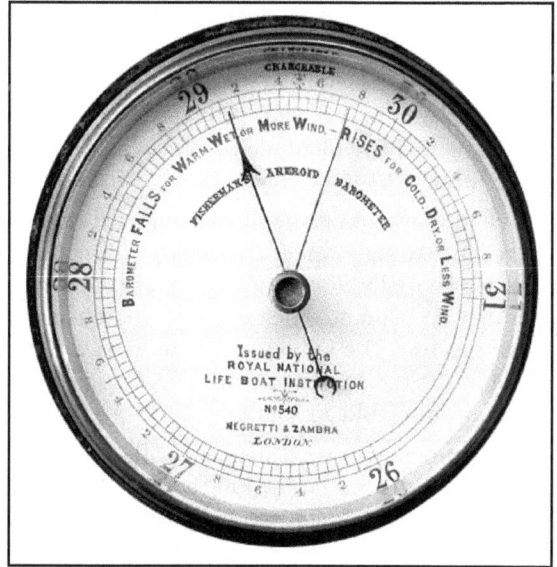

Figure 5.1-3 *Temperature predictions on a "Fisherman's barometer" from the FitzRoy era. These fishermen must also have been mountain climbers, since it goes down to 26", a pressure altitude of about 4,000 ft. Photo compliments of Derek Rayment (antique-barometers.com).*

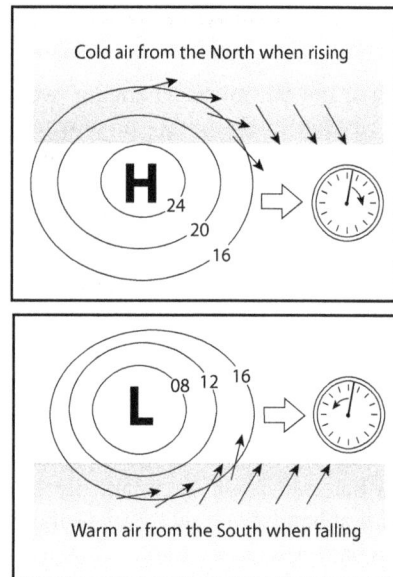

Figure 5.1-4 *How barometric pressure can affect air temperature—rising bringing cold air, falling bringing warm air. In the Southern Hemisphere, the flow around Highs and Lows is reversed, so the same behavior is observed.*

warm air, but in the big picture, the air is warmer to the south, toward the equator.

In the Southern Hemisphere, the wind flows clockwise around the Lows, but this still brings air from the equator toward higher latitudes. In this sense the rule is good for both hemispheres.

A High moving in or building brings a rising barometer and typically colder air from the north. Large Highs are generally not as mobile as are Lows, but when they do build or slide east, they would tend to behave this way. The famous Arctic outbreaks experienced in the U.S. are exactly this effect. Highs over Canada, sending cold air south.

This is not always what happens with a rising or falling barometer, but on the long average it is likely true. In short, though still not gospel on any plane, this is not such a bad label on a barometer.

A recognized good sign for improving weather is thermometer and barometer rising together, but a thermometer rising with a falling barometer is often a sign of coming rain.

5.2 What Causes the Pressure to Change

When we see the barometer changing, we typically think the weather is changing—or maybe going to change. But this is not always such a simple conclusion to draw. It boils down to figuring out what exactly is changing. A first question to ask is whether or not the barometer itself is moving. At sea the barometer is more likely moving than not. The barometer on your wall at home is obviously not moving. The barometer in your watch could be at rest or it could be moving at 70 miles per hour, depending on the speed limit.

As mentioned earlier, the one in your watch is also extremely sensitive to your elevation. Driving down a hill your barometer will rise markedly, but that is not the issue at hand. For now we are looking at what can cause a barometer *at sea level* to change. There are four answers.

1. The pressure pattern is actually changing

If you have a *stationary* Low over your location and the forces of nature are causing that Low to deepen,

then you will see your barometer drop. The most dramatic drop of a stationary Low is something like a 24-mb drop in 24 hours in extreme midlatitude storms called "meteorological bombs." The rate of deepening in these systems is actually much higher than in typical hurricanes and typhoons.

Likewise a huge High can be parked over your location, not moving at all but just getting higher or lower, but not often changing very fast if it is not moving.

2. The pressure pattern is not changing, but the whole pattern is moving toward or away from you.

It is common to have pressure patterns of Highs and Lows that are not changing much, but the whole pattern is moving. As a rule, Lows move faster than Highs, but a Low can also move very slowly. Typical speeds of a Low are between 10 and 25 kts (nautical miles per hour), but there are extremes (maybe 50 kts in the Roaring Forties of the Southern Hemisphere). Outside of the Tropics, Lows generally move toward the East, but it could be toward the NE, E, or SE.

As an example, consider this system. We have a 1016-mb isobar running due north along the West Coast of the U.S., and another one parallel to it 150 nautical miles offshore to the west, with a pressure of 1012 mb. This pressure system (2 straight isobars) is then moving due East at 15 kts. The isobars are not changing their values at all, just sliding East. What would we see as this pressure pattern passes over us?

At 15 kts, it takes 10 hr for the isobars to move 150 nmi, which is the distance between 1016 and 1012 mb of pressure. So we would see a pressure drop of 4 mb in 10 hr as these isobars passed overhead.

That was a benign example. A deep, fast-moving Low with close isobars can move rapidly toward you creating a dramatic pressure drop, even though the system itself is not changing at all.

3. The pressure pattern is not changing and not moving, but you are moving into or away from it

At home this is a non-issue. But when moving this can be a significant factor. In the last example, consider the isobars completely stopped, but you are headed west on a highway at 60 mph to visit friends. On a several-hour trip, your watch barometer would show a pressure dropping 6 times faster than in our last example, at a rate of 24 mb per 10 hr. You would be tempted to warn your friends of an impending "meteorological bomb" or worse. When headed east back home, you would conclude that you cheated nature, because no bomb showed up, and now the pressure is rising rapidly. All of course wrong thinking.

On a vessel at sea, the effect is more often present and it can be more insidious. Under the same stationary isobars, a vessel headed due west from the coast at 15 kts would observe a steady pressure drop of 4 mb/10hr within a pressure system that is neither changing nor moving. This does not mean we do not care about this. We are in fact headed toward a Low. But it would be h wrong to conclude a system is moving toward you or that the weather overhead is itself deteriorating. The important point is, wrong knowledge might lead to wrong decisions.

The VOS program receives pressure reports from moving vessels throughout the day, and these reports include observed pressure tendency over the past three hours. If these reported trends are to be used productively, they have to be corrected for the course and speed of the reporting vessel, which is always included with the reports.

4. The most likely case— a combination of the above.

Nature is rarely so kind as to have just one of these sources affecting our observed pressure at any one time, so we are right back to a theme that permeates this book. To do the best we can with pressure data we often have to do a bit of reckoning. It is rarely a matter of looking at the pressure alone and drawing a useful conclusion. The task of this book is to show the value of this extra effort. When evaluating pressure trends, we must at least consider the items on this list before drawing conclusions about what is actually taking place.

5.3 Estimating Wind Speed from Pressure Reports

We have discussed in Chapter 2 how wind speed depends on isobar spacing—the closer the isobars, the stronger the wind—and we discussed the flow direction of the wind, clockwise around Highs, counterclockwise around Lows. Now we want to make this description somewhat more quantitative, but only so far as to give a numerical feeling for the magnitudes involved.

We also need this background to appreciate some of the concepts behind barometer labels and rules of thumb that use wind direction as a factor for determining the meaning of pressure changes—types of rules that date back to FitzRoy, if not earlier.

Table 5.3-1 Surface Wind Speed (kts)*

Latitude	*4-mb isobar spacing in degrees of latitude*								
	1	**1.5**	**2**	**2.5**	**3**	**3.5**	**4**	**4.5**	**5**
20°	94	63	47	38	31	27	23	21	19
25°	76	51	38	30	25	22	19	17	15
30°	64	43	32	26	21	18	16	14	13
35°	56	37	28	22	19	16	14	12	11
40°	50	33	25	20	17	14	12	11	10
45°	45	30	23	18	15	13	11	10	9
50°	42	28	21	17	14	12	10	9	8
55°	39	26	20	16	13	11	10	9	8
60°	37	25	19	15	12	11	9	8	7

*** Table Notes**

1. This table assumes the isobars are straight. For curved isobars, winds will be somewhat less around a Low and somewhat greater around a High.

2. The table values assume the surface wind has been reduced by friction by 20%. On rough land or rough seas, this reduction could be as much as 40%.

3. To find wind speed, measure the 4-mb isobar spacing from a weather map in units of latitude degrees (1° = 60 nmi), then find wind from the table. Example: if at latitude 45° the 4-mb isobars are 120 nautical miles apart (2° on the latitude scale), then the expected surface wind is 23 knots.

4. Wind direction is figured separately. It is directed clockwise around the high pressure, pointed some 25° out of the High, or counterclockwise around a Low and 25° into the Low, as shown in Figure 5.3-1.

For those who wish more details on wind and isobars, please refer to *Modern Marine Weather*, which covers the subject in more detail.

Because the strength of the Coriolis force increases with latitude, the wind speed you expect depends not just on the isobar spacing where you are, but also on your latitude. Table 5.3-1 shows a coarse summary of the values to be expected. This table assumes the isobars are more or less straight where you are, and it assumes an average correction for the frictional reduction of wind speed as it flows along the surface of the land or ocean. It is still a workable approximation for a basic understanding of how pressure creates the wind.

These are the wind speeds you might expect in the open ocean or on a more or less unobstructed, large open plain on land. As soon as hills and valleys or mountains (or rows of tall buildings) become involved, all bets are off. The terrain can focus the wind to several times these predictions, or they could block strong wind to a dead calm.

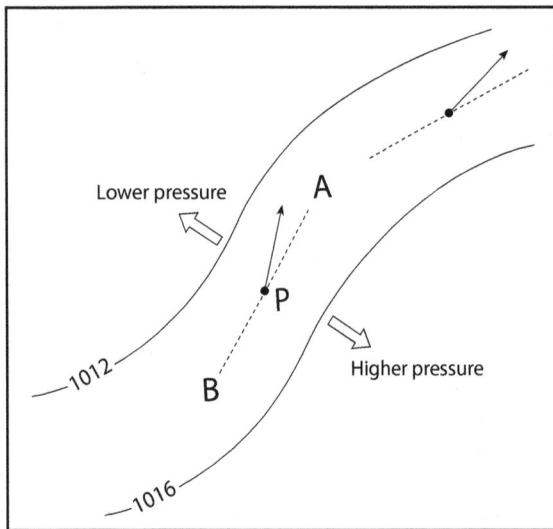

Figure 5.3-1. *Figuring wind direction from isobars in the Northern Hemisphere (NH). At any point P, for example, draw in an artificial isobar parallel to the ones on either side. The wind is then flowing toward A or toward B. Choose the direction that puts the low pressure on your left-hand side when in the NH. Then alter that direction about 25° toward the low pressure as shown. (In the Southern Hemisphere, the direction is toward B, and then again shifted into the low, which would be to the right.)*

What this table shows is just the potential wind power within a large pressure pattern. It also does not help much with winds near the centers of deep cyclonic storms, hurricanes, or tornadoes. These are tightly curved isobars and the rules are different.

The direction of the wind flow, no matter what kind of pressure pattern you have, hurricane or gentle sea breeze, is best pictured by using the Buys Ballot Law backwards. And this in turn, is best done in two steps.

First, look at the isobars, and imagine the wind flowing right along parallel to the isobars in the direction that puts the low pressure on your left as you proceed forward with the wind. Then you have it about right, but now you need to shift the direction slightly toward the low-pressure side, about 25°. Then you have the wind direction associated with that pressure pattern, so long as you are well away from irregular terrain.

We have to be so careful with the prescription here because of the way wind directions are defined. We are talking here about figuring out which way the wind is blowing, meaning the direction the wind flows to-

RISE. FOR N. ELY. NW.--N.--E. DRY OR LESS WIND. EXCEPT WET FROM N. ED.

FALL. FOR S. WLY. SE.--S.--W. WET OR MORE WIND. EXCEPT WET FROM N. ED.

Long foretold, long last; Short notice, soon past.

First rise after low, Foretells stronger blow.

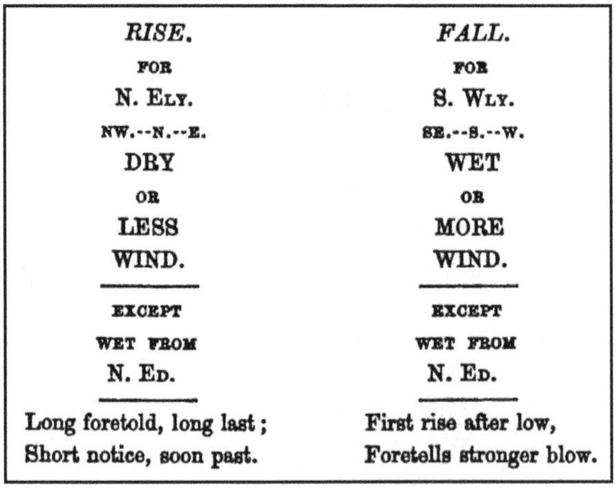

Figure 5.4-1. *FitzRoy barometer labels intended to predict wind and rain based on the pressure and associated wind directions. The labeling is briefly discussed in FitzRoy's* Barometer Manual, *which we have expanded upon in the text here. The primary source of the ideas along with much supporting data is W.H. Dove's* Law of Storms, *1827—the 1862 English edition was dedicated to FitzRoy to acknowledge his support.*

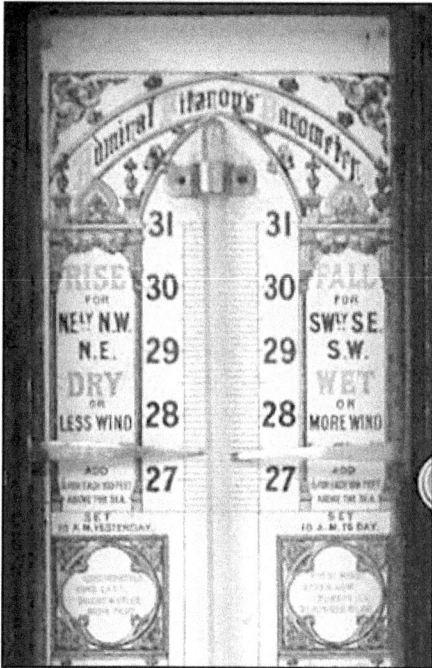

Figure 5.4-2. *A typical FitzRoy label on a mercury barometer. Some also included a Rain, Change, Fair type label, either in the short or long forms of Table 5.1. The two marker hands are for comparing yesterdays' reading with today's.*

Figure 5.4-3. *A contemporary 6-inch dial aneroid with a dial labeled in the classic FitzRoy style, available from barometerworld.co.uk.*

ward. Once you find the wind is flowing toward the south, you have to then say this is a "north wind," because winds are always named after the direction they come from. Examples are given in Figure 5.3-1.

5.4 Rules with Associated Wind Directions

In Section 5.1 we discussed ways to learn as much as possible from the present reading on the dial, without knowing anything else. We could do better if we knew how the dial reading had been changing with time. We would know even more of what is taking place if we knew the wind speed and direction.

This fact was known to the earliest explorers of the barometer, and was made famous by FitzRoy, who not only preached the value and wrote about it in his books, he also arranged to have it printed on many barometers of the day, mercury, as well as aneroid in-

struments. Throughout this period and on to the present, barometers with this labeling are called FitzRoy barometers. Originals are still available from antique barometer specialists in the U.K. and in the U.S.

The most common full form of his labeling is shown in Figure 5.4-1. It obviously takes some explaining. As with the earlier label discussions, our goal now is to read into these as much as we can that would be consistent with known correlations. Even with wind data as a guide, all rules are guidelines to likely outcomes, never the gospel.

Samples of the labeling are shown in Figures 5.4-2 and 5.4-3. There are numerous variations, sometimes including in addition the full labels shown in Figure 5.4-1.

The message provided is actually very generic and could be true throughout the midlatitudes of the Northern Hemisphere. It is not restricted to the British Isles where it originated. Whenever we speak of wind and pressure changes, however, we have to be aware of another factor that is not so obvious. As Benjamin Franklin first taught us, the direction a storm moves is not related to the direction of the surface wind it creates, but the pressure drop or rise does depend on the direction the storm is moving.

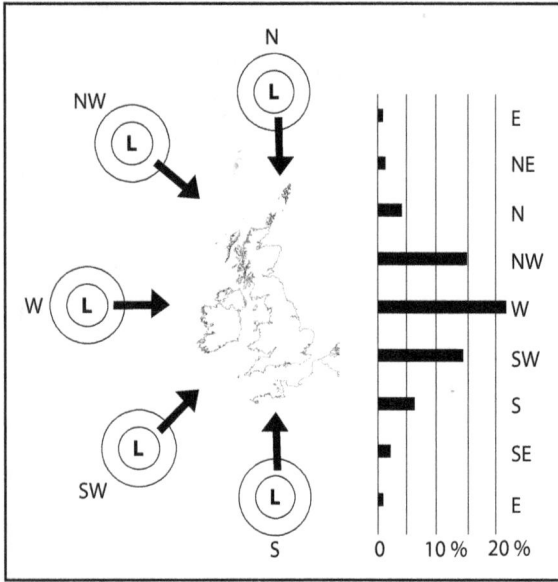

Figure 5.4-4. *Probabilities of the directions that storms approach the British Isles. The small probabilities of an eastern approach are not illustrated. The numerical data were kindly provided by the UK Met Office Library. This graph is for winds aloft data, not actual storm tracks, and we have limited the approach to winds aloft > 40kts.*

Thus we have to be aware of the probabilities of storms approaching from various directions. These data for the U.K. are shown in Figure 5.5-4. Storms approach mostly from the west, with about equal chances of the southwest and northwest. These data are also fairly generic, meaning we would expect about this distribution throughout the higher mid-latitudes of the Northern Hemisphere.

What is less generically true are FitzRoy's observations and declaration (in some publications) that the highest barometer readings tend to be with NE winds, and the lowest pressures with SW winds (a concept directly from Dove's *Law of Storms*). Had he lived in Siberia, for example, he would have stated that the highest pressures come with calm wind. Nevertheless, he broadened his observations to indeed make the label rules more generic than that one statement.

From these observations he defined "northeasterly wind" with a rising barometer as a sign of improving weather, namely dry and less wind. The implication is that either one of these observations alone is not as reliable a sign, which is true.

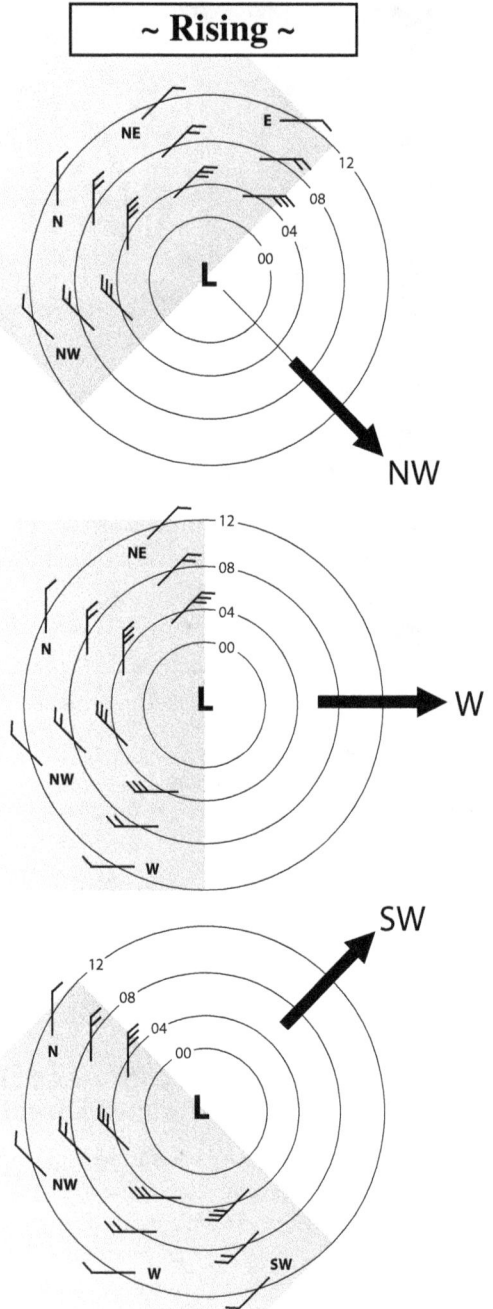

Figure 5.4-5. *Wind and pressure patterns for storms approaching from various directions. The shaded ares are places where the pressure is rising.*

Then to cover the fact that storms could be coming from anywhere in the western quadrant, he broadened the definition of "northeasterly" to include all winds from the range NW to N to NE to E. He was not thinking of storm tracks as we do today, but he had observations that dictated this range was appropriate to the prediction.

We can have pressure rising with a building High or with a Low that is finally moving past us. The case of the High is easy. The east side of an approaching High has NW to N to NE wind, depending on where we are relative to the center of the system. So that High can either just remain stationary and get higher or it could move in over us. In either case the winds get lighter, and the air dryer, as the barometer rises.

Behavior with a passing Low is not as easy to picture without a picture. In Figure 5.4-5 the shaded areas are the places under the moving Low where the pressure is rising. Forward of that it is still dropping, which is not part of this rule. The figure shows the three likely cases of an approaching Low. In all cases, if you choose a place in the shaded area that has wind in the NW to E range, and then draw a line through your position parallel to the direction the Low is moving, you will see that the pressure is dropping and the wind is getting lighter as the Low progresses eastward. As you get farther from the Low center, the isobar spacing increases, and the wind diminishes.

His rule does not address the cases of a W or SW wind with a rising barometer. That circumstance could lead to dryer air and lighter winds, as shown in Figure 5.4-4, for the W and SW approaches of a Low passing north of you, but these winds are equally likely to be associated with approaching Lows, and in particular he singles out the SW wind as a more likely sign of bad weather when the barometer is low, rising or falling.

As for the Falling barometer part of the rule, again we can have decrease in pressure with a retreating High or with an approaching Low. The High part is still easy. The trailing edge of a High has winds from the SE, S, or SW. So a falling barometer with these winds indicates the High is diminishing or moving away. It could be sliding east, or it could be pushed to the south with an approaching Low.

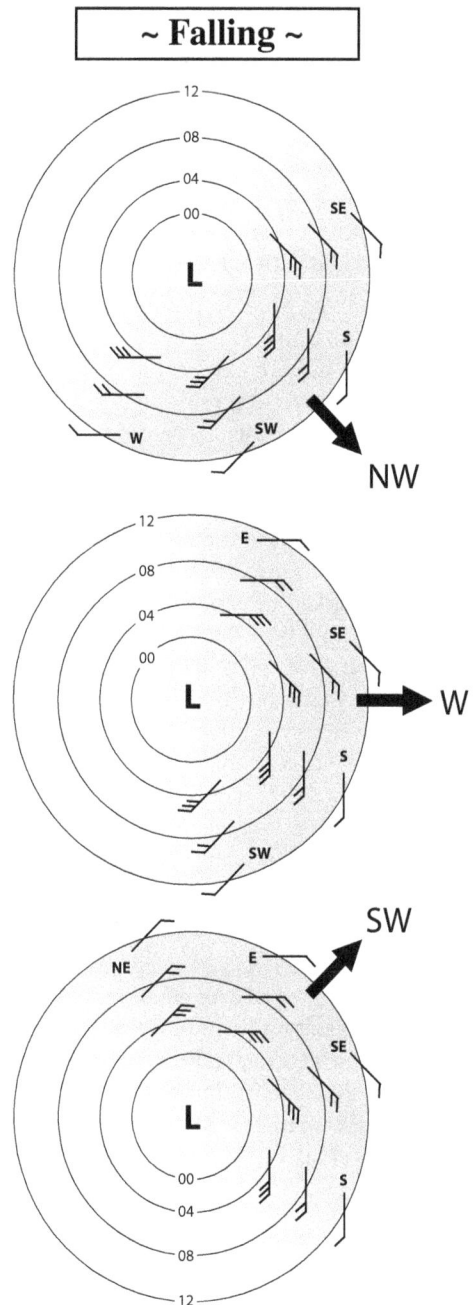

Figure 5.4-6. *Wind and pressure patterns for storms approaching from various directions. The shaded ares are places where the pressure is dropping.*

The approaching Low situations are shown in Figure 5.4-6. The forecasted wind range for wet and more wind is "southwesterly," defined as SE to S to SW to W. As in the last example, choose any place with these winds, then draw a line through it parallel to the storm track, and you will see the pressure is dropping and the wind increasing.

FitzRoy's Exceptions

The exceptions FitzRoy points out for both rising and falling barometer are winds from the NE, for which he states in both cases could be Wet. No mention of wind, just Wet. Also since it is listed with both rising and falling barometer, presumably it applies to stationary pressure as well. This forecast is not quite so transparent.

There is NE wind on the top and NW corner of a Low, and on the bottom and SW corner of a High. So a Low that is parked or passing slowly some distance away to the S or SE of the Isles could bring an extended period of NE wind without necessarily bringing dramatic changes in the local wind. Likewise, a High to the north or northwest could do the same. I do not know enough about weather in this part of the world to say more, except checking the Met Office online archives of flooding records, they show 8 record events, 6 of which had a High to the North or a Low to the South, or both, with light NE winds. These are extreme events, but it could be a hint to what FitzRoy was describing.

For a modern, much expanded, set of FitzRoy-like rules on barometer and wind-direction forecasts, see Appendix 5. They seem overly complex to me as well as optimistically specific, but they are published by several national weather services, so they likely have a level of value, at least in some regions.

The bottom of the common FitzRoy labels often includes two famous aphorisms (Figure 5.4-1), which may have been his making. Both are quite good.

Long foretold, long last;
Short notice, soon past.

The "long foretold" means a long (12 to 24h) procession of lowering clouds, falling barometer, backing wind, and continuous steady rain. This full combination is almost proof positive of the approach of a large Low, or the progressive deterioration associated with an approaching warm front. Both are large systems and present long periods of bad weather.

"Soon notice" means either a squall or a cold front. These systems show up quickly (20 minutes to a few hours) and go away quickly, but they do bring bad weather for a short time. This is not so much an aphorism, as a statement of fact.

The other one is much less general, but none the less important.

First rise after Low,
Foretells stronger blow.

When most Lows go by, the pressure drops as the wind increases, and then when the barometer starts to rise as it passes, the wind diminishes with it. So this rule is not always true, probably not even the common case, as just described. But the exceptions can be so severe that it is worth thinking that this is always a possibility.

In the more common Low, the isobar spacing is more or less symmetric around the Low. Then coming in and going out are the same. But it turns out that oftentimes the worse kind of storm has the isobars much closer together on the backside of the Low. After the lowest pressure is reached, the pressure starts back up, but it increases at a much faster rate than it went down. The higher rate of pressure change then gives rise to higher wind speeds. FitzRoy was obviously aware of this possibility, but he did not know what caused it. These days such systems are called bent back occlusions, or, as described by the Norwegian group that first identified them, "the sting in the scorpion's tail."

This important rule is to remind us not to automatically think the worst is past when the barometer starts back up from its lowest point. In these few cases, the bad conditions we are in will just get worse.

For more about other aphorisms of weather analysis and forecast that actually do work, see *Modern Marine Weather*.

Short Form of FitzRoy Rules

Mariners over the years have used a compressed form of the FitzRoy label rules, being simply that a falling barometer with northerly wind is a definite warning of potential bad weather that should not be ignored. In Lecky's classic *Wrinkles in Practical Navigation* he calls this a "red-ink warning." On the other hand, a rising barometer with southerly wind is often a good sign the weather might improve—keeping in mind always that you might be riding down the back of a scorpion, in which case this conclusion is as wrong as possible!

In the Southern Hemisphere, change northerly references to southerly, or to have it apply to either hemisphere, change northerly to "polar" and change southerly to "equatorial."

A Better Rule for Wind and Pressure

The FitzRoy rules work as discussed, but there is a simpler, even more generic way to think of this. And just like everything else in weather, the key is using trends, not just present values. So instead of relating trend in barometer with present winds, it is best to relate trends in barometer with trends in winds, namely how has the wind direction been shifting as the barometer rises or falls.

The definitions of wind shifts are crucial to the rule. Namely a wind shifting to the right (ie NE to E) is called veering, and a wind shift to the left (ie NE to N) is called backing. Then we can state rules that are very good in many conditions.

When in good weather to begin with, a falling barometer along with a backing shift in the wind is very clear warning that the weather might deteriorate. It is not guaranteed, but the strength of the rule is that if the weather does indeed go from good to bad, it will almost certainly be preceeded by a backing shift in the wind and a falling barometer. It is in that sense a necessary, but not sufficient condition for bad weather.

Likewise, when bad weather improves to good, it is usually preceded by a rising barometer and a veering wind—remember, though, the important exception of the "sting in the scorpion's tail."

The beauty of these rules is they do not depend on the specific wind direction, only on which way it is shifting. Chances are the winds will be more or less as described in the FitzRoy rules, but this formulation is easier to remember. It does require us to log the wind data along with the barometer, which is good practice in itself. For the Southern Hemisphere, interchange veering and backing.

A Sailor's Rule

The "Short Form" and the "Better Rule" just described can effectively be combined into a sailor's rule that depends on the tack of the sailing vessel. It was well known to sailing masters of the 19th century, but is less often on the minds of modern sailors.

The tack of a sailing vessel specifies which side of the vessel the wind is coming from. If you sail with the wind on the right side, you are on starboard tack. Sailing with the wind on the left side, you are on port tack. Strictly speaking, this definition does not depend on the point of sail (your heading relative to the wind direction), but in this rule we use a common interpretation of "tack" to mean the wind is somewhere forward of the beam.

From the Buys Ballot law, we can note that in the Northern Hemisphere when sailing on a starboard tack you are always sailing into higher pressure. Essentially anywhere in the open ocean, well away from the equator, if you sail through an unchanging, stationary pressure pattern on a starboard tack, the barometer will rise as you proceed. Likewise, on a port tack, the barometer will fall as you proceed.

Thus the rule is that a *falling* pressure on a starboard tack is another red-ink warning of potential change for the worse. Likewise, a *rising* barometer on a port tack is good sign of potential improvement. The reason the rule is strong is you are getting just the opposite of what you expect.

Summary

Except for the regions we called "Definitely Good" and "Definitely Bad," the barometer reading is not intended to indicate the present conditions of the weather, but rather it is the barometer's direction of change and rate of change that can help us forecast what might happen next.

Generally the time frame the barometer helps with is 12 to 24 hours ahead. It will not help with forecasting imminent events such as squalls or tornadoes, and though you may watch long slow consistent trends over several days, at any one moment your conclusions have to apply to the next 12 to 24 hours or so.

The exception is when you are using the barometer to monitor *a forecast you already have* from other sources. For example, you could be told that a front will pass over you this afternoon. A good barometer will then tell you very specifically when it passes. Fronts are always long, narrow troughs of low pressure, and you will see the minimum as it passes very notably if it is a sharp frontal boundary. A cold front could pass with a steady barometer followed by a distinct onset of a rise at the passage. (Pressure properties of fronts and other systems are covered in *Modern Marine Weather.*)

In the following section and throughout much of the earlier discussion, we try our best to forecast the onset of bad weather while still within good weather. But if we allow the Lows to get a bit closer, then the barometer and wind direction does give a pretty good measure of what is going to happen next.

WIND BAROMETER INDICATIONS*

When the wind sets in from points between south and southeast, and the barometer falls steadily, a storm is approaching from the west or northwest, and its center will pass near or north of the observer within 12 to 24 hours with wind shifting to northwest by way of southwest and west.

When the wind sets in from points between east and northeast and the barometer falls steadily, a storm is approaching from the south or southwest, and its center will pass near or to the south or east of the observer within 12 to 24 hours with wind shifting to northwest by way of north.

The rapidity of the storm's approach and its intensity will be indicated by the rate and the amount of the fall in the barometer.

Figure 5.4-7 *This notice was printed verbatim on all U.S. weather maps from 1904 to 1941. Refer to Figure 5.4-6 to see the basis of these indications.*

Figure 5.4-7 shows what were called "Barometer Wind Indications." These guidelines, in the exact words shown, were printed on every U.S. weather map from about 1904 to 1941. After that, they simply disappeared. (Though much did change on a global scale in 1941, weather was not one of them.) You can refer to the FitzRoy rules along with Figures 5.4-5 and 5.4-6 to see where these Indications come from.

5.5 Trends and their meanings

To proceed further with the interpretation of barometer readings for forecasting, we need to look more closely at pressure trends, both the terminology and specific numeric values.

The precedence of pressure trends over the actual value of the pressure has been touted since the very first application of the instrument for weather forecasting. In Halley's 1700 report of the first use of a barometer at sea, he praised its benefits as a forecaster (see Section 1.2), then added:

> "... the rising and falling thereof are the things chiefly remarkable in it, the just height being barely a curiosity."

Luckily, some of those who followed in his footsteps did not agree with that, and as a result over the years we gained enough accurate global pressure data to let people like William Ferrel begin to understand the wind. But for the most part, practicing ship captains over the years and into modern times do not exercise the extra effort needed for accurate pressures, but rather use their barometers primarily to monitor trends and rates of pressure change.

And there is little surprise in this, because in modern classic texts such as *Chapman's Piloting*, used by essentially all mariners at some stage of their training, we read from the latest edition:

> "It is not the actual barometric pressure that is important in forecasting; it is the direction and rate of change of pressure."

Chapman and Halley are of course both right. Barometric changes are the main things we have to keep an eye on to spot changes in the weather. They were simply not aware of several modern applications where the magnitude of the pressure itself can also be of value. Nor were they aware of the modern resources available to the ordinary mariner for actually obtaining that information. We no longer have to be a scientific research vessel or a highly trained deck officer with very expensive equipment. Things have changed. But that is not meant to distract from the fundamental role of understanding pressure changes.

Terminology

The WMO defines *pressure tendency* as the barometer change in the past 3 hours. This number is literally the difference in mb values between the recorded pressure at report time and the value recorded 3 hours earlier. This difference is then multiplied by 10 to remove the decimal. This value does not take into account how the pressure changed during that 3-hr period. Thus, 1016.5, 1017.5, 1018.5, is a pressure tendency of +20, just as is 1016.5, 1014.5, 1018.5 is also +20. This difference in pressure behavior is reported in WMO code using the values shown in Table 5.5-1. The first example would be code 2. The second example would be code 3.

It is important to understand this definition when you are calibrating your barometer using weather map data when you do not have your measurement at the precise synoptic time of the report. At best you get an average over the last three hours. With a station report of 998.0 at 12z, along with a tendency report of -30, you have to note a bit of uncertainty if your observation was at 11z or say 13z. The temptation is to say that this pressure is dropping near 12z at 1 mb per hour, so at 11z it would have been 999.0 and at 13z you would expect 997.0 mb. But you could be off a full mb if the actual trace was 1001, 998, 998, which would be better interpreted as no pressure change in these 2 hours. The error could be worse if the pressure had actually gone down, then up, such as 1001, 997, 998. This still gives a tendency of -30, but the actual pressure is going up. An assumption of 997 at 13z would be wrong by 2 mb, and 999 would have been a better estimate.

So if we are relying on maps for the pressure, we need to get out the magnifying glass and try to see the code symbol that is printed next to the tendency on the station report.

The same caution is called for when using text reports from various sources such as the NDBC. They give a table of the pressures, one for each hour, but for each hour they also list the pressure tendency. In this case, we can just ignore the tendency and see what the actual pressure was at the preceding hour and use that to adjust our observations that are not on the exact whole hours they report.

Table 5.5-1 Pressure Characteristics for Station Reports*			
Trend	Code	Symbol	Description of past 3 hr
Pressure higher than 3 hr ago	0	∧	Rising, then falling
	1	⌐	Rising, then steady—or rising, then rising more slowly
	2	/	Rising steadily or unsteadily
	3	✓	Falling or steady, then rising—or rising, then rising more quickly
No change	4	—	Steady, same as 3 hr ago
Pressure lower than 3 hr ago	5	∨	Falling, then rising, same or lower than 3 hr ago
	6	_	Falling, then steady—or falling, then falling more slowly
	7	\\	Falling steadily or unsteadily
	8	∧	Steady or rising, then falling—or falling, then falling more quickly

The numerical value of the pressure tendency is (P at report time - P 3 hr ago) x 10.

If the pressure were 1020.5 at 15z and then 1021.9 at 18z, the 18z report would have a pressure tendency of 14, and it would be coded as 0,1,2, or 3, depending on what happened at 16z and 17z.

Notice that with all this specific information, there is still not a definition of what is a fast or slow rate of change. Most textbooks just use generic terms "slow." "fast," "very fast," and so on without definition. *Chapman's*, mentioned earlier, is one of the rare books that actually defines some rates. It calls 2 mb/3 hr a "slow" rate of change, and 5 mb/3hr a "rather high" rate of change. These are reasonable, but a finer-toothed comb might be more useful. Five mb per 3 hr, for example, is typically well beyond the realm of any long-term "forecasting." In other words, these two terms alone take us from barely at the edge of a typical warning to well over the precipice of strong winds.

The NWS defines only one rate of pressure change. Rising or falling "rapidly" is defined as equal to or greater than 2 mb per hour, which is 6 mb per 3 hr. This is considered a significant enough observation to be an additional element of some reports, beyond just the tendency value. (Table 5.5-2).

They also add a puzzling restriction that the "total drop" must be at least 0.7 mb. It is difficult to see the significance of this, since the observations are made every hour and the "total" is presumably over the full 3-hr period of the tendency report. This rules out things like down 2 mb, then up 1, and up 1, to leave no change? But if that is the logic, that would then rule out up 1, up 1, and down 2.6, which it seems should not be ignored.

The best set of definitions I have seen are those provided by the U.K. Met Office shown in Table 5.5-3. They are used specifically for their "Shipping Forecasts," which are well known throughout the world. The WMO does not provide definitions for pressure change rates.

Generally any pressure drop approaching about 1 millibar per hour deserves our attention. A drop of 2 or 3 mb in 3 hours can mean gale conditions are approaching, although it is still calm at the time, especially if this occurs for two consecutive 3-hour periods.

From a study of many barometer traces for approaching gales and storms at sea from around the world, it can be noted that in many cases there is a slow steady drop of about 2 or 3 mb per 3 hours for up to half a day or so before the severe pressure drop at the storm itself. A few samples for *severe* storms are shown in Figure 5.5-1. We have many more such data for gale-force wind.

The traces shown here are for extreme storms that are usually well forecasted, so none of these would be sneaking up on you. Nevertheless, a sharp eye on the barometer might alert you that its arrival is ahead of time or late. At sea, we typically only get updates every 6 hr outside of the tropics. Within the tropics, we get updates every hour for any system with a name.

Other pressure systems are less prominent and your barometer forecasts could be much more useful.

Table 5.5-2 NWS Definition of Rapid Change[1]		
Term	Pressure change over 1 Hour	Minimum change over 3 Hours
Rising or falling rapidly	2 mb or more	at least 1 mb

1. From the Federal Meteorological Handbook No.1. *The term is essentially equivalent to the Met Office definition below, except for the proviso on the minimum change required.*

Table 5.5-3 Met Office Definition of Pressure Change[1]		
Term	Pressure Change Over 3 Hours	Pressure Change Over 6 Hours[2]
Steady	Less than 0.1 mb	Less than 0.2 mb
Rising or falling slowly	0.1 to 1.5 mb	0.2 to 3 mb
Rising or falling	1.6 to 3.5 mb	3.2 to 7 mb
Rising or falling quickly	3.6 to 6.0 mb	7.2 to 12 mb
Rising or falling very rapidly	More than 6.0 mb	More than 12 mb

1. Used by the U.K. Met Office in their Shipping Forecasts. These are not official WMO terms, but they serve as the best source for this terminology and could fairly be used in other contexts.

2. The 6-hr values are not part of the Met Office definitions, but just for comparison with the "4-5-6" values in Table 5.5-4.

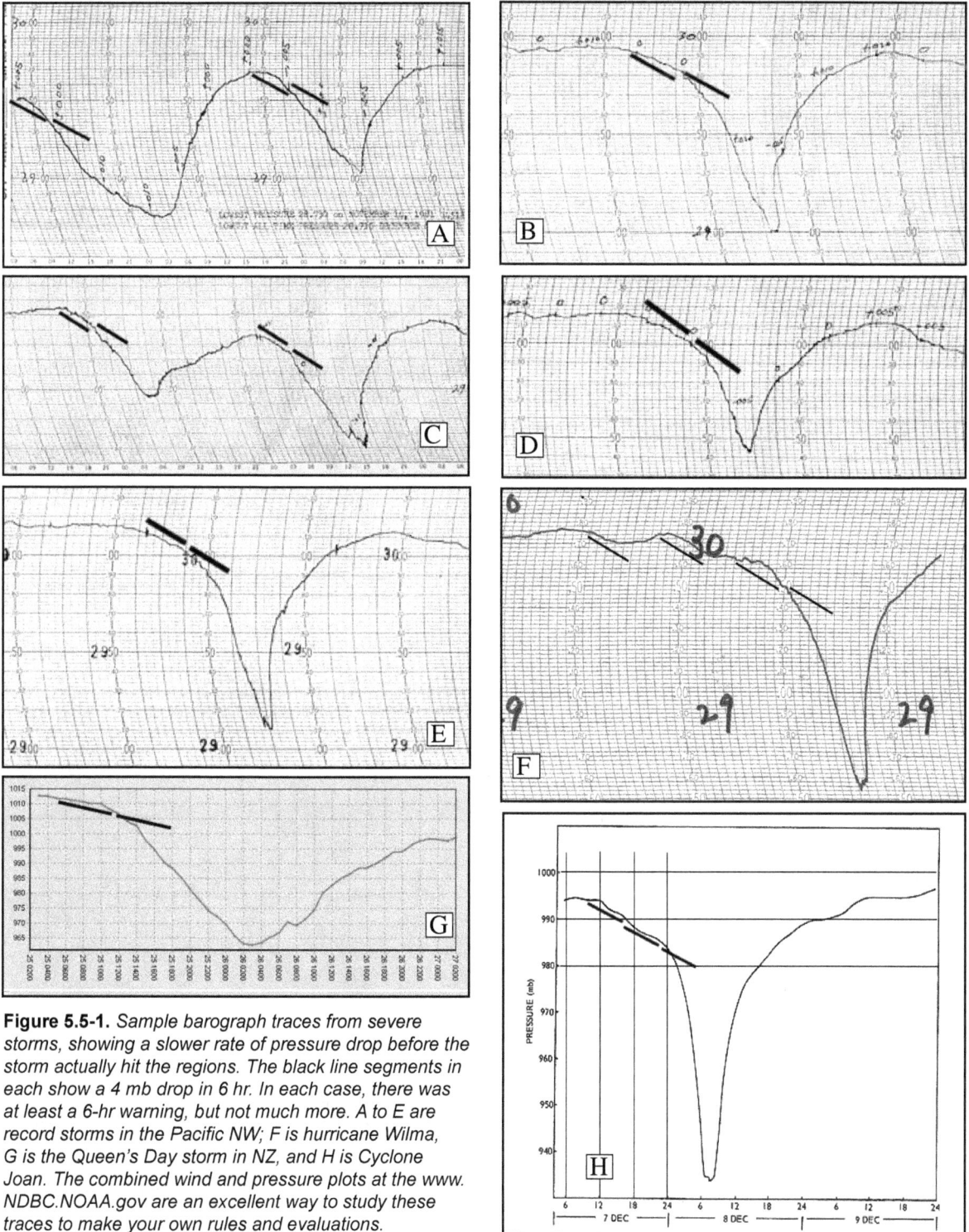

Figure 5.5-1. *Sample barograph traces from severe storms, showing a slower rate of pressure drop before the storm actually hit the regions. The black line segments in each show a 4 mb drop in 6 hr. In each case, there was at least a 6-hr warning, but not much more. A to E are record storms in the Pacific NW; F is hurricane Wilma, G is the Queen's Day storm in NZ, and H is Cyclone Joan. The combined wind and pressure plots at the www. NDBC.NOAA.gov are an excellent way to study these traces to make your own rules and evaluations.*

An ideal way to study the relationship between pressure drop and wind development is readily available for locations worldwide at the National Data Buoy Center, at www.ndbc.noaa.gov. Select the location of interest from a graphical display of observations, then choose the "combined plot of wind and pressure data." Examples are shown in Figure 5.5-2.

This does not represent the rate of pressure drop at edge of a storm itself. These will be higher. Severe storms and typhoons have pressure drops of 5 to 10 mb per 3 hours as the actual storm passes, and record drops are much higher near the eyes of hurricanes, and phenomenal in the very small centers of tornadoes.

Remember, though, that for *forecasting* we want to know what to look for *before* the actual storm is upon us, so it is the lesser steady drops to watch for. One way to express the guideline to help remember it is "4-5-6," that is, 4 or 5 mb in 6 hours is a definite

Table 5.5-4	
"4-5-6" Guideline to Pressure as Wind Forecaster	
Likely Significance	*Steady pressure drop over 6 Hours*
Alert	Less than 3 mb
Caution	3 to 4 mb
Definite warning	4 to 5 mb
Too late for forecasting	More than 5 mb

warning that something is on the way. This guideline is presented in Table 5.5-4.

We presented this guideline back in the 90's and over the years have had good feedback from mariners who found it useful. It is important to remember, however, that you can get strong winds earlier than 4-5-6, especially on inland or coastal waters where the winds might be channeled to some extent. The notes in Figure 5.5-2 explain how to test this. The

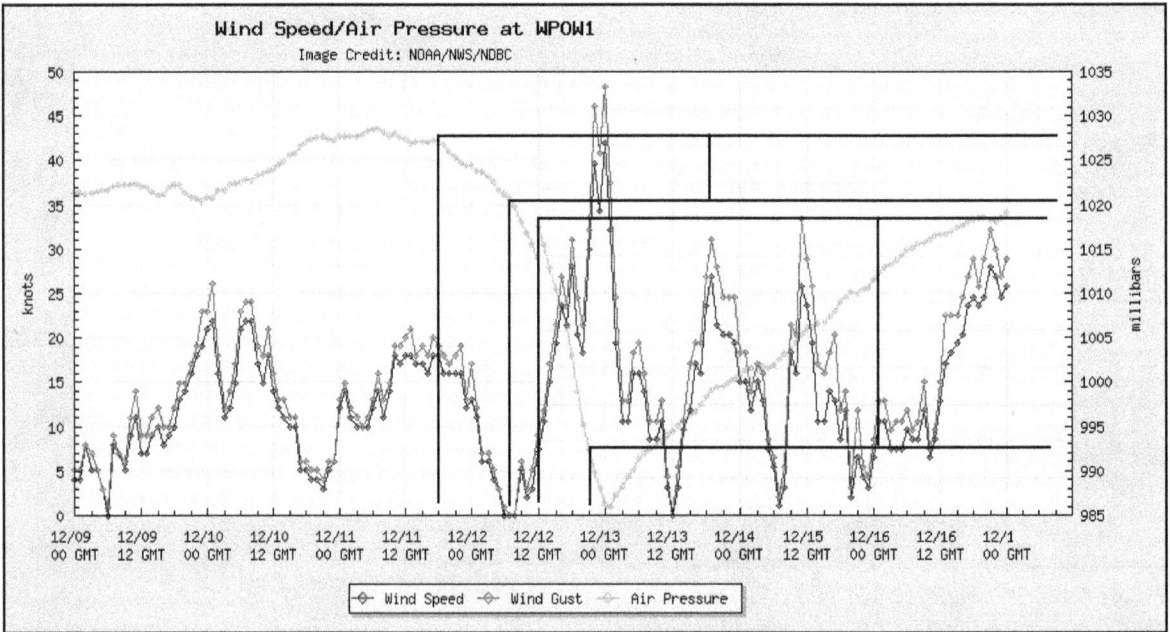

Figure 5.5-2. *Combined wind and pressure plot from www.ndbc.noaa.gov. The ideal way to study relationship of pressure to wind or other parameters. For combined plots (many, but not all, stations offer these) you have to choose between m/s and mb or kts and inches of mercury. Here we have two pictures using each, pasted together, and hence the slight jog at 12/12. For the 14 hr before the plunge and before the wind built, the barometer dropped from 1028 to 1020, for a rate of 8/14 = 3.4 mb/6hr. But during the first 6hr the drop was 5/6h. At the plunge the drop was about 25 mb in 9hr or about 17 mb /6hr. At this stage it is not forecasting, there is 30+ kts of wind. This is just a random example. It roughly supports the guidelines, but more importantly it shows how you can test these ideas.*

4-5-6 guideline is easy to remember, and then use 3 in 6 hr as a caution.

For completeness, if the barometer drops faster than the 4-5-6 warning for longer than 12 hour then you might be facing a "meteorological bomb." The drop rate for this explosive Low development depends on your latitude. It was first named by Tor Bergeron from the Bergen, Norway Group, as a 24 or more mb drop over 24hr. But they were working at Lat 60, and meteorologists have since discovered that it takes rather less than this at lower latitudes to get into this class of storm. Table 5.5-5 defines the conditions described as a meteorological bomb.

It is the total drop in 24 hr that defines these systems, not the rate or rates on the way there. The rate could be slow for a while, then faster, etc as long as the total drop in 24 hr matches, or exceeds, the values in the table. Practicing meteorologists that work with storms sometimes use a term made up to honor Tor Bergeron—he made many fundamental contributions to meteorology besides work on this topic. A pressure drop that meets exactly the terms of Table 5.5-5 is called 1 Bergeron. Thus a pressure drop of 18 mb in 24 hr at 40 N (or S) is called 1 Bergeron. If the pressure dropped 27 mb in 24 hr, it would be called 1.5 Bergerons, and so on. Exceptional "bombs" might be as much as 2 Bergerons.

5.6 Diurnal Variation

The pressure drops to expect depend on where you are. A change of 1.5 mb per 3 hours has a very different meaning at high latitudes than it does in the tropics. Careful barometer use in low latitudes requires us to be aware of the relatively large diurnal (twice daily) variation of the pressure due to an atmospheric "tidal action."

The atmospheric tides are caused by solar heating and cooling, which creates 3 cycles having periods of 4, 12, and 24 hours. The 12-hr cycle has the largest amplitude, being in the range of 1 to 2 mb at lower latitudes.

This daily pressure variation also takes place at higher latitudes but it is weaker and usually masked by normal variations in the pressure that accompa-

Table 5.5-5 "Meteorological Bombs"			
Latitude (N or S)	Total mb drop in 24hr	Avg. Rate per 6hr	Avg. Rate per 3hr
60	> 24	4.0	2.0
50	> 21	5.3	2.6
40	> 18	4.5	2.3
30	> 14	3.5	1.8

This class of serious explosive storm is defined in terms of the total drop over 24 hr. The 6-hr and 3-hr rates shown are just for comparison with earlier discussion. Interpolating the table, a 24-hr drop at latitude 35 of about 16 mb would be called a "bomb," and the pressure drop would be called 1 Bergeron. A drop of twice that much would be called 2 Bergerons. The average rates may be misleading. These storms can deepen very rapidly once they start, so much of the drop could be in the last 6 hr or so.

ny moving weather systems. Even in the tropics, it is strongest near the equator and grows weaker with increasing latitude. The effect is stronger over land than over water.

The peaks are usually at about 10 AM and PM local time, with minimums at about 4 AM and PM. Local time of 10 AM means 2 hours before local apparent noon, when the sun is at its peak height in the sky. Four PM local time is 4 hr after local noon.

The effect of the 24-hr and 8-hr cycles is to make the morning peaks slightly larger than the nighttime peaks, while the afternoon minimum is slightly lower than the early morning minimum. Since the highs and lows are caused by solar heating, the range of this effect can depend on the local cloud cover and humidity.

The diurnal variation must be taken into account when monitoring pressures in low latitudes to watch for approaching systems. A sample is shown in Figure 5.6-1. These days this type of data can be readily obtained from the NDBC.

With the exception of this daily variation, pressures in the tropics are generally very stable. Hence any deviation from the average pressure should be regarded with suspicion. With an accurate barometer and knowledge of the average pressure for your month and location, along with the standard deviation of that average pressure (Chapter 10), you can be very specific about your observations of the pressures and what they might imply—which could be very valuable if you have lost wireless contact with your forecast sources.

Table 5.6-1 shows that if you look very carefully at the wonderful data archives from the National Climatic Data Center (NCDC) you can see diurnal variation at higher latitudes, even when it is much smaller than the standard deviations in the data. Notice the maxima and minima are at about the right local times, and we can even see the effect of the weaker cycles making the 10 AM peaks higher and the 4 PM minima lower each day, throughout the year. The agreement in local mean times (LMT) would be even better if we accounted for the exact longitude of Nantucket Island, as well as a 15-minute solar time correction called the equation of time.

(This table shows why meteorologists average the daily pressures when reducing station pressure to sea level as discussed in Appendix 3. Section 10.3 explains how to obtain this data from the NCDC.)

5.7 Icons on Electronic Barometers

Some portable electronic weather stations include measurements of temperature and relative humidity as well as pressure. These units could in principle make more sophisticated algorithms for turning on such icons as shown in figure 5.7-1. They could, for example, safely turn on the Rain symbol when the relative humidity was approaching 100%, and a rising barometer with a rising thermometer is usually a good sign for improving weather, which could show a Sun, and so on. But even plain electronic barometers include these icons, so these at least are basing the guesses purely on pressure.

Figure 5.6-1. *Diurnal pressure variation in the tropics at Lime Tree Bay, VI, 17.70N, 64.75W. To figure the proper local time, take the longitude divided by 15 to get the time zone and then subtract that from GMT. In this case, 64.75/15 = 4.3 so Local time = GMT - 4. Note they show it at 3h, which means they must be on daylight saving time. The predicted local times are shown on the plot. Halfway points between the full range on each cycle show how the actual ambient pressure is changing over these 5 days— slowly rising from about 1016.5 to 1019.0 mb, with an indication of a down turn taking place. Note that the expected difference between morning and nighttime peaks (about 0.5 mb) is masked on Apr 2 by the rise in the*

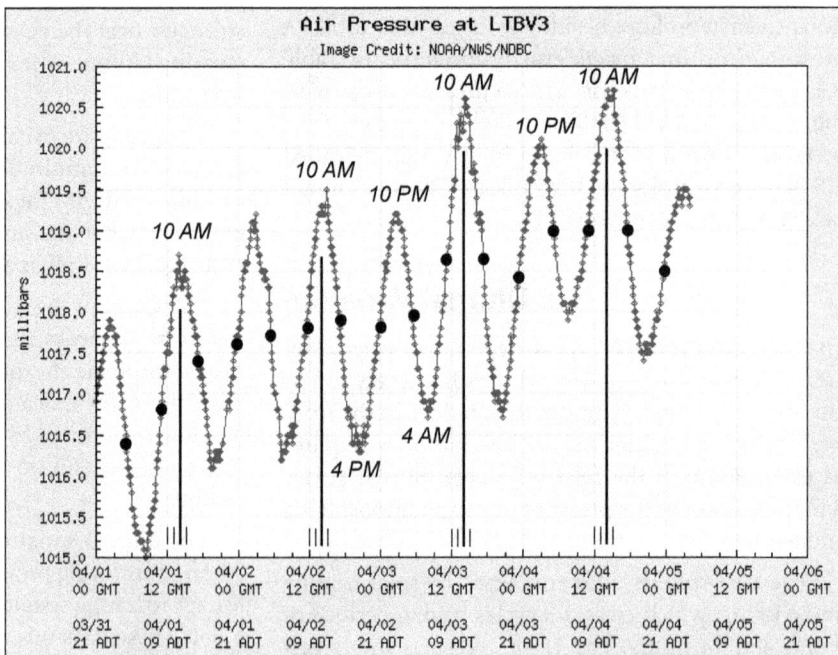

ambient pressure over that period. To watch for an approaching tropical storm, we need to extract an actual pressure drop from a pattern like this one. Knowing ahead of time how much of a change is due to diurnal fluctuations lets you discover the real drop, which could be masked during its initial hours unless you correct for this. Using the data from Chapter 10, we can learn that the average for March at this location is 1016.7 with a standard deviation (SD) of 1.7mb. Thus this pressure of 1019 is about 2 SD higher than normal, making it a rare occurrence (about 3% probability).

Table 5.6-1 Diurnal Variation at Higher Latitudes* — Nantucket Island, MA, 41° N 1988 - 2008

UTC	LMT	JAN	FEB	MAR	APR	MAY	JUN	JUL	AUG	SEP	OCT	NOV	DEC	ANNUAL
00		1016.7	1014.9	1015.0	1013.3	1014.8	1014.5	1014.1	1015.6	1016.5	1016.5	1016.7	1016.3	1015.4
01		1016.9	1015.2	1014.8	1013.4	1014.9	1014.6	1014.5	1015.8	1016.6	1016.5	1016.9	1016.5	1015.6
02		1017.1	1015.1	1014.8	1013.0	1014.9	1014.6	1014.5	1015.6	1016.6	1016.3	1016.7	1016.1	1015.4
03	10 PM Max	1017.2	1015.0	1014.8	1013.0	1014.8	1014.5	1014.6	1015.6	1016.5	1016.6	1016.7	1016.2	1015.5
04		1017.1	1014.8	1015.0	1012.5	1014.8	1014.4	1014.2	1015.5	1016.3	1016.4	1016.7	1016.1	1015.3
05		1016.6	1014.8	1014.8	1012.4	1014.4	1014.1	1014.0	1015.3	1016.2	1016.3	1016.6	1015.6	1015.1
06		1016.9	1014.7	1014.4	1012.0	1014.3	1014.0	1013.7	1015.1	1016.0	1016.1	1016.6	1016.0	1015.0
07		1016.7	1014.5	1014.1	1012.1	1014.2	1013.8	1013.7	1014.9	1015.9	1015.8	1016.3	1015.9	1014.8
08		1016.4	1014.6	1014.2	1012.1	1014.2	1013.9	1013.9	1015.1	1015.9	1016.2	1016.6	1015.8	1014.9
09	4 AM Min	1016.6	1014.8	1014.4	1012.3	1014.5	1014.2	1014.1	1015.3	1016.1	1016.2	1016.7	1015.9	1015.1
10		1016.8	1014.9	1015.0	1012.8	1014.8	1014.1	1014.4	1015.5	1016.4	1016.5	1016.9	1016.1	1015.4
11		1017.0	1015.1	1015.3	1013.4	1015.0	1014.6	1014.6	1015.8	1016.6	1016.7	1017.2	1016.2	1015.6
12		1017.5	1015.5	1015.2	1013.4	1015.2	1014.7	1014.7	1015.9	1016.8	1017.0	1017.6	1016.4	1015.8
13		1017.3	1015.5	1015.6	1013.6	1015.3	1014.8	1014.8	1016.1	1016.8	1017.2	1017.7	1016.8	1016.0
14		1017.9	1015.5	1015.5	1013.6	1015.4	1014.8	1014.7	1016.2	1016.8	1016.9	1017.9	1016.9	1016.0
15	10 AM Max	1017.1	1015.2	1015.0	1013.3	1015.2	1014.7	1014.9	1016.0	1016.8	1016.7	1017.3	1016.4	1015.7
16		1016.6	1014.6	1014.7	1012.9	1015.1	1014.6	1014.6	1015.8	1016.4	1016.4	1016.7	1015.3	1015.3
17		1016.2	1014.1	1014.3	1013.0	1014.8	1014.4	1014.5	1015.5	1016.2	1015.9	1016.5	1014.9	1015.0
18		1015.6	1013.6	1014.2	1012.4	1014.6	1014.3	1014.2	1015.2	1016.1	1015.6	1016.0	1014.7	1014.7
19		1015.8	1013.7	1014.2	1012.3	1014.3	1014.2	1014.2	1015.1	1015.8	1015.6	1016.0	1015.0	1014.7
20		1015.6	1013.7	1014.1	1012.2	1014.3	1013.9	1014.1	1015.1	1015.8	1015.6	1015.7	1015.4	1014.6
21	4 PM Min	1016.0	1013.9	1014.0	1012.4	1014.2	1013.8	1013.9	1015.0	1015.8	1016.0	1016.2	1015.8	1014.8
22		1016.4	1014.4	1014.5	1012.4	1014.3	1013.9	1014.0	1015.1	1016.0	1016.3	1016.5	1016.0	1015.0
23		1016.7	1015.3	1014.7	1012.4	1014.0	1014.3	1014.1	1015.3	1016.3	1016.8	1016.4	1016.1	1015.2
00		1016.7	1014.9	1015.0	1013.3	1014.8	1014.5	1014.1	1015.6	1016.5	1016.5	1016.7	1016.3	1015.4
Monthly mean		1016.7	1014.7	1014.7	1012.8	1014.7	1014.3	1014.3	1015.5	1016.3	1016.3	1016.7	1015.9	1015.2
Standard deviation		9.9	9.5	10.2	8.6	7.1	6.6	5.1	4.9	6.8	8.6	9.4	10.3	8.1
Diurnal variation		2.3	1.8	1.6	1.4	1.2	1.0	1.0	1.2	1.0	1.6	2.2	1.9	1.4

* Each hourly pressure represents the average of 160 to 210 observations during the indicated month.

System A

The programmer's manual for one popular pressure sensor uses these rules for the icons. Store the pressure when the unit is first turned on and show the Change icon. Then as the pressure changes, compare it with that stored initial value. If that pressure increases above the stored value by 2.5 mb, then turn on the Sun. If instead of increasing by more than 2.5 mb, it decreased by more than 2.5 mb, then turn on the Rain. In this model, there is no clock, just pressure values, so these icon changes could happen in 2 hour or 2 days. Once the Rain is showing and the pressure keeps going down, the Rain icon stays showing. Likewise once the Sun is showing, it does not change as long as the pressure is rising.

Once the pressure stops going up and starts back down, then the turn point is recorded and used as the new reference. If it goes down more than 2.5 mb, then it turns on the Change icon. If it goes down another 2.5 it turns on the Rain icon, and so on. In this sense these icons are just showing the direction of change, and at the same time letting you know the change has been *at least* 2.5 mb.

System B

Another guideline used for icon warnings, or for selecting alarms, or textual warnings in electronic barometers are outlined in Table 5.7-1. Whether or not these are viable has been the subject of this chapter. Certainly in very dry climates, you are not going to get rain very often, regardless of what the barometer does. In any event once you discover how your icons or warnings actually are programmed in your unit, you can simply use them as visual indictions of how the pressure has changed, and not be concerned that they reflect the actual weather at hand. In this sense, our earlier discussion of labels on aneroids is pertinent.

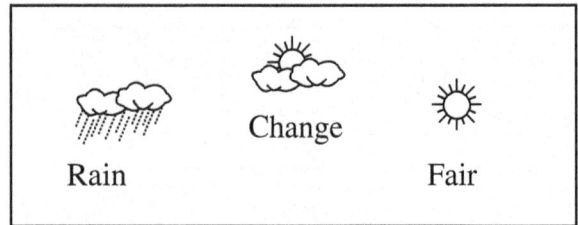

Figure 5.7-1 *Electronic barometer icons.*

System C

Several electronic barometers let users define themselves how the warnings and icons are to be displayed. I have seen two systems. One lets you numerically define the warning rates used for alarms in terms of actual mb settings or mb per hour. Another brand, which also stored the history of the pressure, lets the user define the recent history of the barometer with the label they choose. Then if this pattern shows up again it will show that label or icon. The former option is a simple way to build in the 4-5-6 guideline for significant pressure drops.

Table 5.7-1 Guidelines used in electronic barometers	
Pressure change (mb/hr)	*Description*
more than +2.5	Intermediate high pressure system, not stable
between +0.5 and +2.5	Long-term high pressure system, stable good weather
between -0.5 and +0.5	Stable weather condition
between -2.5 and -0.5	Long-term low pressure system, stable rainy weather
more than -2.5	Intermediate low pressure, not stable

Much of this book has been directed toward obtaining accurate pressure from a barometer. Essentially any application of barometric pressure is done better with accurate data. Even those applications that have historically relied only on trends and rates of change are dependent on an instrument that responds proportionally to the natural changes in pressure.

In this chapter we come to several specific applications of accurate pressure, which were in large part the initial motivation for the work presented in this book. As with the weather topics of Chapter 5, however, this presentation is only intended to cover the basic ideas. For details and nuances please refer to *Modern Marine Weather*, which covers a broader range of weather analysis and forecasting. For now we look specifically just at the use of barometric pressure.

6.1 Perspective

Historically mariners and other barometer watchers looked for trends and rates of barometric pressure change to indicate changes in the weather. Slow steadily rising pressure is broadly a sign of improving weather, slow steadily falling, a more likely sign of deteriorating weather. Rapid changes in either direction usually mean strong wind and more imminent changes.

Northern ocean mariners have long known that a backing wind and a falling barometer are together a strong sign that the weather will worsen, without any specific reference to wind direction, nor to the actual value of the barometer reading. These signs and the value of them remain crucial to the use of a barometer, even if we do not know the calibration of the device—assuming of course that it is at least dependable enough to show trends properly.

If we insure that we have a quality instrument based on the testing of others, or we take the trouble to study our barometer and develop a calibration curve for it, then we can go beyond these traditional applications, often with much improvement to our insights into the weather around us and into what might be on the horizon.

In the simplest sense, if we know the right value of the pressure we read, then we can know if that pressure is normal or not for this time and place. Just look up the average pressure that is expected from the data in Chapter 10 along the with probability of having what you have. There is certainly no guarantee that if you have normal pressure, you will have normal weather, but it is more likely that if you do not have normal pressure, you will not have normal weather. The data of Chapter 10 even tell you how far off the normal a particular pressure is.

At higher latitudes, we can only make very general conclusions about the actual magnitude of the pressure. This type of reasoning, however, is much more pertinent in the tropics where the pressure changes very little from day to day, unless perturbed by an approaching storm. So within the tropics an accurate pressure can be very helpful in confirming a storm warning or making one of your own if you do not have contact with weather agencies. Details of this application are presented at the end of this chapter.

Beyond these basics, there are specific applications that might be thought of as going the extra mile to do the very best you can with the weather data you have. One application is the identification of specific (target) pressures that will mark your location within a specific pressure pattern that you assume is correct as plotted on the map. It is just one more way to test your understanding of where you are relative to the pressure pattern you must sail through.

Another application in this category, perhaps the most crucial, is almost the opposite of the last example. We don't fully accept a weather map as valid and act accordingly until we test the map with our own observed pressure with a calibrated barometer.

In other words, once we are convinced that our barometer is right, if we see a weather map that does not agree with our pressure, then we know the map is not right, and we must respond accordingly. This can be a crucial step in practical weather analysis, especially in parts of the ocean where there are few ship reports to help the NWS lay out the isobars. It can be even more important for mariners using raw computer model output for their forecasts (GRIB maps), because these maps have not been vetted by a professional meteorologist.

These barometric applications are specialized, but they could, in the broad array of circumstances we meet at sea, make the difference between a right and wrong decision at some point in time—and they definitely can make the difference between winning or not winning an ocean yacht race. You can fairly think of these techniques as marking the threshold between doing good weather work and doing the best you can. In short, you simply cannot do the best you can without accurate pressure.

6.2 Target Pressures

The marker needle on the face of an aneroid barometer can be used to mark the present pressure and then as the pressure changes, you see at a glance which direction it is going. Record the time you set the needle and then you have a quick view of the rate as well, without referring to the logbook. You can write the set time right on the glass dial of the instrument using a Vis-à-vis overhead projector marker. These have fine points, they dry to be very durable to the touch, but wipe off easily with a damp cloth.

There is another use of this marker needle, which makes the barometer a much more interactive device. When you have a weather map in hand, you can tell where you are relative to the pressure pattern around you. This pattern is usually in motion and you are usually in motion. Your best route is often determined by this pattern, so your relation to it is crucial. In several circumstances covered below, you might spot specific pressures that will mark important waypoints (target pressures) in your interaction with the pattern.

The process is analogous to laying out your course line on a chart, and noticing you will be crossing over a prominent underwater shelf that should show up nicely on your depth sounder. So you mark this "target depth" as the place the depth sounder should plummet if you are on course. Then watch to see if you are right. In chart navigation and in weather analysis, it is just another way to check that things are the way you think they are.

Sailing around Highs

Most summertime transoceanic sailing routes involve going around a large mid-ocean High. The reason for going around is there is no wind in the middle of the High. The situation is shown schematically in Figure 6.2-1. You can flip, mirror, or rotate this picture for other oceans or routes.

The fundamental step is to know you have to go around, and start off with that climatic knowledge. In other words, regardless of what the forecasts say about the wind at the location of the High when you depart, it takes too long to get there, and the map could be different by then. Statistically it is even likely to be so—meaning if you see wind there now when you are not supposed to, then chances are it will be gone when you do get there. We are looking here some 600 miles ahead, which could be 4 or 5 days away.

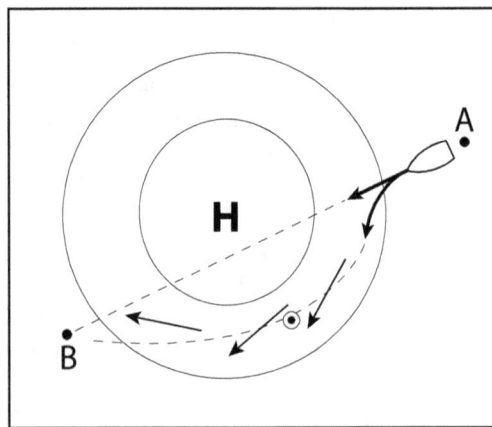

Figure 6.2-1. *Going around a large High to preserve your wind when sailing. Generally staying 2 isobars off the peak pressure when it is seasonable is a conservative route to keep your wind. The dot shows the target pressure that should mark the peak pressure at the corner if nothing changes.*

The usual tactical decision then is how close can you cut the corner and not run out of wind. Keys are judging the stability of the High from its surface shape and location and from the 500-mb maps (*Modern Marine Weather*)—and a good barometer!

From the weather map in hand you can read the highest pressure you expect as you round the corner and set that as a target pressure to watch for. If all goes as planned, the pressure will start down again once you reach that peak. If it does not, you have to consider that the High is building, or moving toward you. If the pressure starts back down before reaching the target pressure, then the High is weakening or slipping away from you.

Crossing a ridge

A similar choice can be confronted when approaching the top of a ridge (Figure 6.2-2). One side is down wind, the other side is to weather. When on a route across the top of it, you might have the opportunity to get from wrong side to right side, or to stay on the right side if you are already doing well. Again, due to the slow speed of a sailboat, it is not feasible to make major adjustments, but sometimes you can

maneuver enough to make a difference. The forecast maps plus your dead reckoning are the only way to evaluate this.

Crossing a trough

The best laid sailing plan around the corner of a High can still get invaded by a low pressure system where we don't want it. You are not going to maneuver around giant extratropical Lows, but you might just end up on the wrong side of a much more localized trough of low pressure. You might, for example, be headed down the east side of a near stationary trough in head winds for several days, whereas if you fell off for a while and crossed the trough you would bite the bullet for a day and then get into downwind conditions (Figure 6.2-3). Look at the forecast maps to see if your speed and position on the alternative courses pans out with this reasoning. Watch the pressure to judge your progress. The pressure will be at a minimum as you cross the trough line. You should be able to monitor your progress with the barometer and know when you are across it. If the trough is sliding toward you this could be a very efficient maneuver. If it is slipping away from you, on the other hand, this might not work at all.

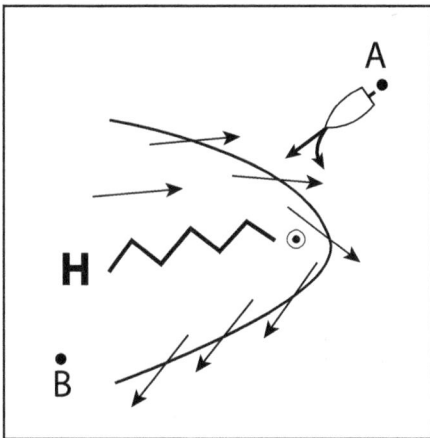

Figure 6.2-2. *This sailing route from A to B will be fastest in the following winds below the stationary ridge line. Anticipate stronger winds at the sharp bend in the tip of the ridge. By recording a target pressure of the crossing from a weather map you can use your barometer to keep track of where you are relative to the ridge top. On an aneroid device, you can mark it right on the dial. If the wind veers around and the barometer remains steady, you know you are following an isobar around the corner.*

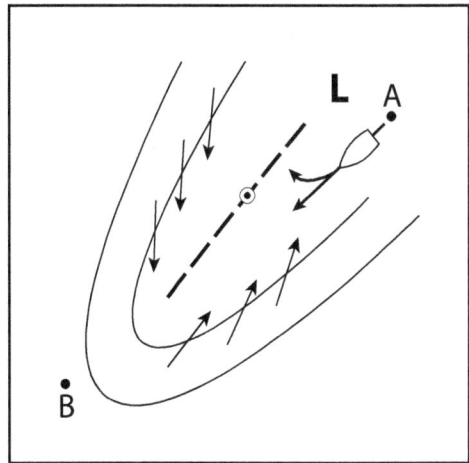

Figure 6.2-3. *The sailing route from A to B will be fastest in the following winds above the trough line. The trough line will be at local minimum in the pressure so it should be detectable underway. This maneuver would work best when the trough is moving toward you. The target pressure marking the minimum pressure expected at the trough line is shown as a dot.*

6.3 Checking Weather Maps and Model Forecasts (GRIB)

We have discussed how the barometer contributes to our own forecasting of what might happen next in the weather. To make a forecast we combine the barometer reading and its trends with wind trends and trends in cloud patterns, and with practice we can do as well on our own or better than mariners have done worldwide for two hundred years.

Realistically, however, we will usually not be left on our own; we will have at hand some form of forecast provided by an official weather agency or one of its associates. The role of the barometer then changes from forecaster to validator. We have outlined the procedure in Sections 2.5 and 4.7.

When you receive the surface analysis map valid for, say, 06z—which you will not receive before about 09z—then you can go back to your logbook to see what pressure you recorded for your position at 0600z. This particular recording will be in your logbook because you know you must make a record at the synoptic times (00z, 06z, 12z, and 18z) if you hope to take advantage of this method. Then on the surface analysis map carefully plot your position from 06z, and then carefully interpolate the isobars for the mapped pressure at that location as shown in Figure 6.3-1.

Next you have to decide how close does this mapped pressure have to be to the one you observed at that time and place in order to call the map right—or at least potentially right. Remember that a pressure confirmation is not proof that the lay of the isobars and their spacing is correct; it only confirms the magnitude of the pressure. On the other hand, if the pressure magnitudes do not agree, then that is positive proof that the map is not right.

The agreement required depends on a couple factors. First it depends on how accurate your barometer is. If we assume for the moment that the official isobars are exactly right, then we can consider the map potentially right whenever it agrees with our observations to within our own pressure measurement uncertainty. If we are confident our barometer is accurate to ±1mb, then if the plotted pressure is within 1 mb of our reading we are in agreement. In practice,

if your barometer is that accurate or better—relatively inexpensive electronic barometers can be set accurate to ±0.5 mb—then you will be surprised how often the maps will be right on what you measure. These weather products are usually very good. In fact, having an accurate barometer is one way to appreciate the fine job the NWS and their counterparts around the world are doing these days.

There can be exceptions, however, and that is where we wander into "doing the best we can." Namely, we have to spot those less-likely cases when the maps are not as good as usual. Keep in mind that even in the best of circumstances, meaning not a complex weather pattern, that the NWS and other weather agencies around the world, have a lot to do to filter though the reports they get from vessels at sea. It is not just a matter of reading the reports and using them. Ship reports are the key input that leads to the location, magnitude, and orientation of the isobars over the ocean, so like any other crucial input data they have to be evaluated.

The weather services are dealing with pressure reports from thousands of ships, every 6 hours, and even though the ship's crew are trained and their barometers checked by PMOs around the world, there can still be some uncertainties and actual errors in the reports. At least 80% of the ships are using aneroid barometers and there is a spectrum of quality among these. The PMOs can check the barometers, but it is not often they can actually calibrate those on foreign vessels. Because of potential hazards in physically removing, setting, and remounting someone else's precision equipment, the barometers that are checked are not typically set, but rather posted with the observed correction. (A sample notice of this type appears later in the book, in Figure 8.2-4.)

But there are other factors besides the calibrations that can affect the results. The draft of a large cargo ship can change by 30 ft when fully loaded, which means the barometer would change by 1 mb. In smaller vessels the effect is smaller, which makes it more likely to be overlooked. Likewise even the tide height in some parts of the ocean or coastal waters could contribute a few tenths of a mb. Also as mentioned earlier, a strong wind outside of the pilot house could cause a change of a mb or more in some cases.

In short, barring outright mistakes in reading or recording, there is a potential for an uncertainty in many of the reports of about ±1 mb. This level of uncertainty was acknowledged by a UK Met Office study reported by Bruce Ingleby in the Journal of Atmospheric and Oceanic Technology in 2001. Data gathering has likely improved since then, but this is probably still a fair estimate of the pressure uncertainties that go into the map making.

Actual errors can periodically slip through, but this would be rare because each report is tested by comparison with the pressure at that location from 6 hours ago, and with neighboring reports. In some cases the weather services apply known fixed corrections for specific vessels. The location of the vessel at the synoptic time is another factor that has to be manually typed into the report, so there is also an outside chance for an error there, which could be just as serious as a pressure error.

So if we conclude that our pressure is accurate to ±1 mb and the maps are accurate to ±1 mb, then we can conclude that the maps agree with our pressures whenever they agree to within in ±1.4 mb. That may look like funny math, but it is a statistical result that accounts for the fact our two uncertainties are independent. We could be too high when they are too high, which is a smaller difference than when one is high when the other is low. Two independent errors A and B combine as the square root of $(A^2 + B^2)$. In our case, square root of 2 is 1.4.

Remember too, these are uncertainties: how much they could be off, not how much they will be off. You will be surprised how often the maps are spot on with the pressures you measure if you have an accurate barometer, which only emphasizes the value of being able to detect cases where there is a question. A sample is shown in Figure 6.3-1. This example was chosen purely at random, being the current map at the time of writing this section. It turned out to be one with examples of what are likely good reports as well as some that are questionable—or at least the model making the isobars had some challenges with it.

Figure 6.3-1 is a surface analysis map compiled by a professional meteorologist at the OPC. Mariners underway also have access to part of the raw data that meteorologist was looking at when he made that map. It is the computer model analysis of the 00z ocean weather made by the NWS's Global Forecast System (GFS). The raw output from the GFS model is readily available to the public, but all sources that provide it warn that it is computer output that has not been vetted by human intelligence.

The GFS analysis and predictions are usually presented in the GRIB (gridded binary) format, which makes the data very convenient to use. Unlike graphic-image maps which are static pictures, the GRIB maps are vector products that can be scaled, layered, and interpolated to present the information in just about any desired format. If you want to see the isobars every 1 mb apart instead of 2, just push a button for a new display. Or better still, just move the cursor around the map and read the predicted pressure to the nearest tenth of a mb everywhere on the map. And you can do the same with wind speed and direction, as well as precipitation and more.

In short, if you can convince yourself that the GRIB data is dependable, then these maps are much easier to use. Checking the pressure at your location is one step in that process. You can of course also check your wind speed (as a measure of the isobar spacing) and your wind direction (as a measure of the orientation of the isobars.) A sample is shown in Figure 6.3-2 for the same time and place as Figure 6.3-1. A few examples are itemized in Table 6.3-1.

The GRIB maps are viewed with special software called "Grib viewers." There are several freeware versions available and several commercial versions. Each has its own virtues. Most of these viewer programs include automated ways to select and download the weather maps from the Internet or by email request while underway. Sample GRIB viewer sources are listed in Table 6.3-2.

The goal in comparing the maps with your observations is to verify that the weather service understands properly what is taking place in the region you wish to transit. You must ultimately make your decisions based on the forecasts, not on these surface analyses, which are all history by the time we get them. So we are making the tacit assumption that a minimum cri-

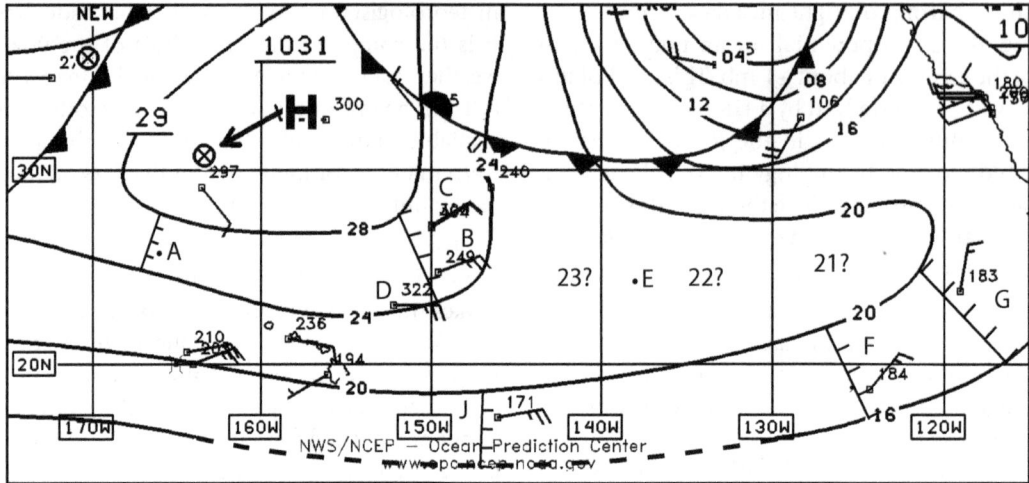

Figure 6.3-1. *Section of a surface analysis (00z, Feb 15, 2009) prepared by the OPC that might be used to compare a shipboard observation. Small rulers have been added to help interpolate the isobars. If our position had been point A, the map shows 1025.5. The ship report at Point B (1024.9) agrees well with the isobars. There are two illegible reports at Point C. Online at NDBC we learn these are 1040.3 and 1030.1 mb with 8 kts and 12 kts of wind respectively, both at 060. The reports are 6 miles apart. These pressures are almost certainly wrong. According to the isobars, they should be 1026 mb. If we were located somewhere near Point E, we would have to guess, and maybe 1022.5 might be a reasonable guess, assuming a weak ridge along that region. The report at G (1018.3) agrees with the isobars, but F at 1018.4 is about 1 mb off. It is a good exercise to make comparisons between ship reports and isobars to get a feeling for the uncertainties involved. This can be done any time with the online maps. This section of a random chart had more discrepancies than usual. It should also be clear that an accuracy level of about 1 mb is what we need for this work.*

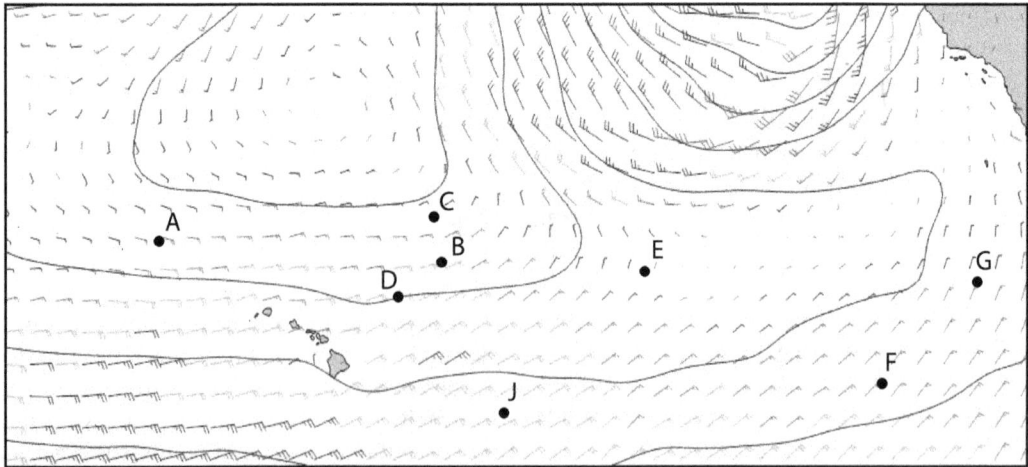

Figure 6.3-2. *Section of a surface analysis from the GFS model at the same time as Figure 6.3-1. The model output does not include frontal lines. The data shown in Table 6.3-1 are obtained from this file using a PC GRIB Viewer (Ugrib in this case), in which you place the cursor on the map in the place you wish to read the data and it is displayed digitally.*

teria for an accurate forecast is being able to explain what is taking place at the moment.

When you find agreement, you can be more confident to carry on with your plans. If you do not find agreement, then a good working philosophy might be just do half of what you want to do until you get a confirmation of the map. That will be in 6 hours when the next map is available.

Consider that you are under sail and have to make a jibe decision. You want to stay on the course you are on, and if the map is right that is good. But if the map is wrong you will get into trouble, and you should jibe right now that you have recognized the threat. In a case like this, you might either wait 3hr and then jibe, or jibe now and then in 3 hr jibe back to this desired course. In short, doing half of what you want till the full 6 hr pass and you see the new map.

If you had more freedom in headings and wanted to turn 60° to meet favorable conditions ahead, but if the map is wrong that will not be a good call, then maybe turn just 30°, and wait till next report. In both of these examples, keep an eye on your barometer to anticipate or confirm what the next map will say.

In regions where ship reports are sparse the isobars could be off somewhat till more reports are available, or the overall pattern begins to firm up. So it is not uncommon in such cases to see the maps off on one report, but then by 6 or 12 hr later they have it figured out. This is especially the case along the corners of the Highs, which are the typical ocean sailing routes. The wind is also light in these regions, so the wind speed and direction reports might not be as precise as they are in other places, which in turn is detrimental to locating the isobars. However, it must be said that the reports in all parts of the oceans are getting better each year, thanks to the good training provided by the PMOs.

You can get near live ship reports at sea by email by sending an email to shipreports@starpath.com with your decimal latitude and longitude in the first line (i.e. 42.123N, 72.456W). This will provide barometer readings, wind and sea state from vessel reports within 300 nmi of your location within the past 6 hours. A blank email to the same address with the

Table 6.3-1 Comparing Isobars and Station Reports at 00z, Feb 15, 2009*

ID	Location	Station Report	OPC	GFS
A	25.7°N, 166.1°W	None	1025.5	13.2@102 1026.1
B	24.8°N, 149.8°W	25@070 1024.9	1025.0	15.9@071 1025.8
C	27.2°N, 150.0°W	8,12@060 1040.3, 1030.1	1027.0	8.6@066 1027.7
D	23.1°N, 152.2°W	25@090 1032.2	1024.1	18.9@076 1024.4
E	24.3°N, 138.0°W	None	1022.5	6.3@011 1023.2
F	18.8°N, 124.4°W	15@040 1018.4	1017.0	15.6@045 1017.8
G	23.8°N, 119.1°W	15@010 1018.3	1018.7	11.1@021 1019.1
J	17.3°N, 146.2°W	25@080 1017.1	1018.5	19.0@066 1018.2

Table notes. Pressure data from Figure 6.3-1 (station reports and OPC) and from Figure 6.3-2 (GFS). The agreement is pretty good, though we could find exceptions. These are the data we must compare with our own observations.

Table 6.3-2 Grib Viewer Software*

Name	Source
ViewFax	saildocs.com
Ugrib	grib.us
Grib Explorer	ocens.com
GribPlot	xaxero.com
Expedition	iexpedition.org
GribView	gribview.com

Table notes. These software programs display weather maps in the GRIB (gridded binary) format. The first map of each sequence is the analysis, the following maps in a sequence are forecasts. Only the analyses can be fairly compared to the OPC produced products. GRIB maps usually first appear about 6 hours after the valid synoptic time of the map—in contrast to the the OPC maps, which are available about 3 hours after the valid synoptic times.

word "help" in the subject line will get you the instructions and list of abbreviations used.

6.4 Storm Warning in the Tropics

There are two things unique about barometric pressure in the tropics. First, the pressure undergoes the diurnal variation discussed in Section 5.6, which causes it to oscillate about the mean value by about ±1.7 mb, with two highs and two lows each day. To find the true mean pressure for the day, you need to average out these variations, and likewise to detect a trend in the pressure throughout the day you need to find and track the midpoint of each cycle throughout the day as shown in Figure 5.6-1.

The second unique feature of tropic pressures is they are remarkably steady. Atmospheric pressures in the low latitudes where tropical storms form and travel for most of their lives are significantly more stable than corresponding pressures at higher latitudes. At higher latitudes there are more systems coming by with larger and more varied pressure changes taking place.

At Long Island Sound, NY, for example, in the month of March, the average pressure is 1016.3 mb with a standard deviation of 9.7 mb (Chapter 10). For comparison, in San Juan, Puerto Rico in September, peak of the hurricane season, the average pressure is 1013.5 mb with a standard deviation (SD) of about 2.0 mb.

The SD is a measure of how far from the average a typical pressure might be, as shown in Table 6.4-1. A pressure of 1 SD below the mean has a reasonable probability of 16%, but 2 SD below the mean has less than 3% probability of occurring. In Puerto Rico in September, if you see a pressure 4 mb below the mean value (1013.5 - 4 = 1009.5) then that is a strong warning of a tropical storm approaching. There is only a 2.3% chance this is part of the *normal* distribution, and a 98% chance this is an *abnormal* pressure signaling the approach of a storm. In New York, on the other hand, a pressure 4 mb below the mean has little significance. That happens some 40% of the time, with or without bad weather.

With tropical SDs of just 2 or 3 mb, you do not have to be much below average before the (mental) flag should be up to alert you. Needless to say, you need an accurate barometer to take advantage of this warning.

The pressure distributions (standard deviations) show why this is useful knowledge for storm warning in the tropics, but not at higher latitudes. If the pressure drops to 4 mb below the average in, say, San Francisco or Annapolis, it does not tell us anything at all about the weather, but this identical drop on St. Croix or Mauritius is essentially a red light, turned on to warn us to pay attention.

To keep things in perspective, we should remember that tropical storms are extremely well forecasted by the National Hurricane Center and related agencies (called Regional Specialized Meteorological Centers) around the world. As soon as the wind starts moving in a circle, they are on top of it, keeping the world posted on predictions and movements. If you have a radio or other wireless contact with the outside world, there is very little chance any of these systems can sneak up on you. The observations we are describing here are most valuable when you have lost wireless contact with your forecast sources. Otherwise you know almost hourly where the storms are located and how they are moving. With a forecast in hand, the barometer can be used to gauge the approach of the systems.

Table 6.4 -1 Tropical Pressures*		
Observed pressure	*Probability*	*"Storm chance"*
0.5 SD below MSLP	31%	69%
1.0 SD below MSLP	16%	84%
1.5 SD below MSLP	6.7%	93%
2.0 SD below MSLP	2.3%	98%
2.5 SD below MSLP	0.6%	99%
3.0 SD below MSLP	0.1%	100%

Table notes. *These probabilities are common to all "normal distributions." MSLP = mean sea level pressure. SD = standard deviation. What is here called "storm chance" is just 100% minus the normal probability. Mean pressures and standard deviations are presented in chapter 10.*

Weather and altimetry are the primary applications of atmospheric pressure in our lives, but there are others as well, which to some may be more important than these two main ones. Here we discuss several areas where pressure can have an influence on our lives, with an effort to put them into perspective with regard to significance and dependability.

7.1 Pressure and Tide Height

Tides roll in and out of estuaries around the world, raising and lowering the water depth into typically two high waters and two low waters each day—in some regions there is only one high water and one low water. Tides are driven by the gravitational pull of the moon and sun. The location of the more important moon as it circles the earth determines the times of the tides, and the phase of the moon relative to the sun determines the size of the tides. When they work together, on the same side of the earth (new moon), or on opposite sides of the earth (full moon), we get tides about 20% larger than average, called spring tides. When the moon and sun pull on the oceans at right angles to each other (the two half moons each cycle), we get tides about 20% lower than average called neap tides.

The predicted heights and times of these tides are some of the most reliable oceanographic data we have. They can be predicted accurately long into the future. Prudent navigators, nevertheless, have learned to avoid planning a route or a maneuver that requires them to rely on predicted tide heights to be more accurate than about 2 ft in the midlatitudes. This safety factor varies, of course, from place to place. In south Florida, for example, the tide barely goes up and down 2 feet at all, so this is an overestimate of a safety factor there. In Cook Inlet, AK, where the tides go up

and down as much as 40 feet, this is an underestimate of a safety factor we should consider.

One of the factors that contributes to the uncertainty of the predicted tide height is the atmospheric pressure. The relative locations of the sun and moon can be predicted very precisely, so the only uncertainty is how much air the tide has to lift as the water rises. Since we live "at the bottom of an ocean of air," as Torricelli put it, we are not aware of this weight, but we do know that each square inch of water has on it about 14.7 pounds of weight from the air above it. That's a ton on every square foot. If the atmospheric pressure changes by just 1%, the force on a bay a mile across changes by 360,000 tons. When the annual book of predicted tides is computed they do not know what the atmospheric pressure will be at the times they predict, so they do not make any corrections for pressure. In short term predictions they can account for this, as is often done in emergency announcements of storm tides

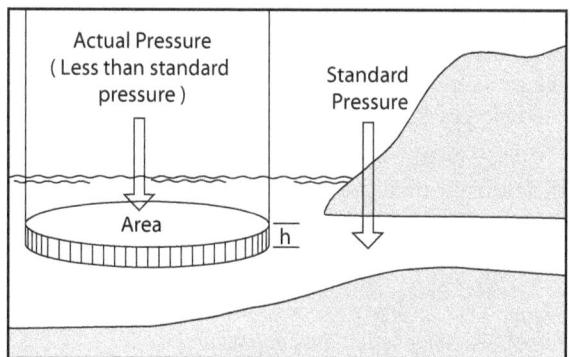

Figure 7.1-1 *Inverse barometer effect. Higher than average pressure gives rise to lower than average tides, whereas lower than average pressure gives rise to higher than average tides. The effect is small, and can be masked by other factors such as winds and river runoff that are also outside the average at the time.*

The effect of atmospheric pressure on the tide height is called the "inverse barometer effect" (IBE), because the waterway acts just like a giant barometer in response to the pressure. It is also easy to compute the size of this effect from the same principles we use to understand a barometer. When the pressure is below the normal pressure used in the tide predictions, the water rises above normal predictions. Referring to Figure 7.1-1,

Weight of water above normal level / Area
= Pressure drop below normal pressure.

Or,

Area x h x (density of sea water) / Area
= Pressure drop

The Area factor cancels out, and then using a 1-inch change in tide height (1/12 of a foot) and a density of sea water equal to 64 lbs per cubic foot, we get, 64/12 lbs/sq ft = 5.3 lbs/sq ft, which equals 0.0368 lbs/sq inch. From Table 2.2-1 you can convert this to 2.54 mb. Thus we can state the inverse barometer effect as: 2.54 mb of pressure drop below normal = 1 inch change in the predicted tide height. A common way to express the IBE is the equivalent expression:

1 mb = 1 cm.

For every 5 mb above the normal pressure, the actual tide is expected to be 2 inches lower than predicted, and for every 5 mb lower than normal pressure, the actual tide height will be higher than predicted by 2 inches.

It is fair to ask at this point what is meant by normal pressure. The pressure drop that enters this formula is "normal pressure" minus actual pressure. The tide

Figure 7.1-2 *Inverse barometer effect in Puget Sound for higher than normal pressures. All instances of pressure above 1030 during 2008 showed results similar to these, giving rise to about a 1-ft adjustment to the predicted tides, which is about the magnitude expected. The full results are presented at starpath.com/barobook.*

data that enter into the tide predictions are gathered over many years from tide gauges in the waterway at each station. In principle these gauges could record the pressure as well as the tide, but that is not the way they work. They just record tide going up and down each day, throughout the month, and throughout the year. Thus the tides we get reported in the books are whatever they have been in the past on the time and date in question whenever the sun and moon were exactly as they are now. This would have been sometimes under high pressure, sometimes under low pressure. So when the tide books say that at 1400 on August 8, 2008 at Elliott Bay (Seattle, WA) the tide height is 5.6 feet, we have to assume this is the value for the mean sea level pressure at Elliott Bay in August. We also have to assume that the winds were about average, and the river runoff was about average and so on. The tide book values are for the average conditions at that time of year.

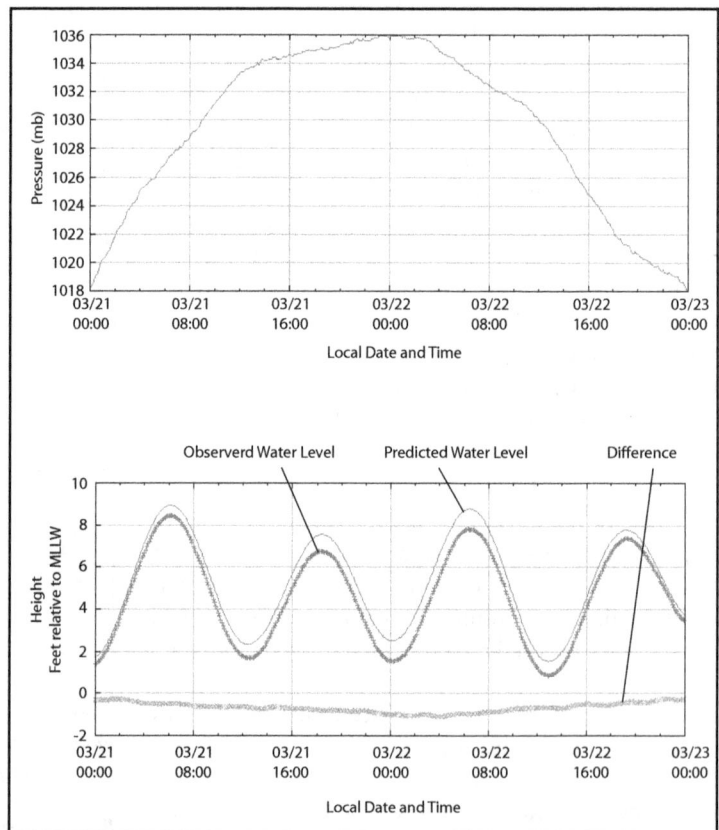

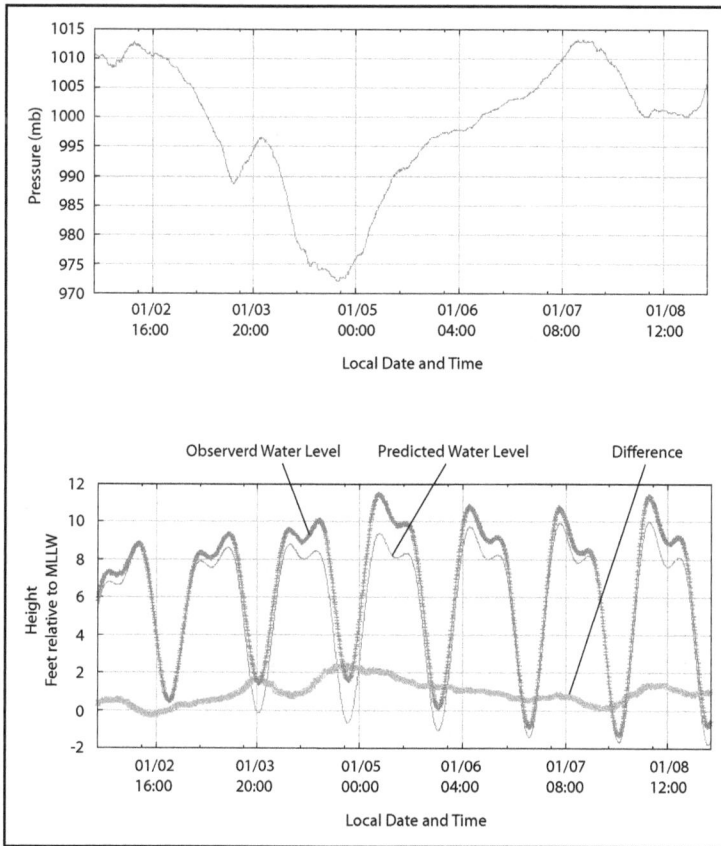

Figure 7.1-3 *Inverse barometer effect in Puget Sound for lower than normal pressures. All instances of pressure below 1004 mb during 2008 showed results similar to these, giving rise to about a 1-ft adjustment to the predicted tides, which is about the magnitude expected. The full results are presented at starpath.com/barobook. Lows often bring strong winds which can mask or reverse this effect in some cases, or enhance it as in this case.*

20 mb, which is a tide suppression of 20 cm, about 8 inches.

Referring to Chapter 10, you see that in Jan on both coasts of the US, the mean pressure is about 1017 mb from latitude 45N to 50N, with a standard deviation (SD) of about 10 mb. The 20-mb deviation from the normal we discuss here is 2 SD off the mean, and from Table 10.1, we know this implies there is a 2.3% chance that the pressure is equal to or greater than the Mean value + 2SD (1017+2x10) = 1037 mb. Thus in this case "not uncommon" means a 2.3% chance!

Then when you ask, so what is the mean sea level pressure in August in Elliott Bay, we have to say you can look it up in Chapter 10 of this book. If you did not have this book, you could look it up in the Appendix B of the *US Coast Pilot, Vol. 7*. The Coast Pilot lists mean monthly pressures for several large ports in each volume. Or if you did not have this book or the Coast Pilot, then you could just guess that the normal pressure was 1013 mb (the standard atmospheric pressure), which will be about equal to the yearly average in many places. Northwest Washington state is a bit of an exception, where the mean monthly pressure only varies annually from 1016 to 1018 mb, and it is mostly 1017.

In the Puget Sound area, for example, it is not uncommon to have a pressure of 1037 mb in the winter (rather than the average value of 1017), which would suppress predicted heights corresponding to 37-17 =

We present this idea as it applies to tide height—even though it applies to all large bodies of water, even those without tides—because this has direct and frequent application to navigation, especially to small craft like kayaks. For a kayak that draws only 6 inches of water, the entire lay of its available waterway for miles around can change completely with a 6-inch change in the tide level.

The low pressure side of the standard atmosphere can have more effect. When the pressure is very low, the air is light and the tides rise higher than predicted. A 980 mb low corresponds to a 33 mb change, with a corresponding tide rise of more than 1 foot over predictions.

These effects of the IBE are often obscured by other factors such as wind (for both high and low pressures) and storm surges, usually associated with very low pressures. If the pressure pattern brings in strong wind, this wind creates an unpredicted wind-driven surface current of up to some 3% of the wind speed. This extra current interacting with the predicted tidal current will either increase or decrease the tide heights. If a very high pressure system, which is suppressing the tide height, happens to create a strong wind blowing in the ebb direction, it would hinder water running in on the flood direction. With less water running in, you can end up with significantly lower tides than predicted. Vessels that can barely get out of a channel at high tide, or barely get up to the fuel dock at the high tide, may not be able to do what they want to do, and might get in trouble if they try. On the other hand, if you are just barely not getting under a bridge near high water, you may still get under if the pressure is high and save having to wait several hours for the tide to fall.

Storm surges are much in the news these days because of all the tragic storm interactions we have had along the Gulf coast. A storm surge is an abnormal rise in the water level caused by high storm waves rolling in with the tides. The total surge in water height is a combination of the waves plus the IBE. In the early hours of Saturday, Sept 13, 2008, the predicted tide heights in the vicinity of Galveston, TX, were about 0.5 ft. When hurricane Ike crossed the shoreline at about 2 am local time, the pressure dropped to about 952 mb. That is 61 mb below 1013, corresponding to 61 cm or 2 feet rise in the water level height. This made the effect of oncoming storm waves even worse. The total surge height was over ten feet. The term "storm surge" means the effect of IBE plus waves.

As mentioned above, the IBE applies to all water levels, which means it is an important factor to take into account when measuring small changes in global sea level heights as when monitoring the effects of global warming. Since the slope of the water surface affects ocean currents, this is also a factor that enters into Gulf Stream predictions and things like the sometimes dramatic Great Lakes seiches.

Studies have shown that this simple solution for the IBE given above is actually quite accurate (5 to 10%), outside of the tropics. Within the tropics the effect can be smaller. But in the mid and high latitudes where the tides are a big factor to navigation this is an important effect to know about.

So this question comes to mind. With such an important effect that is so easy to predict quantitatively, how is it that this is not common knowledge to all navigators and coastal residents? I think the answer comes back to our general knowledge of barometers. If we have a barometer on board or at home that is not accurate, this type of reasoning simply cannot be done, so it has not been done. This is another example of how we can benefit from getting more involved with our barometers and their calibration, so that we become more aware of the effects and meaning of atmospheric pressure.

We should add that like several other areas of practical marine navigation, the fact that something is not well known now, does not mean it was not well known once. The IBE was in fact well known in the early 1800's, when there were sayings such as "frost nips the tide" or "fog nips the tide," which means that periods of fog or frost can correspond to lower tide heights than expected because they are often associated with periods of high pressure. High pressure leads to clear skies and cold nights when temperatures can drop below the dew point. By the mid 1800's it was even known that a 1-inch rise on the barometer corresponded to 1-foot drop in the tide (right to within about 10%), and FitzRoy warned mariners who were relying on a very close tide calculation to keep an eye on their barometers.

7.2 Health and the Barometer

If there is any doubt about the effect of pressure on our wellbeing and health in general, just go to some place like Telluride, CO, elevation 9,000 ft, and run a marathon. At 9,000 feet there is still 21% oxygen in the air, as there is at sea level, but the mean pressure is only 724 mb, which means the density of the air is 76% of what it is at sea level (Appendix 3). You get 24% less oxygen into your lungs on each breath.

No one is surprised that respiratory ailments and emergency room visits go up when we are socked in with a temperature inversion that locks in smog and pollution. This is clearly "weather" affecting our health—but it can also happen on a much more subtle level.

The U.S. National Weather Service has not till recently focused much on the topic of weather and health. In Germany, on the other hand, *Biowetter* and *Gesundheitswetter* are popular topics on many weather websites. These are topics that specifically relate various health risks to present weather conditions. Atmospheric pressure is always one of the components of these forecasts. Environment Canada also has extended discussions online about the role of weather in human health.

In November of 2008, the Cooperative Program for Operational Meteorology, Education and Training (a collaboration of the University Corporation for Atmospheric Research and the National Weather Service) introduced a new training course called "Weather and Health." It is directed toward broadcast meteorologists with the intent of broadening their understanding of the impacts of weather on public health. The goal is to have broadcasters incorporate health messages into their daily weathercasts so the public becomes more aware of the relationships.

Unlike the German counterparts of these planned weathercasts, however, there is—at least for now—no specific discussion in this training course of the possible relationship between atmospheric pressure and health, but the very fact that health and weather are being related is of interest to those using barometers. Whatever your goal is in watching the weather, an accurate barometer remains the number one tool to your own observations.

You can, of course, usually get a report of the pressure from the TV, radio, or Internet, but most of these sources do not save the history or provide a trace of how the pressure is changing at your location. For this you need your own observations. Also, once you do have a barometer that you understand and trust, you can take it with you to places that might not have convenient, frequent reports, and you will have accurate pressure if you lose your electric power.

Headaches and Atmospheric Pressure

In the March, 2009 issue of the scientific journal *Neurology*, several doctors from Harvard University led by Kenneth Mukamal published a paper entitled "Weather and Air Pollution as Triggers of Severe Headaches." They studied over 7,000 patients who

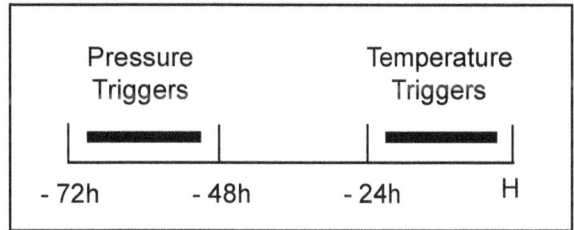

Figure 7.2-1 *Timing of headache triggers according to Mukamal, et al. H is the time of hospitalization. Temperature and pressure triggers occurred at different times and did not overlap.*

had been admitted to an emergency room in Boston with severe headache, between the years 2000 and 2007. They correlated these incidents with the archived weather (temperature, pressure, and humidity) as well as with several pollution levels for three days prior to the admittance.

They found no correlation between severe headache and pollution, nor with relative humidity. There was, however, a significant temperature and pressure correlation with severe headaches. In the temperature studies, they found a 7.5% increase in risk of headache for each 9°F increase in temperature during the 24 hours prior to admittance. There were also notable temperature correlations between the cold months and the warm months, and differences between severe headaches diagnosed as migraines versus those called nonmigraines. There was no headache correlation of any kind, however, with the temperature for the second and third days prior to admittance (Figure 7.2-1).

Of more interest in the present context are the results of their pressure studies. They found a 7.1% increase in headache risk for each 6.7 mb drop of the barometric pressure below the normal value during the period 48-to-72 hours prior to hospitalization. There was no correlation with pressure during the two days before the hospitalization. Pressure was, in this sense, an earlier warning of the onset of headache than temperature was.

These statistics are for individual personal risks, and they are relative to the climatic mean pressures and temperatures at their location. For example, consider how these results would apply to a person who has on average 8 severe headaches each year, spread evenly across all seasons. Their personal risk of a headache on any random day is 2.2% (8/365).

If the normal pressure on, say, April 27th at their location is 1015 mb, but on this particular Monday, April 27th, the pressure throughout the day was 1008.3 mb (i.e. 6.7 mb below the average), then this person expects an increase to their personal risk of getting a headache on Thursday by 7.1%. Their new risk would be: 2.2% + 0.071 x 2.2 = 2.36%. If the pressure were even lower at 1001.6 (normal - 2 x 6.7 mb), the compounded risk would be: 2.36% + 0.71 x 2.36 = 2.52%.

When a storm passes by with a pressure of 981.5 mb (normal - 5 x 6.7 mb) the personal risk compounds to 3.1% for this individual. An even larger pressure drop brings with it a proportionally larger increase in risk, but there is some statistical limit to the likelihood, because of typical annual pressure distributions, as shown in Figure 7.2-2 for the site of this study.

We see that at a higher latitude location like Boston, a pressure drop leading to 2 or 3 times the 7% increased risk is readily possible within the normal fluctuations of their pressure. They do not need a storm for this level of variation. At lower latitudes, on the other hand, the pressure is much more stable throughout the year. In St. Croix, Virgin Islands, for example, you cannot even get the required drop for a 15% increased risk without a tropical storm coming by.

These newly documented correlations between headache and pressure are obviously not huge effects, even with temperature going up as the pressure goes down, which could double or triple the effect, but they are real, statistically significant results. There has been extensive anecdotal evidence over the years for a correlation between headache and pressure, but this brand new research is being heralded as the strongest experimental evidence to date. It is a first step toward understanding a relationship that many headache sufferers have long avowed.

There is obviously more to be learned. The two-day lead time on the pressure trigger is consistent with the timing of many other types of triggers reported for migraine headaches. Unfortunately, migraine

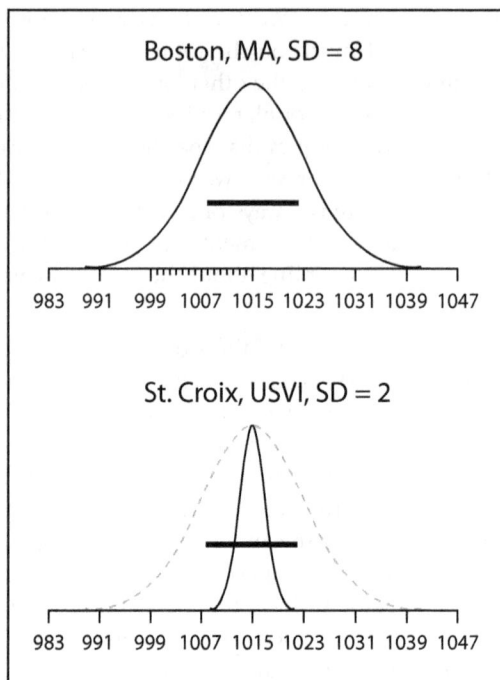

Figure 7.2-2 Annual sea level pressure distributions in Boston, MA: mean = 1015.7 mb, standard deviation (SD) = 8.2 mb, and in Saint Croix, USVI: mean = 1015.5 mb, SD = 1.6 mb. The Boston distribution is shown for comparison as a dashed line in the Saint Croix data. The horizontal line (14 mb) represents the predicted pressure drop associated with a 15% increase in the personal risk of headache. Except during the relatively rare passage of a tropical storm, this pressure drop is very unlikely in low latitudes where the pressure is much more constant throughout the year. Chapter 10 shows how pressure stability varies with location and season, worldwide.

sufferers will have to wait for more insight into this effect. The Mukamal et al study found *temperature* correlations with migraine and non-migraine headaches, but the *pressure* effects were all associated with those diagnosed as non-migraine headaches. They added, however, that this classification remains one of the uncertainties in their results, as was their not knowing when the symptoms actually started, but just the time of the hospitalization. We can also reasonably assume that there were during this period many severe headaches that did not result in a visit to the emergency room.

It is well known that headaches have many triggers that differ amongst individuals, and that these triggers are cumulative. Thus with this new information, those susceptible might be more conservative with their other known triggers on days when the temperature is rising or the barometer is falling. The larger and more sudden the changes, the more likely the influence.

Weather in itself is complex, and how the human system interacts with weather is even far more complex. It is obvious that weather affects humans on many levels. The extent that atmospheric pressure affects an individual can only be tested with real data, collected by the individual, and that is an exercise that requires an accurate barometer.

7.3 The Barometer In Sports

Sometimes atmospheric pressure enters into our daily lives in ways we might not have thought of, though maybe we should not be too surprised. We live, work, and play in the air, so is it a surprise that the remotest nature of the air affects much of what we do?

Anything moving through the air is subject to frictional drag from the air. If you think of walking straight across an empty room, compared to walking straight across a room filled with people, you see the problem. You have to push these people out of your way to get across. An object flying though the air has to push the air molecules out of its way, which consumes some of its energy and thus slows it down.

From this room analogy, it is easy to imagine that the strength of the frictional resistance through a fluid of air, just like through a fluid of people, depends on the shape of the object, the speed of the object, and the density of the air. The faster the object moves through the air, the more work it has to do to clear the path. In fact, the resistance increases with the square of the object's speed. Consequently, air resistance is very sensitive to speed, and it is not much of a factor for things moving slowly.

Picturing the room again, we appreciate that the denser the air, the more resistance it creates. Air density varies with the temperature, humidity, and pressure, as illustrated in Table 7.3-1. The density changes with each variable as expected, but it is not easy to guess which factor dominates when several are varied.

Dry air (20% relative humidity) is more dense that moist air (100% relative humidity), because wa-

Table 7.3-1. Air Density (kg/m3)*								
	Relative Humidity %	At high elevation		At sea level				Saturated vapor pressure
		8,080 ft	4,780 ft	Low	Normal	High		
°F		750 mb	850 mb	980 mb	1013 mb	1046 mb	°C	mb
0	100	1.022	1.159	1.336	1.381	1.426	-17.8	1.5
	20	1.023	1.160	1.337	1.382	1.427		
30	100	0.958	1.086	1.252	1.295	1.337	-1.11	5.6
	20	0.960	1.088	1.254	1.297	1.339		
60	100	0.897	1.018	1.175	1.214	1.254	15.55	17.7
	20	0.903	1.024	1.181	1.221	1.261		
90	100	0.835	0.949	1.097	1.135	1.173	32.22	48.0
	20	0.851	0.966	1.114	1.152	1.189		
120	100	0.764	0.872	1.012	1.048	1.084	48.89	116.3
	20	0.802	0.910	1.051	1.086	1.122		

* The formula for air density is given in Appendix A2b. As rough guidelines, the air density decreases about 1% for a pressure drop of 10 mb; an elevation rise of 300 ft; or a temperature increase of about 3°C (5° F).

ter molecules are lighter than nitrogen and oxygen and there is a fixed number of molecules needed to create a given pressure and temperature. The humidity contribution to the density, however, is relatively small for low and moderate temperatures. At higher temperatures it matters more, because then there is more water vapor in the air at saturation. In any application where air friction might play a role, it is the density that matters, and each of these factors contributes to it.

Baseball

There is a reason baseball batters love to come to the plate at Coors Field in the mile-high city of Denver, CO. Chances of hitting a home run are higher, because baseballs fly farther though the thinner air at that elevation. As noted above, temperature and humidity can be as important as pressure, but that big step up to 5,000 ft gives a giant boost to begin with. A warm day there is far better for batting than a warm day in San Francisco.

Baseball must be the human activity with the most recorded statistics. Everything is recorded, for every play of every game, for every player. Thus it is easy to study the results to evaluate these effects on home runs. Analysts have developed factors that account for the distance of a home run based on temperature at the time and the pressure altitude of field, which includes the local sea-level pressure at the time. These factors specify how much of the full distance of the home run in feet is due to a temperature different from 70°F and a pressure different from 1013 mb.

The data for 2008 for three fields are shown in Table 7.3-2. Coors Field adds an average of over 20 feet to the typical home run. On a warm day with lower than average pressure, the boost could be twice that much. At a sea level field like McAfee in Oakland, you get no help from the pressure, and the temperature could be with you or against you.

So the message is, if you want to fine tune the estimates of home run predictions at any field, take a look at the temperature and pressure. They might just add another 10 or 20 feet to the range and put a couple extra over the fence.

Golf

Golf is another sport with small round projectiles moving rapidly though the air. Whereas well hit baseballs leave the bat at some 105 mph, golf balls can leave at more than 150 mph. Aerodynamics in golf are even more crucial. Baseballs have not been aerodynamically designed, but golf balls most certainly have been. The famous dimples in golf balls are critically designed to minimize air resistance. Make them just a bit bigger or a bit smaller and the ball will not travel as far.

Furnace Creek Golf course in Death Valley (214 ft below sea level) prides itself in being more challenging because of the air density, noting that experienced golfers can tell the difference and adjust for it. It ranks among the "50 toughest golf courses," in part for that reason.

Table 7.3-2 Home Run Distance Factors due to Air Density, 2008 Season*									
		Temperature factor in ft				Pressure factor in ft			
Stadium	*Elevation*	*Range*	*Median*	*Mean*	*SD*	*Range*	*Median*	*Mean*	*SD*
McAfee Coliseum Oakland, CA	9 ft	-8 to +9	-2	-1.9	3.2	0	0	0	0
Kaufman Field Kansas city, MO	891 ft	-12 to +12	+3	+2.1	4.4	0 to +5	+4	+3.6	0.8
Coors Field Denver, CO	5,197 ft	-13 to +12	+1	+0.3	4.7	+16 to +32	+21	+21.4	4.6

* These factors are how much of a home run's total distance is attributed to temperature relative to 70°F and to pressure relative to 1013.25 mb. The elevation dominates the pressure factor. The raw data for individual home runs was taken from www.HitTrackerOnline.com. Median is the most likely value; Mean is the average; SD is the standard deviation. The total numbers of home runs were: Coors 174, McAfee 125, and Kauffman 123.

Home runs of some 400 ft in Colorado go some 20 ft farther than at sea level (a 5% effect), but golf balls in Colorado travel some 10% farther, meaning the effect on the smaller, faster balls, even with their aerodynamic design, is twice as large.

There are patents on handheld devices that compute the effect of air density on golf ball range, and there are CD courses on the market on how to take air density into account in your golf swing. To the extent that these aids actually help, this might be a good application for a watch with a barometer in it, providing you have checked that it works properly.

Car Racing

Air density plays a key role in car racing for two reasons. The first relates to aerodynamics, which are crucial to the ultimate speed that can be reached. A car that would slide off a curve at 80 mph can increase that speed to 115 with well designed aerodynamic adjustments (spoilers). The fastest of these cars are essentially "airplanes flying upside down," in that the downward force of the spoilers can be larger than the weight of the car. The proper setting of these aerodynamic adjustments based on air density can make the difference between winning and losing a race.

In professional races, the weather is monitored throughout the race and the spoiler angles are adjusted to match the density of the air. Usually it is a changing temperature over a long race that calls for the most changes, but the elevation of the track and its associated pressure are always the starting points. The ambient pressure goes into each computation as well.

The other application relates to engine tuning. The right setting depends on the density of the air as well as the humidity and oxygen content. These values are measured at the track and then entered into computer programs on site that tell the technicians how to best tune the cars and select the right jetting for the engines. Obviously, for both applications, accurate station pressure is mandatory. All of these applications can benefit from a quick calibration using the methods of Chapter 4.

The horsepower of all cars, not just race cars, depends on air density. The standards we read from car specifications can be traced to the Society of Automotive Engineers (SAE) who specify horsepower based on a standard of 77°F intake air temp, 990 mb external pressure (corresponding to an average elevation of 650 ft), and dry air (Relative Humidity = 0).

In warm air at higher elevations, actual horsepower could be just 80% of what it is at lower elevations and cooler air. Formulas and calculators for figuring horsepower are readily available online. Search under "Relative Horsepower Calculator."

Speed Skating

The 2009 World Championships in Long Track Speed Skating were held in March at the new Richmond, BC, Olympic Oval. The best skaters in the world were there. The competition was keen and the racing beautiful to watch. It was an ideal preview of what the upcoming Olympics will be. The ice and the arena were immaculate, but despite this wonderful venue, no world records were set, and no personal best speeds were recorded.

The announcer even warned the audience to concentrate on the skaters and the competition, and do not look for record achievements here, "because the ice is at sea level." The implication was that all such

Figure 7.3-1 *U.S. champion Shani Davis, winning the 1500 meter race at the 2009 World Championships. Second place was 0.13 seconds behind him, and 3rd place was 0.88 seconds back, illustrating the typical closeness of the competition. Photo by Stephen Rusk.*

records and bests in speed skating are achieved at high altitude ovals, and sure enough a quick check of the records will confirm that. Most are from the Olympic Oval at Kearns, Utah (elevation 4,685 ft) or from the Saddledome in Calgary, Alberta, (elevation 3,470 ft). The Olympic Oval in Richmond, BC, on the other hand, is right on the water with an elevation of about 10 ft.

Most speed skaters and those who follow the sport are aware of this; many refer to high altitude ice as "fast ice." Scientists, however, are beginning to learn that this is probably not the best description. Rather, it might best be described as a matter of "fast air."

Speed skating is a highly finessed sport. Every motion optimized, each component finely designed to optimize speed: from ice to skates to skin suits, to the air around the ice. Time differences between the best skaters are measured in hundredths of a second. Examples are presented in Figures 7.3-1 and 7.3-2. And it has all paid off; this is a very fast sport. Speed skaters can reach speeds of up to 40 mph, which is fast enough to expect frictional drag of the air to be a factor.

The skaters' forward thrust is resisted by the ice and by the air, but the contribution of the ice is only some 20% of the resistance, compared to 80% from the air. Table 7.3-1 shows that air density can vary by

20% from sea level to 4,000 ft, so this is a logical candidate to account for the differences in performance. It will take some time, however, before we can be more quantitative. Scientists have only recently discovered that long-held conceptions of how skates move across the ice have not been correct—the weight of the skater *does not* melt the ice under the blade creating a watery "grease" to slide along. The interaction is far more complex, but it is not likely to account for the difference in performance at sea level vs. 4,000 ft.

The answer is most likely in the air, not the ice. Resistance from the air is proportional to the density of the air, so with expected air resistance differences up to 20% or so at sea level vs. 4,000 ft, it is easy to imagine this as a crucial factor in such a fine tuned sport. Significant differences might even occur from day to day at the same arena.

Past US team member and World Cup medallist Patrick Seltsam has drawn attention to this subject for some years. He proposes that barometric pressure should be recorded with every record set. He also suggested, only half jokingly, that we might one day see skating ovals in air-tight buildings that can be partially evacuated to lower the pressure. This is not an entirely foreign concept. Some athletes preparing for events at high elevations sleep in rooms with reduced pressure to adapt their bodies to the elevations where they must perform.

Fishing and Hunting

There are many hunters and fishermen who swear by the barometer when it comes to evaluating their chances for the day's outing. Enough so to spawn an industry of custom barometer dials designed for hunting and fishing. Samples are shown in Figure 7.3-3. There is much written on this application in sports magazines and online discussion groups.

The lore is so extensive there must be some value to it, but chances are it is actually the overall weather that is the factor, and not the barometric pressure itself. It is almost certain, for example, that air temperature (and hence surface water temperature), cloud cover, precipitation, and wind could any one affect the movement and feeding habits of wildlife on land or underwater. So it is logical that the barometer read-

Figure 7.3-2 *Speed skater Masako Hozumi of Japan. The clap-skate design lets the blade separate from the boot heel temporarily to maintain maximum contact with the ice at each stroke—an example of the technology development in this sport. Photo by Stephen Rusk.*

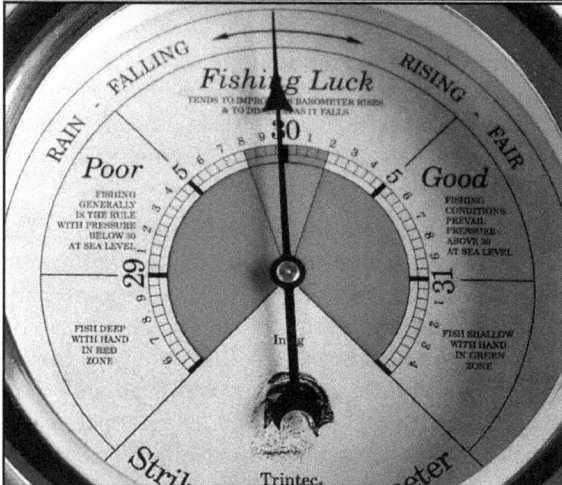

ing is valuable, being the best single piece of information that might foretell the weather.

At least with regard to fishing, however, it is easy to show that weather and not pressure itself is the crucial factor, because fish are underwater and the weight of the water dominates the pressure they feel. Water weighs some 800 times more than air, so our rule of how pressure changes in the air ("point four four per floor," meaning 0.44 mb per 12 ft) can yield a quick answer for the weight of water, namely 29 mb per foot. A more accurate approach would be to consider how tall a 1-square-inch column of water would have to be to weigh 14.7 pounds, which is one atmosphere (1013.25 mb). That answer for fresh water (density 62.4 lbs/ft^3) is 33.9 feet. So 1 ft on a water barometer is 29.9 mb.

Thus, when a fish changes its depth by just 1 foot, the change in pressure that it must accommodate with its air bladder is more than the worse storm would bring by in a full day. So daily changes in the atmospheric pressure are most likely not noticed by fish on any level. In fact, the change of the tides in

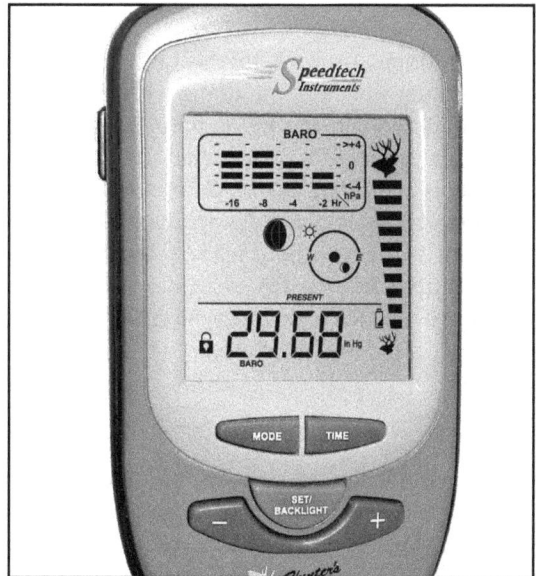

Figure 7.3-3 *Sample dials from hunting and fishing barometers. There is some agreement on the significance of various pressure patterns, and some disagreement. Chances are there are regional influences that affect any potential correlations between weather patterns and fishing and hunting success.*

tidal waters, or even the changing heights of the water with passing wavelets on inland lakes change the pressure on a submerged fish more than the passing weather does.

Atmospheric pressure effects on outdoor game animals and birds is another matter. We have recent science that indicates pressure can be sensed by humans susceptible to severe headache, and we do know that animals are remarkably more sensitive to some natural stimuli than humans are, so it would be difficult to rule it out. On the other hand, if there is a correlation it could be very regional, and observations for one location or season or game might not apply to others. This is apparent from reading the online discussion on the topic. There are many conflicting observations about which pressure behavior is most crucial. This in turn, takes us back to the more likely scenario, which is the barometer is indicating the weather, and the weather is affecting the hunting. In that sense, those hunters who have found good success with their barometer observations are the ones who have been most successful in using the barometer to predict that aspect of the weather that is most influencing their hunting.

Which brings us back to the ongoing mantra, that no matter what you are doing with the barometer, you will do it better if you have an instrument that you are confident is correct. And the only way to know that is to calibrate it with the methods outlined in Chapter 4. This is especially pertinent for hunting and fishing in areas without ready access to wireless pressure reports. In these cases having a calibrated barometer you can take with you to monitor changes in the weather could be a great asset.

7.4 Barometers In Science

Robert Boyle was the first to use a "barometer" in the laboratory to study the behavior of gases, and several still-famous laws of gases were the result. From then on, pressure has been measured inside the lab and out, in various scientific studies. Terminology in use today restricts the word "barometer" and "barometric pressure" to be that of nature's *atmospheric* pressure. Scientists have frequent occasion to measure artificially created pressures; the instruments used for this are generically called "pressure gauges." These can be used for pressures below 1 atmosphere or above it.

Of the hundreds of applications of barometric pressure in science, there is one that stands out in that it not only requires knowing barometric pressure, but it requires knowing it as accurately as possible. It falls into the relatively new research field called GPS meteorology.

GPS Meteorology

GPS (Global Positioning System) is the state of the art, all weather, satellite navigation system now used worldwide for essentially anything that moves, from planes, ships, and cars to cyclists and runners. It provides remarkable accuracy (sub-meter with special equipment) by timing electromagnetic signals between the moving vehicle and GPS satellites, far overhead. There are several potential sources of the very small errors involved in this process, and one of them can be traced to the amount of water vapor in the air.

Scientists recently learned that they can invert the position analysis using signal times to a precisely known location to actually determine how much precipitable water vapor had to be in the air in the region the signals traversed. A fundamental input to this analysis, however, is accurate barometric pressure, so developments in highly accurate pressure measurement were crucial to this new application.

Precipitable water vapor (PWV) is the most important variable gas in the atmosphere. It is a greenhouse gas that protects our environment, as well as the direct measure of the state of the hydrologic cycle that distributes water around the earth. The amount of this vapor present is also the key factor in storm development and accurate forecasts in general. In short, it is one of the most important quantities to measure in all of atmospheric science.

PWV is measured in cm, being the height of the column of water if all the PWV above a point were fully condensed. Typical values are 2 cm in midlatitudes to some 5 cm at the equator. If pressure can be measured to an accuracy of 0.3 mb, the PWV can be determined with this method to within about 1 mm, which is a big improvement over conventional weather balloon measurements. Paroscientific, GE Sensing, and Vaisala are among the pioneer providers of barometers with this high level of pressure accuracy and required stability.

Pressure Waves

Our ears are in a sense a barometer. Ears measure oscillations in air pressure that we interpret as sounds. The "ear barometer" is exquisitely sensitive to pressure changes that occur at rates of 20 to 20,000 times per second. If the pressure on the ear changes more slowly than that we cannot hear it, but we might feel it. Riding in a plane landing or taking off we can feel it and sometimes explosive shock waves are perceived, but generally we are not aware of weaker atmospheric pressure oscillations that take place slower than some 20 cycles per second.

There are incidents in nature, however, that do create pulses of pressure waves that we cannot hear. Some are large enough to see on a common barograph. Atmospheric shock waves produced by volcanic eruptions are one example. They are strong compressive waves driven by rapidly moving (hundreds of mph) volcanic ejecta. They are rare. Most eruptions do not produce them, but when they are created they can be quite prominent. The famous 1883 Krakatoa eruption led to 7 mb spikes in common barograph traces more than 90 miles away. The Mount Saint Helens eruption in 1980 produced measurable barograph pulses around the state of WA, and into OR and ID. A sample is shown in Figure 7.4-1.

There are many more subtle sources of pressure waves, but they take a more sensitive instrument to detect. A sample designed and built by Steve Hansen is shown in Figure 7.4-2. With this instrument he can measure pressure changes relative to a reference volume to within several microbars (0.001 mb). He has also shown that this instrument can be built on the limited budget of an amateur scientist or small school.

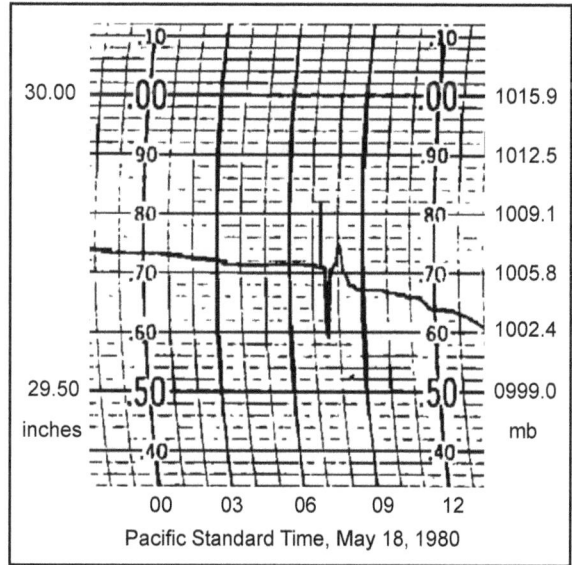

Figure 7.4-1. *Barograph trace of Mt. St. Helens eruption recorded at the Toledo, WA airport, 34 miles away. There was a sharp spike followed by a dip and a rise. This was the closest barograph. Signals were detected on common barographs like this as far as Lewiston, ID, 230 miles away. Numerous traces detected around the state were analyzed by Jack Reed of Sandia Laboratories (Further Reading.) From the theoretical wave strength and other observations, it was concluded that some common barographs had the needles set too tightly against the paper and thus they missed the signal. Microbarographs detected the eruption more than 1,000 miles away.*

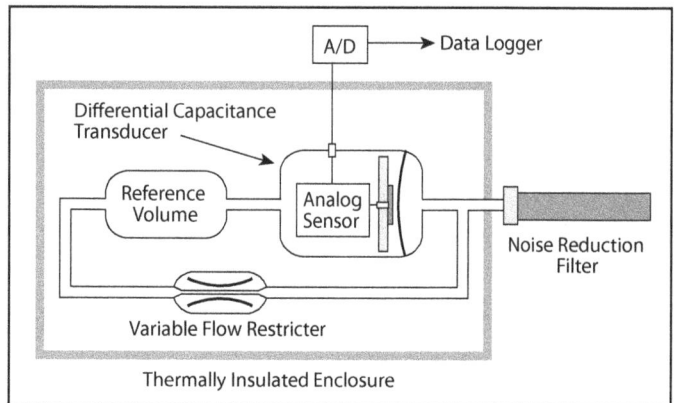

Figure 7.4.2 *Differential capacitance diaphragm gauge (MKS type 223) configured as a microbarograph The measurement side of the sensor is connected to the atmosphere through a length of porous "soaker" hose. The other side is connected to a reference volume connected to the atmosphere through a variable flow restriction (leak). The size of the leak and reference volume determines the time sensitivity of the device. A typical frequency response would be 0.003 to a few Hz. Temperature changes affect the reference pressure, so it is important to maintain a constant temperature environment. Illustration adapted from Steve Hansen's Bell Jar article (Further Reading).*

Research in this area began in the Cold War days as a way to monitor nuclear blasts to supplement underground seismographs. It is still used in a similar way to monitor explosions in strip mining projects. Other projects include monitoring snow avalanches, or detecting the entry of a meteoric fireball. Depending on your relative location, you can detect a train entering a tunnel from quite a distance off of the other end. Figure 7.4-3 shows the atmospheric pressure disturbance of a passing jet plane.

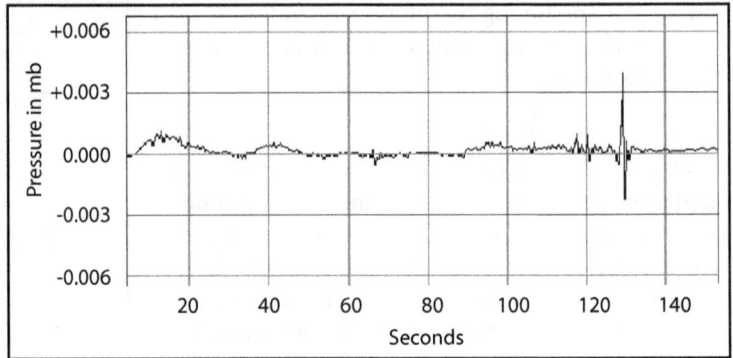

Figure 7.4-3. *Microbarograph signal from a passing jet plane. This was measured with the instrument shown in Figure 7.4-2. In some circumstances the signal from a jet when landing or taking off overhead could yield a stronger signal.*

In this chapter we look at the criteria for selecting a barometer as well as the issues relating to choosing between aneroid and electronic—and why it could be valuable to have both. As noted earlier, we are not considering mercury tubes as an option for working instruments, though they can be a fascinating and accurate way to keep track of pressure on land.

8.1 The Choices

Decorative barometers

When considering a barometer it helps to keep in mind that most barometers on the market today are essentially decorative. They are not meant as dependable instruments and many of them do not serve that purpose. This is not a new state of affairs nor any kind of commentary on our times. Middleton points out in his authoritative *History of Barometers* that this also was the case in the 18th and 19th centuries as well. Barometers have always been popular, but also throughout their history they have not often been used to their full potential, at least by the majority of users.

So the obvious step one—regardless of the style of barometer you desire—is to be sure you choose a device that will meet your needs. If the goal is just to have something that will go up and down, more or less in sync with the actual pressure, and you do not care if the actual values, or even actual rates are accurate, then you can get by with what we might call a "decorative" barometer, electronic or aneroid. Most barometers on the market will function on this level, unless they are outright broken. They cost anywhere from $20 to $500—or more if they have a fancy housing.

Most devices in this category cannot be calibrated, as they do not have dependable behavior. Trying to push such a device to a higher standard will be frustrating and typically unsuccessful.

Precision barometers

Back in Table 4.3-1 we gave the official WMO classification of precision barometers. The discussion in this chapter is intended to give us a way to discuss all barometers, not just the best ones. Thus we can go from the "decorative" category to the complete other end of the spectrum to the category we label "precision barometers." For most of our readers, we guess that this, too, is another category many will not choose. The problem is simply the cost. A precision electronic barometer costs several thousand dollars. The very best aneroid barometers could cost even more, even though their ultimate accuracy is less than the best electronic devices. "Precision" as applied to electronic barometers might be those units with accuracy of better than ±0.2 mb, whereas the word "precision" in aneroid barometers might be thought of as those that are *dependably* better than ±0.8 mb.

For our present purposes, however, we are reserving the description of "precision barometer" to those reference standards used at the NIST along with the several scientific grade electronic units with accuracies better than ±0.15 mb. The accuracy of a precision electronic barometer is beyond the practical needs of most users we address in this book. These devices are intended for official meteorological stations, airports, and various scientific applications. Their quality extends beyond just their extreme accuracy to include long term stability and temperature independence. We expect our repair departments and calibration services to have such instruments, but end users typically will not. Samples of these highest quality precision barometers are shown in Figures 8.1-1 to 8.1-4.

Quality barometers

Thus we are left with a broad range of units between the two extremes of what we have called decorative barometers and precision barometers, which we call simply "quality" barometers. There are no ab-

Figure 8.1-1 *Vaisala PTB330, (7.2" x 4.6" x 2.8"). This is a scientific instrument, with ultra-high accuracy (±0.10 mb) and stability. From Finland. A WMO Class A standard. Price about $2,300.*

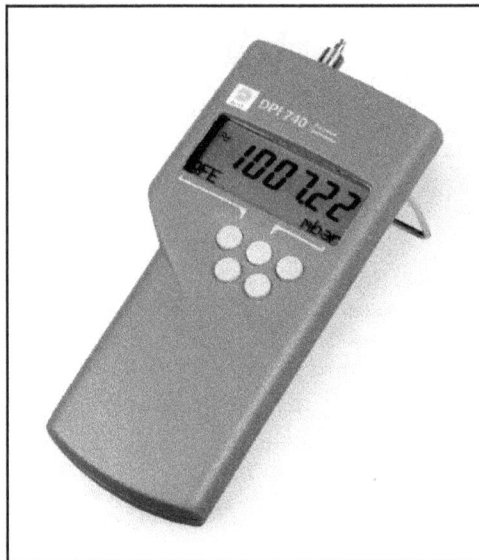

Figure 8.1-2 *GE Druck DPI 740, (7.5" x 3.5" x 1.4"). Another scientific instrument with ultra-high accuracy (±0.14 mb) and stability. It is manufactured in the UK by an American company, GE. Range 745 mb - 1151 mb. A WMO Class A standard. Price about $2,600.*

solute standards implied here, and there is certainly both "quality" and "high-quality" in this category. The category applies to both aneroids and electronic units alike.

The goal is to have a unit that is dependable to within ±1 mb, but twice that uncertainty could be useful in some applications, as we have seen from earlier chapters. It should also be accurate over a reasonable range of likely temperatures, as well as having minimum hysteresis and long term drift. Likewise we have seen that some crucial applications for mariners are not met if the device is much worse than that.

Generally it is easier to find an electronic unit with these specifications than it is an aneroid, but if care is taken with the aneroid selection, that can be achieved as well, and there can indeed be value to the effort in some applications. First there is a certain satisfaction to be had in the use of an accurate instrument that does not depend on batteries and electronic circuits in order to function. You do not have to rely on a computer too long in life to appreciate this. And this is especially true when headed off to sea in a small boat. Ocean-going mariners are accustomed to self-reliance and back-up systems. They practice it from one end of the boat to the other. They are the ones that keep the fine art of celestial navigation alive and

well. Thus our recommendation for mariners would be to have both, a good electronic barometer for ease of use and accuracy and also a quality aneroid with a calibration curve or proven pedigree as a back up and double check.

It is exactly analogous to carrying a sextant to back up the GPS. Then you know if you get cut off from the outside world and eventually use up all your batteries, you still have a way to navigate. The tools are shown in Figures 8.1-5 and 8.1-6.

The same concern applies to your most crucial instrument for monitoring the weather. It might even be more important in this "age of transition" from aneroids to electronic barometers to keep a good marine tested aneroid at hand. Several of the aneroid models have been specifically made for maritime use and are known to withstand the marine environment, whereas many of the new electronic devices have little experience at sea. The combination of warm moist air, salt spray, and the rough ride through a seaway can be detrimental to electronics.

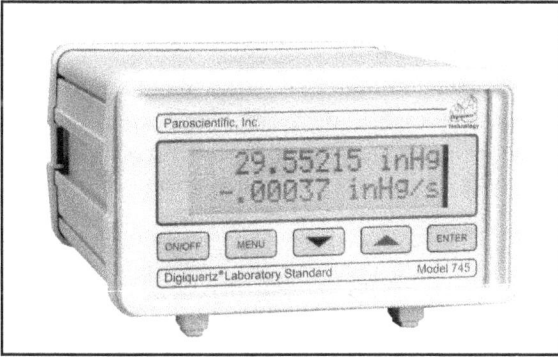

Figure 8.1-3 *Paroscientific Model 745, (6.1"x3.9"x8.2"), a scientific instrument with ultra-high accuracy (±0.08 mb) and a 3 year 0.1 mb/year stability warranty. Range 500 to 1100 mb. Made in Redmond, WA. A WMO Class A standard. Price about $5,800. This instrument is often described as one of the most accurate and most stable barometers in the world outside of the NIST.*

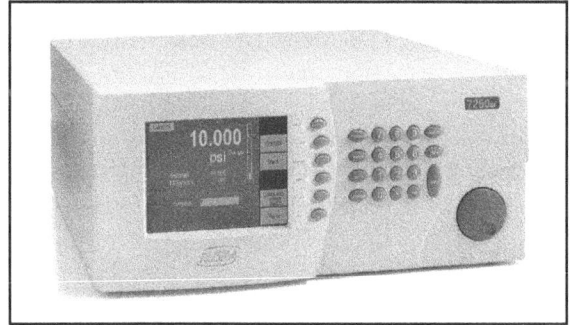

Figure 8.1-4 *GE-Sensing Ruska Model 7050, (7"x16.5"x19"), a scientific instrument with ultra-high accuracy (0.005% of reading = ±0.05 mb at 1000mb) with < 0.0075% annual drift. Ranges custom designed for users. A WMO Class A standard. Price about $14,000. This instrument is often described as one of the most accurate and most stable barometers in the world outside of the NIST. (Shown is a similar looking, but different model.)*

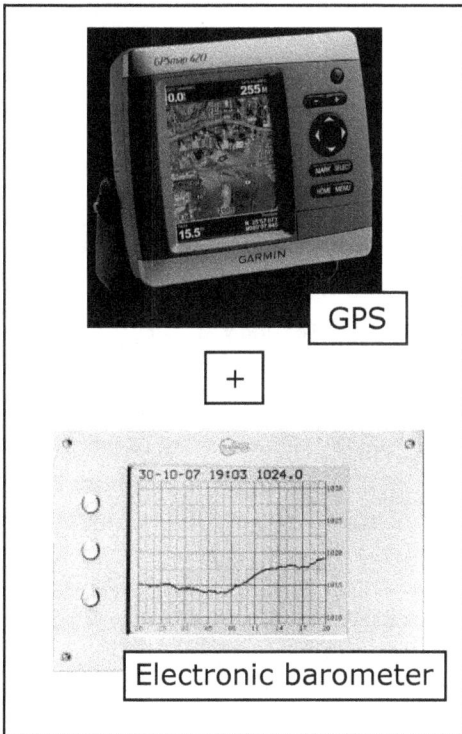

GPS

+

Electronic barometer

Figure 8.1-5 *The electronic solution for navigation and weather. It requires batteries and all circuits functioning. The GPS is a Garmin model; the electronic barometer with graphic display is from Barigo in Germany.*

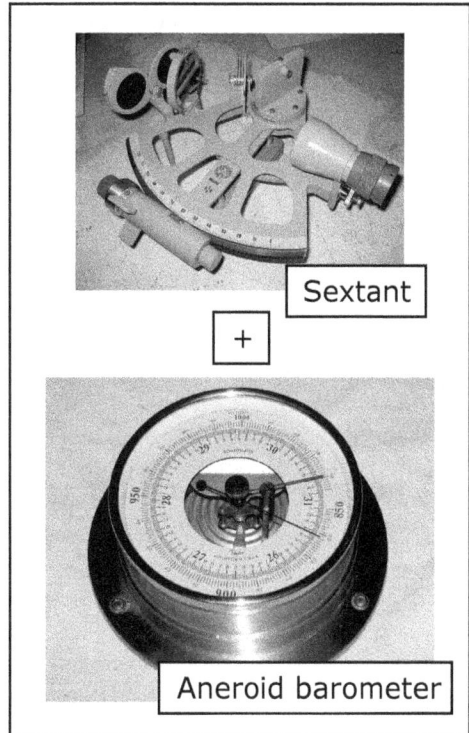

Sextant

+

Aneroid barometer

Figure 8.1-6 *The non-electronic alternative for navigation and weather. No power requirements, no dependence on functioning circuits. The sextant is a German Freiberger model, sometimes called a drum sextant. The barometer is a classic, high-quality Taylor model, refurbished to like-new condition at BarometerMan.com.*

In the next two sections we look at some specific issues in selecting a barometer. To date the advertising specifications of many units, especially the aneroid devices, are not as helpful as we could want. Often the accuracy is not given at all, or it is confused with the reading precision, or specified in an ambiguous manner, such as ±2 mb "over the mid range of the dial," but then not saying what the mid range is. Thus we are left to make the best call possible, and then do our own testing to be sure it is right.

On the other hand, some units, electronic and aneroid, are being sold with a guaranteed certificate of performance provided with them. This is an obvious bonus. But remember if you follow the calibration procedures given here, you can on your own turn a quality instrument into a high quality instrument and maybe save several hundred dollars by doing so.

Price is always a tricky factor when it comes to barometers. There are some outlets that carry only high quality instruments, new or refurbished. The price of their units are usually a true reflection of their value. But more frequently outlets may carry a wide variety of products, spanning the full range from decorative units to high quality units. Over this full spectrum, price is not always a dependable gauge of quality. This is true for both aneroids and electronic units, especially if we consider the electronic barometers that are included with so-called weather stations (barometer, thermometer, and hygrometer, and maybe more.) Some of these may in fact be quite dependable, but they need to be tested.

8.2 Choosing an Aneroid Barometer

Here is a list of items to consider when purchasing an aneroid barometer.

A1. Movement and bellows.

You can't tell very well what is inside an aneroid, even on those with an open face; this takes professional or written verification. Generally, the larger the bellows surface area, the better the device. This is accomplished by adding several individual aneroid cells or using larger single cells. Generally a unit with 4 or 5 cells (as in a barograph) would be more accurate than a unit with 1 or 2 cells. On the other hand, some of the best aneroids ever made have just 1 or 2 large cells.

In many cases, a company offers two barometers of the same size that look very similar, but one is more expensive. Generally, the more expensive one has the better movement in it. These might be referred to as premier, deluxe, etc., but only rarely does the advertising include specific information about the inner workings or the accuracy of the instrument. In some cases, the movement is identical in the expensive and inexpensive versions, with the housing being the determining cost factor. Also it seems that there are only a few factories worldwide making the movements these days, so it could be that models from different sources actually include the same movements, which might account for why they pretty much all look alike from the outside. There is at least one popular source in France and two in Germany.

Again, we cannot tell by looking from the outside, but jeweled movements are superior to those without jewels. Generally they will state it if they have jewelled movements. Some high-quality units point out in their specifications that they contain precision movements with very low friction. Others will have

Table 8.2-1 Belfort 6079 Specifications
Range: 900 to 1060 mb
Accuracy at 70°F
910 - 927 mb = ±1.00 mb
928 - 961 mb = ±0.80 mb
962 - 1030 mb = ±0.65 mb
1031 - 1047 mb = ±0.80 mb
1047 - 1060 mb = ±1.00 mb
Temperature Change Error ±0.015 mb / °F, (+ 30° to + 120°F)
Jeweled movements Sensing element NI-SPAN-C diaphragm
The case is air-tight, with a 1/8-27 NPT vent that can be closed for shipping.
Mirror ring to eliminate parallax errors
Dial Size is 5.4", Weight = 4.6 lbs

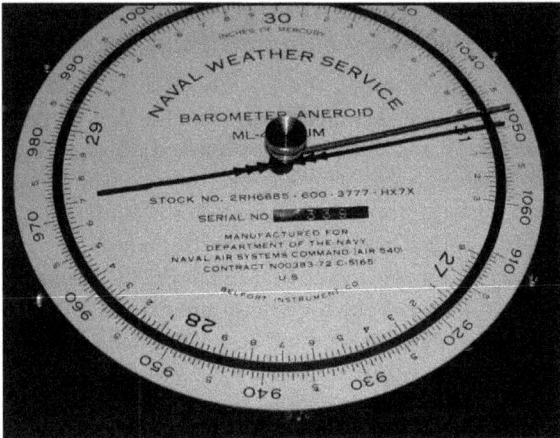

Figure 8.2-1 *Belfort model 6079, one of the top aneroid barometers in the world today. Its accuracy specifications are listed in Table 8.2-1, which serve as a benchmark for all aneroid instruments. It has jeweled movements, and is fully sealed in an aluminum housing with a single pressure input which can be closed off for shipping. They are made in Baltimore, MD. Photo compliments of Merrill Kennedy.*

Figure 8.2-3 *Fischer aneroid from Germany, with a 5.5" dial and a 5-cell movement is among the best of the aneroids available today. This instrument has an accuracy of better than ±0.7 mb over its full working range of 890 to 1050 mb. Fischer aneroids have been used at sea for 60 years. Its double needle design removes parallax error.*

Figure 8.2-2 *Airflo Model 9038 is made specifically for the U.S. Navy by The Airflo Instrument Company of Glastonbury, CT. Surplus instruments are available periodically. Airflo has made precision barometers since the 1970s, including model ML-102 instruments like those featured extensively in the* Manual of Barometry. *Photo compliments of The Airflo Instrument Company.*

Figure 8.2-4 *Yanagi Keigi is the premium barometer from Japan. They are world class instruments, dating from the 1940's. This model has a unique time dial that can be set to label the marker dial with the time it was set. Newer models are from Utsuki Keigi company in Tokyo. Notice this one from a salvaged vessel has a correction to sea level posted as -6.8 hPa, with another note that its elevation is 28m (92 ft). This is a large offset, since the elevation correction would otherwise have been +3.4 hPa. Photo compliments of Manish Ponda.*

to be maintained more frequently. Jerky motion or a sticking needle is a call for maintenance.

A2. Units and Pressure Range

It would be best to have your units of choice on the outer dial, as that would lead to the highest precision in reading. As mentioned earlier, mb (hPa) are best for maritime or international use, but for use on land in the U.S. you might prefer inches.

The pressure range from lowest to highest numbers on the dials of aneroid barometers can be puzzling. Recall that the world record low surface pressure was 870 mb in the center of Typhoon Tip and the world record high surface pressure was 1084 mb in the center of the Siberian High. Thus one might argue that this range 870 to 1084 mb (25.7" to 32.0") might be a reasonable range to cover for units to be used at sea level. That would cover all the cases ever heard of.

But if you cover that broad of a range (214 mb) you sacrifice a lot of reading precision for pressures you are very likely never going to see. More typical extreme pressures are 950 to 1050 mb, which is only a 100-mb span. If this were the full range on the dial instead of the record range, then the space between each mb tick on the dial would be 2.14 times wider, and we could get more precise readings.

Logic, however, does not seem to dominate the dials. You will see all sorts of ranges. The ideal for sea level would be something like 950 to 1050 mb, which is the same as 28" to 31", and sure enough some units are made this way. Often you also see 27.5 to 31.5, which is another good choice.

Sometimes you see models referred to as "high sensitivity" because they spread the full dial size over just 28.5" to 30.5". This is 965 to 1032 mb, which is low enough but frankly not quite high enough. Check Chapter 10 data to see that much of the world experiences pressure well over 1032 fairly frequently. This would be better at 31.0 (1050).

Keep in mind that some barometers are specifically made for high elevations, meaning the dial goes to very low pressures. This would be required if you live at high elevation (see Table 3.1-1), but not very useful for sea level work. It won't hurt anything, it just

reminds us that an expanded scale matching sea-level ranges would lead to higher precision in the reading.

Strangely enough, the FitzRoy aneroid from the late 1800's that was specifically called a "Fisherman's barometer" was almost always marked down to 26", some times to 25". The low end here is way below anything to be seen when fishing. Perhaps this was an early attempt at a multi-tasking instrument that could also serve as an altimeter, in those days called "mountain barometers." The highest mountain in the British Isles is Ben Bevis in Scotland at 4,400 ft, which would be at 862 mb = 25.5 inches.

A3. Accuracy

As mentioned throughout, our goal is to know the pressure to within ±1 mb. This is frankly going to be difficult to achieve with a common aneroid device, but is achievable with a calibration curve. There are high-quality aneroids on the market that come with a calibration curve demonstrating their accuracy, and others can be calibrated on your own. If you are considering aneroids as a back up to an electronic unit, a dependable ±2 mb aneroid could meet that need, but a higher quality one is still preferred. In any event, a calibration curve is needed.

Table 8.2-2 Star names in the used-barometer constellation*	
Airflo	U.S.
Belfort	U.S.
Bendix	U.S.
Fischer	Germany
Frieze	U.S.
Fuess	Germany
Kollsman	U.S.
Lufft	Germany
Taylor	U.S.
Wallace & Tiernan	U.S.
Yanagi / Utsuki	Japan

* **Table Notes** *These are models in production for 50 years or more. If you see one of these units on the used barometer market and you are assured it is in working or repairable condition, then you can be confident it is a high quality device. This list includes the best aneroid barometers available. Several are still in production.*

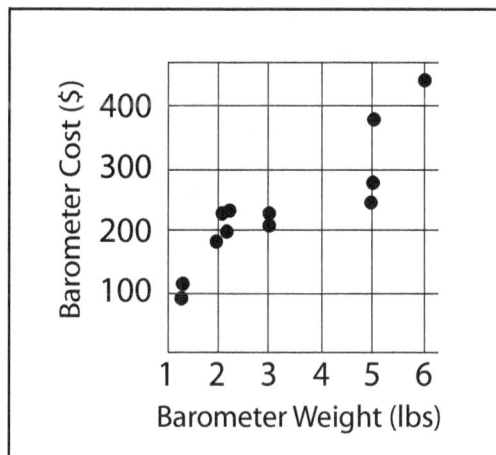

Figure 8.2-5 *Weight versus cost for all barometers in one particular catalog from about 1990. This is not science! — just an informal way to show that barometer cost is often in the price of the brass.*

But even with a calibration, we must start off with a quality device, and as mentioned, this is not always easy to determine. A few units do in fact come with a stated accuracy. I have seen them from about ±1 mb up to about ±3 mb. Some say nothing more. Some

say "over the mid range of the dial" without defining mid range. However, I have also purchased units that did not give these specifications at all, and yet I was able to measure a calibration curve that rendered the readings accurate to about ±1 mb over the full working range.

On the other hand, there are a few proven aneroid brands that do come with certificates of accuracies better than ±0.7 mb, that have withstood the test of time at sea.

Chapter 4 explained how to do a calibration yourself over a period of time, using the pressures nature gives you, or using a tall building or ride to the mountains, but there are also commercial services at reasonable costs that provide that curve for you using test equipment. Thus if you buy an instrument for $200 and pay $100 for a calibration curve, then you can think of it simply as buying a higher quality instrument for $300, which would be an exceptional price for a calibrated barometer.

Besides specifying accuracy as an actual number of mb, such as ±1.5 mb, you will occasionally see accuracy specified as percentage of full scale (FS) or as a percentage of working range. So an instrument stating

Table 8.2-3 Samples of Aneroid Barometers with Published Accuracy*						
Brand	*Model*	*Accuracy*	*Dial dia.*	*Range (mb)*	*Cost*	*Manufacturer/Source*
Barigo	1500	±1 mb	5"	950 - 1075	$500	www.barigo.de
Belfort	6079	±0.65 mb	5.5"	910 - 1060	$5,800	www.digiwx.com
Fischer	103-001	±0.7 mb	5"	890 - 1050	$650	www.starpath.com/fischer
Fuess	15PMN	±0.7 mb	5"	910-1090	$1,700	www.rfuess-mueller.de
Lufft	2187.70692	±2.7 mb	5"	870- 1050	$995	www.lufft.de
Maximum	Proteus	±2.7 mb	4.5"	930 - 1066	$400	www.maximum-inc.com
Oakton	03316-70	±1 mb	4.5"	930 - 1070	$273	www.4oakton.com
Robert White	BAP-111	±1.7 mb	4.5"	930 - 1066	$250	www.robertwhite.com
Wallace-Tiernan	FA-160426	±0.6 mb	6"	880 - 1066	$3,400	www.bucksales.com
Weems & Plath	Atlantis	±2 mb	4"	965 - 1033	$328	www.weems-plath.com

* Table Notes *The only requirements to be listed here are published accuracy specifications and currently in production for the public. Several companies listed offer several models with accuracy specifications. There are other high-quality instruments as accurate as some of these, but they do not publish accuracy specifications. Note too, that the fact that the specifications are given here does not guarantee that the instrument is as accurate as advertised. In some cases, a design or model type is capable of the specifications, but not all examples on the market meet the specifications. All barometers must be tested, and as needed, calibrated using the methods of Chapter 4. A barometer advertised at one level could in practice be more accurate with use of a good calibration curve.*

accuracy of ±1.5% of *full range*, with a range of 870 to 1050 mb, would mean 0.015 x (1050-870) = ±2.7 mb. If the accuracy were presented as 0.2% of *full scale*, then this one would be 0.002 x 1050 = ±2.1 mb.

A4. Access to set screw and setting

Most aneroids on the market today have the set screw on the back, so the issue of how to access this once mounted arises. There are several solutions. The most awkward is you have to unscrew it from the wall to get to the set screw. Check this issue on the model you are considering. Others are built into a threaded cylinder, so you grab the whole unit and turn it to remove it from the mount attached to the wall. Still others are built like a port light, with hinges so you can loosen a knob and then rotate it open. Some of the early high precision Navy barometers had the adjustment screw on the side, directly accessible.

Also, it is very valuable to ask the sales person to demonstrate setting the barometer. Just choose a desired pressure different than on the dial and ask to see it set there. On some units this works very well, others it is almost impossible to set to a desired pressure. If you cannot set it to the pressure you choose, right on the money, then that is a problem. I would look for a different model, or maybe a different sample of the same model would behave differently.

A5. Dials, needles, and scales

A large dial face is preferable because it is easier to read. Generally, a 4-inch diameter should be considered minimum. Five- or 6-inch diameters are better, but they are more expensive, and increasingly more rare. The ones that are 3 inches or less across are just too small to read. And in all cases, thin needles are much preferred over wide needles.

It's best to have the outer scale be in the units you prefer for daily work, which as we have stressed would be millibars or hPa for maritime work. The outermost scale is the one that is spread out the most and easiest to read.

Also, strange as it may seem, check that you can actually read the dial though the glass. I have seen one model that would almost pass muster at just 3.5 inches diameter with mb on the outside edge; but then there was a decorative bevel cut in the glass along the outer edge, right over the scale, that essentially prevented it from being read!

And finally, also in the category of "why do we have to say this," check that the needle actually crosses the scale you wish to use. In some units you find a nice mb scale along the outer edge, marked every mb, but the needle does not reach to the scale. It is as if that scale is there for decoration alone, and they want you to use the inside scale. It is not easy to read the dial when you have to visually project the needle forward to be on the scale.

A6. Dial labels

As discussed in Section 5.1, the labels on the dial (Rain, Change, Fair, etc) do not have much significance and should not be considered a factor in choice. Furthermore, they won't really vary that much from one unit to the other, outside of the two systems discussed earlier. If, on the other hand, you run across a unit with labels that do not match either of these traditional ones, that might be a cause to pause.

On the other hand, the very best, as well as several other high quality instruments, have no such labels at all, and one quality German model has a line at 1013 with an arrow to the left saying *Tief* and one to the right saying *Hoch* (Low and High), which is fair enough. There are no real rules on this.

A7. Dial surface

A shiny or silvered face sometimes acts like a mirrored dial so you can tell from looking at the reflection of the needle whether or not you are properly aligned when reading it. Some of the best barometers, however, come with flat black or white dials, which do not allow for this trick. As noted earlier, reading errors of up to 0.5 mb are easily possible from this parallax problem, which is an even bigger concern for smaller units. If the dial has a mirror strip to eliminate parallax, that is usually a sign of a quality instrument.

A8. Temperature compensation

Temperature compensation is mandatory if the instrument will be exposed to significantly varying temperatures. Typically the instrument will be in actual use in at least a semi-controlled environment, but temperatures could easily vary from 60°F at higher latitudes to over 100°F below deck in the tropics. It is not easy to test for temperature effects, so it is best to have a unit that offers some specifications on this. One of the main differences between quality instruments and decorative ones is the level of their temperature compensation.

A9. Housing

Traditionally, barometers made for boats have heavy brass housings, usually with a matching clock. These are nice looking, but not very practical. They add weight to the boat and cost to the instruments. A racing sailboat, for example, would instead prefer a very light-weight housing. Any brass on this instrument is purely decoration that can add up to 3 or 4 pounds to the boat without serving any function.

Some very high quality barometers come in relatively lightweight brass housings, whereas some elegant heavy brass housings encase low quality movements. Some time ago there were good units in lightweight acrylic housings, but I have not seen these in a while. In short, other than for decorative purposes, the housing does not matter, and cannot be used to evaluate the quality of an instrument. An exception are some military aneroids meant for use in the field, and these typically have written specs calling for heavy housing—even in this case the logic is not entirely clear, unless the idea is to protect it from things falling on it.

A10. Cost and Where to Buy

The price of an aneroid barometer does not guarantee its quality, but the inverse is more dependably true. A high quality aneroid is not cheap. It is hard to guess actual costs since there is such a range of instruments available. Some quality instruments sell for as low as $250 or $300, others for twice that, or ten times that. Generally once into the high-quality category, you do get what you pay for. Some refurbished older units that sell for $300 to $800 were originally instruments that sold for four times that much, and they work just as well now as then.

Also keep in mind one of the main messages of this book. The value of barometer calibration. Sometimes a careful calibration can turn a $200 barometer into one that is effectively worth $600. The difference

might simply be with the one you make your known corrections at various readings and the other one does not need corrections. Besides, you should do this calibration procedure no matter what the instrument costs, so it is in that sense not even extra work.

An instrument maker or repair shop that sells barometers is usually the best place to look for a quality aneroid barometer. Several of the oldest stores in the country are nautical instrument makers, in continuous business for 100 years or more. They know the best units and can explain the features and virtues to you along with comparison with other models. There are also antique dealers who specialize in barometers and who are experts in the devices, as well as retired Navy barometer experts who carry on their trade in private business.

And there are numerous other outlets for both mariners and weather buffs who have taken the time to learn the history and nuances of good units. Hopefully the background obtained from this book will help you evaluate the purchase setting and options you have available.

Used or refurbished Army, Navy, or NWS (called Weather Bureau originally) surplus barometers are another option to consider as they become available. In any event, a reliable professional source familiar with the instruments is crucial. Buying from those not trained in barometers could be risky. Names of some famous brands of high quality instruments are listed in Table 8.2-2.

And the punch line is, how do you know you have a good one (regardless of how you came about it)? Answer, do a calibration as outlined in Chapter 4. That is the *sine qua non* of every barometer.

8.3 Choosing an Electronic Barometer

At first it might seem easier to select an electronic barometer than it is to select an aneroid one. At least we do not have to worry about the size of the mb divisions on the scale or whether or not the needle reaches the scale. And we also won't have anywhere near the number to choose from. There are hundreds of models of decorative aneroids, with the few high quality units almost hiding among them. There are

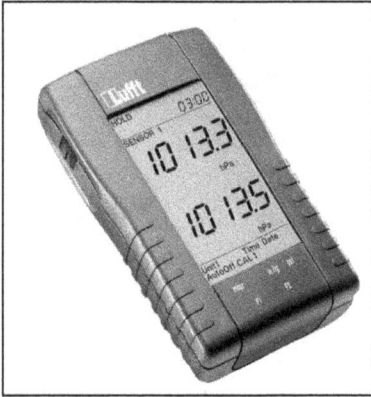

Figure 8.3-1 *Lufft electronic, C300, Germany. Has dual pressure ports and real-time clock. 6" x 3.3" x 1.5"*

Figure 8.3-2 *Castle Group Electronics, GA690, U.K.. 4.2" x 2.6" x 1.2"*

Figure 8.3-3 *Control Traceable 1870, U.S.. 4" x 3" x 1". Has PC output.*

much fewer electronic units to be considered, depending on the application, and typically their product descriptions are more specific. Only the best aneroids come with any documentation at all.

Nevertheless, there are still a lot of criteria to consider, many of which are the same as with the aneroids. Accuracy remains the key factor, but unlike many aneroids, the accuracies of electronic units are almost always given in their specifications. Here again are some points to keep in mind when making your selection.

E1. Accuracy and stability

Not counting the very best aneroids, affordable electronic barometers offer the potential to be more accurate and dependable than typical aneroid barometers, but this is by no means guaranteed. And there are numerous nuances to knowing what to expect from the printed specifications.

Some manufacturers list the inherent accuracy of the internal pressure sensor as being the accuracy of the final device, but this is not valid without special care and quality control. The very design of the circuit board could influence the final output of the device. There are also internal calibration constants that need to be checked or adjusted to obtain the optimum accuracy of the sensor.

Though it is rather rare to witness such a demonstration, if you have an outlet selling an electronic ba-

rometer with a quoted absolute pressure accuracy of ±0.5 mb and you are looking at several of them, all set internally the same way, with displayed pressures that vary by ±2 mb, then you know that the published accuracy is inherently incorrect. On the other hand, it might not be so bad as it seems. This could be a simple matter of quality control. In such an experiment, you may find that if you remove the highest and lowest one or two showing, the remainder then fall well within the published accuracy.

This test does not mean the pressure is right on the "good ones," it just shows that the specs are not rigorously correct. The units could all still be perfectly good if they have a set option. The key issue with electronic barometers is often not so much their absolute accuracy, straight out of the box, but rather their linearity and stability. If a unit has a quoted absolute accuracy of just ±2 mb, but it has a guaranteed linearity of ±0.2 mb over its full working range, then once you

Figure 8.3-4 *Fischer model 1500. Shows pressure to the tenth of a mb in LED. Range 900 to 1050. Accuracy is ±0.5 mb. Size 5.6" x 5.6" x 2.5". Includes analog voltage out as well as display.*

take the trouble to set it accurately you then have a working accuracy of much more like ±0.2 mb. We will come back to this important point.

Before continuing with the mundane issues of earthly barometers, refer back to Figures 8.1-1 to 8.1-4 to see what the stars look like. These represent the state of the art, the industry standards worldwide in electronic barometers. They are scientific instruments, not what most of us would choose for our barometer needs. They are here to show what the benchmark specifications look like.

E2. Readout precision

Most electronic barometers on the commercial market read out the pressure to the nearest millibar or to the nearest hundredth of an inch. As explained in Section 3.3, these are not the same precision. The inches display (precise to 0.01″) is about 3 times more precise than the millibar display (1 mb = 0.03″).

The ideal, however, would be to have the millibar (hPa) display reading in tenths of a mb. Then if the unit had options of hundredths of an inch or tenths of a mb, the mb scale would then be about 3 times more precise. The display with a precision of 0.1 mb is preferred because that is the WMO and NWS standard for recording and reporting atmospheric pressure.

Furthermore, this is a level of observation that I have confirmed over many years of practice on land and underway as valuable for early detection of pressure changes. This is just one more data point in support of the WMO-NWS standard pressure precision, but in the personal observations I referred to this has a broader significance.

A broader significance in this regard: I am recording and caring about the tenths of a mb on devices that I know for certain are inherently not accurate to that precision. In other words, when we write down 1028.7 mb, we do not bet the farm that this is the exact pressure to the tenth. In fact, most of these past units have been calibrated and found to be reliable to only about ±1 mb. So if I wanted to be formally correct, I might record the pressure as 1028.7 ±1 mb, which is really the same as 1029 ±1 mb. The reason for keeping and stressing the tenths however, is the experience that they do indeed show an early indication of the trends.

When the environmental pressure is rising for some reason it does not just bounce straight up by 1 or 2 mb units. That would be very rare. Of course it looks like that if you only show whole mb units, but in practice with a higher precision readout you will see the real pressure change by the tenth. In very slow changes, these tenths give you a much earlier warning than if you had to wait for a full mb change—or more precisely 0.5 mb change, since they are rounded. In some tactical situations, this early warning is quite valuable.

Furthermore, having the tenths displayed helps tremendously with getting an accurate calibration.

Figure 8.3-5 *Vion 4000 from France. Size 4.5″x5.5″x1.3″. Price is about $140, published accuracy ±1 mb, linearity ±0.2 mb.*

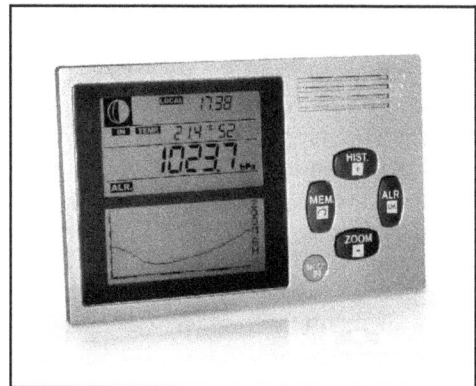

Figure 8.3-6 *Weems-Plath 4002. Size 4.5″x6″x1.3″. Price is about $190, published accuracy ±0.5 mb, linearity ±0.2 mb. Many versatile options, menu driven.*

Most sources of accurate pressure give the pressure to the tenth, so if you are recording to the tenth as well, you will home in on a more accurate calibration curve more quickly. This is not to say you cannot get an accurate curve with just whole mb readouts. If you average a lot of data, you effectively learn the corrections to better than 1 mb. But the process goes faster if you an work in tenths.

With a low priced electronic barometer that shows tenths of a mb it is best to check that they are stable. I have seen two different models that have more jitter in this his decimal place than nature has. In contrast, some average over larger time intervals, which stabilize the display, but they miss sudden changes. Moving the instrument up and down 12 feet should show you a 0.44 mb shift and show you the averaging time in the process.

Again the issue of linearity is related. If the device is linear to ±0.15 mb, then even though the absolute accuracy is off by 2 mb before you set it, once you set it right, you can start believing what you see within that linearity uncertainty. In this example, any change of ±0.2 mb should be real.

It is a waste of a high precision linearity if you cannot read the dial to a high precision. Figures 8.3-5 and 8.3-6 show two low-priced units from France that show the pressure to the tenth of a mb.

Note that from a practical point of view, there is no advantage to go to even higher precision, such as 0.01 mb, as shown on the high precision units. In many practical applications, this would be too much. That last digit would be undergoing quite natural oscillations with pulses in the local pressure, zephyrs of warm or cold air, or even the ship going up and down in the waves. Recall the jingle for elevation corrections, "point four four per floor " meaning 12 feet (a floor) is 0.44 mb. So 3 feet change is 0.11 mb. Even an essentially calm sea will oscillate at 0.03 mb.

E3. Range

Unlike an aneroid device, you can't tell the pressure range covered by an electronic barometer by just looking at it. It shows the present pressure but not the end points. All electronic devices, however, also have a set working range, just as aneroids do. The full working range should be given in the specifications. It is valuable to know this for several reasons.

For one, if you live at high elevation you want to be sure it will work there, and related to that, if it does work at pressure altitudes of 10,000 feet or so (700 mb) you can feel more confident in it's ability to go for a plane ride. Table 3.1-1 itemized high-elevation barometers ranges.

Another reason for knowing the working range is some units specify the accuracy as some percentage of the full range. If you do not know the range, you cannot figure the quoted accuracy. Some companies refer to percentage of "full scale" or "FS," but actually they mean full range. In short, you may have to check with them to clarify the definition.

And finally the full range gives you some measure of the sensitivity of the unit. Although it is difficult to make specific estimates, it seems a unit with a working range of say 800 to 1060 mb should be more sensitive than one with a range of 50 to 2000 mb. Some of the sensors used for atmospheric pressures are actually sensitive pressure gauges over very wide ranges of pressures. Since accuracy or electronic sensors is often a percentage of the range covered, when you can choose the working range you wish, it is best to choose one to match the atmospheric range.

For example, if you have a unit with accuracy of 0.25% of full range, it will have twice as good accuracy for 800 to 1000 mb (±0.75 mb) compared to a 500 to 1100 mb (±1.5 mb). Put another way, if you need one to work at both high elevations and sea level, you may have to sacrifice some level of accuracy.

E4 Temperature dependence

All electronic pressure sensors are sensitive to the temperature of the device. Most units monitor the temperature of the sensor and control the output to minimize this effect. In that sense, most electronic barometers are also electronic thermometers, and some capture this reading and display it, but not all.

Most units specify the accuracy of the device at one specific temperature and then provide a range of errors that might occur at other temperatures away from this calibration temperature. (This is also true for aneroid devices, but we very rarely get this level of

Table 8.3-1 Accuracy vs. Temperature — Brand 1	
Temperature (°F)	Accuracy (mb)
+59 to +77	±0.3
+32 to +104	±0.6
-4 to +113	±1.0
-40 to +140	±1.5.

Table 8.3-2 Accuracy vs. Temperature — Brand 2	
Temperature (°F)	Accuracy (mb)
+68	±0.6
+32 to +104	±1.2
-4 to +122	±2.0
-40 to +140	±2.5

specification with them.) Another way to specify temperature dependence is to give separate accuracies for different temperature ranges. Top of the line models offer the types of specifications shown in Tables 8.3-1 and 8.3-2

We see that even in the top of the line models, once you leave the normal temperature range, the accuracy suffers, but you have to go to extremes in temperature or pressure to have an effect. If we looked at the actual data showing pressure ranges as well, it would not look so bad. The temperature deviations typically occur at the extreme ends of the pressure ranges.

Other more modest units might specify the effect this way: accuracy is ±0.5 mb at 68°F and then temperature uncertainty adds ±0.02 mb/°F different from 68. So at 40°F, the uncertainty would increase to (68-40) x 0.02 = 0.56 + 0.5 = ±1.1 mb at 40°F.

These days, even the most basic sensors are well compensated for ambient temperature so long as we remain in normal temperatures and are working with normal atmospheric pressures. If you live at a high elevation or you take your barometer into a mine or cave, then you might check this more carefully, but generally the temperature effect in normal conditions is not a major factor in modern electronic barometers.

E5. Numerical display

Not all digital displays are the same. Some are LCD (liquid crystal display) and some are LED (light emitting diodes). The former can be large or relatively small. They can be back lighted or not. Back lighting is a definite battery drain, and some of these back-lighting options are very faint at best, so you still need a flashlight to read them in dim light. After several

hundred years of unlighted aneroid barometer usage, it is hard to think of back lighting as a required option. The LEDS, on the other hand are bright and sharp, but sometimes the numbers are not very big. Nevertheless, in some pilot houses at night, these displays may be too bright. This is something to consider if they might be in view of the helmsman.

In many applications, the size of the numbers is the key issue, and a couple of units stand out nicely for having very large numbers. The large dials that you can see across the room or across the pilothouse are a big virtue to those who want to keep on top of the pressure. Equally valuable is some icon or graphic that lets you know the pressure trend also from across the room. On the other hand, we recommend that the instruments be mounted near the nav station or your working desk at home so you see them even when the numbers are not oversized. Figure 8.3-7 shows samples of big numbers in a simple display and smaller numbers in a more complex display.

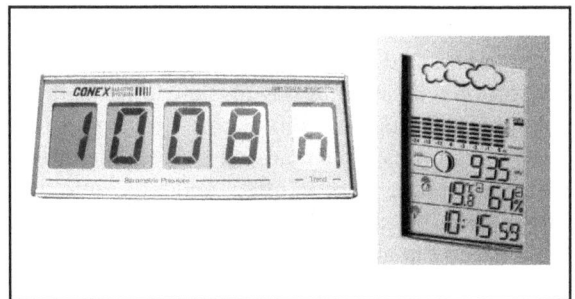

Figure 8.3-7 *A simple display and a complex display. The digits on the left are about 1.5 " tall, the ones on the right are about 0.5" tall. On the left we see the pressure and the trend, falling rapidly in this case. On the right we see the pressure, a bar graph of past values, cloud icons, phase of the moon, battery meter, temperature, humidity, time including seconds, as well as an alarm icon.*

E6. Sampling rate

The sampling rate is how often the device measures the pressure and displays it. Unlike an aneroid which is continuously updating the pressure displayed, an electronic unit must take a measurement and do some computations and then activate the display. The more often they do this, the more power they consume. Thus there is some compromise called for on battery operated units.

In the present market that we know of, the sampling rate varies from 6 seconds to 15 minutes. Many run at a compromise value of 1 or 2 minutes. Most tell you this rate. Strangely, some others do not. It is particularly tricky to set and calibrate a barometer if you do not know how often it is updating!

Frankly, for most practical applications the 15-minute reading would do, but this long period can make it more difficult to calibrate—all of the tricks, for example, like going up and down a tall building do not work for a slow sampling rate.

Also note that if you are experiencing a meteorological bomb, with a pressure drop rate of about 24 mb in 24 hr, then this is 0.25 mb per 15 minutes, and we are missing a lot of the action if we just get to read it every 15 minutes.

Some versatile units let you program the sampling rate which could be a valuable option. In any event, we need to know what it is. A minute or less would be nice.

E7. Battery operation

As mentioned above, battery life can be directly proportional to sampling rate in some units. Without using backlighting or audio alarms, you might find one unit that gets more than a year from one or two batteries. Sample twice as often, and this same unit might decrease battery life to 6 months. Backlights and buzzers can also eat up the batteries.

But the key point to look for with battery operation is a low-battery warning of some kind. Most of the sensors behave erratically when the battery voltage begins to fall off. If you do not have a warning to change batteries, you may go through a period with wrong pressures.

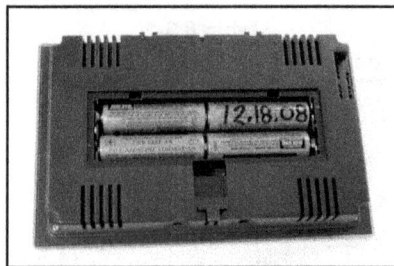

Figure 8.3-8 *A simple note on the batteries marking when new ones were installed can be a big asset to learning about battery life and help you avoid running out at an inopportune time.*

In some cases, you can tell if the batteries are low because the LCD (liquid crystal display) starts getting weak (lower contrast). But by that time you may already have lost some accuracy.

With that said, we must note that there are a couple units on the market that are otherwise excellent dependable devices, but they do not have low-battery warning. This is a known issue with each of them. With these units, and with any battery operated instrument, it is good policy to use high-quality batteries and mark the date on them when you install them (Figure 8.3-8). This way you gain knowledge on how long they last.

Some battery operated units also offer an optional AC or DC power source, which is a safer way to avoid accuracy changes with battery life.

E8. Pressure adjustments

The option to adjust the pressure on an electronic barometer is fundamental. Without such an adjust-

Table 8.3-3 Sample Scientific-grade High-accuracy Electronic Barometers*			
Brand	*Model*	*Price*	*Accuracy*
GE Ruska	7050i	$14,000	0.003%
Paroscientific	745	$5,700	±0.08 mb
Vaisala	PTB-330	$2,470	±0.10 mb
GE Druck	DPI-740	$2,600	±0.14 mb
MKS Baratron	120AA	$3,650	±0.05%

* *These instruments each have unique specifications that affect their function and price, which is only estimated here. Two give accuracy as percentage of reading.*

ment, you cannot set it to a desired pressure, so no matter what you choose to show on the dial, you will have to make corrections for every reading. It is by far best to be able to set the device to the type of pressure you want to read (sea level or station).

Most units have some option for adjusting the pressure, but some are much easier to use than others. In some units, there is one button, maybe marked "calibrate," or "set," and you just push it and the displayed pressure starts slowly up. Stop and press it again, and it starts slowly down, and so on till you get it to exactly what you want. Alternatively, you may have to step through a long menu system, and then find the option to change the pressure using generic [+] and [-] keys on the device.

Still other units do not let you change the pressure itself, but you can change a stored elevation in the device, which in turn changes the displayed pressure according to Laplace's *hypsometric equation* (Appen-

dix 3). This is the least favorable option since some of these are limited to 10-meter steps, which is fairly crude on the mb scale (10 m = 1.2 mb). The best option is both elevation input and a pressure offset option.

In short, a key question to answer before purchase is how you set the device to a desired pressure.

E9. Altitude input

If you have the option to set the pressure (E8) then it does not really matter if you have an altitude input or not. Those that do have an altitude input sometimes offer the option to display sea-level pressure or station pressure, but you have to check this to see exactly how it works.

In some units, for example, once you enter an altitude, the one and only display on the device will increase accordingly. These make the assumption that

Table 8.3-4 Samples of Electronic Barometers*						
Brand	Model	Price	Published Accuracy	Range	Precision	Comments
Barigo	2055	$1080	±1 mb	940-1070	0.1 mb	Includes hi-res trace
Castle	GA690	$130	±3 mb	100-1300	1 mb	Has calibration option
Conex	JBD1	$190	±1 mb	700-1060	1 mb	Super large digits
Control	1870	$153	±5 mb	795-1050	1 mb	Has PC output
Davis	Perception II	$180	±1.7 mb	880-1080	0.1 mb	PC/MAC connect option
Fischer	3312	$811	±0.5 mb	900-1050	0.1 mb	Includes analog output
Luft	C300	$490	±0.5 mb	750-1100	0.1 mb	Max, min, and avg. values
Ramsey	UP24B	$300	±1 mb	700-1060	0.01 mb	Includes history trace, and other features
MetroGraf		$1300	±0.5 mb	940-1070	0.1 mb	Inkless paper trace
Trintec	EB14	$150	±0.5 mb	985-1045	0.2 mb	10" analog dial
Weems-Plath	4002	$188	±0.5 mb	617-1060	0.1 mb	History trace and other features
Greisinger	GPB3300	$150	± 2 mb	300-1100	0.1 mb	Adjustable readout
Vion	A4000	$100	±1 mb	617-1060	0.1 mb	Includes history trace

*Each of these instruments has its own unique features. This table cannot be used to evaluate one model over the the other. Prices are all approximate. To be included here requires only a published accuracy and current availability. All units can be set to the proper pressure, so the unlisted linearity of the instrument is the key to accurate output. Temperature behavior is also a crucial factor not listed here.

you want to show sea level pressure all the time. This is essentially the same scheme that uses the altitude as the only way to set the pressure.

Other units let you enter an altitude and then use it or not, as you choose. With these you can toggle between station pressure and sea-level pressure, usually with some icon on the front to indicate the mode you are in. The most versatile programming lets you not just enter an elevation, but also enter an offset of the displayed pressure. This is best because generally you will not know your elevation to the precision of the barometer, so that last tweak on accuracy is done manually once you learn the correction from the procedures of Chapter 4.

E10. History option

An electronic barometer that stores and displays, or lets you step through, past pressures is an electronic barograph. There are almost as many ways to show the history as there are models that have this option. If you see two that are the same, chances are they have the same sensor and control circuit in them—essentially the same product from different companies.

The value of this history depends on your application. If you are recording the pressure daily, or hourly, then this is not crucial, but the display itself could be informative. Samples can be seen in Figures 8.3-5 and 8.3-6, as well as 8.1-1 and 8.3-3. See also Figures 1.2-11 and 1.2-12. The model shown in Figure 8.3-11 is unique in that it prints the history on a paper chart, just as aneroid barographs do.

Normally we recommend recording the pressure every watch (4 hours) when underway, but in changing conditions, every 1 hour might be called for. In these cases, having this much interaction with your barometer plus having your written record reduces the need for the electronic history. But still, if you anchor out overnight, you are not recording the pressure, and you might want to know what took place overnight. This record in that case is very helpful. The same argument could apply to a barometer at home, but at home we can always check the Internet for pressure histories if we do not have it on our own unit.

Some units have a fixed display, others allow you to zoom the history display, so you can look at the past 2 hours, or the past 48 hr (refer back to Figure 1.2-11).

Also of interest is exactly what pressures are the devices storing? Some, for example, measure the pressure every 1 minute, but when you step back through the history you see just one pressure for each hour. These are either the value at that past hour, or they are the average of the 30m before and after that specific hour. This is not often explained in the manuals, so you have to figure it out from your own records.

There are also different ways to display the times of the past pressures. Some have a user adjustable clock, so they can show pressures at specific times in the past. Others that also have clock time showing, only show relative values of past pressures, such as -1h, -2h, etc. In this format, the pressures are not listed with specific times. All of these are options to investigate when evaluating the history function.

E11. Alarm options

Most electronic barometers offer some level of pressure alarm, which means if the pressure changes faster than a certain rate, the instrument either makes a sound or blinks something on the dial. These are a mixed blessing, useful in some circumstances, annoying in others. In all cases they are a drain to the battery. In Section 5.5 on pressure trends we outlined some of the conventional change rates used for these alarms. It boils down to how fast a drop or rise do you want to set off the alarm.

As with the history option, there are many solutions and approaches to this function. Some are fixed, with no choice but to turn it on or off; others have two levels of alarms, and in fact let you program the rate that sets off the alarm.

For those putting the barometer into the pilothouse or nav station of a vessel, remember you likely have half a dozen instruments near it that also have alarms, so you want to be sure that the pressure alarm is showing something prominent on the face of the dial so you know which instrument is sending the alarm.

E12. Other Options

The modern trend in electronics is to have single units serve many functions. Our cell phone these days might also be our camera, music player, and GPS. It might even have a barometer in it! Our radio dial

Figure 8.3-9 *Trintec EB14 from Canada. A unique and effective combination of a large analog dial (6" to 14") connected to an electronic pressure sensor with a precision motor. Dial can be interpolated to within few tenths of a mb, published accuracy is ±1 mb over full range, but linearity is much higher, resulting in higher practical accuracy. Similar movements also available in marine housing. Prices begin at $150, depending on housing.*

Figure 8.3-10 *Davis Instruments Perception II barometer with temperature and humidity, about $150. Has a PC connect option ($150). One output can be selected for a precision display. A popular and long-tested instrument.*

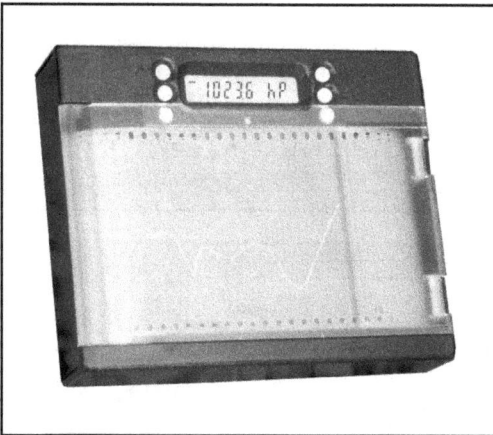

Figure 8.3-11 *Metrograf from Switzerland. A unique combination of electronic sensor with a paper print out. 5.75" x 4.75" x 1.4" Range 940 to 1070 mb, linearity of ±0.5mb or better. Numerical pressure display to 0.1 mb. Price about $1,300.*

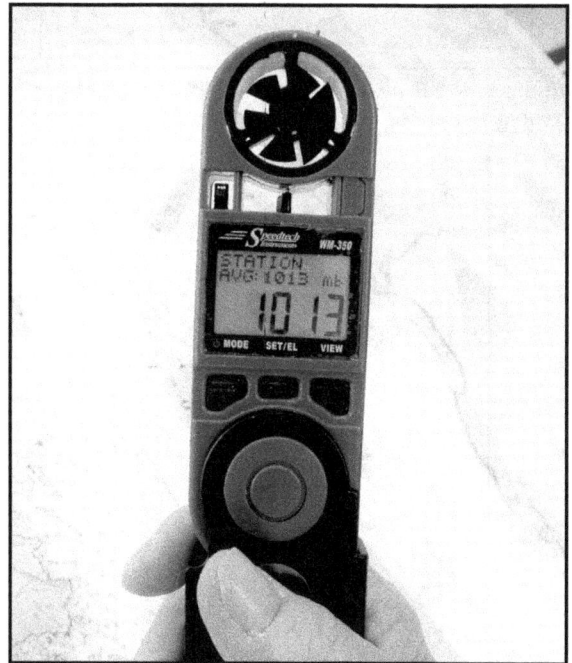

Figure 8.3-12 *SpeedTech WM-350, hand-held weather station with published pressure accuracy of ±1.5 mb over the range 300 to 1100 mb. It has both pressure offset and elevation input. Can display inches or mb. Updates every second. Pressure recording interval selectable from 5 min to 12 hr. Also includes wind speed, temperature, humidity, and a digital compass.*

might be how we set the temperature in the car, or see who is calling us on our cell phone. These days when you look at the radar on your boat, it might be telling you the depth of the water. There are pros and cons to this trend. I am old fashioned and still prefer to have separate instruments for separate tasks. Therefore everything the barometer tells me that is not about pressure is a distraction. But that is obviously just one personal preference, and not likely a popular one, judging from trends in many electronic devices.

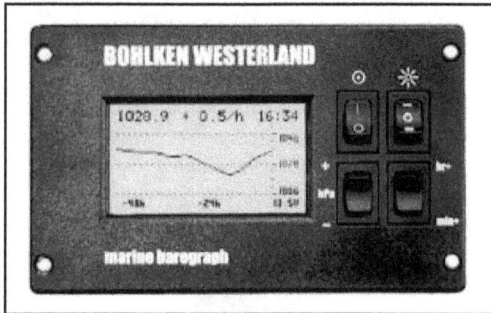

Figure 8.3-14 *Suunto barometer watch, also includes a digital compass and a timer intended for yacht racing starts. Some watch barometers include graphic history.*

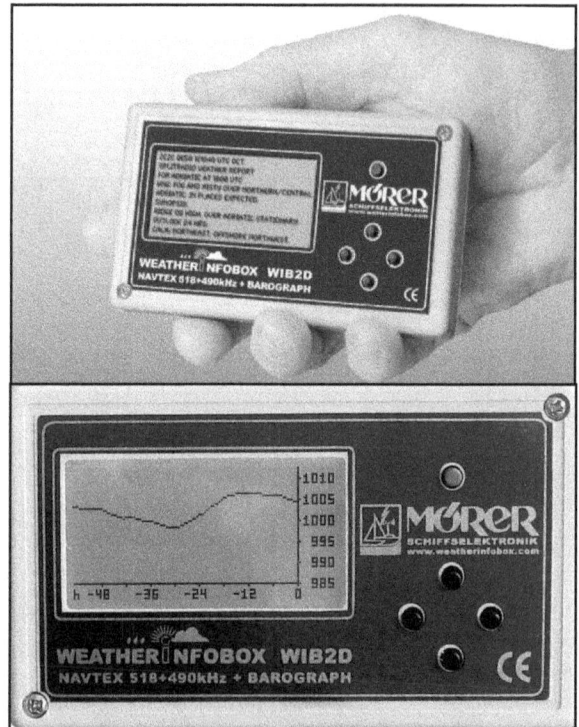

Figure 8.3-13 *Bohlken Westerland. It includes NIMA compatible data export. From Germany.*

Figure 8.3-16 *Geisinger GPB 3300. 4.2" x 2.6" x 1.2". Unadjusted accuracy of ±2 mb, but can be set to higher accuracy. User can input elevation for a correction to sea level. From Germany.*

Figure 8.3-15 Combination barograph and Navtex weather and navigation radio receiver, with many options, from www.wetterinfobox.com. From Germany.

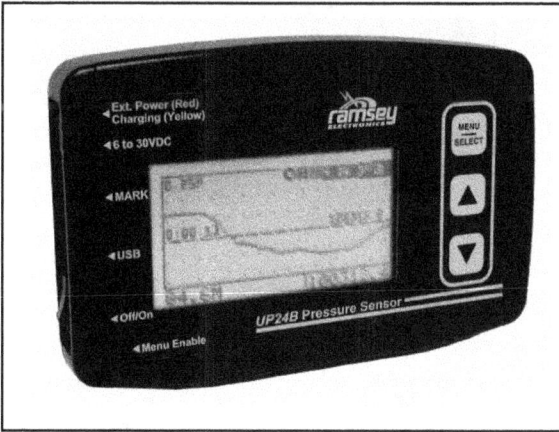

Figure 8.3-17 *Model UP24B from Ramsey. Has USB data export as text file. Includes graph and very high precision readout (0.001 mb). Many options and functions.*

Figure 8.3-18 *A prototype barometer, with digital and electronic analog display. Runs on Li batteries, stays on just 1 minute then shuts off. It can show elevation or pressure, can be adjusted, and shows tenths of mb.*

There are in fact some very high quality "weather stations" that include accurate temperature and accurate humidity along with the time of day and atmospheric pressure. There are other devices, however, that display something called humidity that does not change much if you put it in the shower. And there are some barometers that include the phase of the moon. That seems doubly bad, as that gives some remote implication that these things are related.

Part of the problem is once you have programmable controllers, you can do a lot with them, and sometimes there is a temptation to over do it. The goal of the instrument designer is to be sure they do not add some feature that actually distracts from an otherwise perfectly good barometer.

The options that might show up are varied and will likely change as more users get involved with electronic barometers. One model, for example, has an option of switching to a pressure trend mode. In this trend mode, instead of showing the present pressure, it shows digitally how many mb the pressure has dropped over the past 1 hr or past 3hr. This is obviously a very practical option.

Other units that do not show a graphic display of the past pressures have a nice symbolic display of the present pressure trend, indicating at a glance whether the pressure is steady, rising or falling, or rapidly rising or falling. These displays are very effective, and in fact warn of trends better than an actual graph of the pressures in most cases. An example is shown Figure 8.3-7.

Another option we have not seen that would be useful is the option to press a button and have the barometer report back to you the pressures it recorded at the past 3 or 4 synoptic times. This would make comparison with weather maps very easy, especially if we forgot to record this data.

8.4 Sensors vs. Barometers

When we think of a "barometer" we usually think of a device that both measures the pressure and displays the value digitally or on a dial. Inside each electronic barometer, however, is a barometric pressure sensor, and we can use these devices to record the pressure without necessarily displaying it. The output from the sensor is usually fed into a computer, which stores the data, and the values are then read from a software program.

This offers the end user essentially unlimited versatility with data handling, interpretation, and display. You can also interrogate the sensor every few seconds or so and pass this on to a separate display device or show it on the computer. With that set up you have a "barometer" with a PC output to record the data. Most of the high-end electronic barometers include the option to export the data to a PC. Figures 8.4-4 and 8.4-5 show two sample sensors. Table 8.4-1 lists several popular models. Each has its own special features, so they must be checked individually for a productive comparison. This list ranges from the most economical to the best in the world. A "data logger" is a sensor that will accumulate data that can be downloaded later, whereas the word "sensor" often means the device can only read and record live data.

Figure 8.4-4 *Conex-Electro WJ-10 sensor and data logger.*

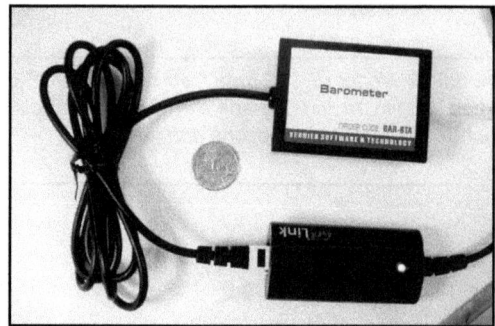

Figure 8.4-5 *Vernier BAR-BTA sensor with required GoLink adaptor.*

Table 8.4-1 Sample of Atmospheric Pressure Sensors[1]					
Manufacturer	*Model*	*Range (mb)*	*Temp. Range (°F)*	*Accuracy[2]*	*Price[3]*
Conex-Electro	WJ-10	677 to 1050	32° to 122°	±0.5 mb	$130
Druck (GE)	RPT410	600 to 1100	14° to 122°	±0.5 mb	$829
Fischer	E331113	900 to 1050	-4° to 122°	±0.5 mb	$870
Honeywell	HPB200	500 to 1200	-40° to 185°	±0.4 mb	$960
Paroscientific	6000-16B	800 to 1100	-40° to 122°	±0.08 mb	$4,700
Ramsey	UP24B	150 - 1550	32° to 122°	±0.5 mb	$300
Setra	270	800 to 1100	30° to 120°	±0.15 mb	$1,249
Setra	276	800 to 1100	30° to 130°	±0.75 mb	$429
Vaisala	PTB110	800 to 1060	32° to 104°	±0.3 mb	$940
Vernier	BAR-BTA	812 - 1066	32° to 122°	±0.75 mb	$132

1 These small or portable units store the pressure, which is then read by a PC. Typically they do not have a digital display, though a couple offer optional readouts. This is just a sample selection; there are many more. This is a far over-simplified list of specifications. Details of each model must be consulted to appreciate its features.

2 Some units have different accuracies for different temperature ranges. For some units, this is the unadjusted accuracy, for others this is essentially the linearity that is maintained once the unit has been set properly. Others have an enhanced precision option.

3. These estimated prices are intended for relative comparison only. Most have multiple options and varying prices.

As you go up in the atmosphere (on land to higher elevations, or above the land or oceans to higher altitudes) the pressure falls, because the air density grows thinner the higher you go. If the rate of this fall in pressure could be accurately predicted, then an accurate measure of the atmospheric pressure would be an accurate measure of your elevation or altitude. The principle is simple enough; the practice is not so simple. The accurate implementation of this principle has occupied engineers and scientists since the conception of the aneroid barometer.

The first question is how accurate does your barometer have to be to get a usable altitude, and second, what is the proper theory for pressure versus altitude, and does this theory change with passing weather patterns.

Answers to the first two questions are closely related, and they make up the primary matter of this chapter. The answer to the last question is a resounding "Yes," and that remains the main challenge of this application.

9.1 The Hypsometric Equation

It started with Toricelli in 1642, who believed the pressure decreased with increasing altitude, but he was not able to prove it. Then Pascal sent his brother-in-law up a mountain with a mercury barometer in 1648 and proved it was true, but he could not write the equation to describe it. Finally Pierre-Simone Laplace (the Isaac Newton of France) used his mathematical genius to explain observations of pressure changes in balloon flights. His result from about 1800 is called the *hypsometric equation*, and it is still used today to relate elevation and pressure.

When the compact, rugged aneroid barometer became available some 50 years later, explorers, hikers,

and climbers were ready to put it to immediate use. Laplace's equation is given below to illustrate two important features. Referring to Figure 9.1-1:

$$H = Z2 - Z1 = (RT/g) \times \ln (P1/P2),$$

where H is the height difference between two elevations, $Z1$ and $Z2$, that have pressures of $P1$ and $P2$. R is the universal gas constant; g is the acceleration due to gravity; "ln" is the natural logarithm. T is the average temperature (Kelvin absolute temperature scale, $°K$) of the air column between $Z1$ and $Z2$. We are not going to solve this equation for now, just discuss it.

Notice first that it is for a height difference, not an absolute height. We always need some reference level at which we know the height and its pressure if we wish to determine altitude from pressure. For altimetry, this reference level is usually taken as sea level, with its corresponding sea-level pressure. The

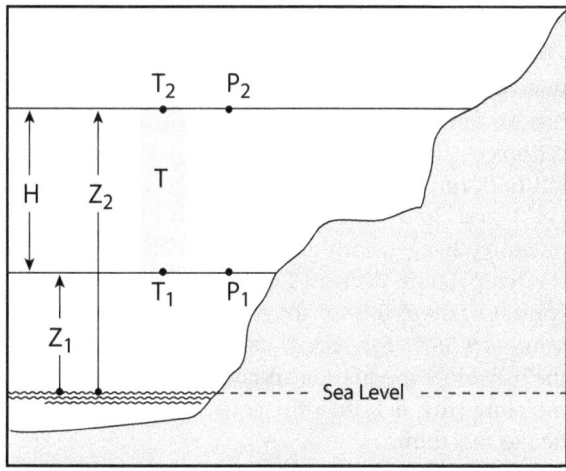

Figure 9.1-1. *Definitions used in the hypsometric equation. For altimetry, the height Z1 = 0; the pressure P1 is the sea level pressure; the temperatures T1 and T2 are estimated from the International Standard Atmosphere. T is the average air temperature of the column shown.*

sea-level pressure at any location is always changing as the weather changes, so an altitude measurement with a barometer is a dynamic process. We must know the accurate sea-level pressure at every moment we wish to learn our altitude from our measurement of the pressure at some higher (or lower) location. Sometimes the pressure is stable over long periods, so we can learn it once and use it for sometime into the future, but this is an uncertainty that remains with this process.

Next we note that innocent-looking "T" in the equation, the average temperature of the air between our elevated location and the temperature at sea level. We can measure the air temperature at our location, but what is the temperature at sea level? In an airplane or balloon above the ocean, this is an understandable concept; it would be what someone measures on a boat directly below us. But what about flying over a high plateau or hiking on a mountain that is 1,000 miles from the nearest place at sea level. This is a temperature that is difficult to know accurately, even in the case of flying over the ocean with a vessel below you. You can learn these two temperatures (on the water and in the air), but chances are very good that the true average temperature of the air column below you is not the average of these two temperatures. Furthermore, the average temperature will also depend on the relative humidity of the air column as well.

This average temperature of the air column remains the main uncertainty in this entire process, but we can work around it for most practical applications of altimetry, including aircraft altimeters. We fall back on the International Standard Atmosphere (ISA), and simply use that prescription for how temperature changes with altitude. Namely, we assume the temperature decreases as we rise in the air at a constant rate of 6.5 C° for each 1 km, which is the same as 3.56 F° for each 1,000 ft. If we fold this into the hypsometric equation and neglect the effect of the moisture (dry air), then the equation can be simplified to this form:

$$Hs = 145366.45 * [1-(Ps/1013.25)^{0.190284}],$$

where Hs is the station elevation above sea level in ft and Ps is the station pressure in mb. (I know some readers must be chuckling at the phrase "simplified form," but I mean there is just one H on one side and one P on the other side, so there is some calculator or spreadsheet program than can solve this, more or less directly.) This equation is equivalent to the one used in Appendix Table A2 to compute pressure vs. altitude in the ISA.

Now we have elevation in terms of pressure alone and this is called the *pressure altitude*. If we take the temperature and dew point into account, we would compute a more accurate altitude, but that is not a procedure used in aviation.

To ensure uniform standards:

> *all altimeter applications are based on*
> *pressure altitude,*
> *without regard to air temperature.*

On the other hand, when meteorologists measure station pressures at elevated locations of known elevation, they want to know what "sea-level pressure" that observation must imply. For this computation, they must account for the air temperature and dew point, and solve the problem of that "T." The procedures are outlined in Appendix 3.

Although not part of their altimeter reckoning, pilots do ultimately care about air temperature because it affects the density of the air. When operating at high elevations in warm air, it reduces their engine horsepower, propeller thrust, and aerodynamic lift, which in turn affects required speeds and runway lengths. It also affects their true altitude, which is needed for clearing obstructions.

9.2 Climbing and Hiking

There are not many "explorers" left these days, but there are many people who care about their elevation when hiking or climbing, or when biking or skiing. Elevation is another component of navigation, which could in principle be valuable on the road as well. It would be analogous to mariners using the depth of the water below them to help locate their position on a chart, or as a way to check a position provided by the GPS. Elevation contours are shown on topographic maps, just as depth contours are shown on nautical charts.

Altimeters for this application come as aneroid devices with analog dials or electronic barometers with digital displays. Some show elevation or pressure; some show only elevation. Analog (aneroid) devices mark off the altitude in intervals of 50 to 250 feet. Many electronic units have a high precision readout (sometimes called "resolution") of maybe 1 to 3 feet or so, but their inherent uncertainty and stability will generally be larger than that. If it shows the elevation to 1 foot, for example, it should be able to measure your height, which is easy to check. Read the manuals carefully and then test them on a known hill. You can use www.starpath.com/barometers to find accurate elevation for known lat-lon positions, which you can get from a GPS.

Portable altimeters and barometers often use custom terminology. The phrase "absolute pressure" usually means station pressure, and the term "relative pressure" usually means sea-level pressure.

To evaluate altimeter specifications, we can fall back on basic barometer values. A full sized, top of the line aneroid provides stable absolute pressure accuracies of some ±0.7 mb, but after reducing the size and beefing up the movements for shock resistance, we would expect to sacrifice some accuracy—though they still might maintain very good linearity over the working pressure range. High quality instruments use jeweled movements. As with any barometer, however, the larger the range the bigger the demands on the engineering. A 20,000-foot range of altitudes corresponds to a working pressure range of some 1050 to 450 mb. We could expect higher accuracy and precision for units limited to half of that or less.

Besides using an altimeter for navigation underway, you can also carry a small recording device with PC output. Once back from the outing you can replay the elevation profile of the trip. This application could use a device called a barometer or called an altimeter.

For any altimeter application, however, you need to set the reference level of the device. The most direct procedure is just to set the device to a known elevation when you are there. Then the altimeter displays changes in your elevation relative to that zero point. For this you do not need to know the actual barometric pressure at your location. If you set an altimeter this way, then take a long hike and return to this same location, but now the elevation is different, then the atmospheric pressure has changed. You can confirm this by checking the local weather data, either from a weather map or a text report. To estimate the values, use 0.44 mb = 12 ft. ("Point four four per floor"). So if the parking lot is now 100 feet lower than when you left, the pressure has risen by (100/12) x 0.44 = 3.7 mb, which is a reasonably likely change over a half a day or so. It could be more, or less.

There is virtue to the aneroid devices, because that is the way they work, and that is all there is to adjust. As soon as you have a microprocessor reading a pressure sensor in an electronic altimeter, you have all sorts of options. Many options can be a virtue or a distraction. Caution is worthwhile in units that have both barometer and altimeter displays.

One such option is to set the proper sea-level pressure into the device (no matter what elevation you are) and then it should read out your proper elevation. If you are then at an elevation you know, but notice the elevation you read is not correct, then you can further adjust by changing the displayed elevation to the true elevation. This last adjustment is taking into account that the ISA prediction of pressure drop with elevation was not correct, as in fact it is likely not to be.

The virtue of a sea-level pressure adjustment is you can reset it underway if you learn the sea-level pressure has changed. For example, suppose the radio report at departure was 1020 mb for your region, and you set that into the instrument. Then when you are at a known elevation you set that into the instrument to calibrate the elevation. Then on the next day if you hear by radio that the pressure in your region is now 1030 mb, you can just change that sea-level pressure setting without being at a place with known elevation. That will then make subsequent elevation readings more accurate. You will not need to have another elevation calibration point. This is a similar procedure to that used in aviation altimeters.

Some electronic altimeters work more like simple aneroid units, and some with more complex options allow you to revert to the simple approach—namely set it to the proper elevation from a known location, and go on, without any background pressure settings.

Contour hiking means traveling along sloped terrain, wishing to maintain the same elevation. On a topographic map, you would be following along a contour line. This can be difficult navigation sometimes, especially in poor visibility. There is a tendency in this situation to walk slightly downhill. The solution is to monitor your progress with an altimeter, perhaps counting off so many steps, or some measured time interval, to learn how far you wander off elevation in a given interval. Then you can correct for it.

If the ambient pressure in your region does not change, then it is a relative measurement to maintain the contour and you are not dependent upon absolute calibrations. We are back to "Point four four per floor," meaning a 12 foot change in elevation shows up as 0.44 mb change on the barometer. But it takes a pretty sensitive altimeter to dependably measure this change. Twice this is more likely detectable (24 ft = 0.88 mb) and three times this (1.32 mb corresponding to an elevation change of 36 feet) should be detectable with a modestly good instrument. An

---

Barometric Altimeter Surveys

A good way to determine the elevation of one place relative to another is to use two identical, recording barometers. Coordinate the times in the two units, then leave one at a reference station while you carry out the survey. As you survey with the moving instrument, mark the times and pressures at the points of interest. Then you can later compare any changes in atmospheric pressure with the reference barometer and adjust the measurements accordingly.

For some applications, however, you might just look up the results from the National Elevation Dataset. Namely, just make a list of the GPS coordinates (to high precision) then access the database to find accurate elevations. www.starpath.com/barometers is one way to get these results.

---

electronic unit is likely to be more dependable for this, but keep in mind that many include an inherent uncertainty of ±15 feet due to a mathematical approximation used in solving the hypsometric equation. Plus recall the usual concerns: be sure it has fresh batteries and remember that strong wind blowing over the instrument could change the reading (20 feet or more) so test this by reading it in different configurations of shelter from the wind.

The problem to keep in mind over a long contour hike is the possibility that the local weather pattern will change. This gives rise to atmospheric pressure changes you may not be aware of, and this in turn leads to perceived elevation changes that throw off your navigation. It is not unusual, for example, to have a pressure drop of some 6 mb or so in half a day or less from within a high pressure system, without notable signs of the weather changing. In short, without wireless communications, you might not have warning of this change from what you see in the sky. If this happened over some 10 hours, then you would think that during this period you were headed up the hill, which you would correct by going down the hill. In this example, you would be going some 164 feet too low every 10 hours, and you would not know it from the altimeter alone.

Or the pressure could rise. If you camp on the slope, and wake up to find your elevation has dropped 120 ft, but you obviously have not moved, then sure enough, over night the atmospheric pressure went up about 4.4 mb.

A good way to learn about your altimeter is the same way we learn about our barometers. Set it to your known elevation at home (ground level + removal correction), and mount it eye level somewhere you go by every day, and just keep an eye on it as the weather changes. When you see your living room going up and down over time, check the weather reports online to see what has been taking place.

9.3 Aviation

An aircraft altimeter, just like a hiker's altimeter, measures only pressure altitude. They do not take into account the actual temperature of the air below them, nor do they account for the moisture in the air. There is some virtue in this apparent oversimplification, in that this is an easy computation that everyone understands and can do in the same way. A more accurate solution is complex, requires more accurate input, and it is open to debate as to which of the various solutions is the best for particular applications (Appendix 3). When two planes approach each other, it is best when they are both computing their altitudes in the same manner.

Much of aneroid barometer development from the beginning of their history to modern times can be traced to needs for accurate and dependable aircraft altimeters. The most famous line of instruments came from the American inventor Paul Kollsman in 1928. Kollsman Instruments remains a leader in this field, worldwide, though the actual design and performance has not changed significantly for many decades. See Figure 9.3-1.

Aircraft altimeters are rugged aneroid barometers with essentially no power requirements, other than those used with "black box" recorders that store the data they receive. Even these, though, are inherently mechanical aneroid devices (Figure 9.3-2).

Figure 9.3-1. *A classic 3-pointer aircraft altimeter. The inside dial is below 1, meaning below 10,000 ft, the next largest dial shows 4,000 ft, and the outer dial shows 140 ft, for a total reading of 4,140 ft. The "altimeter setting" in the Kollsman window is at 29.92". This happens to be a Kollsman instrument, but that window is called "Kollsman window" on all altimeters. The instrument is about 3.25" wide and about 5" deep. They typically include 2 or 3 aneroid capsules. On international flights some altimeters offer two synchronized windows so the altimeter can be set in mb or inches.*

U.S. federal standards for construction and performance for these instruments have been established for many years. The required accuracy is outlined in Table 9.3-1.

Pilots calibrate their devices by entering a pressure correction called the "altimeter setting." It is done with a knob on the front of the panel, and in U.S. airspace this is always done in inches. Thus before an aircraft takes off it will get a radio report telling them the altimeter setting. They then dial this into the instrument, and then the instrument should read out the proper elevation of the runway.

The altimeter setting is thought of as the sea-level pressure that will, under present conditions, yield the correct true altitude on aircraft altimeters on the ground at the reporting station. All approaching aircraft will also be given that setting so they can be calibrated to the airfield they are landing on.

Pilots departing from a remote airfield without altimeter reports, would work the process backwards by adjusting the altimeter setting to the known elevation of the airfield they are on.

As a departing plane rises above the ground, its true altitude becomes more uncertain, but this is not crucial for traffic control because all planes in the vicinity have their altimeters set to the same airfield, so they agree with each other on their indicated altitude. The true altitude may be off some, but they will all be off the same amount. And when they descend to that field they will all find the ground level where

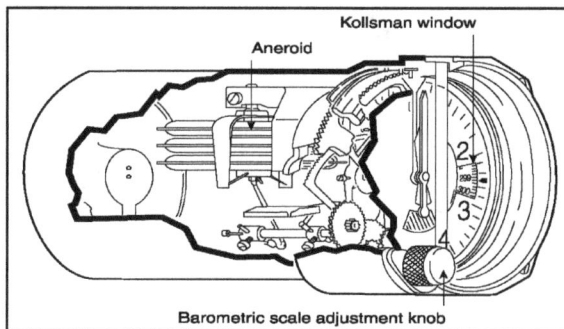

Figure 9.3-2. *The inside of an aircraft altimeter showing aneroid capsules. The bearings are typically all jeweled, and they are built to rigorous shock proof standards, with high durability and dependability. Accuracy specifications are shown in Table 9.3-1.*

they expect it. The true altitude is, of course, crucial for clearing obstacles, and we will come back to this correction in a moment.

As a departing plane leaves the vicinity of the airport that provided the altimeter setting, they enter into regions that can have different sea-level pressures, which would mean the altitude calibration is no longer valid. They would then experience the same errors that the contour hiker confronted, but since they are moving rapidly themselves, the changes could be much larger. The normal procedure is to check in with passing airports at least once every 100 miles to reset the altimeter to meet local conditions. Without this adjustment, two planes could be at the same altitude, yet have their altimeters read different values.

Table 9.3-1 Altimeter Tolerances*			
Altitude (ft)	Equivalent Pressure (in)	Scale ± ft	Sum ± ft
-1,000	31.018	20	32
0	29.921	20	32
500	29.385	20	32
1,000	28.856	20	32
1,500	28.335	25	35
2,000	27.821	30	39
3,000	26.817	30	39
4,000	25.842	35	43
6,000	23.978	40	47
8,000	22.225	60	65
10,000	20.577	80	84
12,000	19.029	90	93
14,000	17.577	100	103
16,000	16.216	110	113
18,000	14.942	120	123
20,000	13.75	130	132
22,000	12.636	140	142
25,000	11.104	155	157
30,000	8.885	180	182
35,000	7.041	205	207
40,000	5.538	230	231
45,000	4.355	255	256
50,000	3.425	280	281

Flying into regions without these reports, or flying between altimeter reports, pilots remember this caution with the jingle, "Cool or low, look out below." This warning is illustrated in Figure 9.3-3. It means if you fly into a region where the proper altimeter setting is lower than you have set (meaning the sea-level pressure is now lower), then you are actually flying at a lower altitude than is indicated. If you knew the change in sea-level pressure, the offset could be figured from the ISA data of Appendix 2. As an example, flying along with an indicated altitude of 5,000 ft with an altimeter setting of 30.36 (corresponding to a sea-level pressure of 1028 mb), you check into a nearby airport and they tell you the altimeter setting is 30.09 (sea-level pressure 1019 mb). Then, as soon as you enter this new altimeter setting, your indicated altitude would go down by about 280 ft. At 5,000 feet the loss of true altitude is about 30 ft per 1 mb. At 14,500 it is about 40 ft per 1 mb.

Without a radar altimeter or accurate GPS altitude, you would not be able to detect this altitude shift from the barometric altimeter alone. A weather map of the region, however, would alert you to the need for this correction until you get another airport altimeter setting.

The warning jingle includes temperature as well as pressure, and that makes sense. The barometric altimeter measures the weight of the air above it, which is determined by the air density, which in turn depends on both pressure and temperature. So ask yourself, if the pressure drops (meaning the air is getting thinner), where do you have to go to get the same weight above you, and that is down. To keep the same indicated altitude, you would have to fly lower and lower as the atmospheric pressure decreases.

Another way to think of it is you are flying along a constant pressure surface, and if that surface descends, then you follow it down, no matter what caused it to go down, but you still read the same altitude. If the air

* **Table notes.** *From* Federal Aviation Regulations, *Part 43, Appendix E. Scale is the main uncertainty, then there is a fixed 25-ft tolerance on the setting window. Setting and Scale add as square root of the sum of the squares since they are independent errors. Other tolerances are specified after large maneuvers related to friction in the movement and hysteresis.*

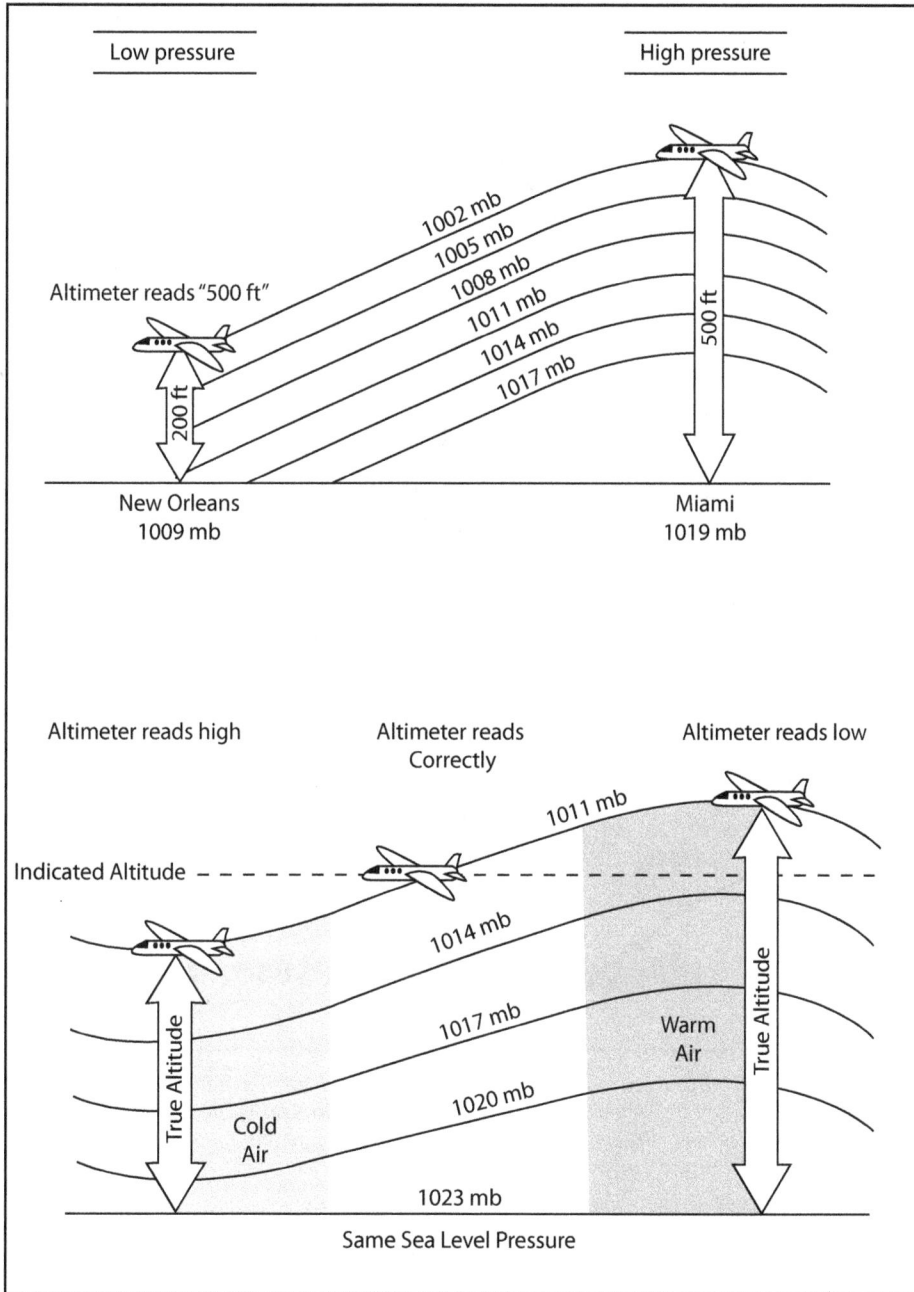

Figure 9.3-3. *"Cool or low, lookout below" is a reminder of two sources of error in indicated altimeter reading. The above are two independent examples, one of each effect. The errors are approximately 100 ft for each 2.7 mb at 1000 ft or 100 ft per 3.6 mb at 10,000 ft (see ISA data in Appendix A2). The error due to temperature is a loss of about 4% of the indicated altitude for each 11°C the air temperature is colder than the ISA predictions for your indicated altitude.*

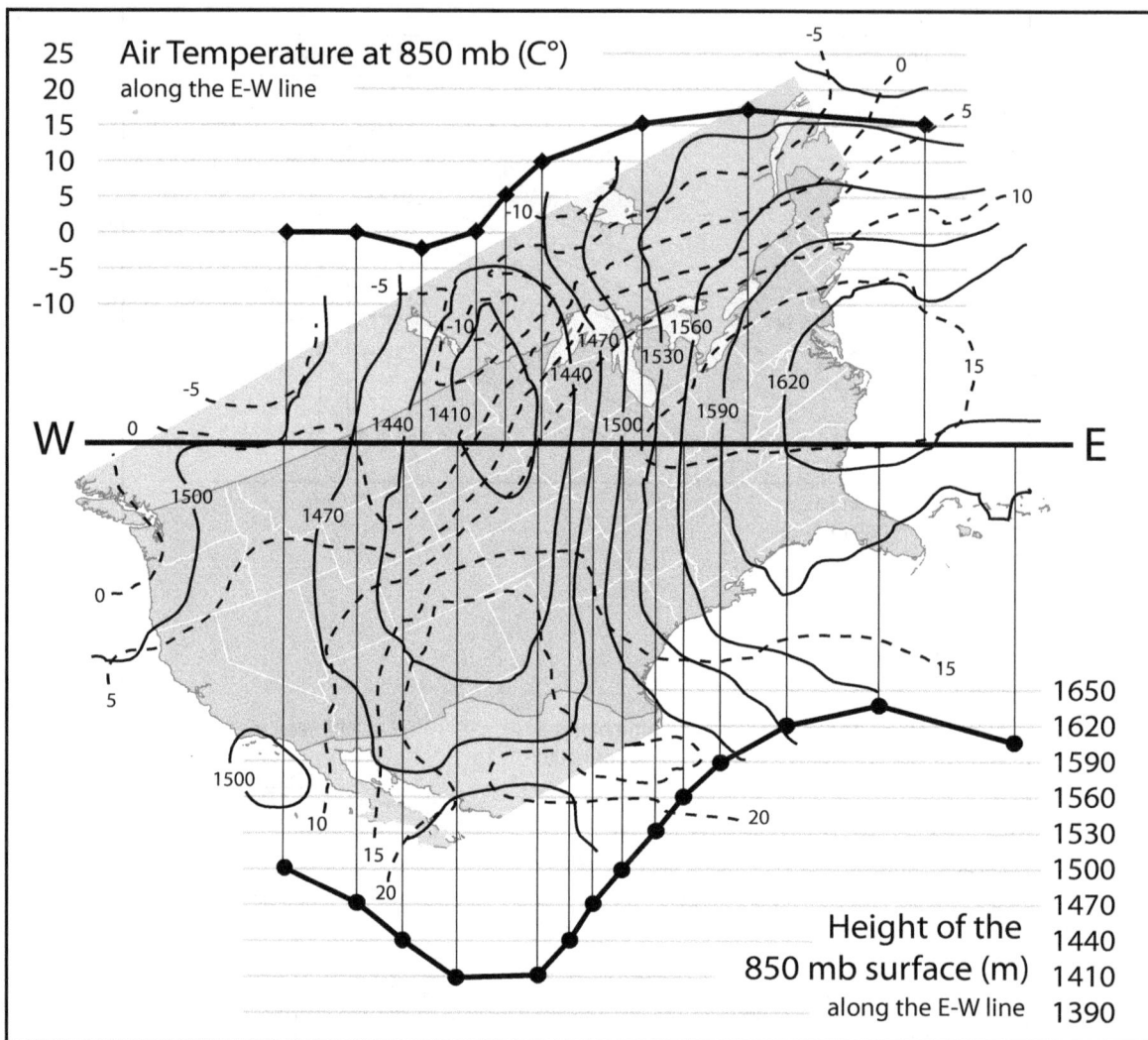

Figure 9.3-4. *Height of the 850 mb surface located at about 5,000 ft (1500 m) in standard atmospheric conditions, corresponding to an air temperature of 5°C. This map was valid 00z on 27 Apr, 2009. The solid lines are the heights (m) of the 850 mb surface above sea level; the dashed lines are isotherms (°C) at that pressure level. The line from E to W was used to plot the profiles of the pressure surface height and air temperature vs distance across the country.*

Along the E-W line, altimeters set in NW Illinois would give good true elevations, but flying east from there without correction they would end up reading about 120 meters low, and flying west without corrections underway they would end up about 90 meters high. Notice that flying from E to W the pressure is dropping and the air is cooling. So "Cool and low, look out below" reminds us that the true altitude is getting lower as we proceed (without corrections) even though the indicated altitude remains the same.

In this example the temperature and pressure are working together as we might expect them to, but this is just one situation. The isotherms could be parallel to the elevation contours or perpendicular to them, so either part of the warning could apply independently.

The air temperature in NW Illinois is about 13° C at 1500 m (5,000 ft), which is about 8°C warmer than the standard atmosphere. This means the density altitude at that location and elevation is closer to 6,000 ft (as shown in Appendix 6).

grows cooler (meaning it weighs more), then all the pressure surfaces descend, and likewise you follow it down not knowing you are doing so. Examples from a real weather map are shown in Figure 9.3-4.

These two reasons the pressure surfaces can descend are closely related meteorologically, but they have different significances in aviation. The warning statement quoted above is a mixed metaphor, in a sense. Pressure has a direct effect on the indicated altitude, but recall that temperature does not enter into that reckoning. A changing air temperature, even if it were known precisely, cannot be used to estimate a change in the *indicated altitude*. Air temperature changes imply changes in the *true altitude*, not the proper indicated altitude. Table 9.3-2 summarizes the altitude concepts of interest to aviators.

The key point is that the *indicated altitude* is a correct *true altitude* when you are on the ground at the airport where you set it, but other than that it is almost better thought of as a "flight level." We want all planes to agree what flight level they are on, even if this level does not correlate exactly with their true altitude above sea level.

How close the indicated altitude is to the true altitude depends on the lapse rate that is present compared to the lapse rate of the ISA. The ISA lapse rate is -6.5°C/1,000 m (3.56°F/1,000 ft). If that is how fast the temperature is dropping in the air where you set the altimeter, then the indicated altitude will be close to the true altitude in that region. But if the temperature is dropping faster, then the pressure surfaces are lower and you get to the indicated altitude before reaching the true altitude. Likewise, if the air is cooling more slowly as you rise, then the pressure surfaces are higher, and you have to go physically higher than the indicated altitude to reach the corresponding pressure surface.

Again, the temperature does not affect your proper altimeter setting, but since it affects your true altitude it is obviously important for flying over

obstacles like mountains. Nonstandard lapse rates could cause the indicated altitude to differ from true altitude by as much as 20%, even a bit more in very cold air.

If you write the hypsometric equation in this form, you can experiment with specific values:

$$H \text{ (ft)} = Z2 - Z1$$
$$= 221.152 \, (T + 273) \log (29.92/P),$$

where T is the average air temperature in °C between Z2 and Z1, and P is the station pressure (inches of mercury) at elevation H. From this you can see that for every 11°C that the air is cooler than predicted by the ISA, you would expect a loss of altitude of roughly 4% (11°/273° = 0.04).

To apply these ideas for actual cases, we must be very specific. Consider a station at elevation Z1 and temperature T1, which was used to set the altimeter for a plane at altitude Z2 with air temperature T2. The indicated altitude will read Z2, and this will be close to the true altitude, providing the actual mean temperature T_A between Z1 and Z2 matches the mean temperature of the ISA (T_S), where:

$$T_S = T1 - 0.0065 \times (Z2 - Z1)/2.$$

Table 9.3-2 Altitudes used in Aviation	
Name	*Definition*
True Altitude	The distance between you and the mean sea level below you.
Indicated Altitude	The altitude showing on an altimeter (in the air or on the ground) that has been set to read the true elevation at a specific time and place on the ground.
Pressure Altitude	Altitude in the standard atmosphere that has the same pressure that you have. Does not depend on temperature. It assumes the sea level pressure is 29.92. In the U.S., aircraft flying over 18,000 ft or more than 100 miles from shore always set their altimeter to 29.92 so they are flying pressure altitude.
Density Altitude	Altitude in the standard atmosphere that has the same air density that you have. Depends on temperature and dew point at your location.

The actual mean temperature we do not know, but we can estimate it as

$$T_A = (T1 - T2)/2.$$

Remember that the indicated altitude is always above sea level, but we can only make corrections to the part above the ground. So we define Hi as the altitude above the station, such that the indicated altitude, $Z_i = Z1 + Hi$ and, correspondingly, we define the true altitude as $Z_t = Z1 + Ht$. Then we can write:

$$Ht/Hi = T_A / T_S ,$$

which is to say,

True height above the station =

(T_A / T_S) x Indicated height above the station.

Remember these are absolute temperatures, meaning $T = T°C + 273.2°$ or $T = T°F + 459.7°$.

In practice, the temperature ratio can vary from 0.80 in very cold air to 1.10 or so for very warm air. To be more precise, the actual temperature T_A has to be adjusted to account for the humidity as explained in Appendix 3, but this is rarely done in altimetry.

Figure 9.3-4 illustrates an example. The ratio of mean temperatures is $(-7.5+273.2)/(2.2+273.2) = 0.965$, and $0.965 \times 7000 = 6,755$ ft. So the true altitude is 245 ft lower than indicated. A pilot can estimate this underway from the air temperature alone by assuming the actual air temperature increases below the plane at the same rate as the standard atmosphere. Since the observed air temp is 11.2°C below the standard, that would make the estimated actual mean equal to 11.2 below the standard mean of 2.2°C, or -9.0°C. Thus the ratio would be $(-9+273.2)/(2.2+273.2) = 0.959$, yielding a true altitude offset of -287 ft.

This same estimate could be obtained from the approximation given earlier, namely the air temperature is lower by 11°C, which corresponds to 4% of 7,000 ft = 280 ft.

Returning to the "mixed metaphor" idea, if a pilot learns underway that the sea-level pressure has changed or has a map onboard showing when it is expected to change, they can (when flying under Visual Flight Rules) immediately reach to change the altimeter setting for a more accurate indicated altitude. But if they note the air temperature has dropped significantly telling them (with some computations) that their true altitude is in fact lower, they cannot change the altimeter, because that would violate the protocol in use. It is just knowledge they must take into account as the flight proceeds. (Flying in conditions of Instrument Flight Rules pilots cannot adjust the atlimeter at all unless provided settings from an air traffic controller.)

These notes here are intended as an overview for those not familiar with aviation. All the nuances of aviation altimetry have been worked out in great detail and are presented in standard training manuals that all pilots must know.

Pressures used in aviation are summarized in Table 9.3-3.

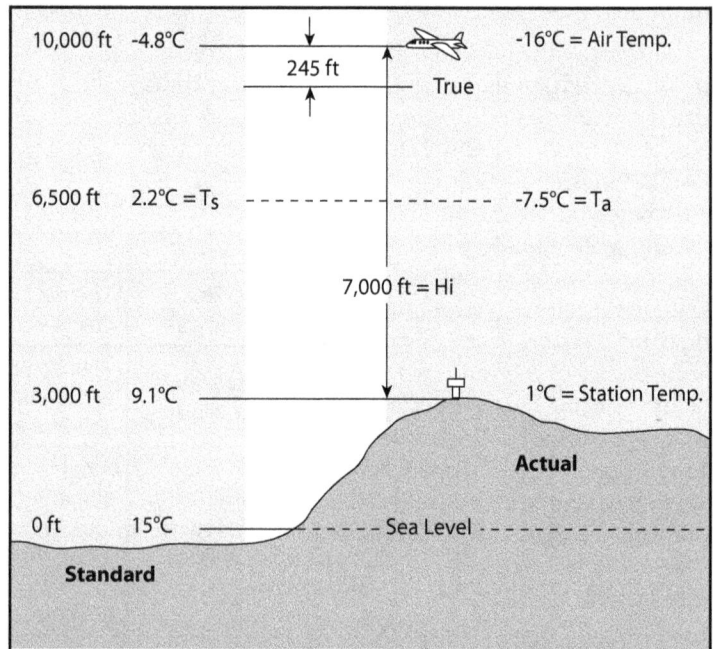

Figure 9.3-5. *Plane with indicated altitude of 10,000 feet and air temperature of -16°C, with altimeter set correctly to a field below at 3,000 ft with a station temperature of 1°C, will be flying at a true altitude of about 245 feet lower than indicated.*

9.4 Skydiving

Skydiving is one of the most crucial applications of a barometer. It is the only application where the manual can rightfully state in bold red letters:

WARNING! — FAILURE TO FOLLOW ALL WARNINGS, INSTRUCTIONS, AND REQUIRED PROCEDURES MAY RESULT IN SERIOUS INJURY OR DEATH.

A skydiving altimeter is in principle like all others. The required absolute accuracy is not even as high as in some other applications, because the speed of the descent limits accurate individual readings, but dependability and durability are crucial, as are several unique precautions. During free fall, the diver is falling at 120 mph, which is 176 ft per second. Once the parachute opens the descent slows to about 6 mph or 8.8 ft per second. Typical sport dives are from 13,000 feet with parachute opening no later than 3,000 ft.

Unlike aviators (in most parts of the world), who want their altimeters to read the airport elevation when they are on the ground, skydivers always want their altimeters to read zero when they are on the ground. Thus pilots keep track of their altitude relative to sea level; whereas sky divers keep track of their altitude relative to the ground level. There is obvious virtue in their choice.

One advantage to skydiving use of altimeters is the total time span from takeoff to subsequent landing is usually short enough that atmospheric pressure

Figure 9.4-1. *The Altimaster skydiver's altimeter from www.alti-2.com. It is set to zero at the drop zone, then it rises with a clockwise turn up to 12,000 feet on the ascent, then on up to 6 on the dial corresponding to as much as 18,000 ft. Then on the descent it makes one uniform rotation back to 0 at ground level. Many sports dives start from about 13,000 feet. The yellow zone (3-2.5) marks the typical elevation for latest parachute deployment. The sector below 2.5 is red. Photo compliments of Alti-2 Inc. (www.alti-2.com).*

changes are not likely to be significant. The procedure is to check and set the devices before each jump. Many skydiving schools or airports provide a pump-out chamber that can test the portable altimeters over their full range ahead of time. A sample skydiver's altimeter is shown in Figure 9.4-1.

Table 9.3-3 Pressures used in Aviation		
Name	*Q code*	*Description*
Station pressure	QFE	The actual barometric pressure measured at the elevation of the runway. A pure measurement. No theory.
Altimeter setting	QNH	An estimate of the sea level pressure that would lead to the observed station pressure at the runway based on the standard atmosphere. It depends only on the true elevation of the runway and the observed station pressure, as well as the fixed pressure lapse rate of the standard atmosphere. It does not depend on temperature or dew point.
Sea-level pressure	QFF	The station pressure for locations with elevation at sea level—or for higher stations, this is an estimate of what the pressure at sea level would be based on the station elevation, taking into account the temperature and dew point of the air. For elevated stations, this is usually closer to what meteorologists would want to compare with neighboring reports than QNH would be. These two pressures rarely differ by more than a few mb.

The caution that must be accounted for is the takeoff point at the airport is likely to be a different location from the drop zone (DZ) where you plan to land. It is the station pressure at the DZ that matters for the calibration of the altimeter. The safest plan is to travel to the DZ to set the altimeters there.

When that is not possible, the relative elevations of the airport and DZ must be accounted for. If the DZ, for example, is 600 ft lower than the airport, then when setting at the airport the altimeter must be set to +600 ft. Likewise it must be set to -600 ft if the drop zone is higher. Manuals from high quality altimeters warn users that they are only to be used in the presence of qualified sky divers. If that last computation is done backwards, for example, the diver could be in very serious danger.

Another caution to keep in mind is the point mentioned earlier that just 20 kts of wind can change a barometer reading some 1 mb or more. At 120 mph this is an obvious factor to keep in mind. Altimeter designers are aware of this effect and compensate in the design as best possible. Nevertheless, turbulent flow when tumbling or when the instrument is held in an unusual position could cause false readings.

Sky diving is definitely an application of barometer use that takes special training, and quality, well-tested and maintained instruments. Military or other parachute missions that involve initial travel over a long distance require special coordination with regard to altimetry. Not only is the elevation likely to be different at takeoff and DZ, the entire pressure patterns over the two locations are likely to be different as well.

We should add that all skydivers are trained to be aware of their elevation so that they are not dependent on any one device to judge maneuver or deployment times. They also typically carry an additional audio altimeter in their helmets, which can include circuitry and sensors for automatic canopy deployment if needed. We are told that industry wide, 90% of younger skydivers use electronic altimeters, whereas many of the veteran skydivers still prefer the aneroid devices.

9.5 Barometers in GPS Units

Several handheld GPS units are available with built in barometric pressure sensors. Some are quite versatile, with barograph plots and various ways to view the pressure history. Some show pressure to the tenth of a mb, others do not. These units are standalone electronic barometers, the same as any other electronic barometer, but with one additional feature—always presented as an asset, but if not understood properly, it could yield misleading results.

The concern is the GPS can also determine your altitude from the same satellite measurements it uses to find horizontal position. This could be called *GPS altitude* to distinguish it from the *barometric altitude* determined from the separate pressure sensor in the device. Both are measured relative to sea level, but they have very different criteria for accuracy.

The barometric accuracy and calibration procedures are exactly as presented earlier. The GPS altitude is a mathematical solution to your elevation that depends on the configuration of the satellites. In very broad terms, the uncertainties in a barometric altitude (if done carefully), and the uncertainties in a random GPS altitude (obtained without special satellites or equipment) are roughly comparable. The best measurement of either type, however, would be better than an average measurement of the other type. In short, it is not clear which method can claim the rights to be "better."

We can think of GPS accuracy separately for horizontal positions versus vertical altitude. Generally the vertical uncertainty is some 1.5 to 2 times larger than the horizontal uncertainty. Most hand-held GPS units that are not specifically made for aviation display the horizontal uncertainty but not the vertical component, so the above guideline can be used as a rough estimate.

The typical horizontal uncertainty in a standard GPS position is about ±15 meters (49 ft) on average. Half that in some cases, twice that in others. GPS accuracy depends on the bearings and elevations of the satellites, which are changing with time. The unit will tell you the present uncertainty in the form of CEP (circular error probable), which means that 50% of all measurements are within this radius, and 95% of all are within twice this radius. It is somewhat analogous to the standard deviation we discuss elsewhere in the book to describe statistical values. Most GPS models do not define this uncertainty factor, but simply call it "GPS accuracy." When checking this, remember it is the horizontal accuracy, not vertical.

For best accuracy and smallest uncertainty you need to see as much of the sky as possible. If you are standing next to a building (tree or hill) that blocks half the sky, you will do much better by stepping around the corner to see more of the sky.

Many hand-held units these days advertise that they are "WAAS enabled." WAAS stands for Wide Area Augmentation System, which is a system developed for aircraft navigation that significantly improves the GPS accuracy for all users. It works by comparing known locations with the GPS position indicated by the passing satellites, and sending out a signal that corrects for any discrepancy noted. To take advantage of this system, you not only need a WAAS enabled receiver, but you also need to see one of the two geo-stationary WAAS satellites, located over the equator: #48 (*Galaxy 15*) at 133.0°W or #51 (*Anik F1R*) at 107.3°W.

From the ground level, these WAAS statellites are not always visible from higher latitudes. From the Canadian border, for example, one or the other is at most 30° to 40° above the southern horizon, which is easily blocked by terrain or buildings. To check this for your situation, turn on the WAAS feature and look for these two satellites in the satellite setup page of your GPS unit. You can find the elevation and bearing to the WAAS satellites at www.starpath.com/waas.

With WAAS enabled and working, your horizontal position accuracy will improve to < 3 m (10 ft) and sometimes close to 1 m! The vertical data will still be some (1.5 to 2) times more uncertain.

These are the matters to keep in mind when comparing a barometric elevation with one from GPS. If you have a good barometer and have the sea-level pressure set properly, chances are it will be better than the non-WAAS GPS elevation. For relative elevations, your barometric measurements (corrected for change in sea-level pressure as needed) will likely always be better than can be done with a GPS.

Here are a few factors to keep in mind when selecting a GPS with barometric sensor:

- Some store the pressure when the unit is turned off.
- Some show pressures in decimal mb, others just in whole mb.
- Some have a barometric altimeter, but do not show barometric pressure.

9.6 Mining and Caving

Altimeters are a natural tool for underground exploration to document the depth of caves and mines. The same guidelines as in hiking apply. A reference level must be established, and changes in the atmospheric pressure noted to correct the observations. Of particular note are explorations of *karst* regions, where the same instruments can be used to document related elevation changes above and below the surface. (Karst are complex landscapes of towers, cliffs, caves, and sinkholes sculpted by water flowing over dissolvable rock for thousands of years.)

Caves are noted for changes in wind and temperature. Strong winds blowing over the altimeter can cause changes in its reading. This is easy to test by varying the configuration relative to the wind flow while riding a bike or through an open car widow. Some cavers have noted that they can predict the winds to expect in their well known caves, based on the atmospheric pressure outside. And in reverse, they can predict a change in the weather on the surface based on the wind they experience underground.

Monitoring the pressure in a cave with a sensitive barometer could help identify which route to follow based on likely wind flow. It could be, for example, that a falling barometer might imply the wind will be flowing into the cave, whereas a rising barometer might imply outflow.

Several cavers have reported in online discussion groups that their inexpensive altimeters were very sensitive to temperature, so this is worth testing before relying on them. Put it in the fridge for a while to see if your room moves.

Barometers can be used to do crucial pressure surveys of mines, which in turn are used to manage the ventilation of the mine. In some environments with explosive gasses, accurate aneroids are favored as they do not employ any electrical or electronic components.

In this chapter we present average pressures world-wide that can be used to evaluate the likelihood of any observed pressure, and also as a way to learn about the world's pressure patterns and how they change throughout the year. Several applications have been mentioned earlier in the text.

10.1 The data

The atmospheric pressure statistics presented here are reproduced from the *U.S. Navy Marine Climatic Atlas of the World, Vol IX*, 1981. The original data set was assembled in the late 1950s and early 1960s from many nations covering over 120 years, largely from ship observations recorded in logbooks. They were then averaged over 5° quadrangles, and smooth lines drawn through these average values.

Potential errors come about because all data are included in the monthly averages, whereas there is no distinction between time of day or time of month. If a particular station had mostly data from early in the day, or only from the end of the month, then that data could be biased. The original text states that there is no indication that this biases the results. According to the Navy Atlas, the "operationally significant accuracy" of the data is considered to be ±1 mb. This accuracy estimate refers to the marine data over the water. The NWS provided average isobars for the land, but the blending together of the data sets is not always uniform. Also there are no standard deviations for the land data.

Another question might be related to the age of the data, now quite old in some cases. Comparable temperature data could in principle reflect some element of global warming, but there does not seem to be any notable trend in this pressure data. We have tested this several ways, and present examples and procedures for doing your own tests in Section 10.3.

The pressures presented are the mean sea level pressure averaged over the month. It is defined in the usual way as the sum of all values divided by the number of values. Also presented here are the standard deviations of the data for each month. The standard deviation (SD) of a set of data is a measure of its variability. It is the average difference of all values from the mean value. When the SD is small, the data are clustered closely around the mean value, when the SD is large, there is much more variation in the values, as illustrated in Figure 10.1-1.

The SD can be used to understand pressure probabilities because studies show that an extended set of pressure measurements for the same location follows

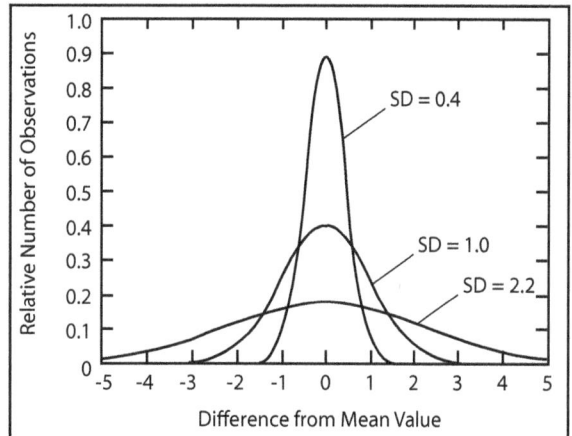

Figure 10.1-1 *Three "normal" distributions of (say) 100 measurements with 3 different standard deviations (SD). When SD is small, the values are all near the mean value (like monthly pressures in the tropics); when it is large they are more spread out (like pressures at high latitudes). To find the SD of a set of numbers, first find the average, then make a list of all the differences between each value and the average, then square each difference (to cancel what side of the average it is on), then find the average of these squared differences, and then take the square root of that. In this sense, the SD is the average difference from the mean for the full set.*

what mathematicians call the normal distribution (bell curve). This curve describes much of what we see in nature that stems from more or less random distinctions. The heights of American women, for example, between ages of 18 and 24 follows a normal distribution with a mean value of 65.5 inches and a standard deviation (SD) of 2.5 inches. This SD determines the spread in heights we might encounter.

In normal distributions it is easy to predict the probability of values that differ from the mean value of the data set, as shown in Figure 10.1-2. From this distribution we can make Table 10.1-1 that tells us about the pressures we might observe and what they can mean.

As an example look at the pressures in January for Anchorage, AK and San Diego, CA. In each case some interpolation is called for to learn that the January MSLP in Anchorage is 1008 mb with an SD of 15 mb, and in San Diego it is 1019 mb with an SD of about 4 mb. In Anchorage, 68% of all January pressures will be between 993 mb and 1023 mb (1008 ±15). Any pressure outside of that range has only a 32% chance of occurring (100-68)

A pressure of 1005 mb, for example, in January in Anchorage is fairly common. It is in the range that occurs 34% of the time. In San Diego in January, however, 1005 mb is 14 mb lower than the mean value of 1019. That is 14/4 = 3.5 SD. That pressure is in the

Table 10.1 -1 Normal Pressure Distributions*	
Observed Pressure, P	*Probability*
MSLP-1SD ≤ P ≤ MSLP +1SD	68.2%
MSLP-2SD ≤ P ≤ MSLP +2SD	95.4%
MSLP-3SD ≤ P ≤ MSLP +3SD	99.6%
MSLP ≤ P ≤ MSLP + 1SD	34.1%
MSLP ≤ P ≤ MSLP + 2SD	47.7%
MSLP ≤ P ≤ MSLP + 3SD	49.8%
P ≤ MSLP - 0.5SD	31%
P ≤ MSLP - 1SD	16%
P ≤ MSLP - 1.5SD	6.7%
P ≤ MSLP - 2SD	2.3%
P ≤ MSLP - 2.5SD	0.6%
P ≤ MSLP - 3SD	0.1%
MSLP ≤ P ≤ MSLP + 1SD	34.1%
MSLP + 1SD ≤ P ≤ MSLP + 2SD	13.6%
MSLP + 2SD ≤ P ≤ MSLP + 3SD	2.1%
MSLP + 3SD ≤ P ≤ MSLP + 4SD	0.13%

The top group references a pressure to either side of the mean value. The second group references pressures on the high side of the mean. The same values apply to the low side of the mean (reverse all signs). The next group specifies all values below a specific value, as was done back in Table 6.4-1. Reverse signs to get the high side values. The bottom group refers to specific ranges of pressures on either side of the mean (reverse all signs for the other side).

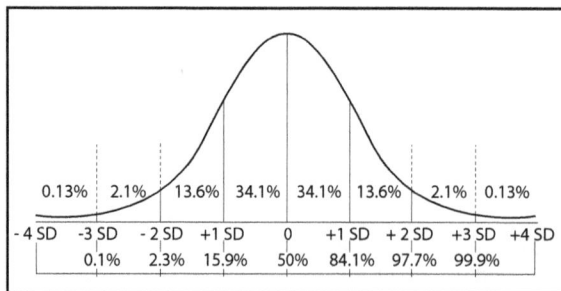

Figure 10.1-2 *Probabilities related to any normal distribution of observations. In a normal distribution, 68% (2x34) of the values are within 1 SD of the mean, half above and half below; 95% are within 2 SD of the mean; and 99.7% fall within 3 SD of the mean. If we carefully figured all the areas under the sections, we would learn that the probability of a value being less than the mean by 1 SD is 16%; less than 1.5 SD is 7%; and less than 2 SD is about 2 or 3%, which is summarized in Table 10.1-1.*

range that occurs only 0.13% of the time. In short, a rare occurrence. If we had this January pressure in Anchorage, we would have no reason to note it. But if we had this same pressure in San Diego, we should pay attention—if we are not already fully attending to the weather.

To further illustrate the table, we can now figure the probability of a 20-year old women being over 6 feet tall. Six feet is 72 inches, which is (72-65.5) = 6.5 inchs above the mean. This is 6.5/2.5 = 2.6 SD. So the probability of a height $\geq 65.5 + 2.6$ SD is about 0.6%. Out of every 1,000 young women there would be about 6 of them over 6 feet tall.

10.2 Overview of World Pressures

Though pieces of the puzzle had been coming together since the mid 1700s, it was William Ferrel in 1856 who gave us the first sound interpretation of the average global winds and pressures, shown in Figure 10.2-1.

The sun heats the earth along the equatorial belt, which lightens the air creating a low pressure band around the globe called the doldrums. The warmed air rises in this low band to an elevation about halfway up through the atmosphere at which point the thermal updraft can no longer overcome gravity pulling it back down, and so the warm air is forced poleward on both sides from the updraft below, to the north and to the south.

As it moves poleward at this high altitude, parts of it then cool enough to begin sinking back to the earth at around latitude 30° to 40°, N and S. This descending cool air creates a broad band of high pressure around the globe, but because of the presence of land masses, isolated large Highs are created in the centers of the oceans and continents. At sea these are the famous subtropical Atlantic and Pacific Highs, and over land they create the great deserts of the world.

This descending air then fans out in all directions when it hits the surface. As it proceeds along the surface of the earth it is forced to the right by the Coriolis effect in northern latitudes and to the left in the southern latitudes. Thus the flow along the equatorial sides of the Highs form the NE and SE trade winds, and the flow along the poleward sides of the Highs form the prevailing westerlies in both hemispheres.

The air aloft moving poleward that did not descend in the subtropical Highs, does finally cool enough to descend in the polar regions to form polar Highs. Upon reaching the surface, the air moves toward the equator in both hemispheres, and is then forced westward by the Coriolis effect to make the prevailing polar easterlies.

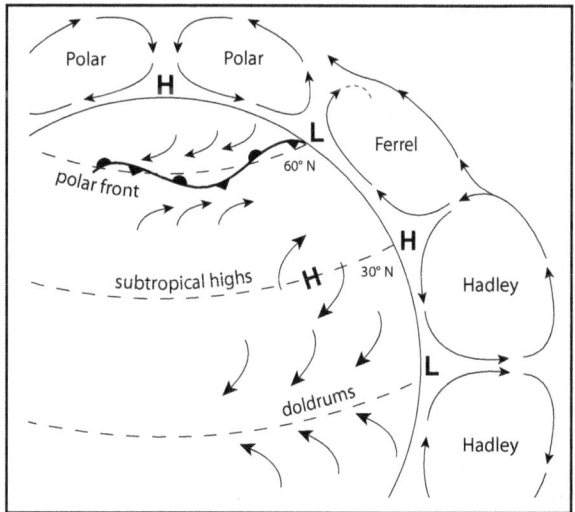

Figure 10.2-1 *Global wind circulation and pressure distributions. H's mark High pressure zones; L's mark Lows. The process is initiated by solar heating along the equatorial belt. The cells of circulation are essentially symmetric in the Northern and Southern Hemispheres.*

The polar easterlies then converge with the prevailing westerlies at about 60° latitude creating rising air along the polar front, along which we find a series of Lows at any one time.

The average pressure profile of the earth can thus be described as a band of low pressure around the equatorial belt, generally centered at about 5° to 10° North; a series of large Highs centered about 30° to 40°; a series of Lows distributed along a latitude of about 60°; and weak Highs at both poles.

These features can each be noted in the monthly maps of the mean sea level isobars. Air temperatures vary little in the tropics, so annual pressure variations over the equatorial areas are very small. In the mid-latitudes, however, the annual variations are notable and can be classified as continental or oceanic.

Over continents, the pressure is maximum in the winter and minimum in the summer. Thus over Asia we see the alternating pressures that give rise to the famous monsoons: the great Siberian High in the winter and the Asiatic Low in the summer. Likewise the California trough (elongated Low) over the SW U.S. in summer has a large influence on several weather patterns, as do cold winter Highs over Canada.

Over the oceans this is reversed, with the maximum pressures in summer and minimums in the winter. Look for the Pacific and Atlantic Highs as an example, as well as the Icelandic and Aleutian Lows.

10.3 Obtaining Mean Pressure Data from the NCDC

The National Climatic Data Center (NCDC) archives weather data from land stations around the world, including standard deviations for most data. The NCDC is an immense resource, so there are many layers to finding the type of data you might want—and hence the value of the instructions below. This is, for example, also the place you would go to find a weather map from some specific date in the past.

To illustrate the use of this resource we will find the MSLP and SD for Nantucket Island, MA (41° 15'N, 70° 04'W) for the past 20 years, from 1988 till 2008. This then we can compare to the data presented here, extrapolated onto the land from marine observations. The marine data extend back in time much longer but ended just before these newer land based data. The steps are presented in Table 10.3-1 and the results for Nantucket Island Memorial Airport are in Figure 10.3-1. Results are compared to Chapter 10 data in Table 10.3-2.

Table 10.3-2 Nantucket Island Pressures*

Month	MCAW <1980 MSLP	SD	NCDC 1988-2008 MSLP	SD
Jan	1016.4	10.0	1016.7	9.9
Feb	1015.2	10.8	1014.7	9.5
Mar	1014.7	10.0	1014.7	10.2
Apr	1015.5	9.0	1012.8	8.6
May	1016.0	6.9	1014.7	7.1
Jun	1015.0	6.1	1014.3	6.6
Jul	1016.0	5.2	1014.3	5.1
Aug	1016.0	5.1	1015.5	4.9
Sep	1017.0	6.8	1016.3	6.8
Oct	1017.5	8.0	1016.3	8.6
Nov	1016.0	9.2	1016.7	9.4
Dec	1016.0	9.4	1015.9	10.3

* MCAW is the US Navy Marine Climatic Atlas of the World. NCDC is the National Climatic Data Center. The former data are presented in this chapter; the latter are available online as outlined in Table 10.3-1. Figure 10.3-2 shows the raw data from NCDC. Except for Apr MSLP, the agreement is good. The SD are within ± 1mb, which we have also seen in other high midlatitude coastal comparisons, even when the MSLP might be off several mb.

Table 10.3-1 How to get Mean Monthly Pressures and Standard Deviation from NCDC

Step	Procedure
1	Go to NOAA National Climatic Data Center at http://cdo.ncdc.noaa.gov/CDO/cdo
2	Select "Data set / Product"
3	Select " Surface Data, Hourly Global (Over 10,000 worldwide sites)." Press Access Data/Products
4	Agree to WMO Resolution #40 and proceed to the next page.
5	Choose "Continue with Advanced Options"
6	Select Country of interest. Choose "Data Summary" as output format. Click continue
7	Select your State/province and then your desired Station(s). Click continue
8	Under #1, Choose "Select 10 year summary from the most recent data—go to step 6"
9	Choose your Summary type (Sea level pressure statistics summary). Click continue.
	A link will be provided to the table data on the screen, or they will email you a link.*

* If the data comes up all blank, check date-range availability at the site you chose from an earlier step. You can also get other data this way, and you can approach it from a graphical search engine at Step 1 to see where the stations are located. There are tremendous amounts of data available at this site (including past surface analysis maps for any time and date), but the interface is complex and takes some practice. Note in Step 1 there is an uppercase and lowercase "cdo."

NNDC CLIMATE DATA ONLINE

Surface Data, Hourly Global: Summaries(DS3505)
ISD Summary
POR 01/01/1988 - 12/31/2007
Sea-Level Pressure Summary for 72506314756/NANTUCKET MEMORIAL AP
1988/01/01 00:00 to 2007/12/31 23:59

HOUR (UTC)		JAN	FEB	MAR	APR	MAY	JUN	JUL	AUG	SEP	OCT	NOV	DEC	ANNUAL
0	mean	1016.7	1014.9	1015.0	1013.3	1014.8	1014.5	1014.1	1015.6	1016.5	1016.5	1016.7	1016.3	1015.4
	stdv	9.9	9.7	9.9	8.8	7.0	6.3	5.6	4.8	6.6	8.5	9.3	10.1	8.0
	#obs	180.0	165.0	179.0	174.0	182.0	189.0	206.0	208.0	199.0	211.0	205.0	214.0	2312.0
1	mean	1016.9	1015.2	1014.8	1013.4	1014.9	1014.6	1014.5	1015.8	1016.6	1016.5	1016.9	1016.5	1015.6
	stdv	10.0	9.5	9.8	8.4	6.9	6.3	5.0	4.8	6.6	8.5	9.2	9.9	7.9
	#obs	178.0	164.0	181.0	175.0	189.0	195.0	209.0	221.0	203.0	212.0	209.0	213.0	2349.0
2	mean	1017.1	1015.1	1014.8	1013.0	1014.9	1014.6	1014.5	1015.6	1016.6	1016.3	1016.7	1016.1	1015.4
	stdv	9.6	9.4	10.0	8.4	7.0	6.3	4.9	4.8	6.5	9.1	9.2	10.0	7.9
	#obs	179.0	165.0	176.0	174.0	185.0	192.0	209.0	212.0	201.0	214.0	209.0	212.0	2328.0
3	mean	1017.2	1015.0	1014.8	1013.0	1014.8	1014.5	1014.6	1015.6	1016.5	1016.6	1016.7	1016.2	1015.5
	stdv	9.6	9.4	9.8	8.5	7.1	6.4	4.9	4.7	6.6	8.3	9.1	10.1	7.9
	#obs	177.0	167.0	184.0	186.0	189.0	197.0	214.0	216.0	200.0	206.0	205.0	214.0	2355.0
21	mean	1016.0	1013.9	1014.0	1012.4	1014.2	1013.8	1013.9	1015.0	1015.8	1016.0	1016.2	1015.8	1014.8
	stdv	10.3	9.7	10.3	8.4	7.1	6.6	4.9	4.9	6.9	8.4	9.5	10.2	8.1
	#obs	178.0	165.0	186.0	179.0	180.0	200.0	211.0	219.0	198.0	211.0	203.0	213.0	2343.0
22	mean	1016.4	1014.4	1014.5	1012.4	1014.3	1013.9	1014.0	1015.1	1016.0	1016.3	1016.5	1016.0	1015.0
	stdv	10.1	9.7	10.0	8.3	7.1	6.6	5.0	4.9	6.8	8.5	9.4	10.1	8.0
	#obs	177.0	167.0	183.0	175.0	179.0	190.0	207.0	211.0	204.0	212.0	204.0	217.0	2326.0
23	mean	1016.7	1015.3	1014.7	1012.4	1014.0	1014.3	1014.1	1015.3	1016.3	1016.8	1016.4	1016.1	1015.2
	stdv	10.0	10.0	10.0	8.4	7.0	6.3	5.0	4.8	6.9	8.5	9.5	10.2	8.0
	#obs	163.0	135.0	160.0	170.0	169.0	183.0	204.0	211.0	201.0	201.0	202.0	210.0	2209.0
Total	mean	1016.7	1014.7	1014.7	1012.8	1014.7	1014.3	1014.3	1015.5	1016.3	1016.3	1016.7	1015.9	1015.2
	stdv	9.9	9.5	10.2	8.6	7.1	6.6	5.1	4.9	6.8	8.6	9.4	10.3	8.1
	#obs	4244.0	3917.0	4342.0	4206.0	4364.0	4600.0	5003.0	5110.0	4816.0	5038.0	4914.0	5090.0	55644.0

Figure 10.3-1 *Pressure data sample from the NCDC following the instructions of Table 10.3-1. The middle section has been omitted. The bottom lines are the summaries shown in Table 10.3-2. stdv = SD, #obs = number of observations. If you need accurate data for stations on land it is best to get it from NCDC, rather than the graphic results shown in this chapter. This is the data set we used to extract the diurnal variation shown in Table 5.6-1.*

The agreement between the older marine data and the more recent land based data is pretty good in this example at higher latitudes. At other high latitude locations the transition from marine to land data along the coast is not so smooth. On Kodiak Island and Anchorage, AK, for example, the mean pressures are off in some cases by 5 mb or so, but this represents only about a third of the SDs, which are on the order of 15 mb. The SDs themselves are typically within 1 or 2 mb in the worst cases. In short, the reminder again, that if you want the best data for coastal or inland stations, it is best to go directly to NCDC. Coastal stations in the tropics, on the other hand, are very close to the marine values in most cases.

January — Sea Level Pressure (mb) — Means

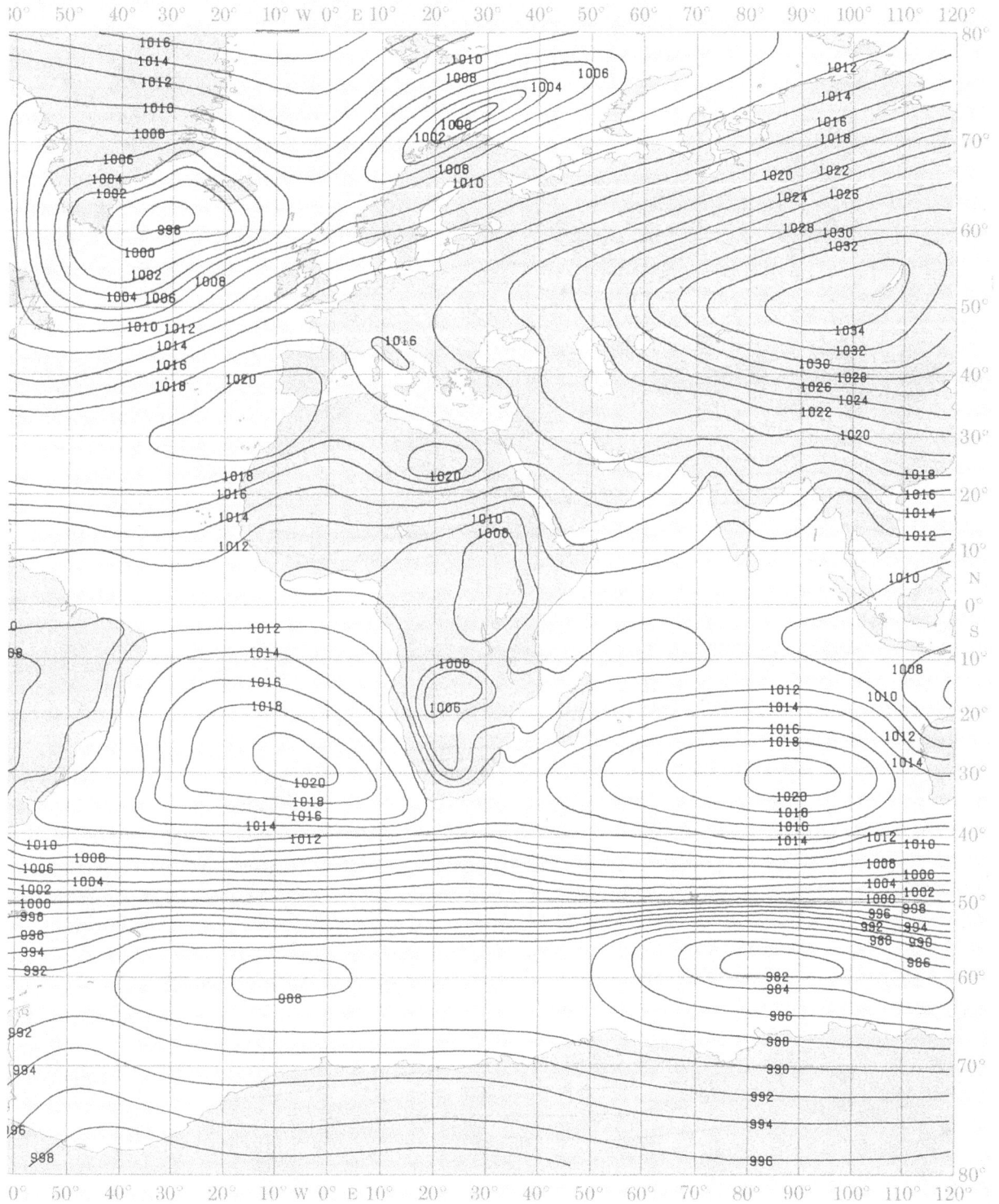

January — Sea Level Pressure (mb) — Standard Deviations

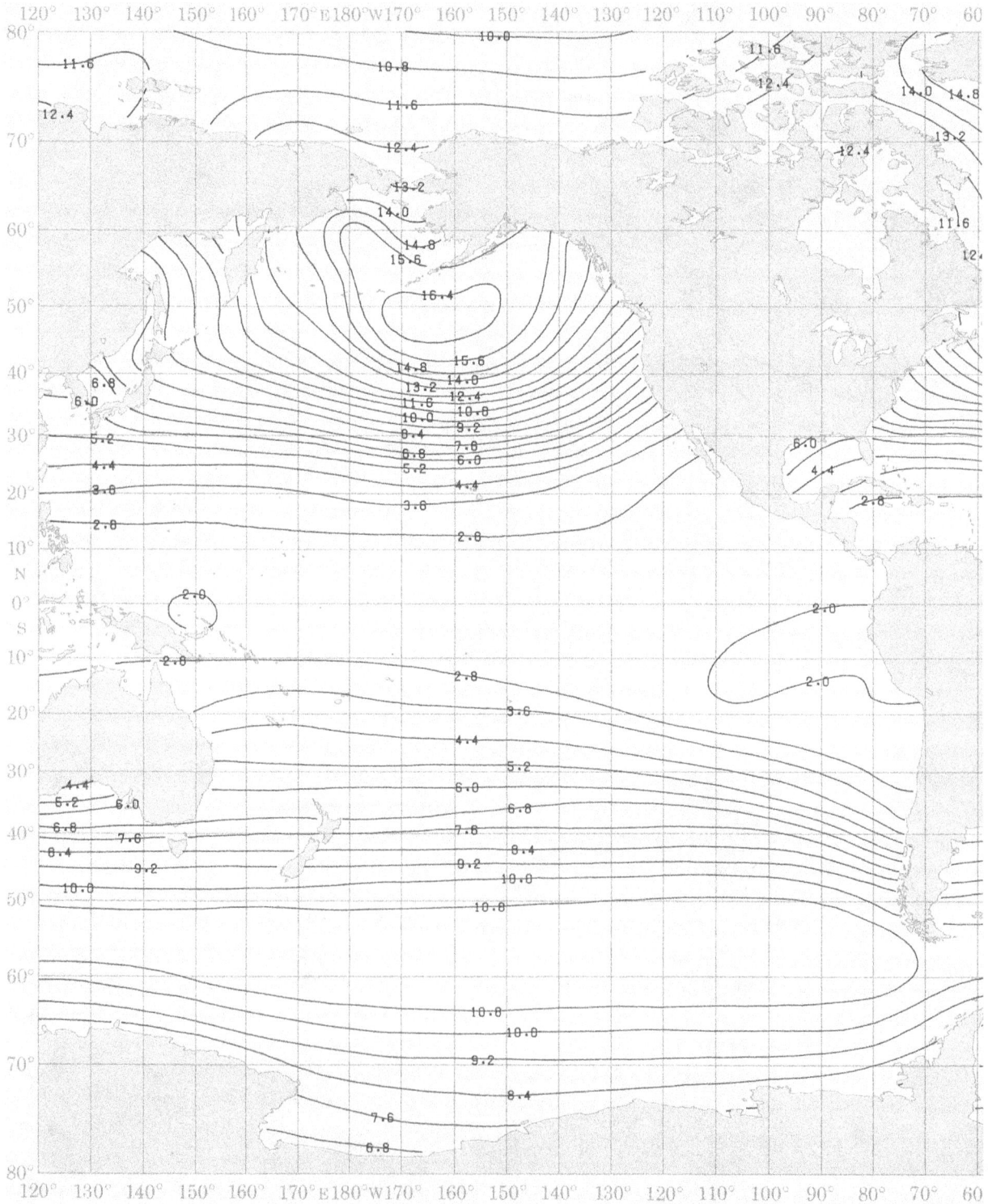

January — Sea Level Pressure (mb) — Standard Deviations

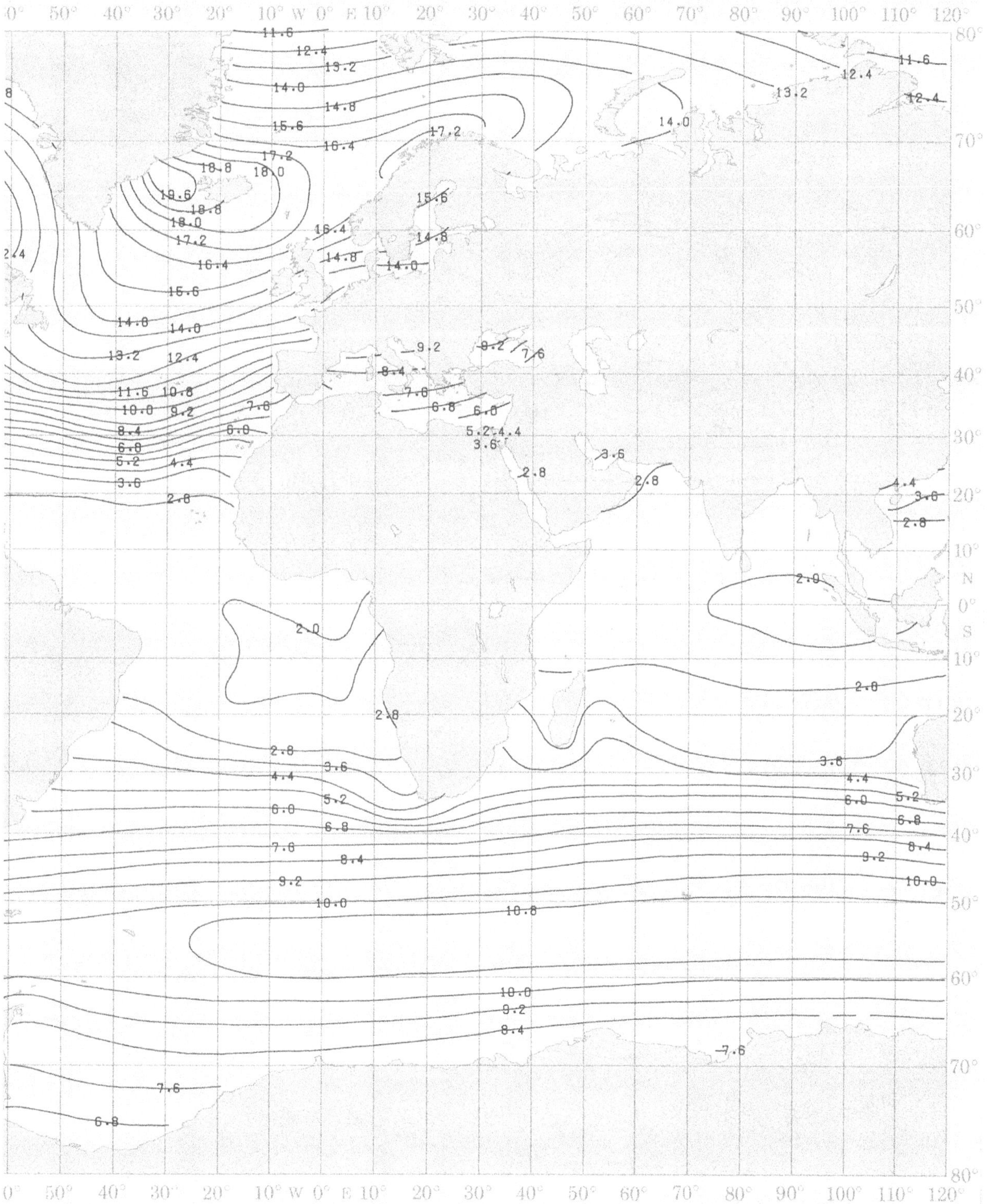

February — Sea Level Pressure (mb) — Means

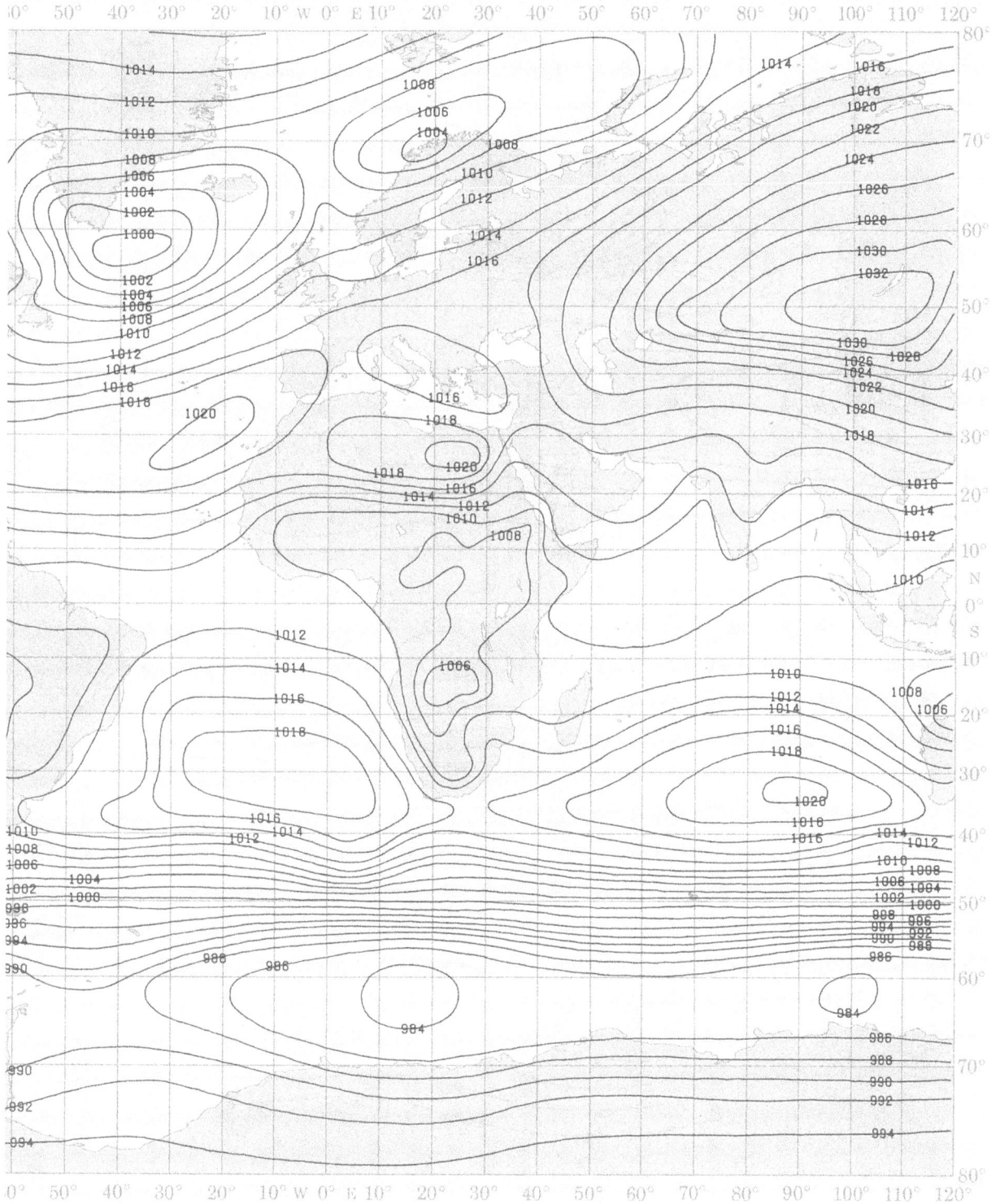

February — Sea Level Pressure (mb) — Standard Deviations

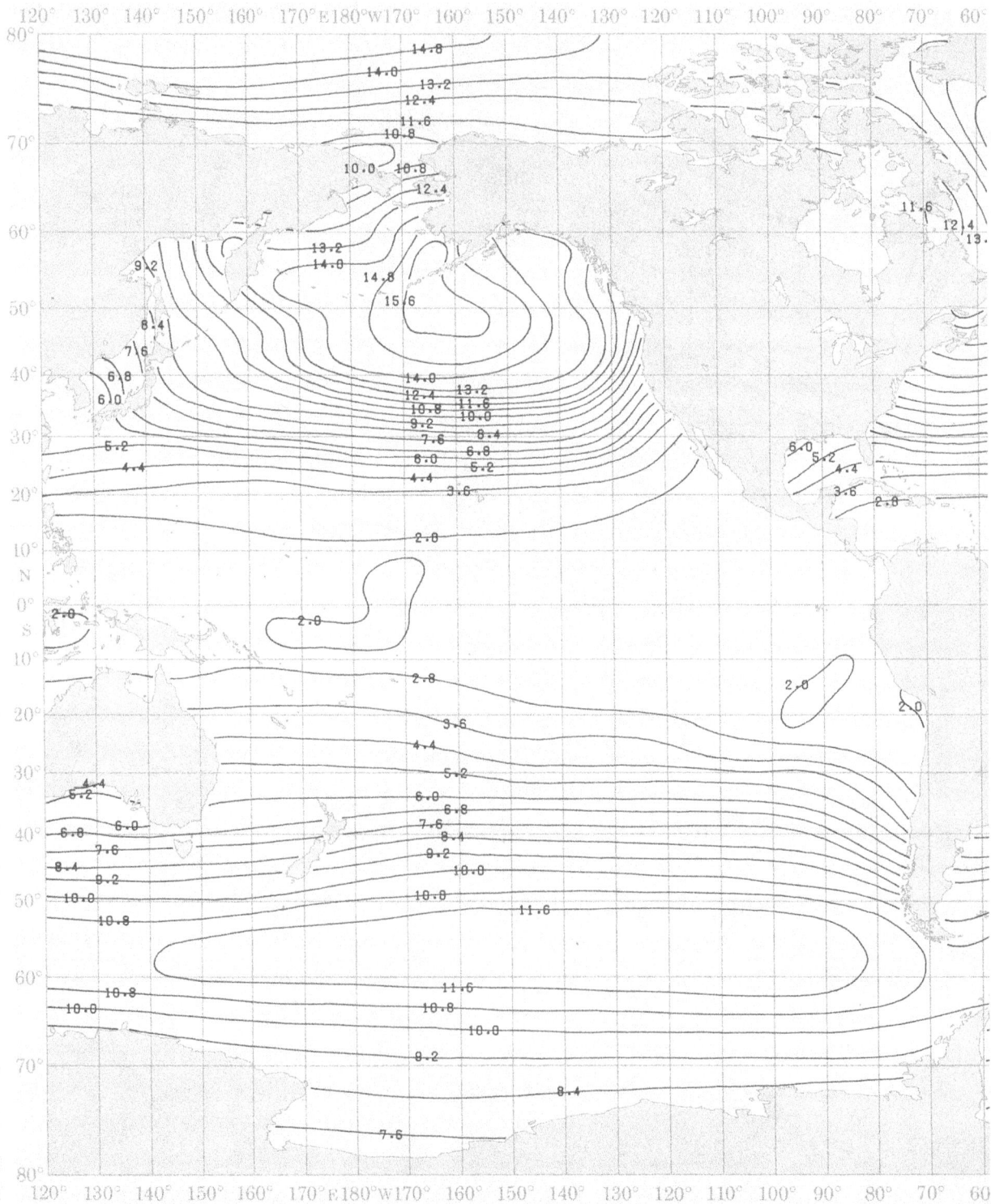

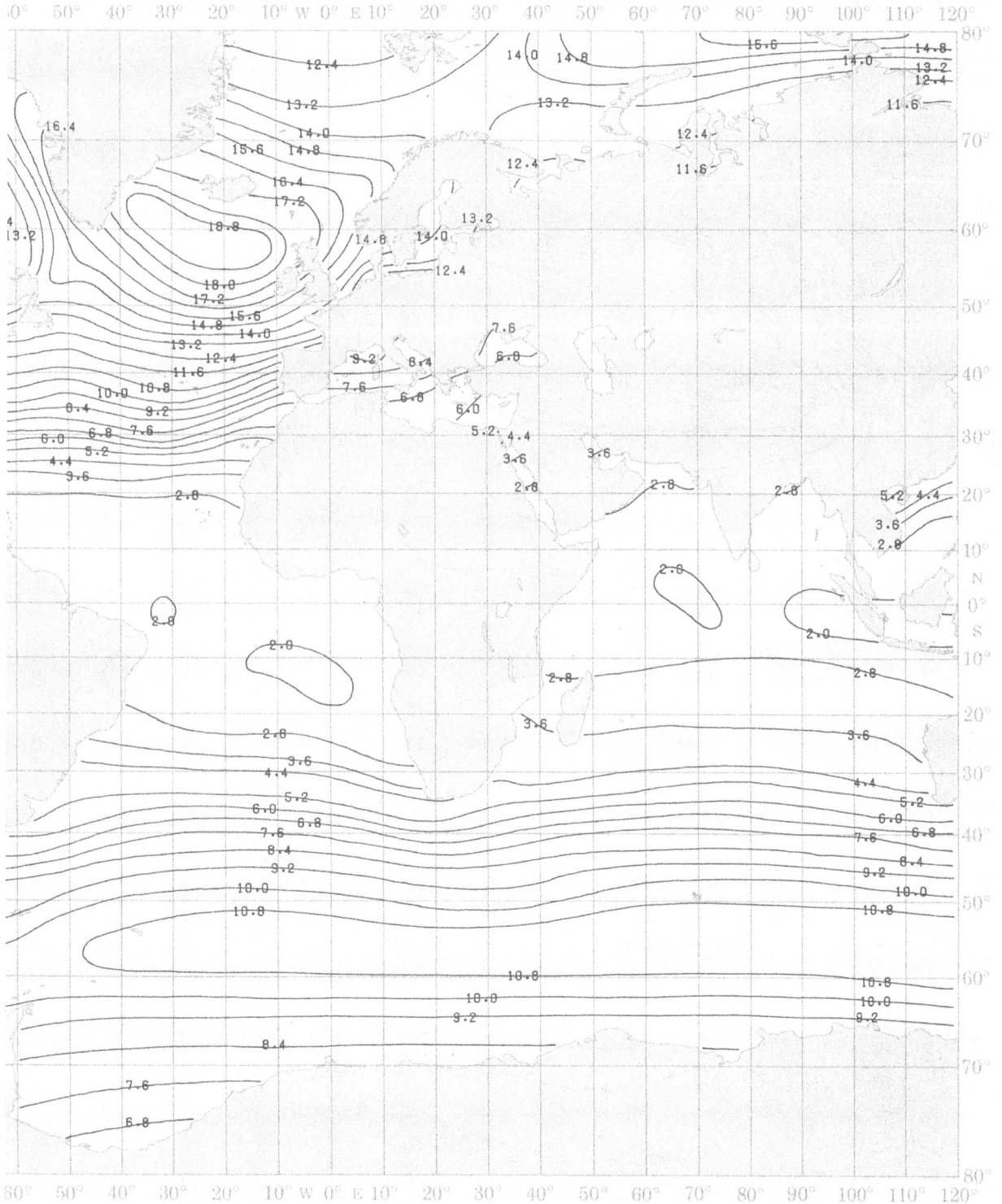

March — Sea Level Pressure (mb) — Means

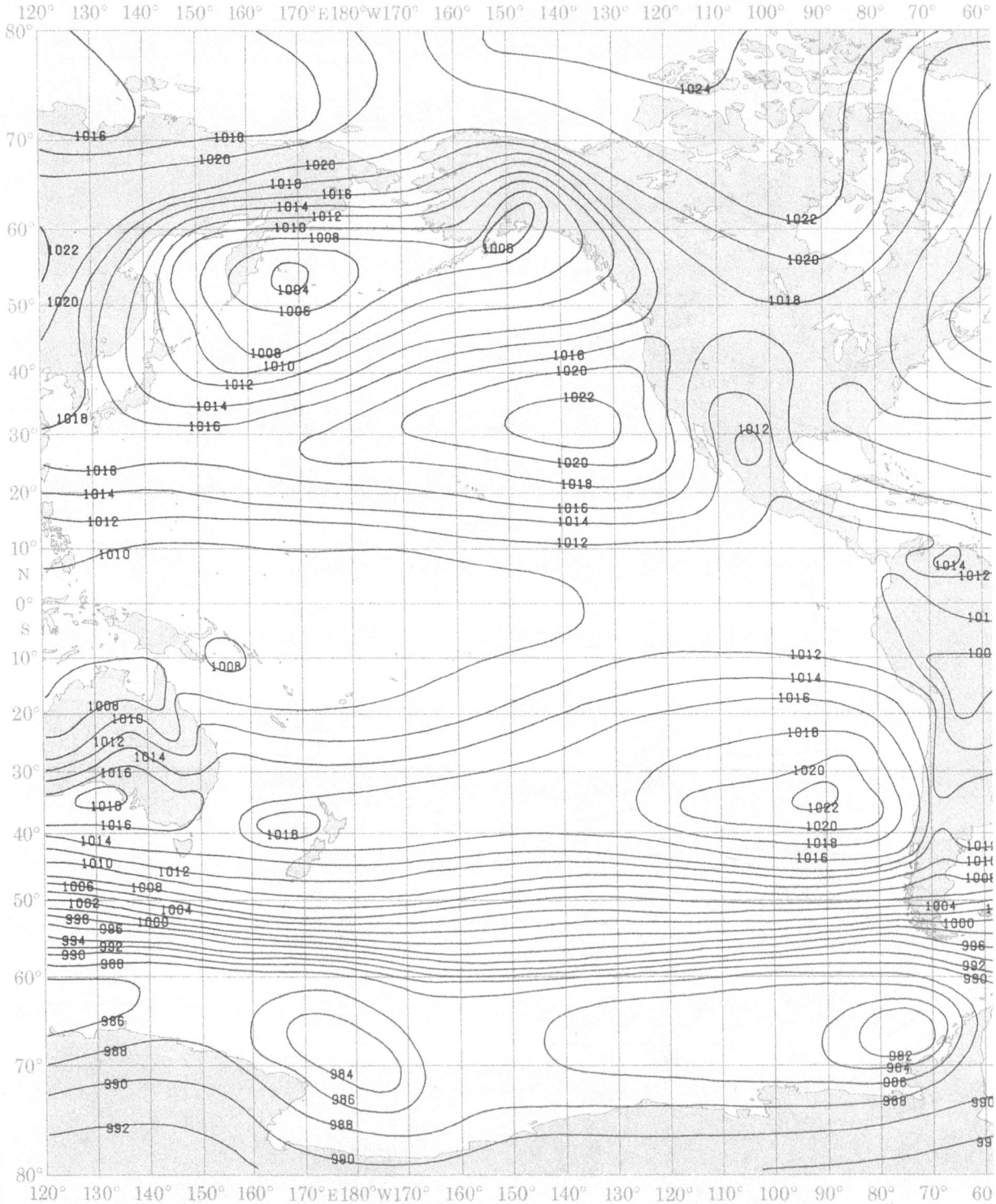

March — Sea Level Pressure (mb) — Means

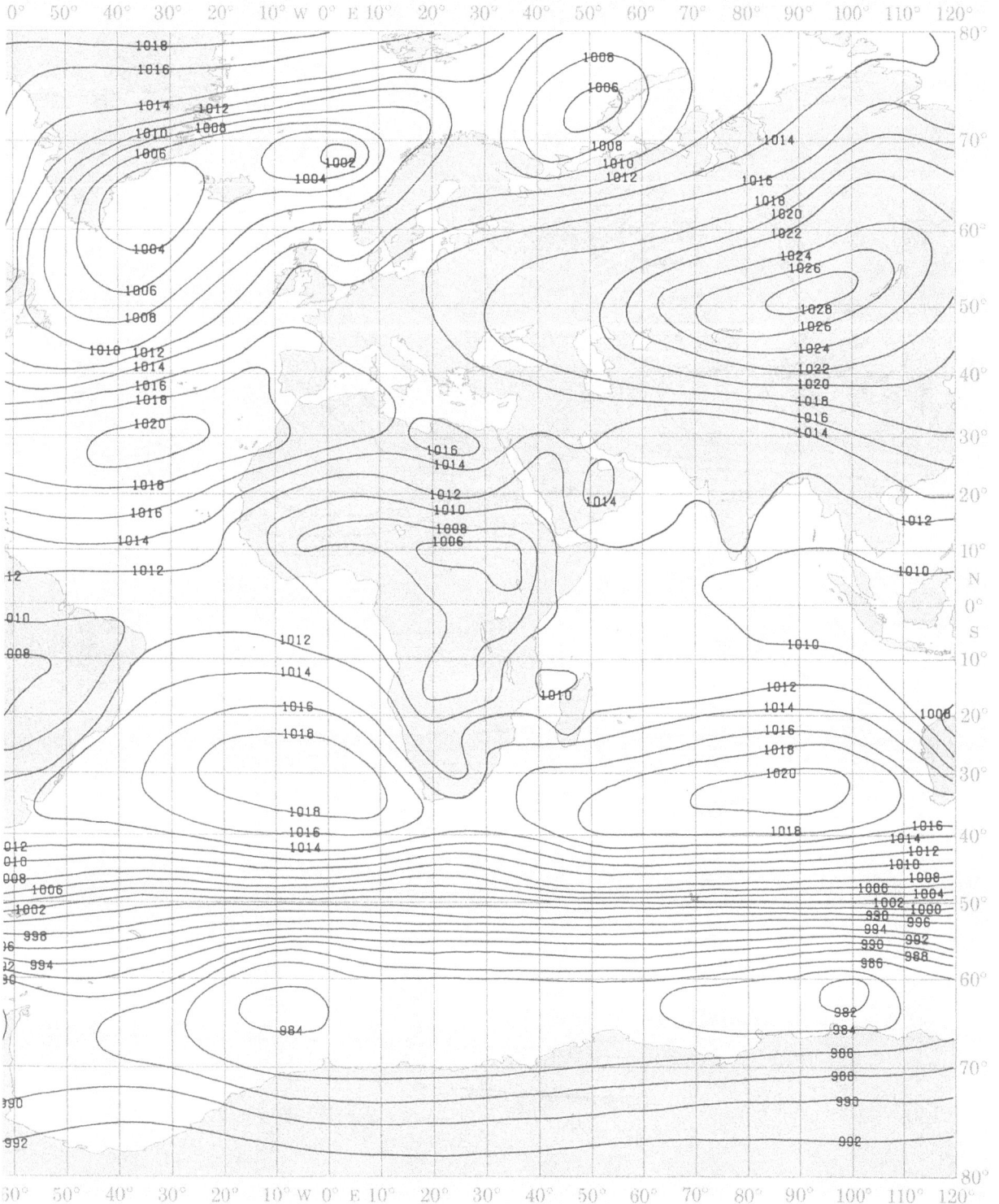

March — Sea Level Pressure (mb) — Standard Deviations

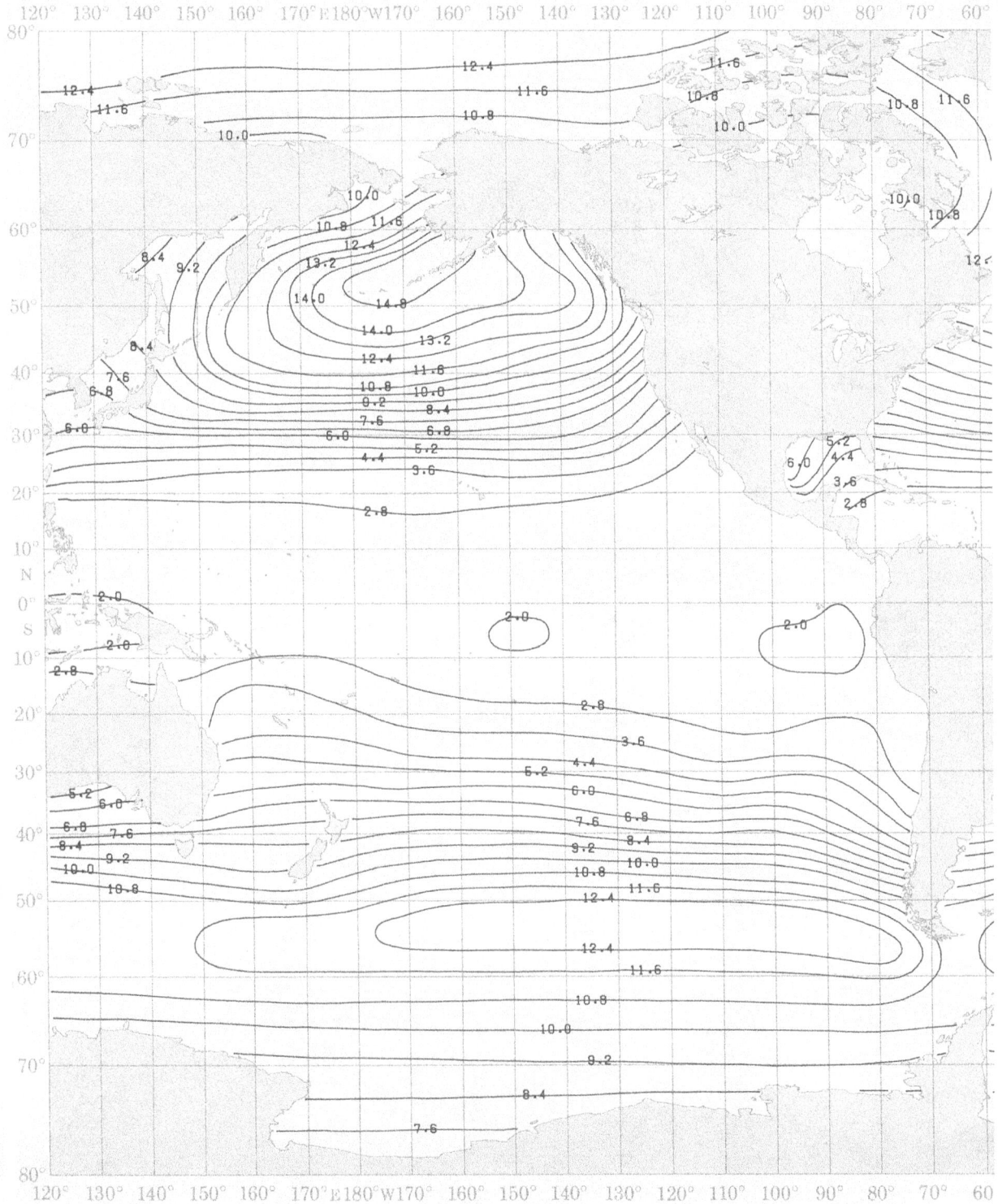

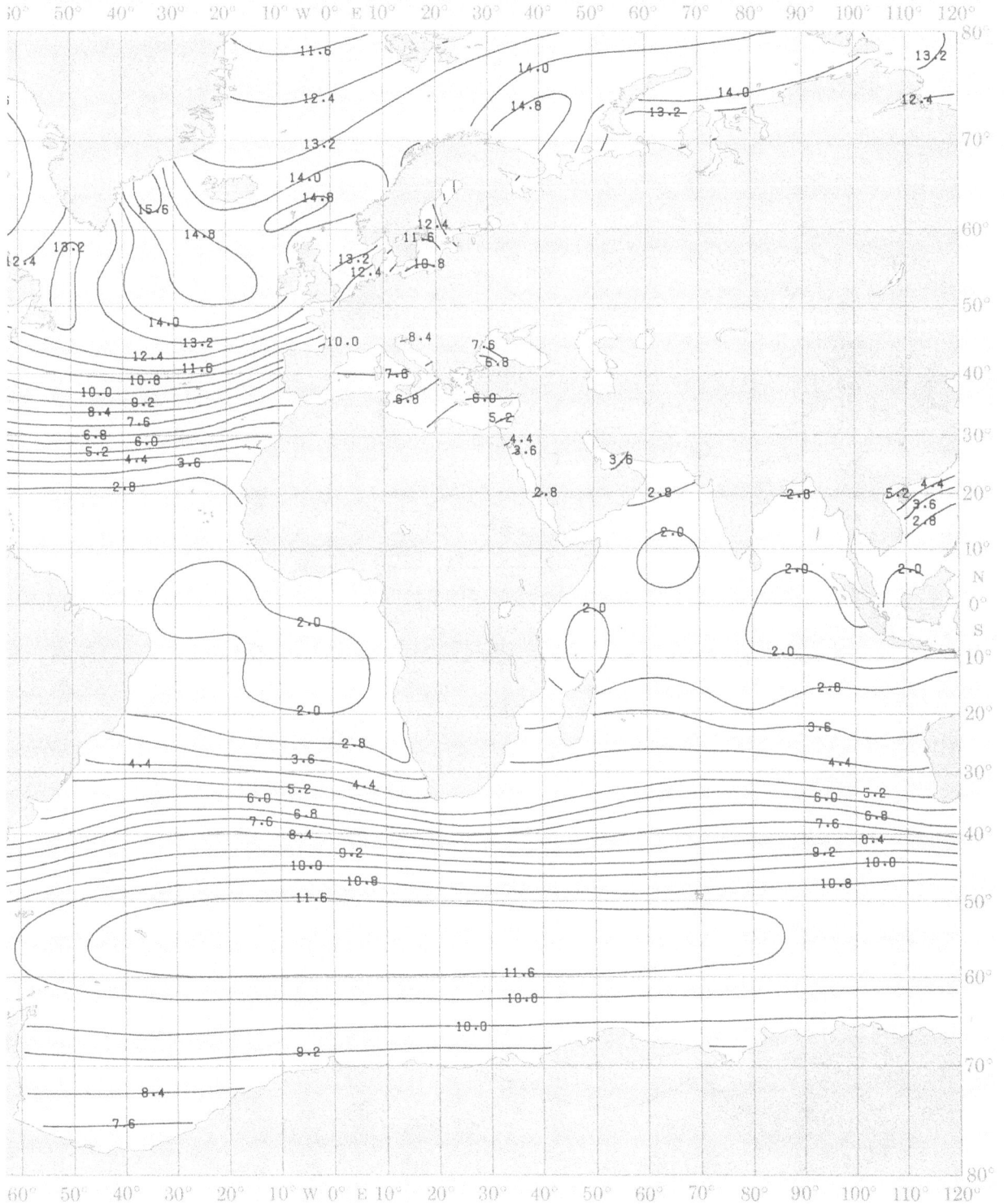

April — Sea Level Pressure (mb) — Means

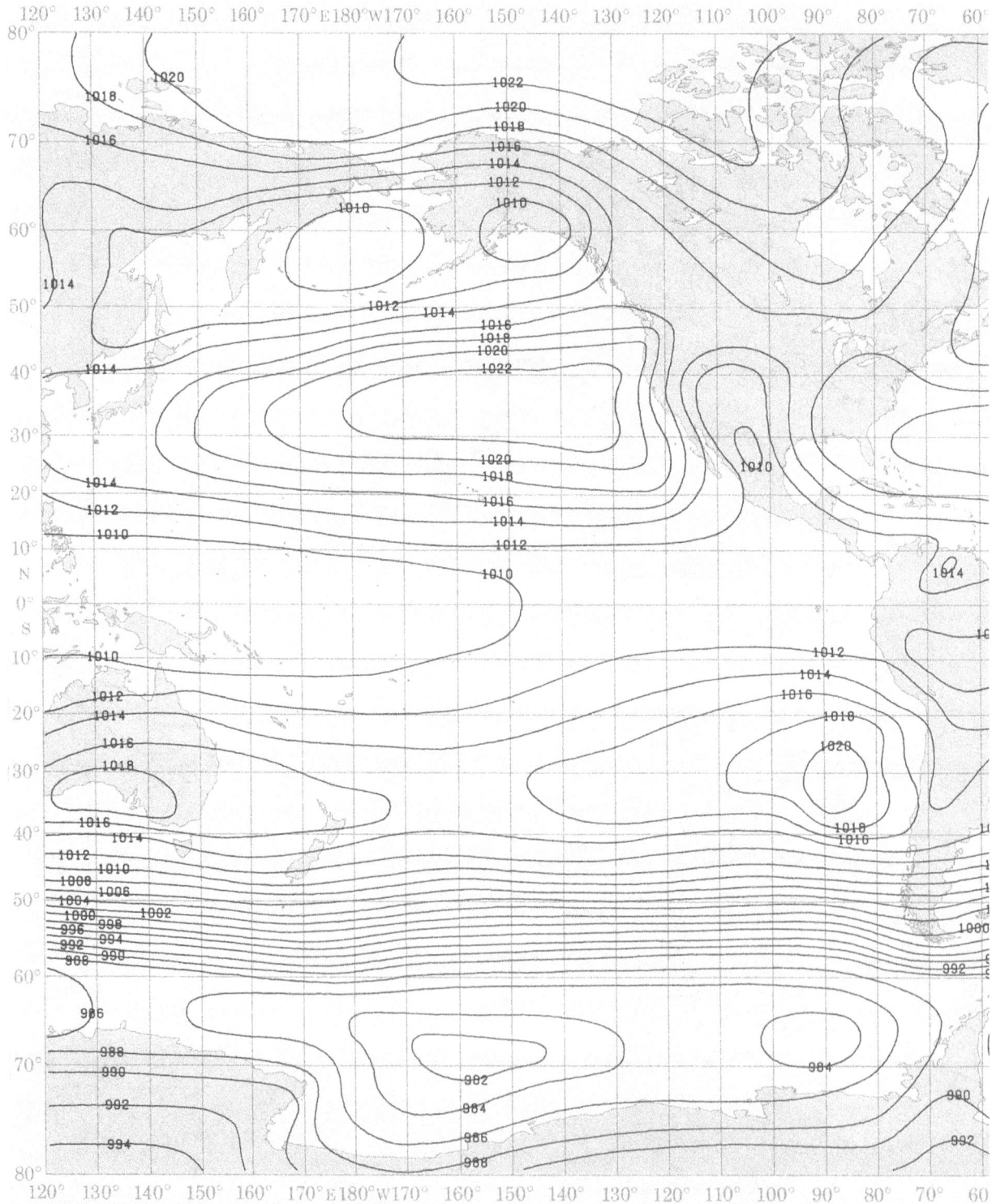

April — Sea Level Pressure (mb) — Means

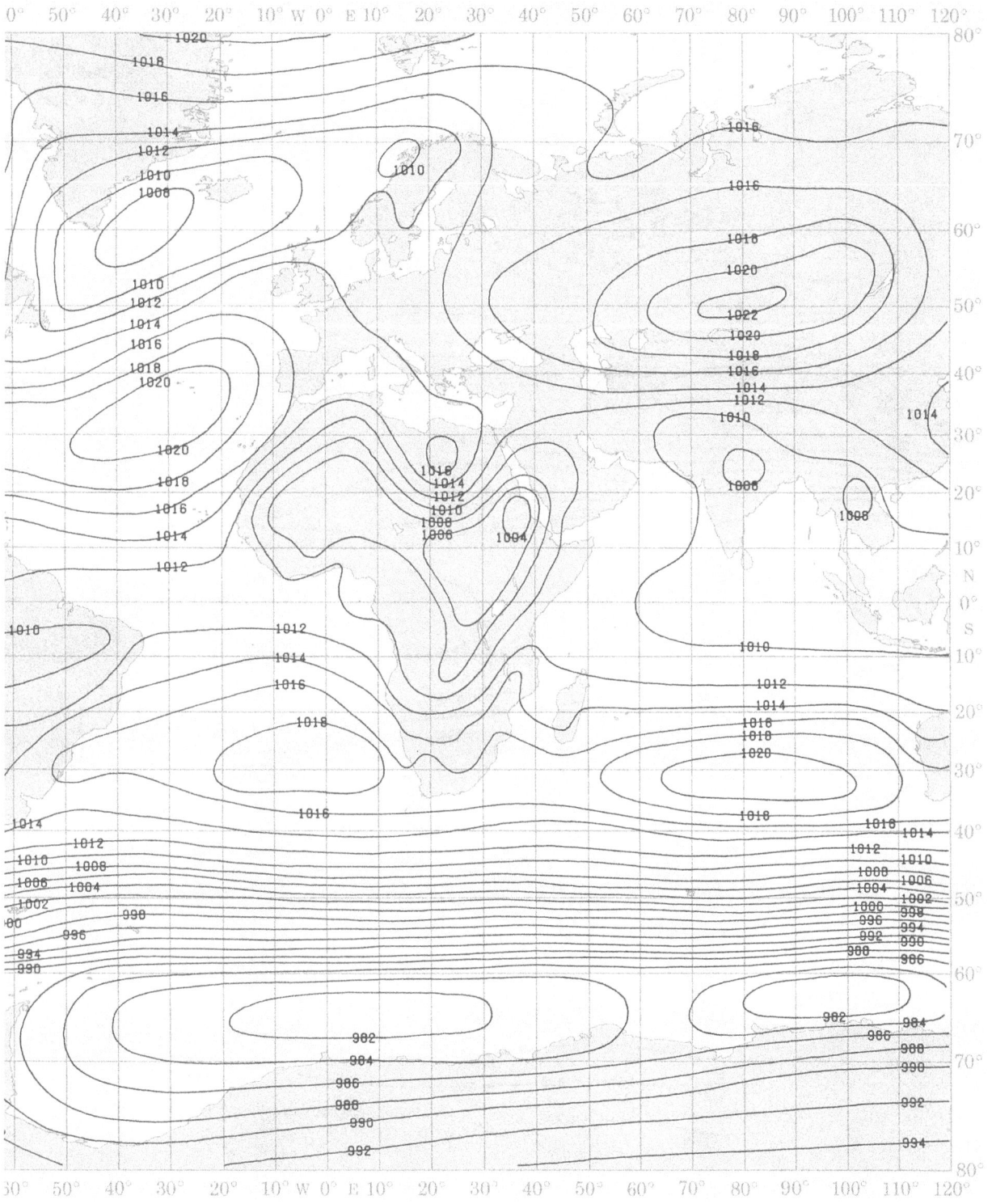

April — Sea Level Pressure (mb) — Standard Deviations

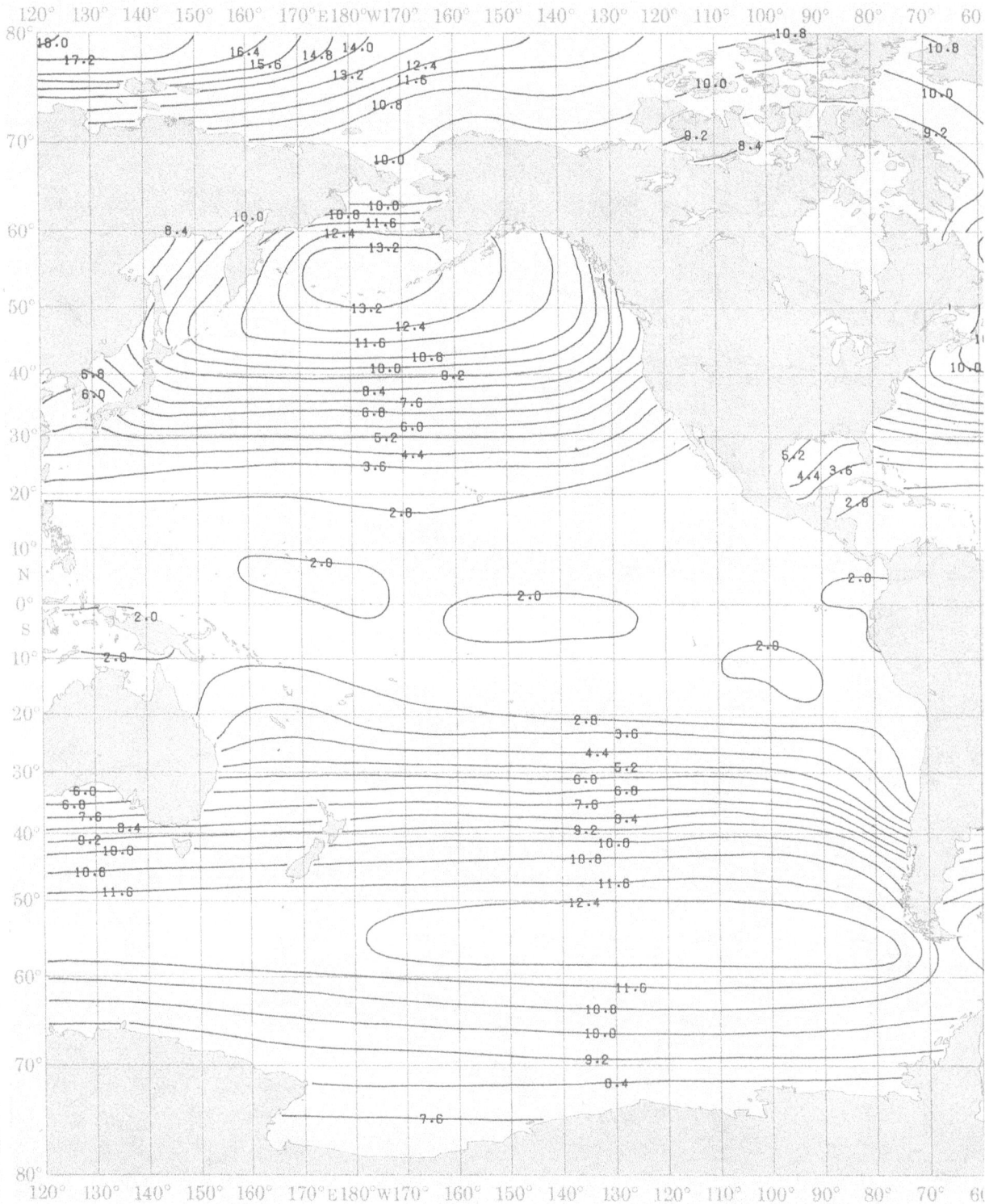

April — Sea Level Pressure (mb) — Standard Deviations

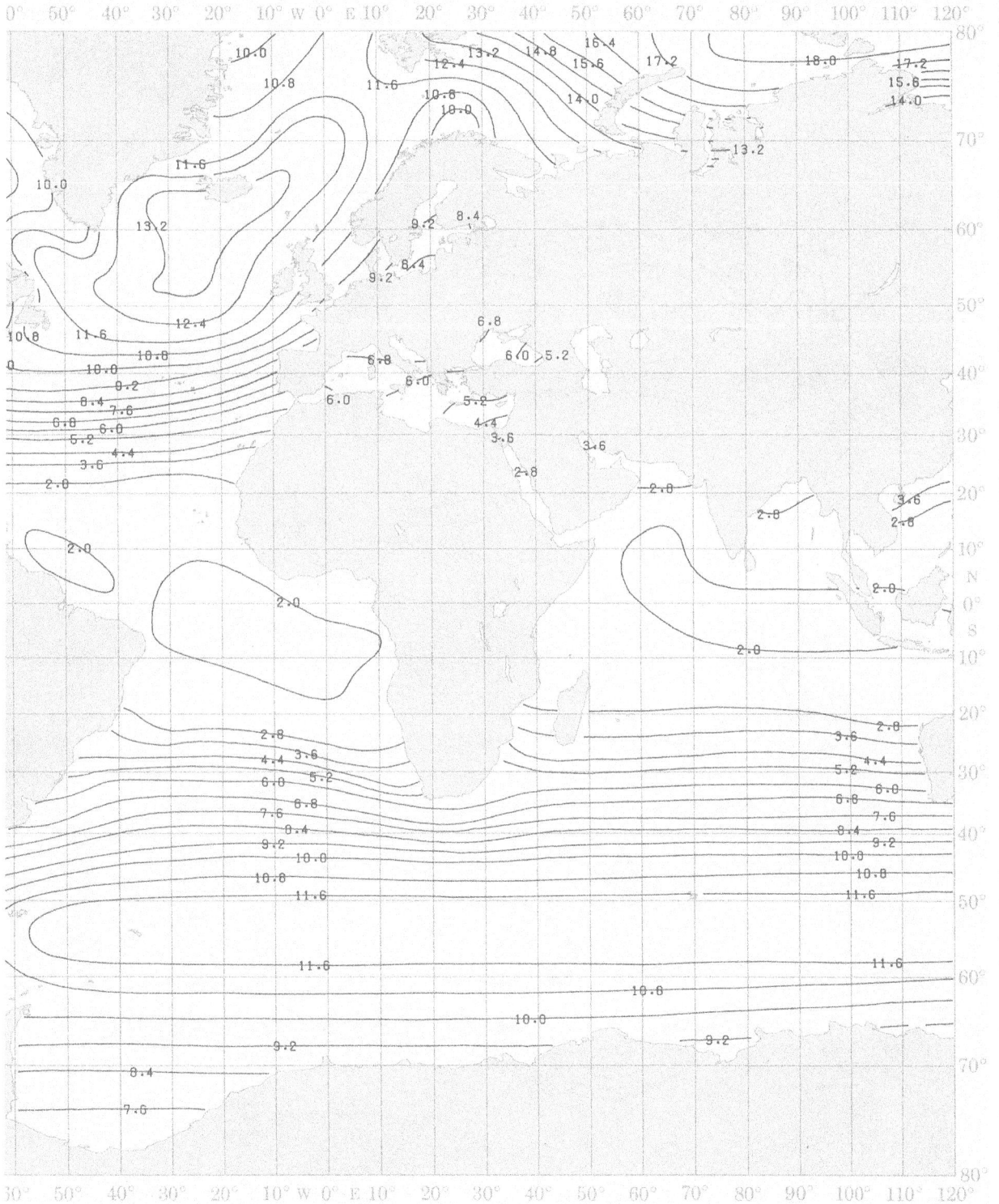

May — Sea Level Pressure (mb) — Means

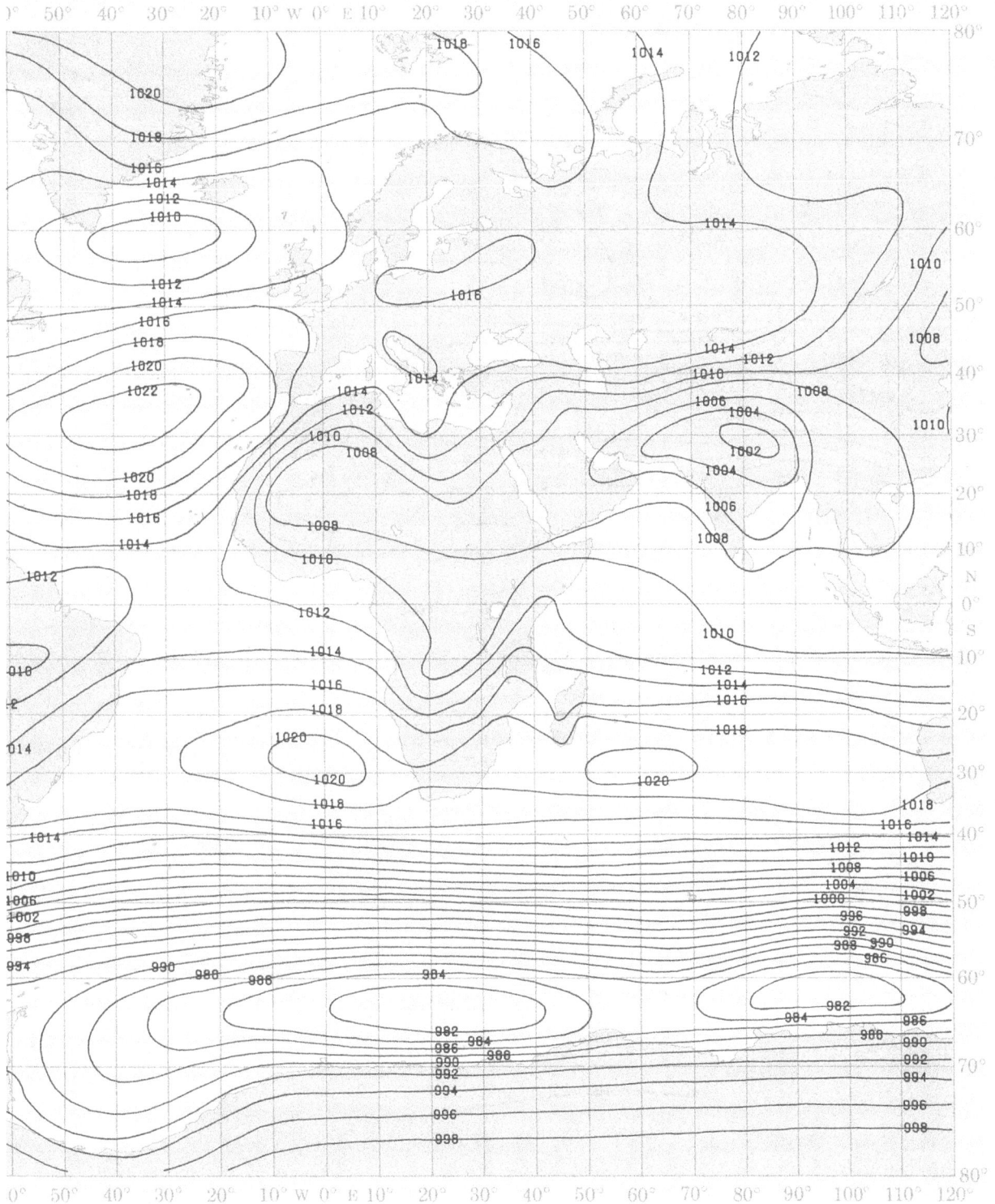

May — Sea Level Pressure (mb) — Standard Deviations

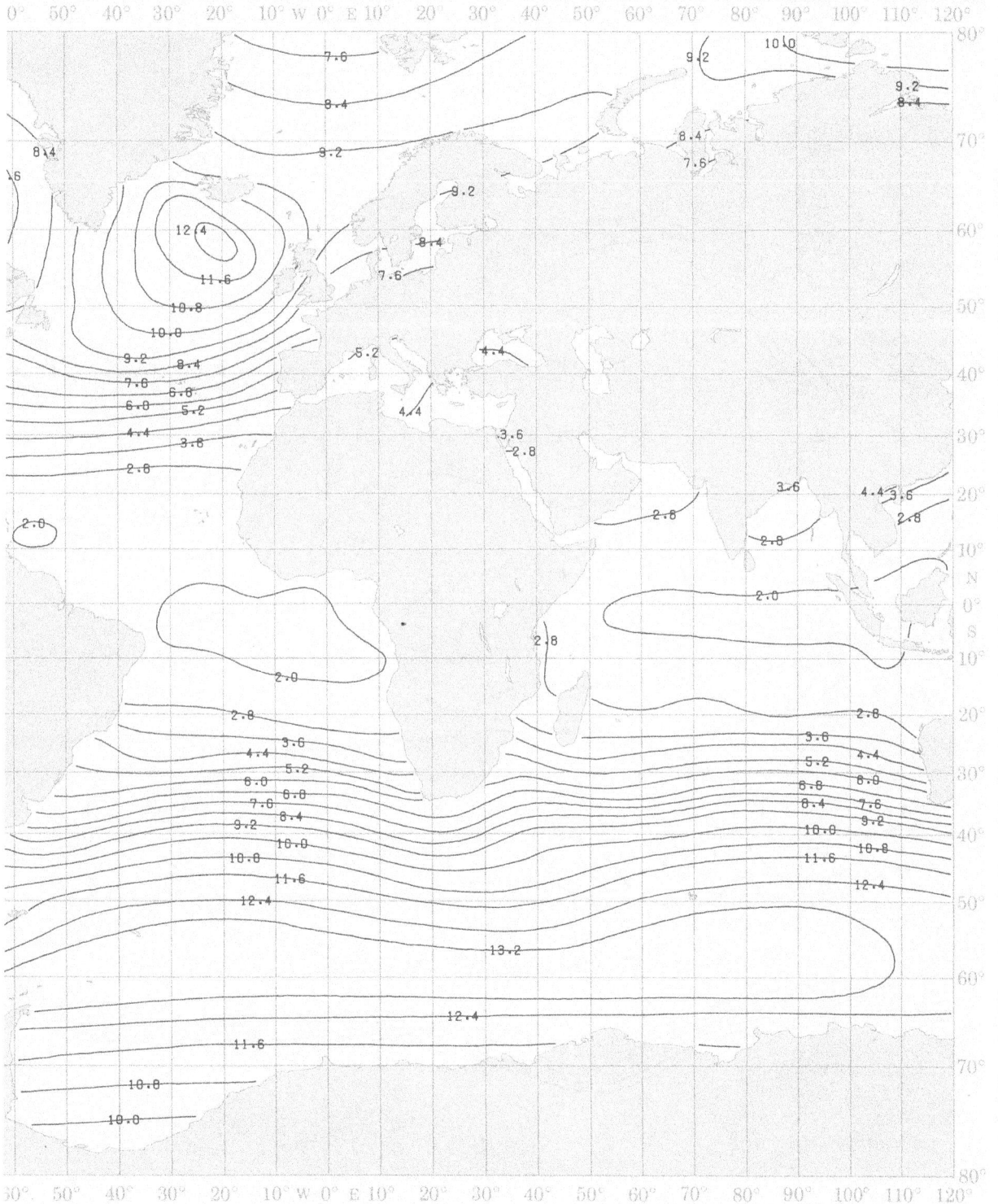

June — Sea Level Pressure (mb) — Means

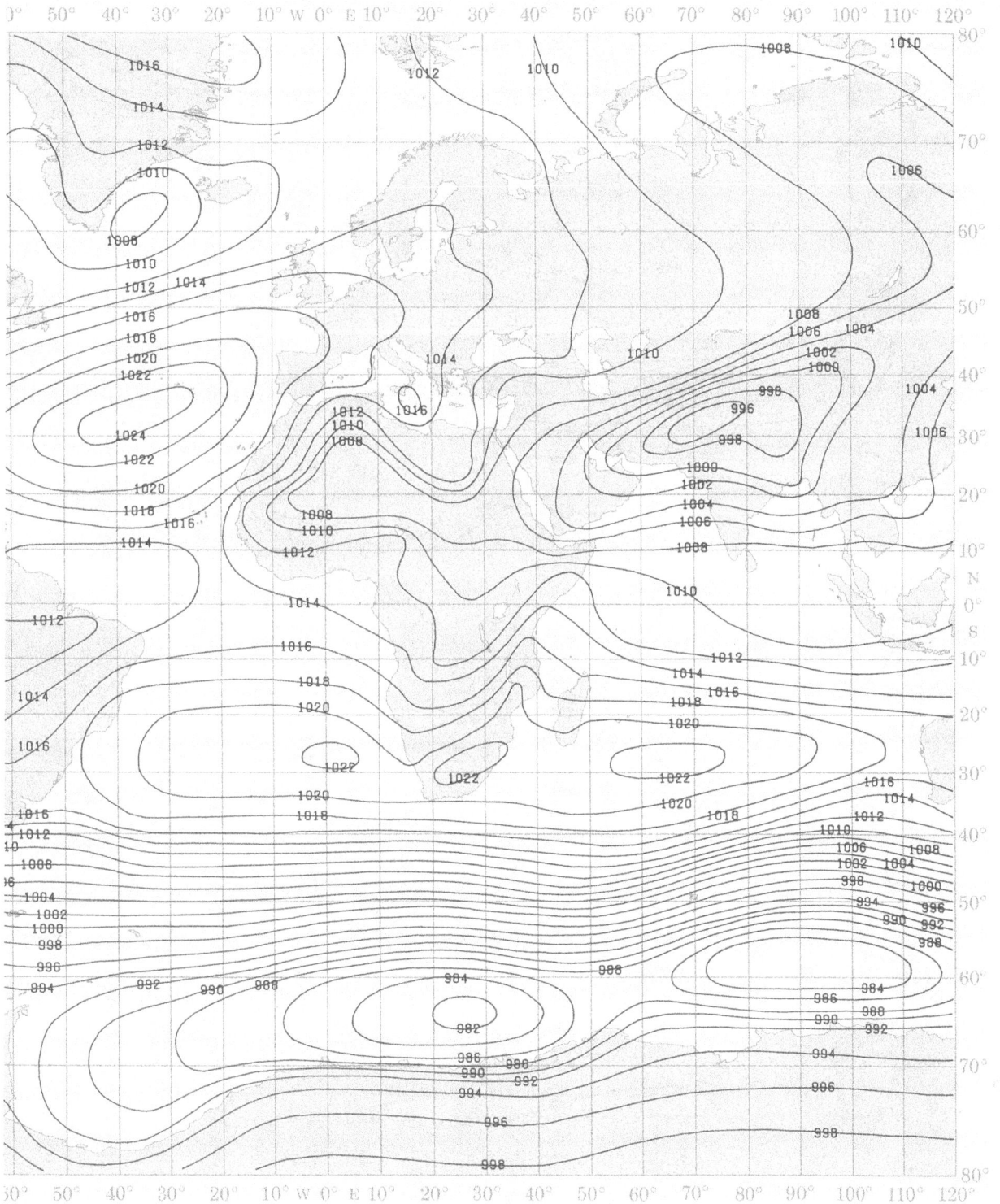

June — Sea Level Pressure (mb) — Standard Deviations

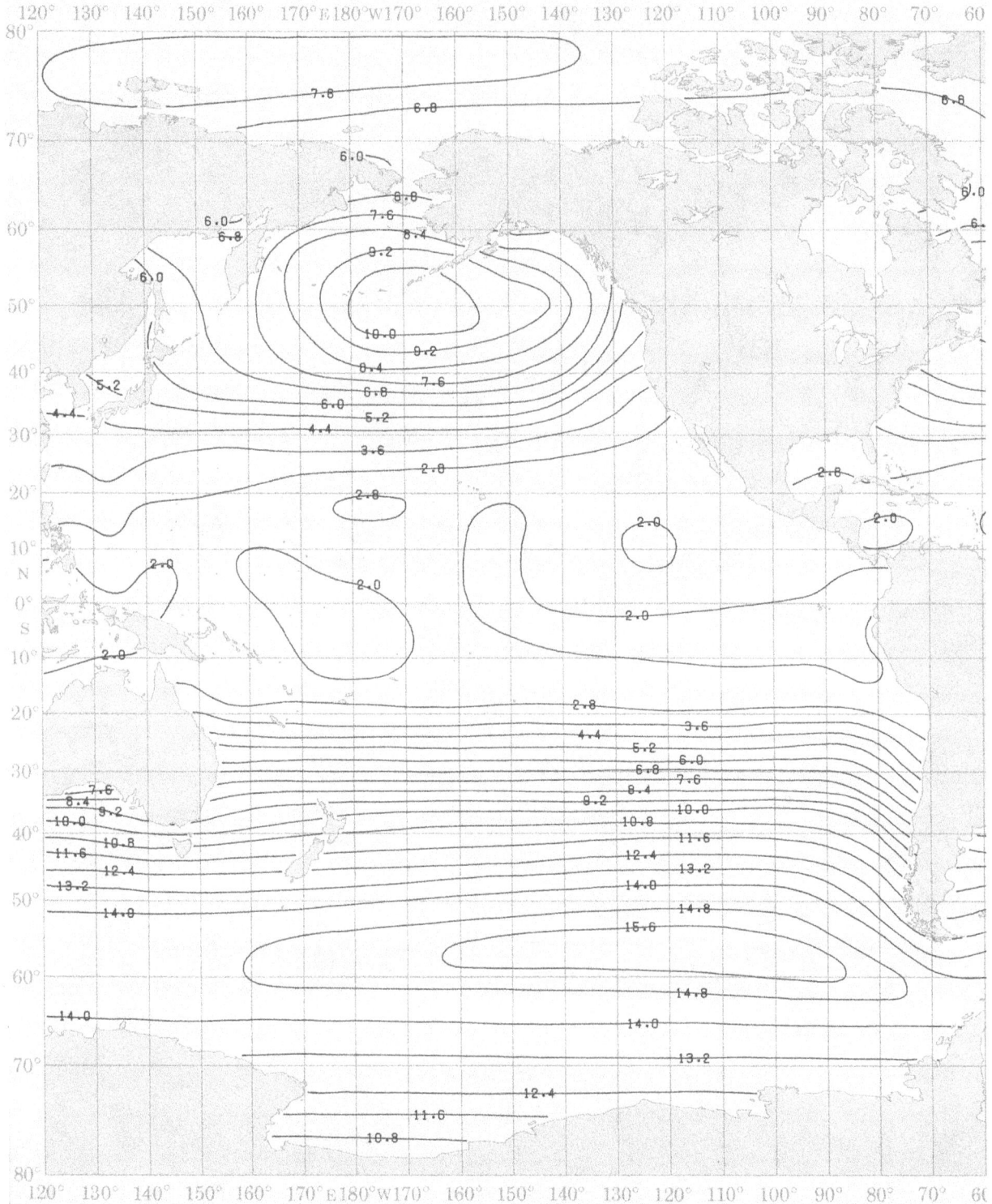

June — Sea Level Pressure (mb) — Standard Deviations

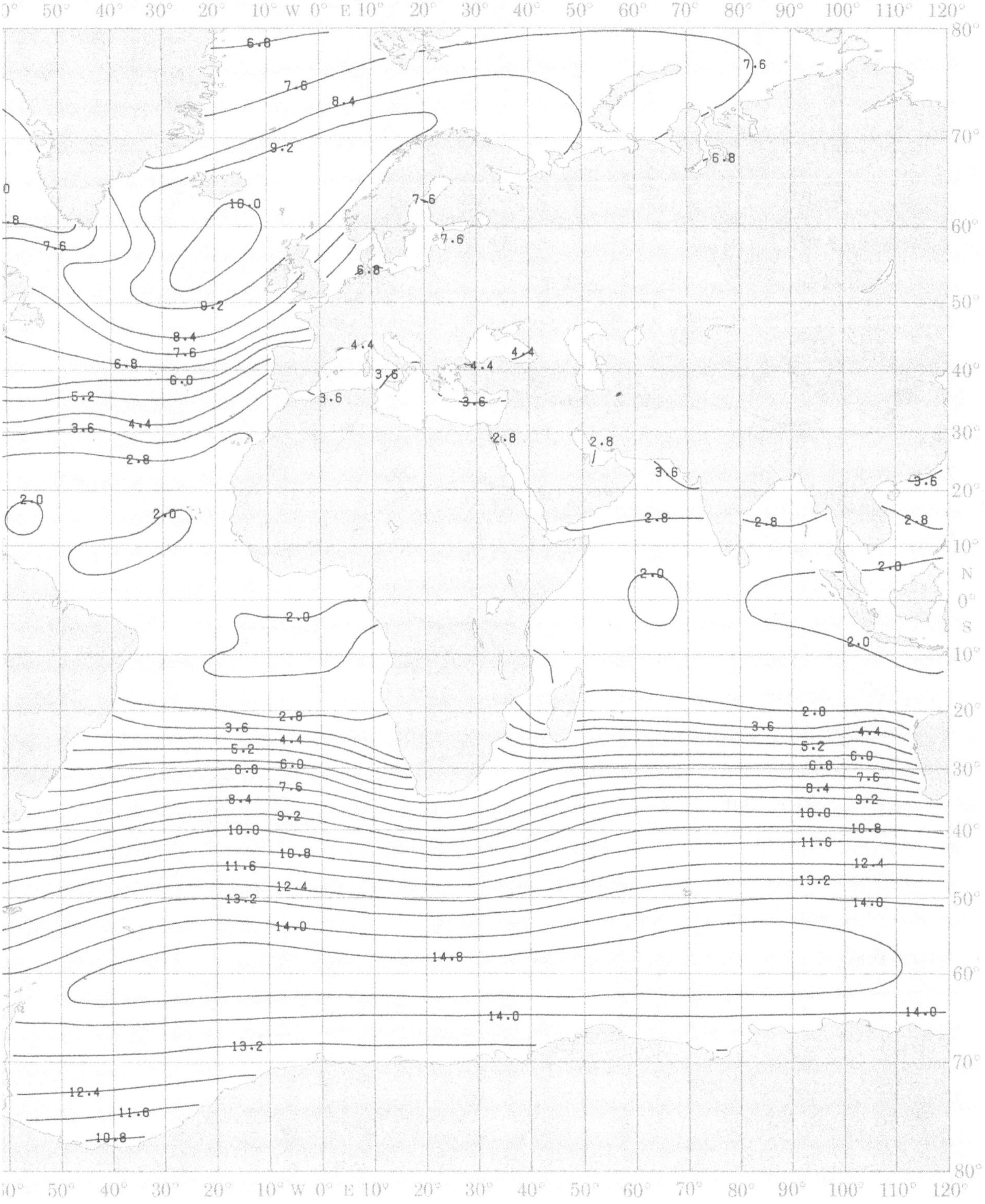

July — Sea Level Pressure (mb) — Means

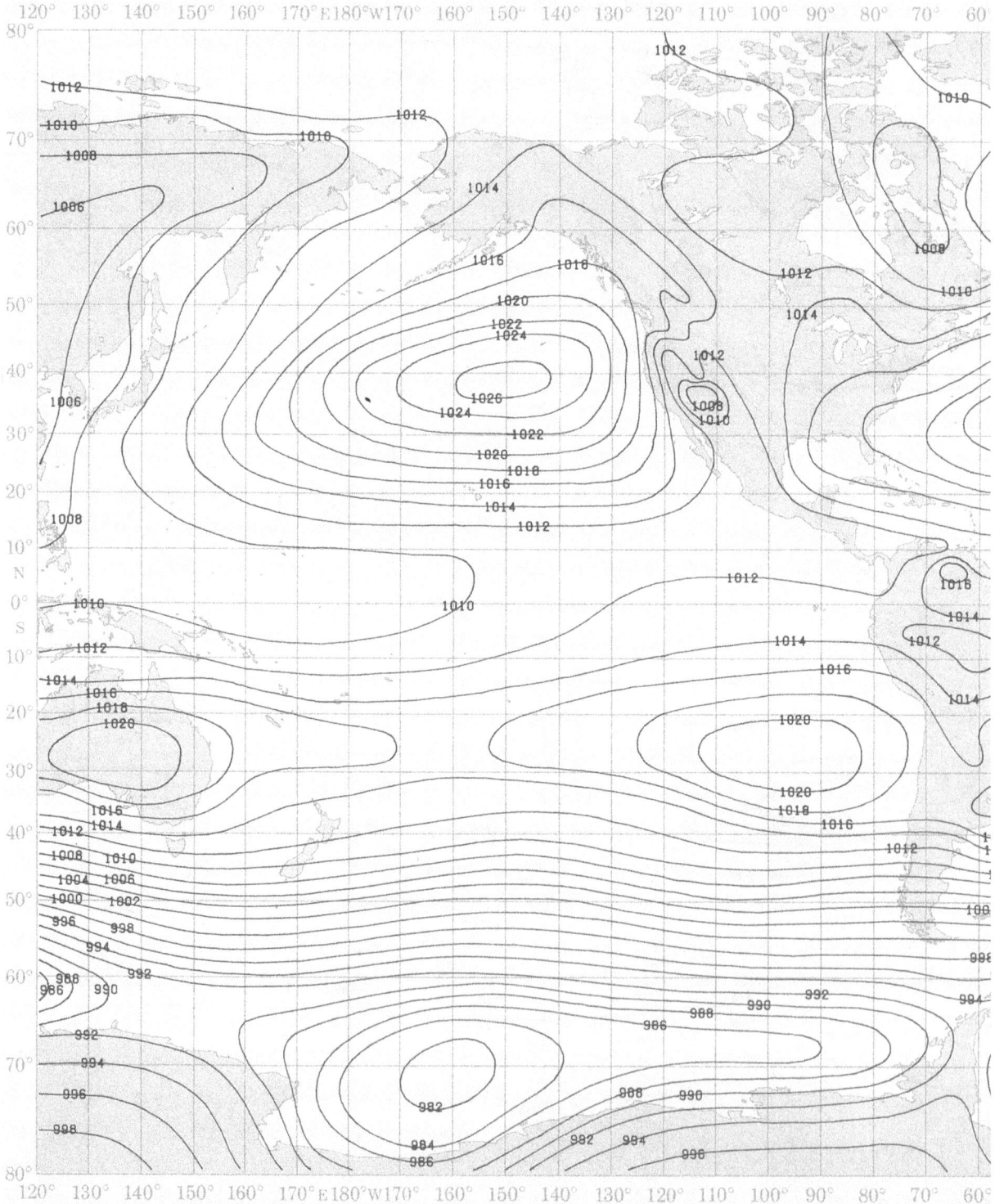

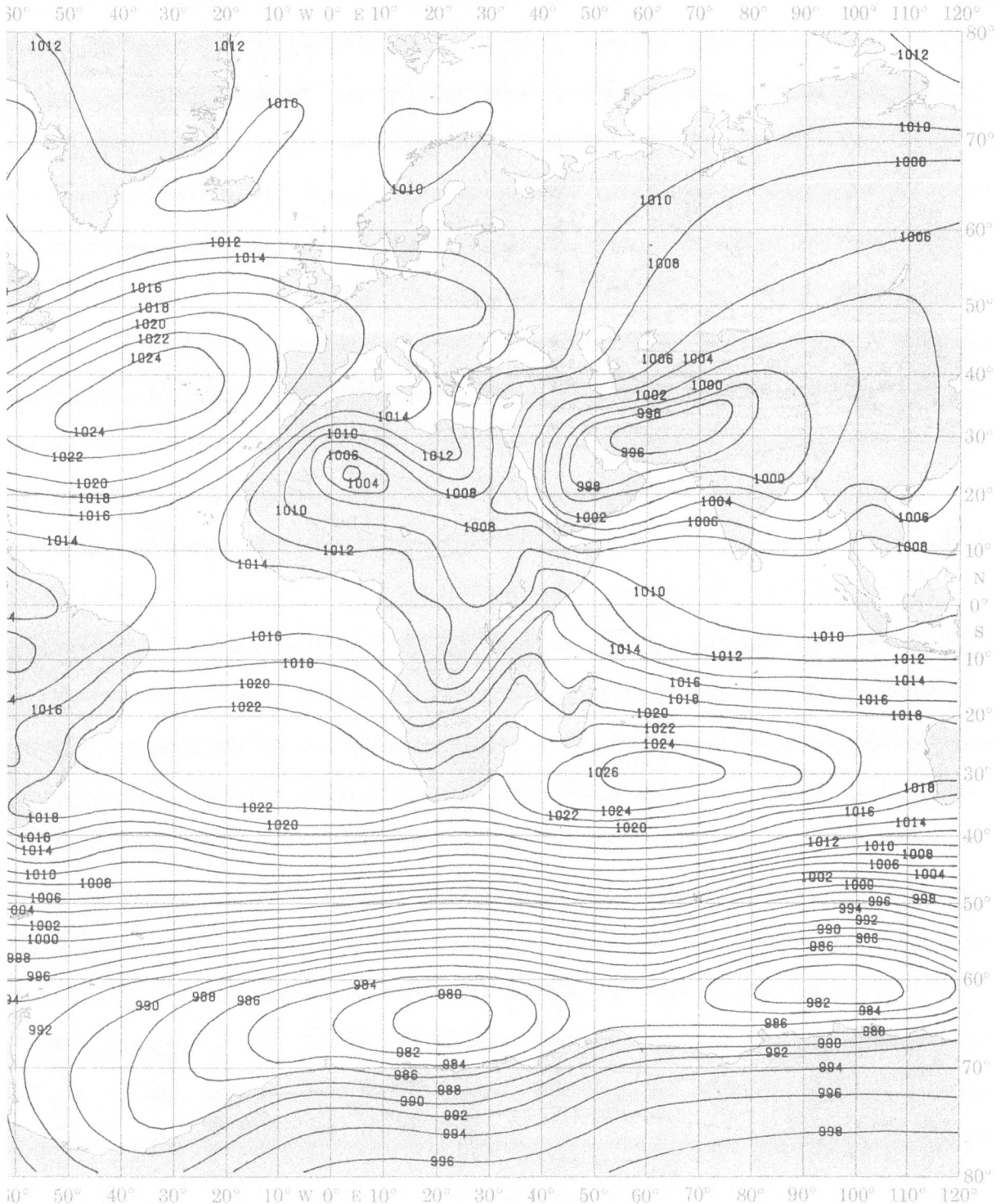

July — Sea Level Pressure (mb) — Standard Deviations

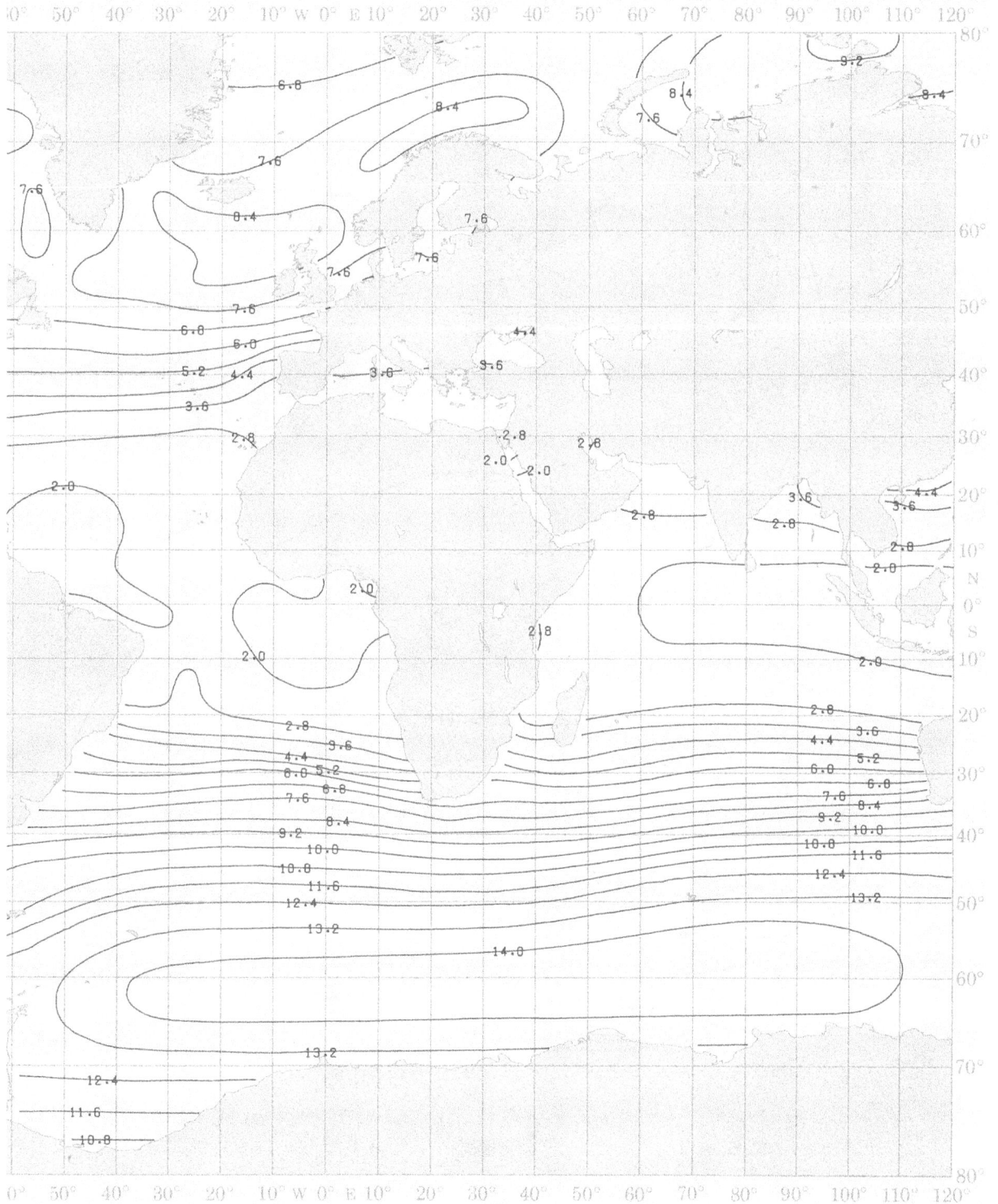

July — Sea Level Pressure (mb) — Standard Deviations

August — Sea Level Pressure (mb) — Means

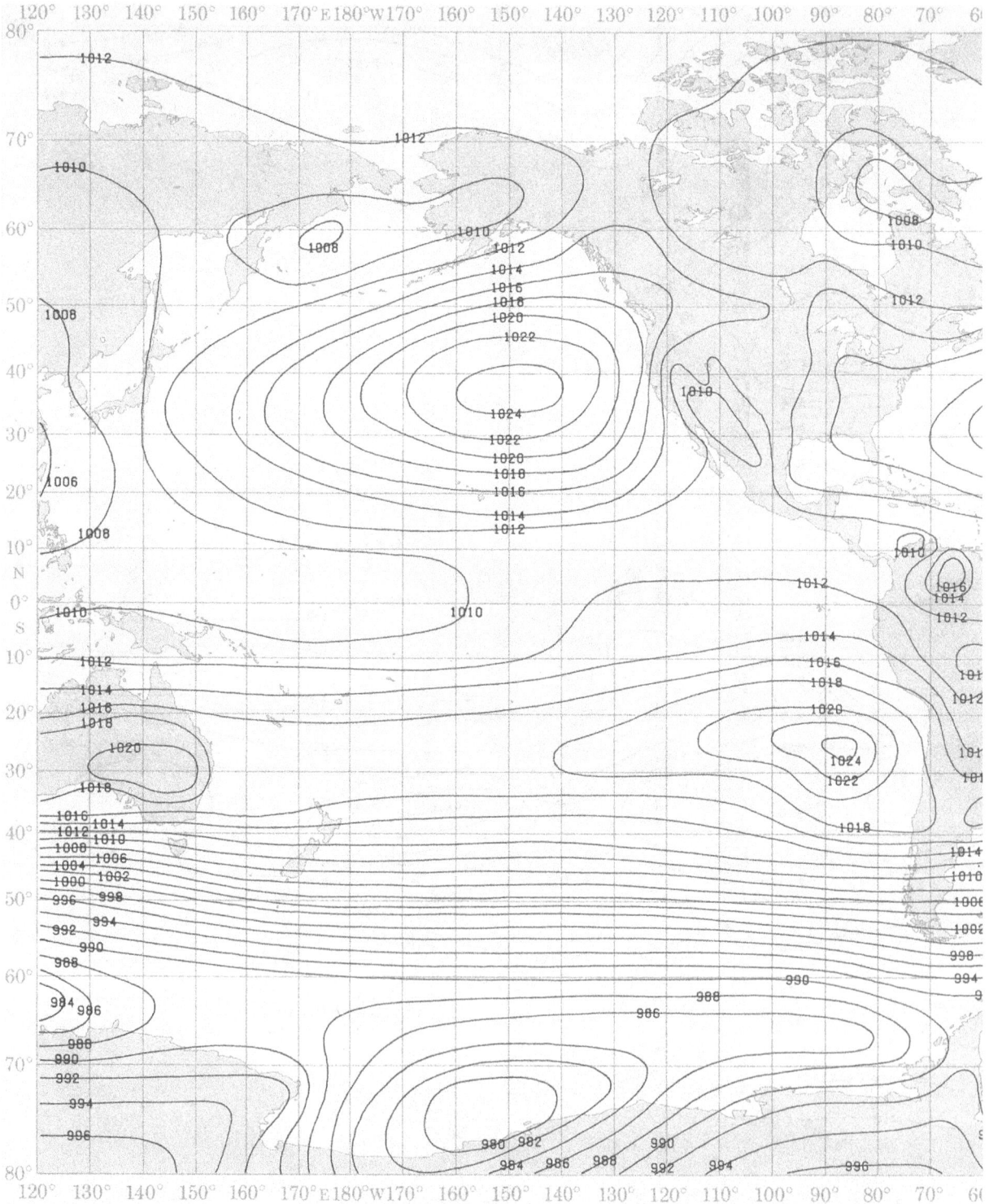

August — Sea Level Pressure (mb) — Means

August — Sea Level Pressure (mb) — Standard Deviations

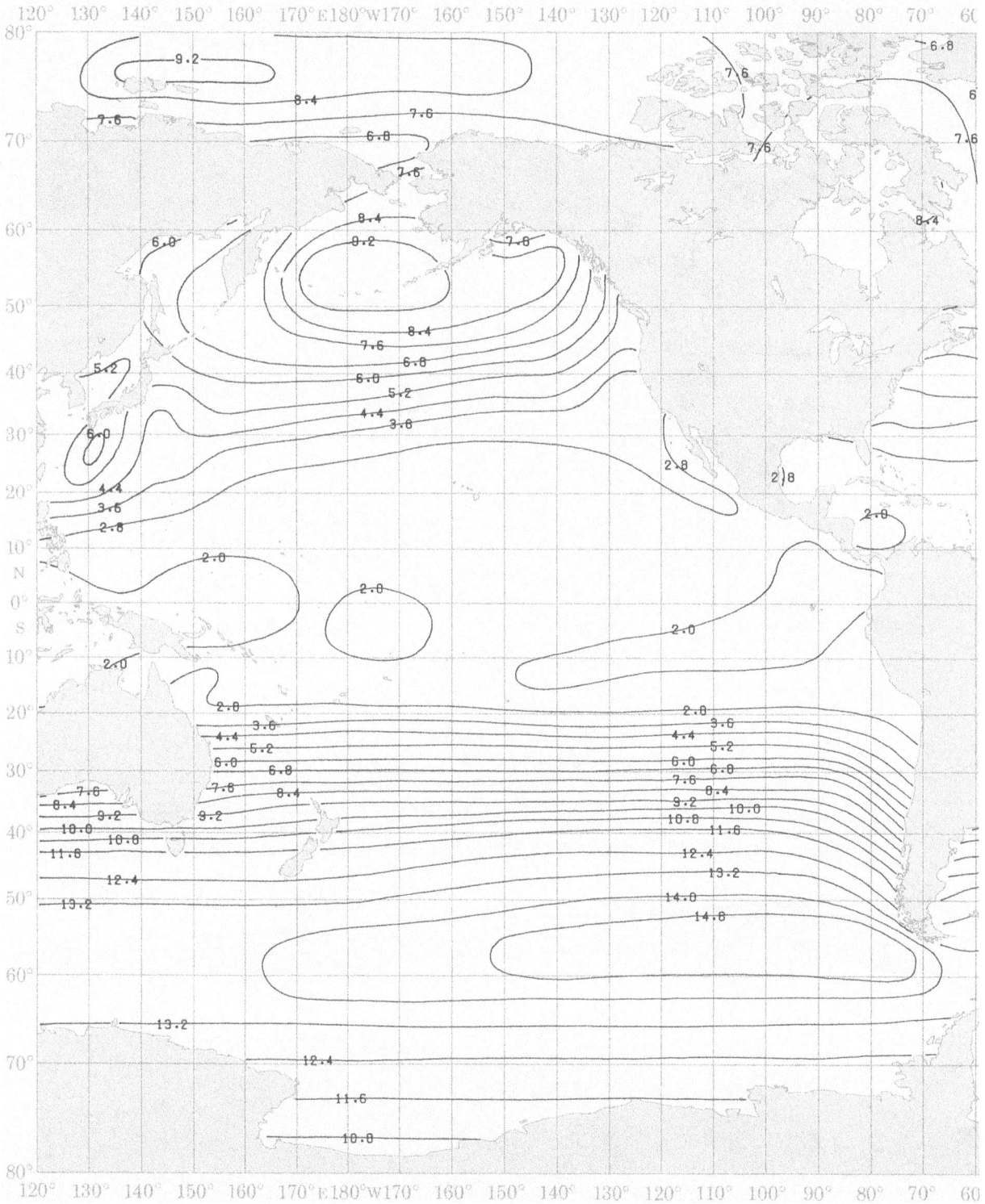

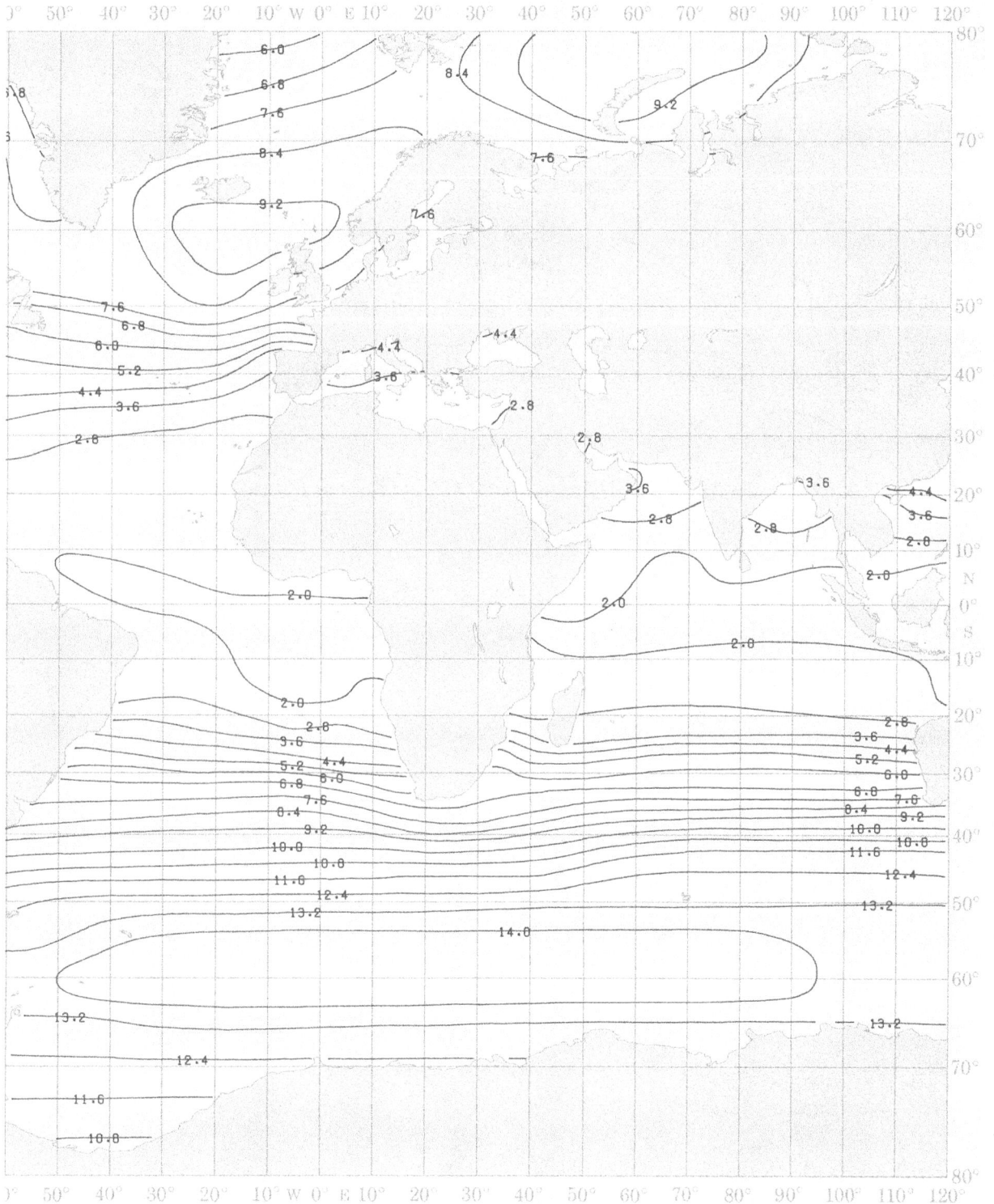

September — Sea Level Pressure (mb) — Means

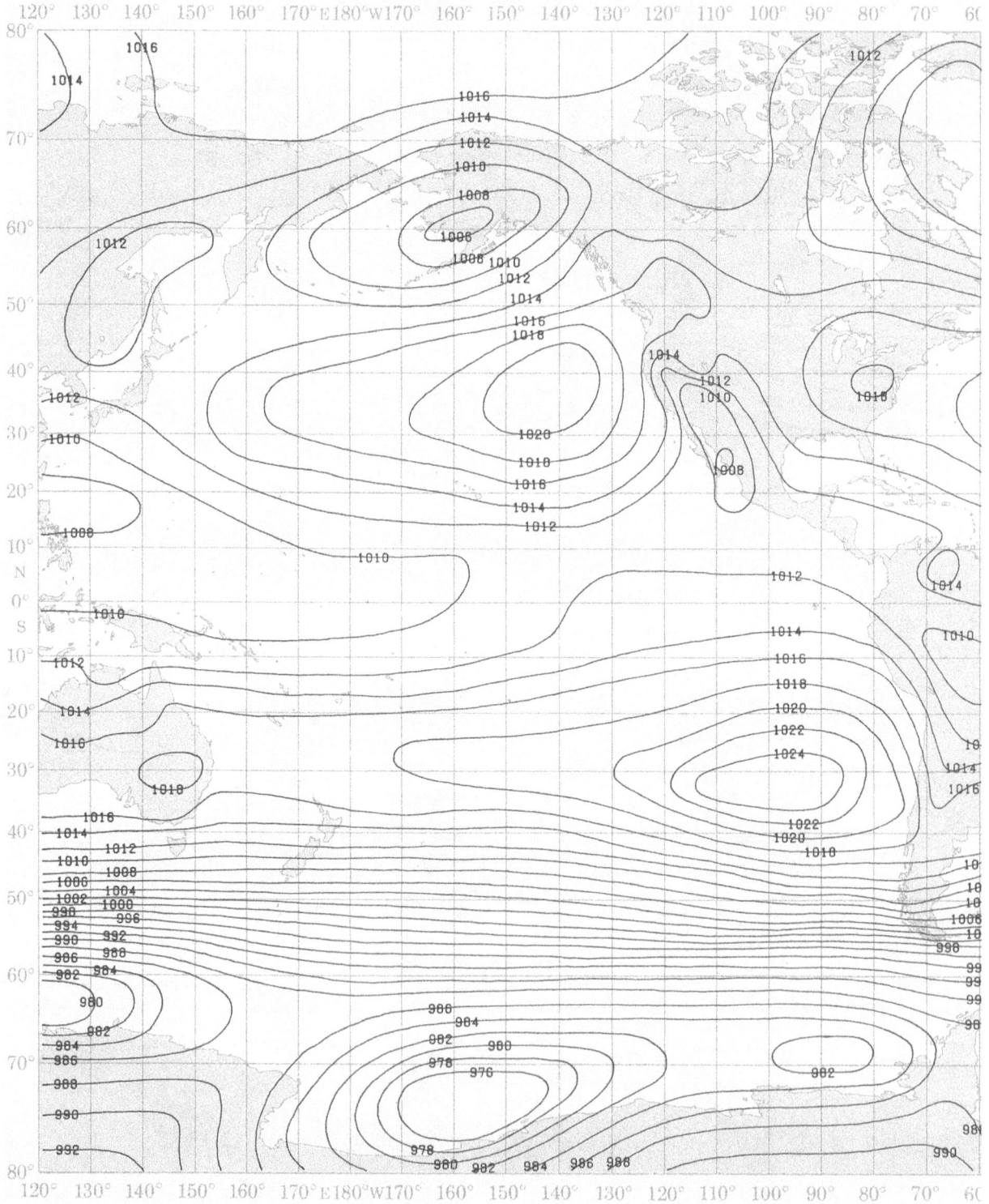

September — Sea Level Pressure (mb) — Means

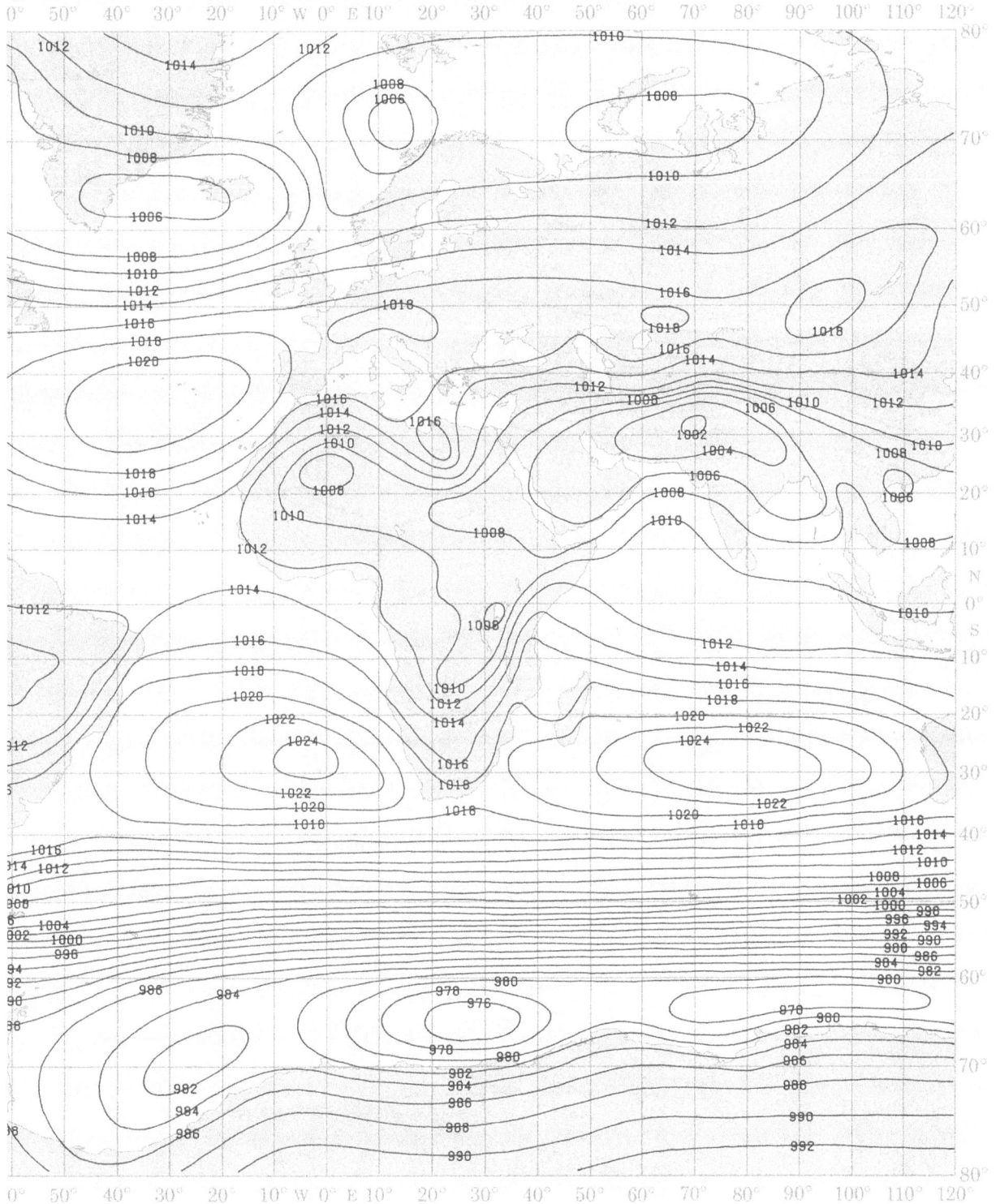

September — Sea Level Pressure (mb) — Standard Deviations

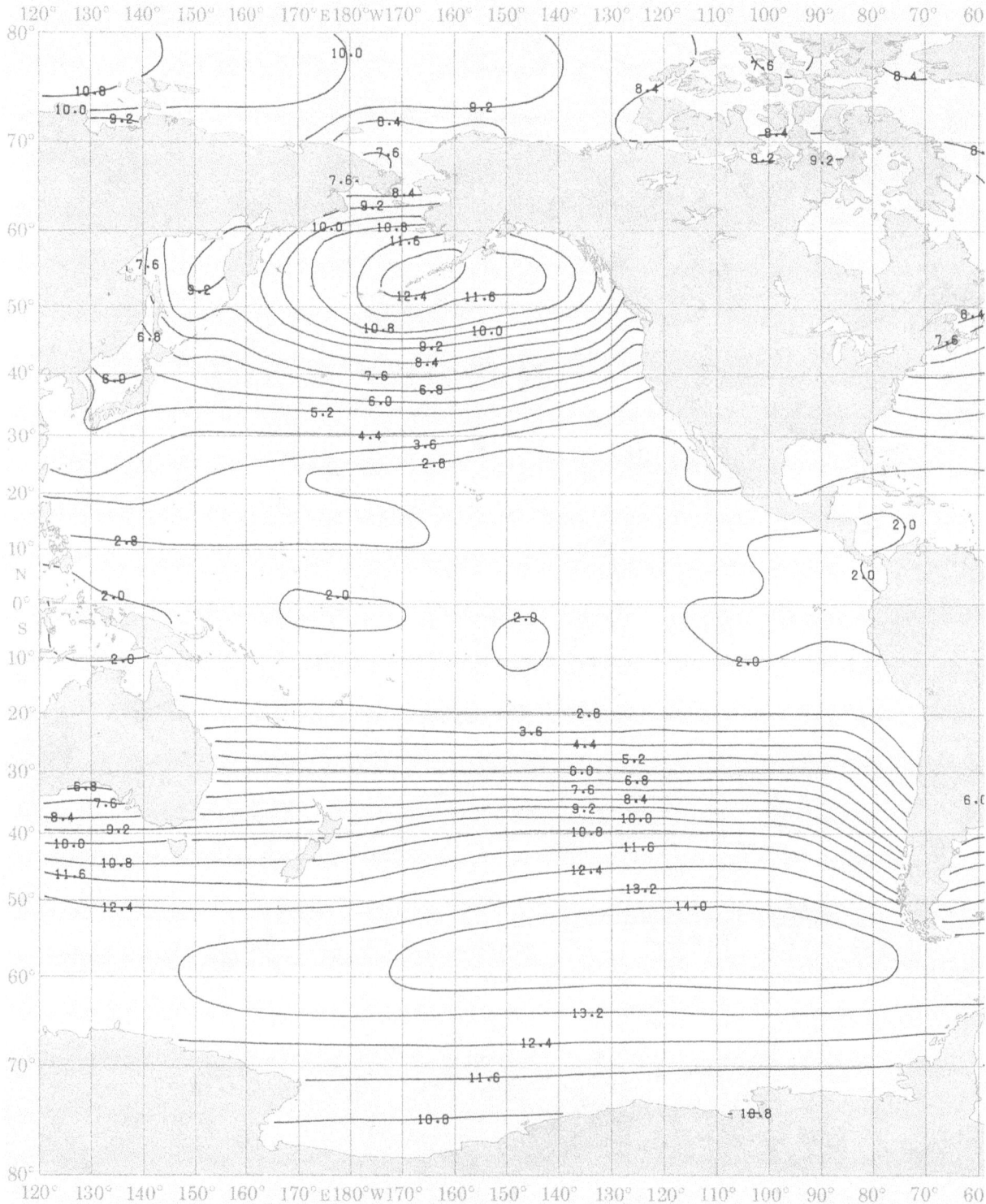

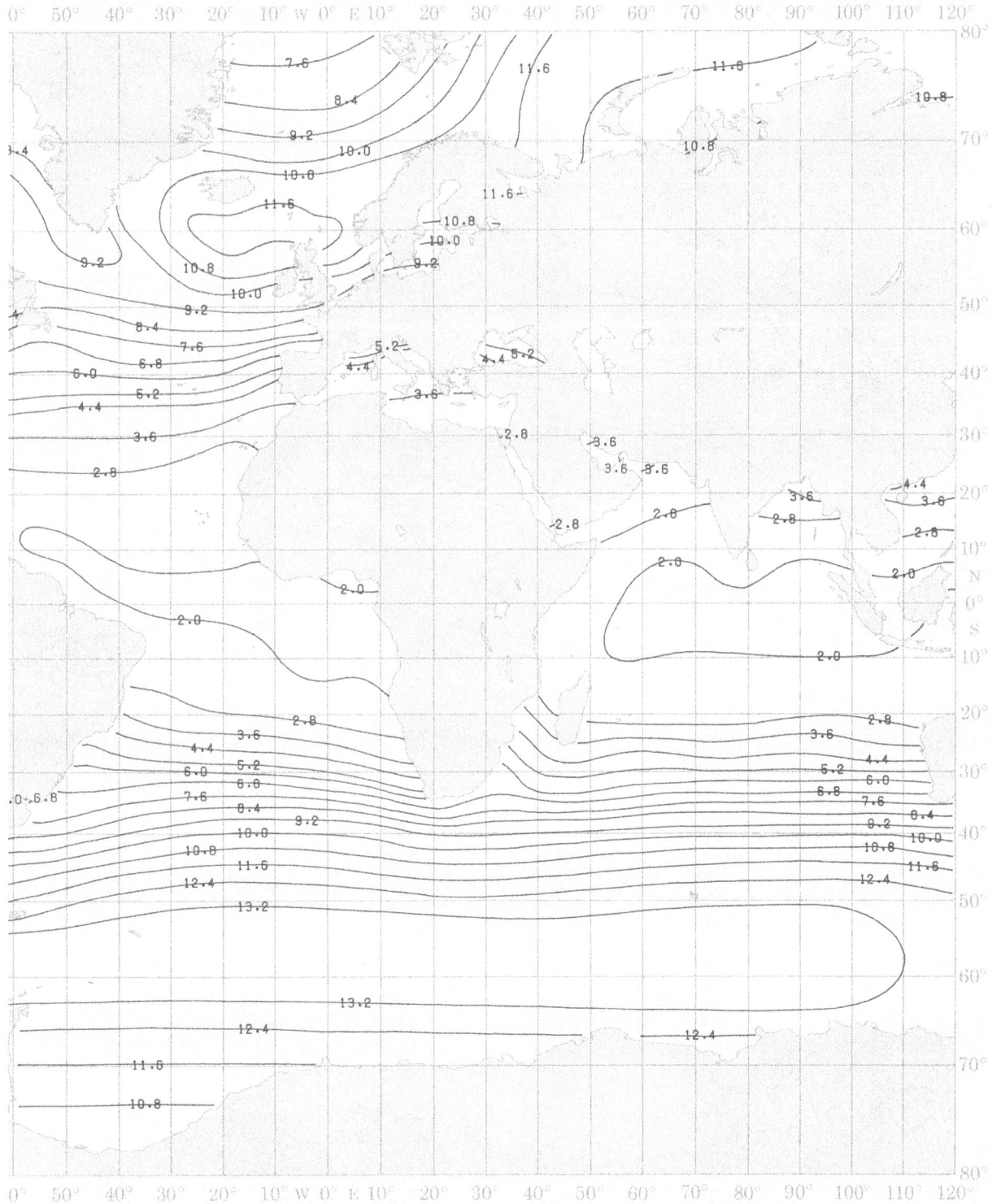

October — Sea Level Pressure (mb) — Means

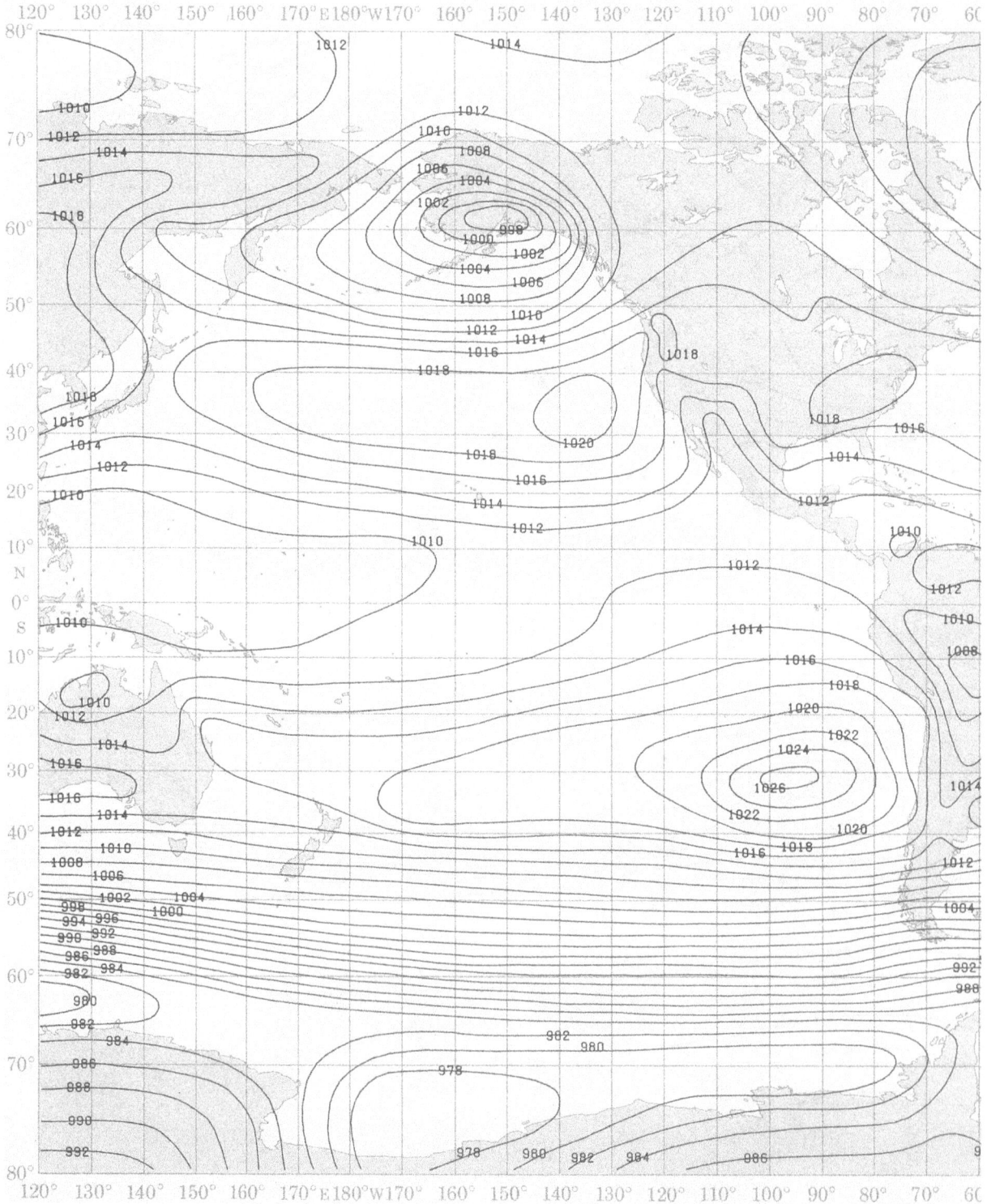

October — Sea Level Pressure (mb) — Means

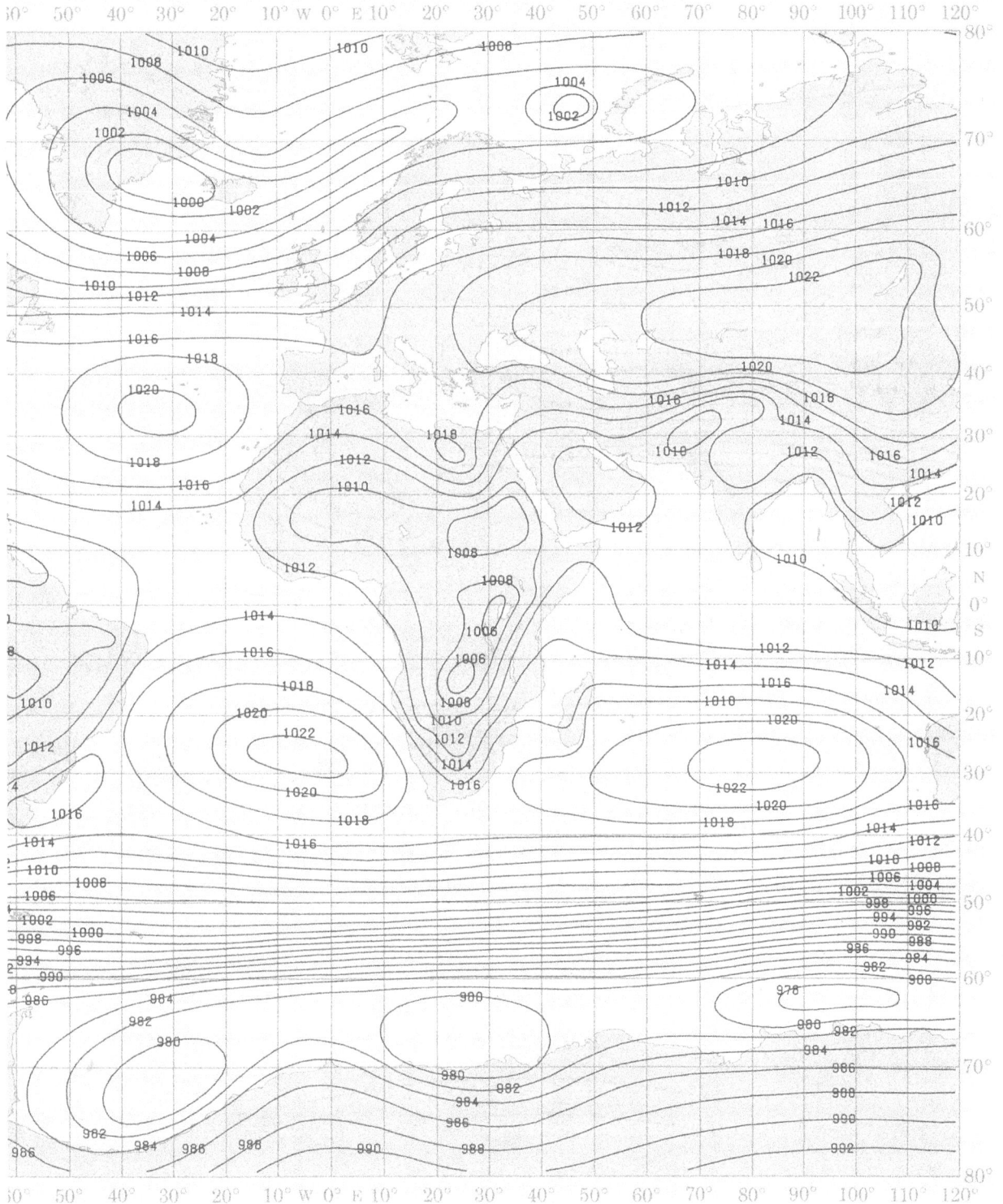

October — Sea Level Pressure (mb) — Standard Deviations

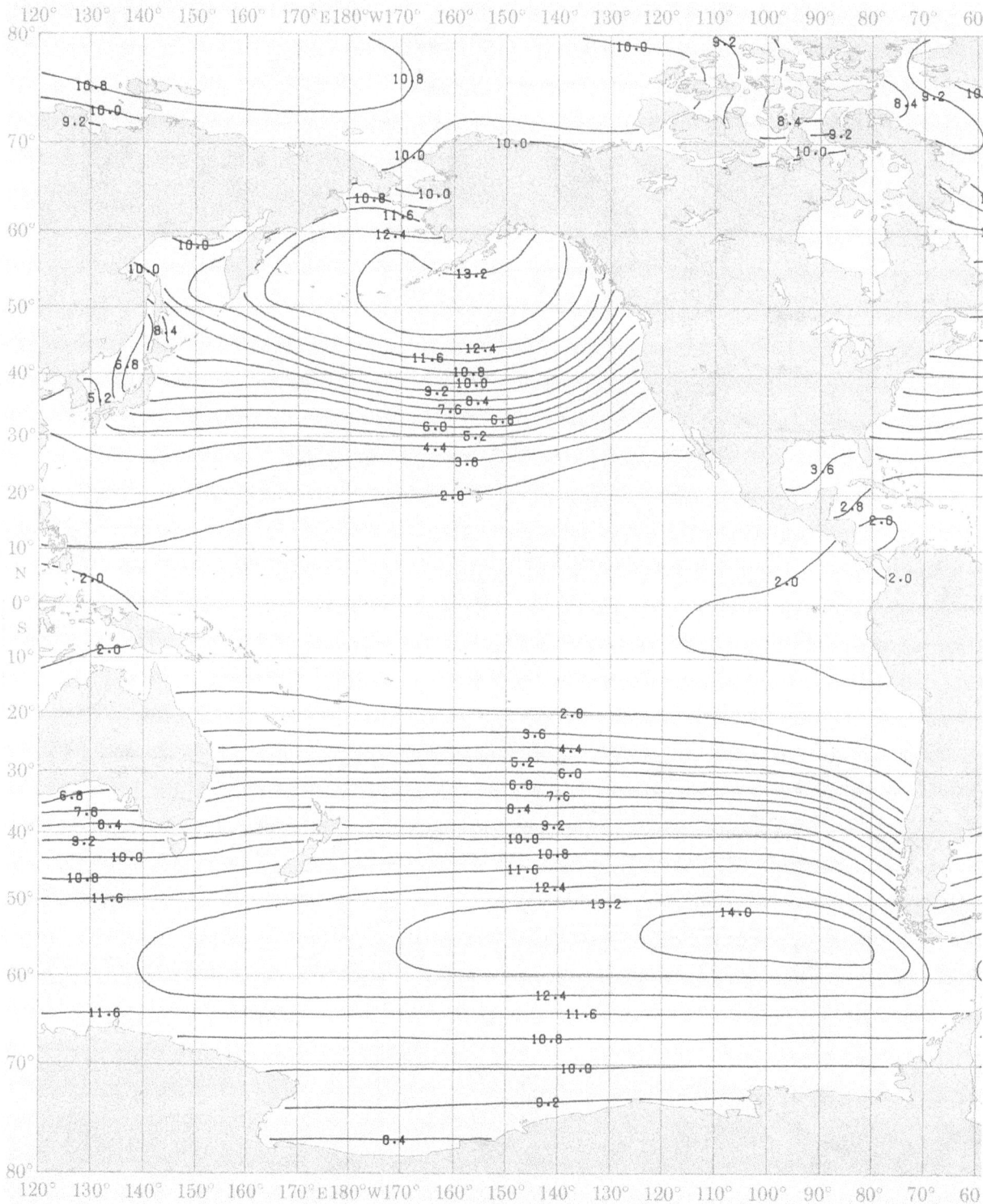

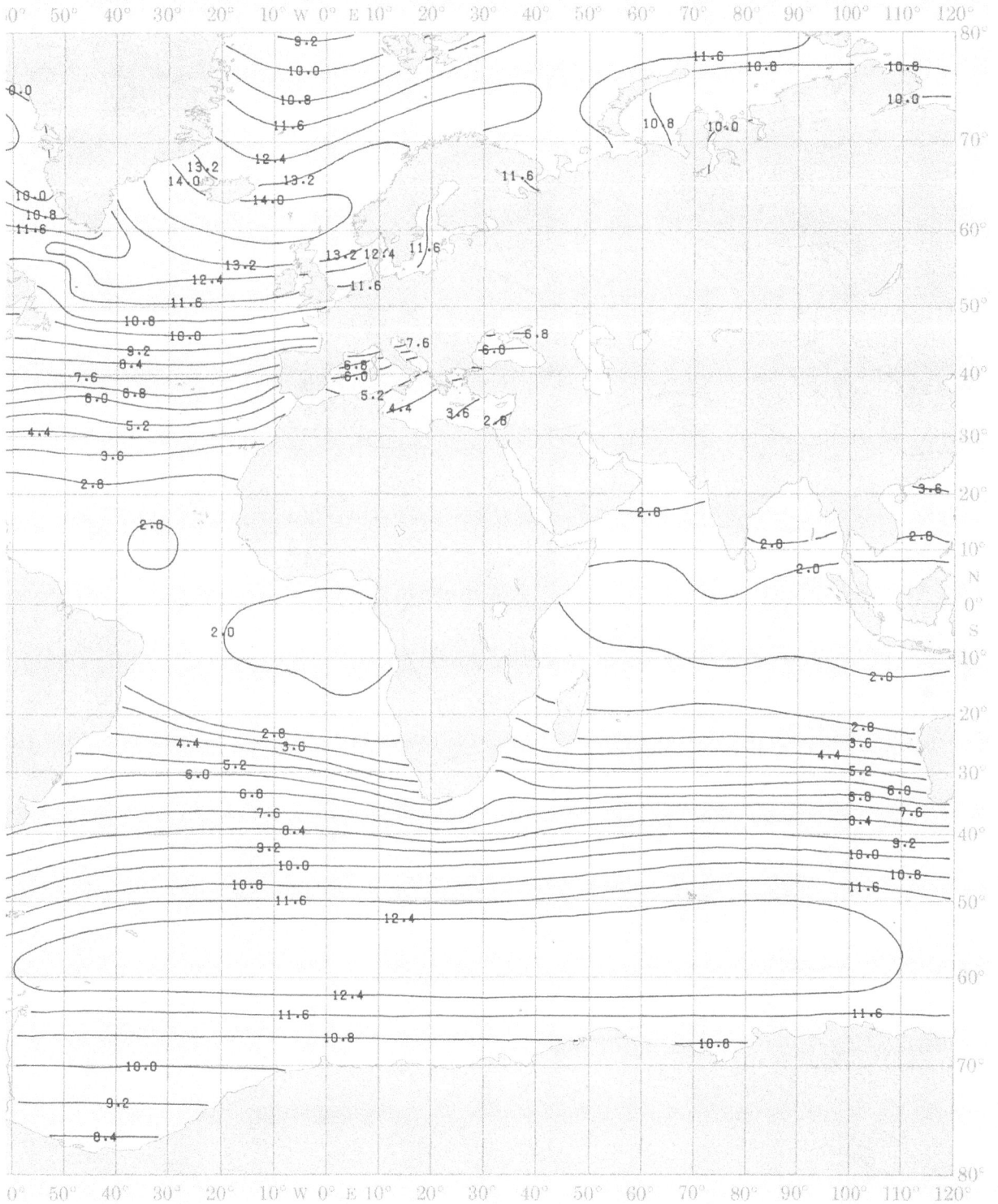

November — Sea Level Pressure (mb) — Means

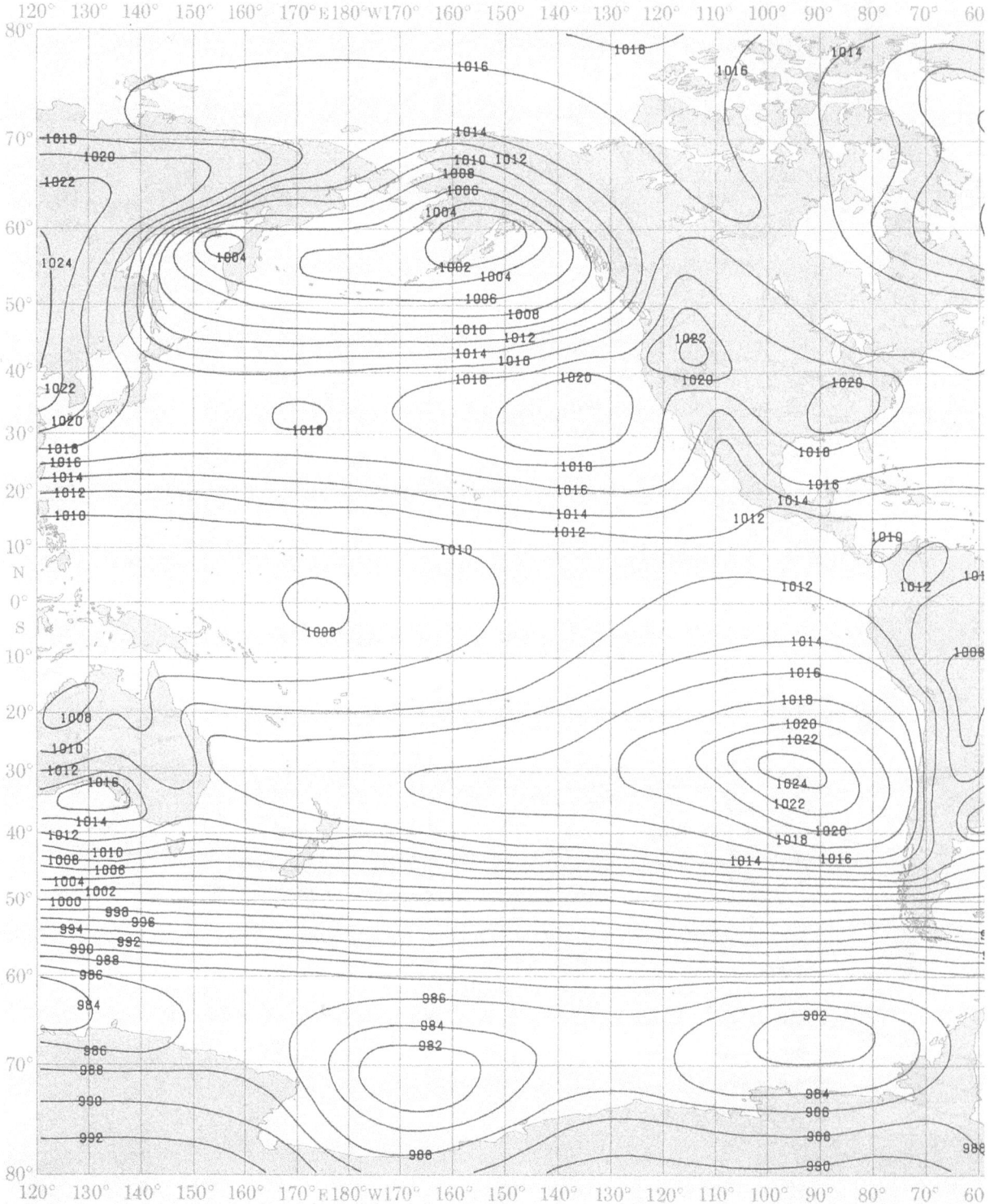

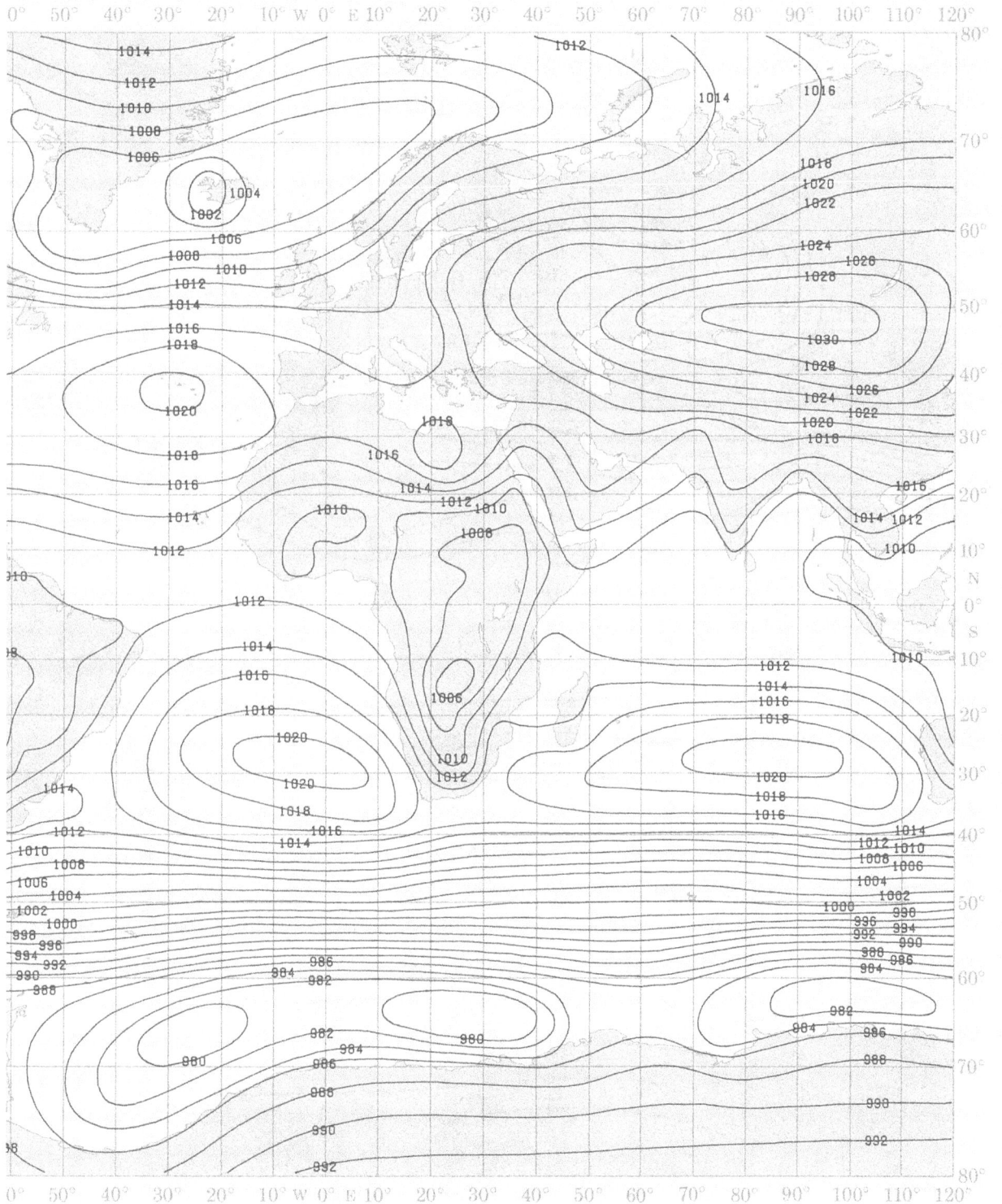

November — Sea Level Pressure (mb) — Standard Deviations

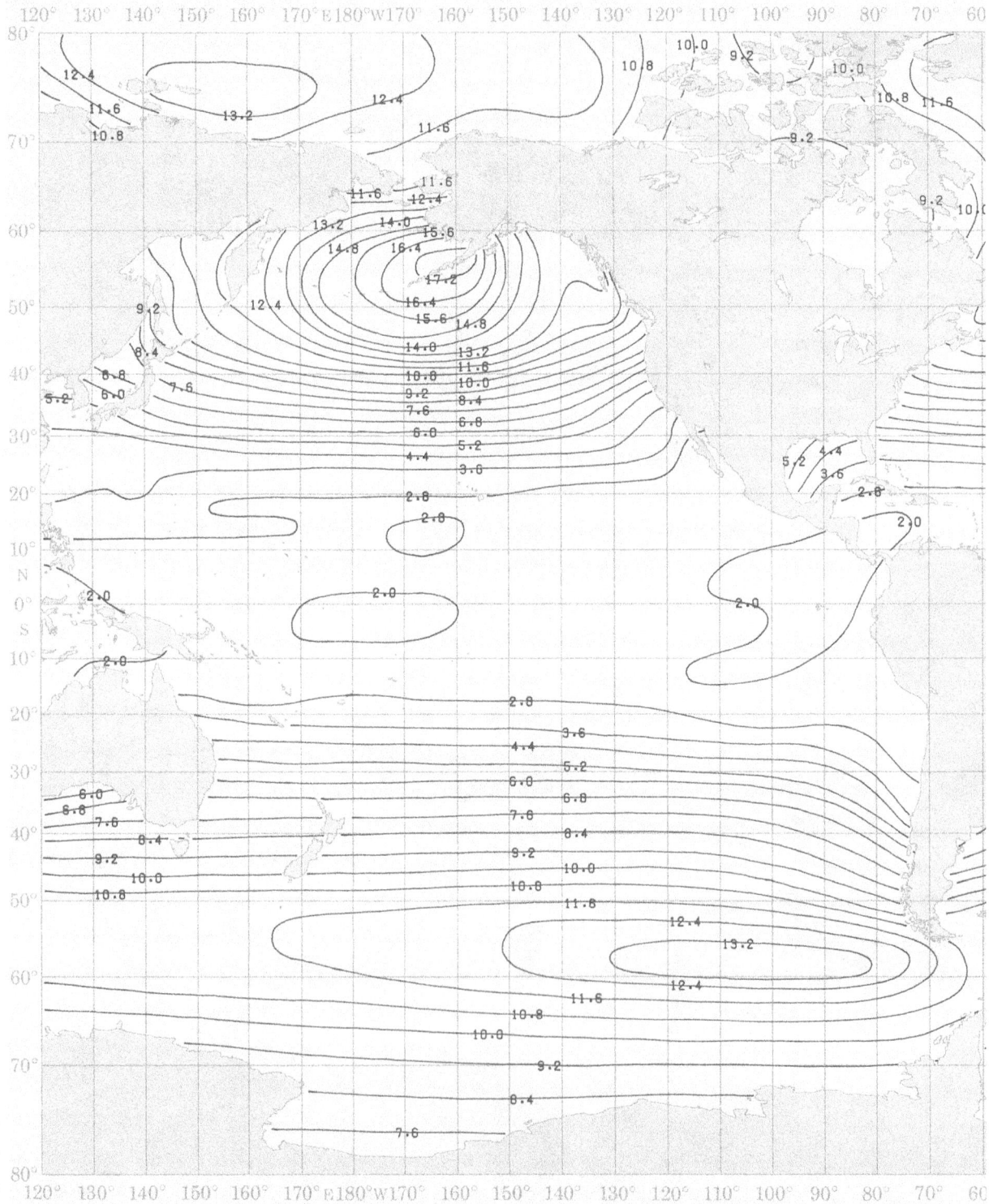

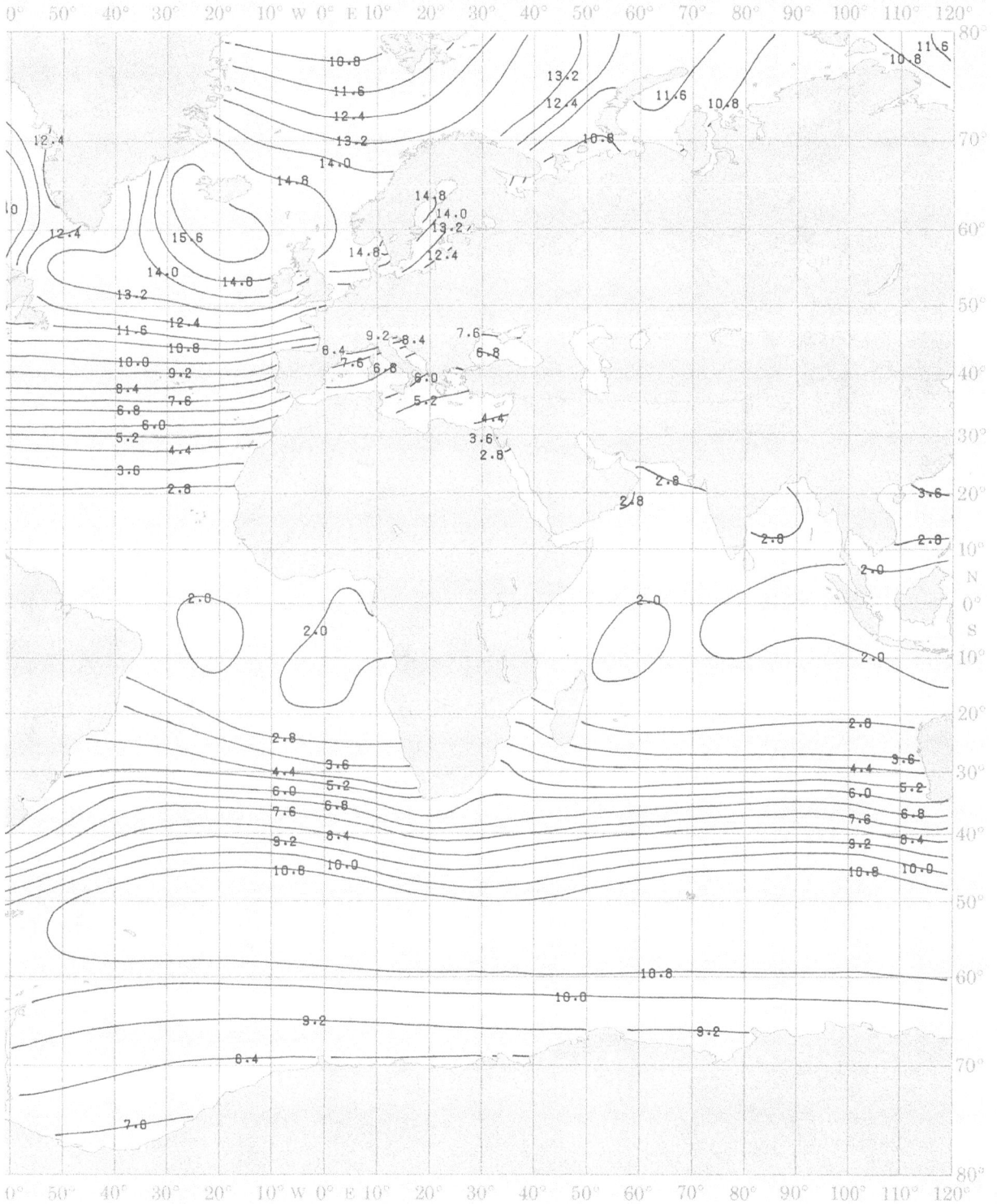

December — Sea Level Pressure (mb) — Means

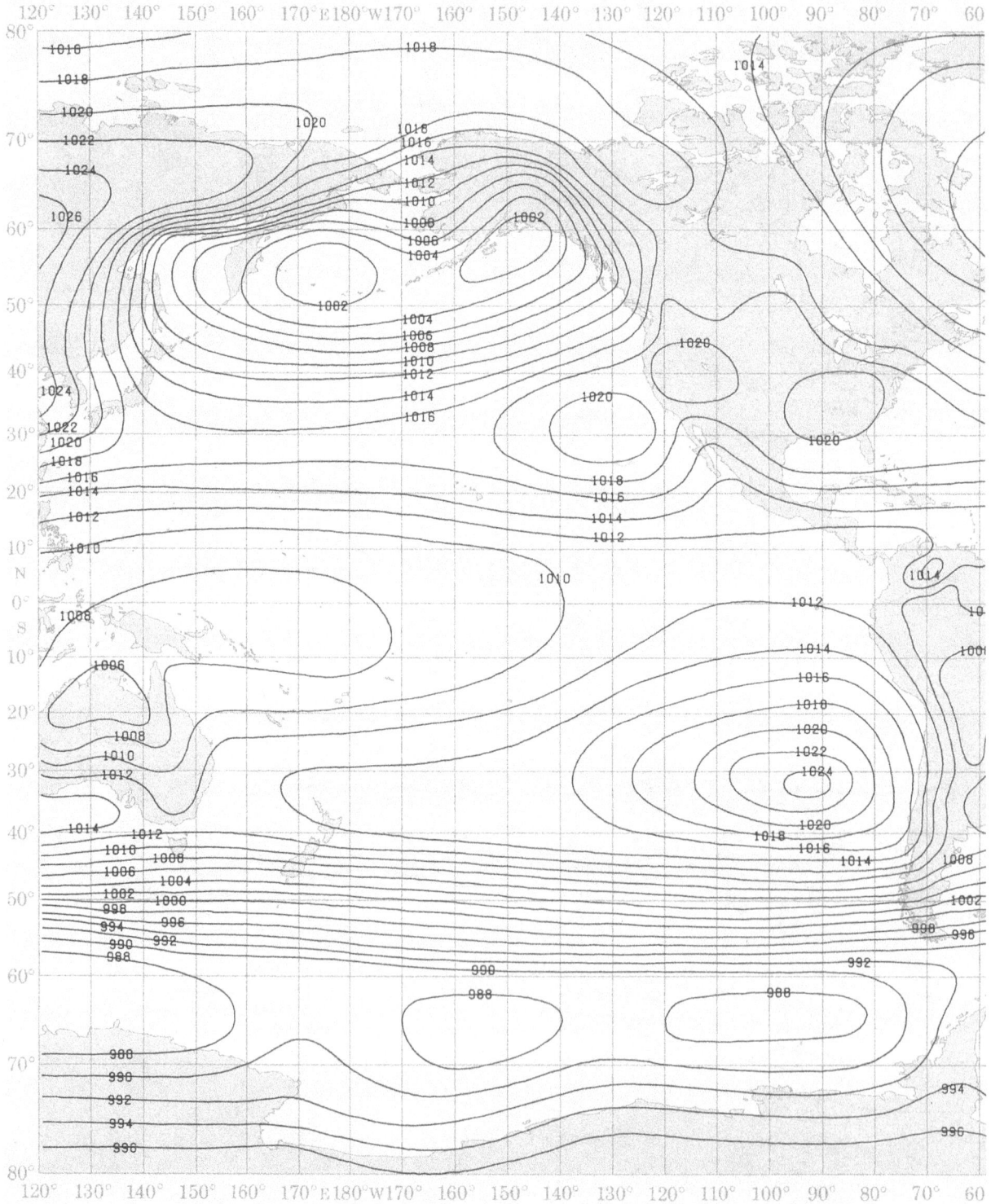

120° 130° 140° 150° 160° 170°E 180° W170° 160° 150° 140° 130° 120° 110° 100° 90° 80° 70° 60°

80°

1018
1018
1020
70°
1022
1024
1026
60°
1024
50°
40°
1024
1022
30° 1020
1018
1016
20° 1014
1012
10°
N 1010
0°
S 1008
10°
1006
20°
1008
30° 1010
1012
40° 1014 1012
1010
1006 1008
1004
1002 1000
50° 998 1000
994 996
990 992
988
60°
70° 988
990
992
994
996
80°

1018
1020
1016
1016
1014
1012
1010
1008
1006
1004
1002
1004
1006
1008
1010
1012
1014
1016

1002

1014

1020

1020
1020

1020

1018
1016
1014
1012
1010
1012
1014
1016
1018
1020
1022
1024
1020
1018 1016
1014
1008
1002
998 996
992
990
988
988

1014

990
994
996

120° 130° 140° 150° 160° 170°E 180° W170° 160° 150° 140° 130° 120° 110° 100° 90° 80° 70° 60°

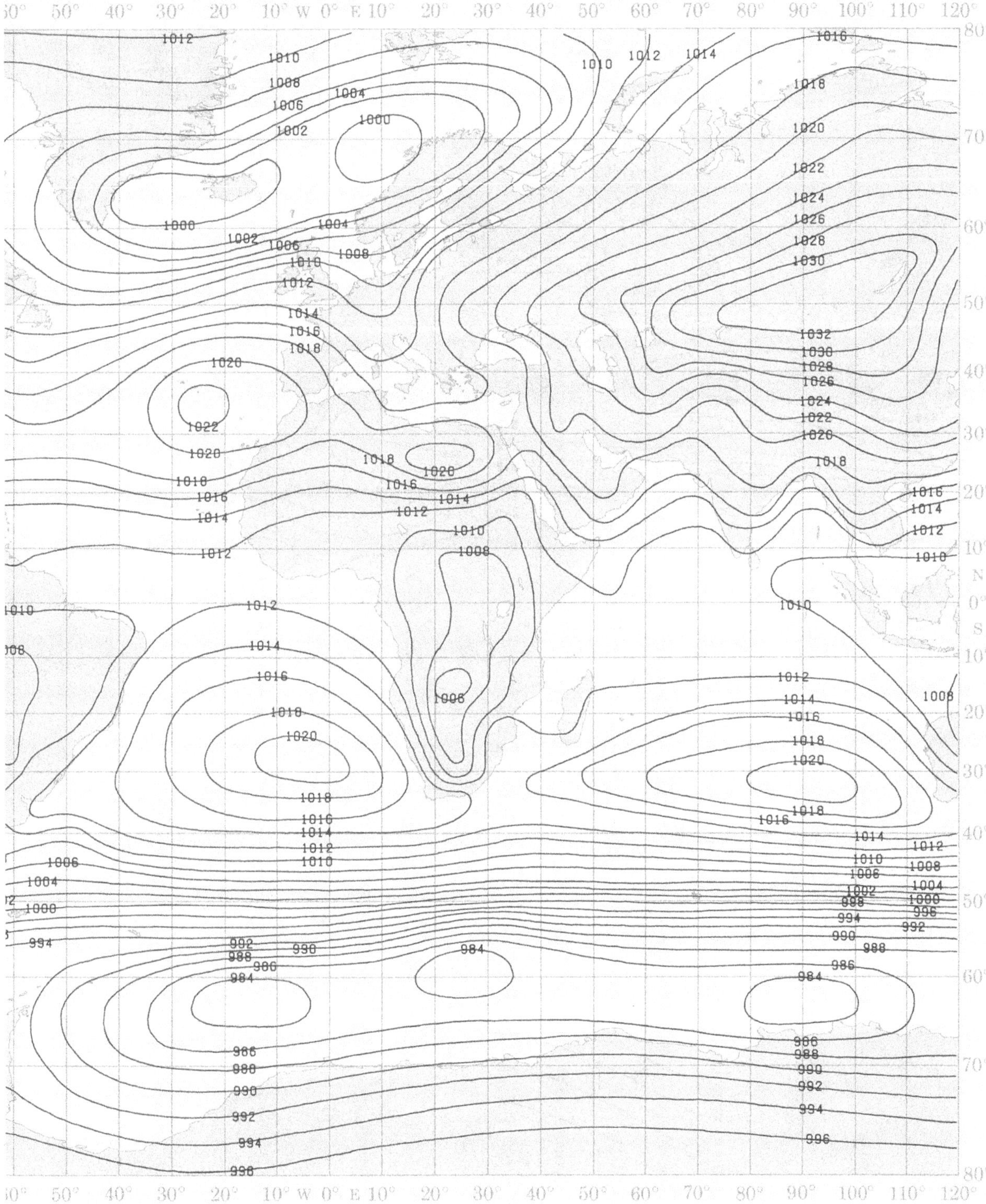
50° 40° 30° 20° 10° W 0° E 10° 20° 30° 40° 50° 60° 70° 80° 90° 100° 110° 120°
80° 70° 60° 50° 40° 30° 20° 10° N 0° S 10° 20° 30° 40° 50° 60° 70° 80°
1012
1010
1008
1006
1004
1002
1000
1014
1016
1018
1020
1022
1024
1026
1028
1030
1032
996
994
992
990
988
986
984

December — Sea Level Pressure (mb) — Standard Deviations

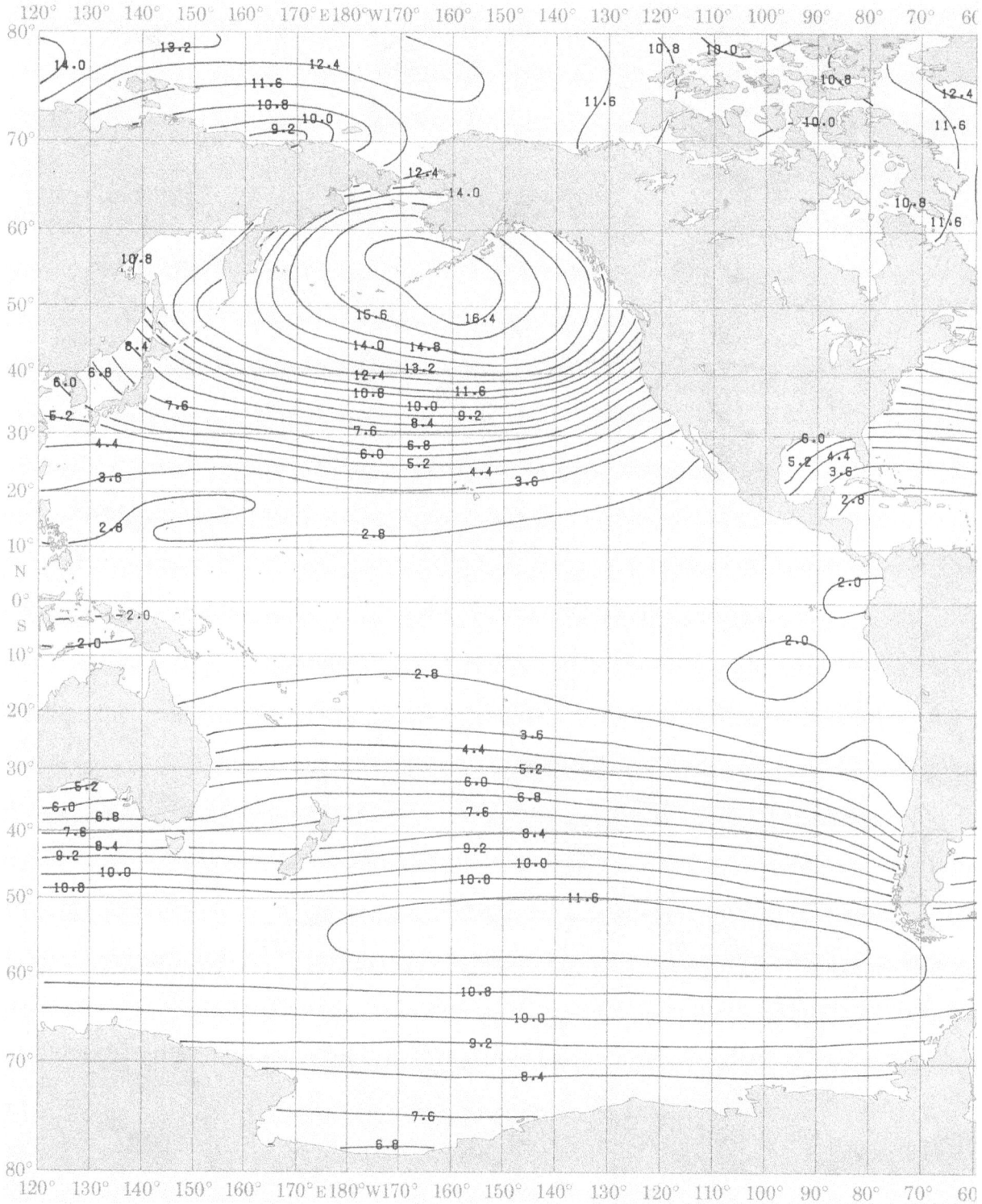

December — Sea Level Pressure (mb) — Standard Deviations

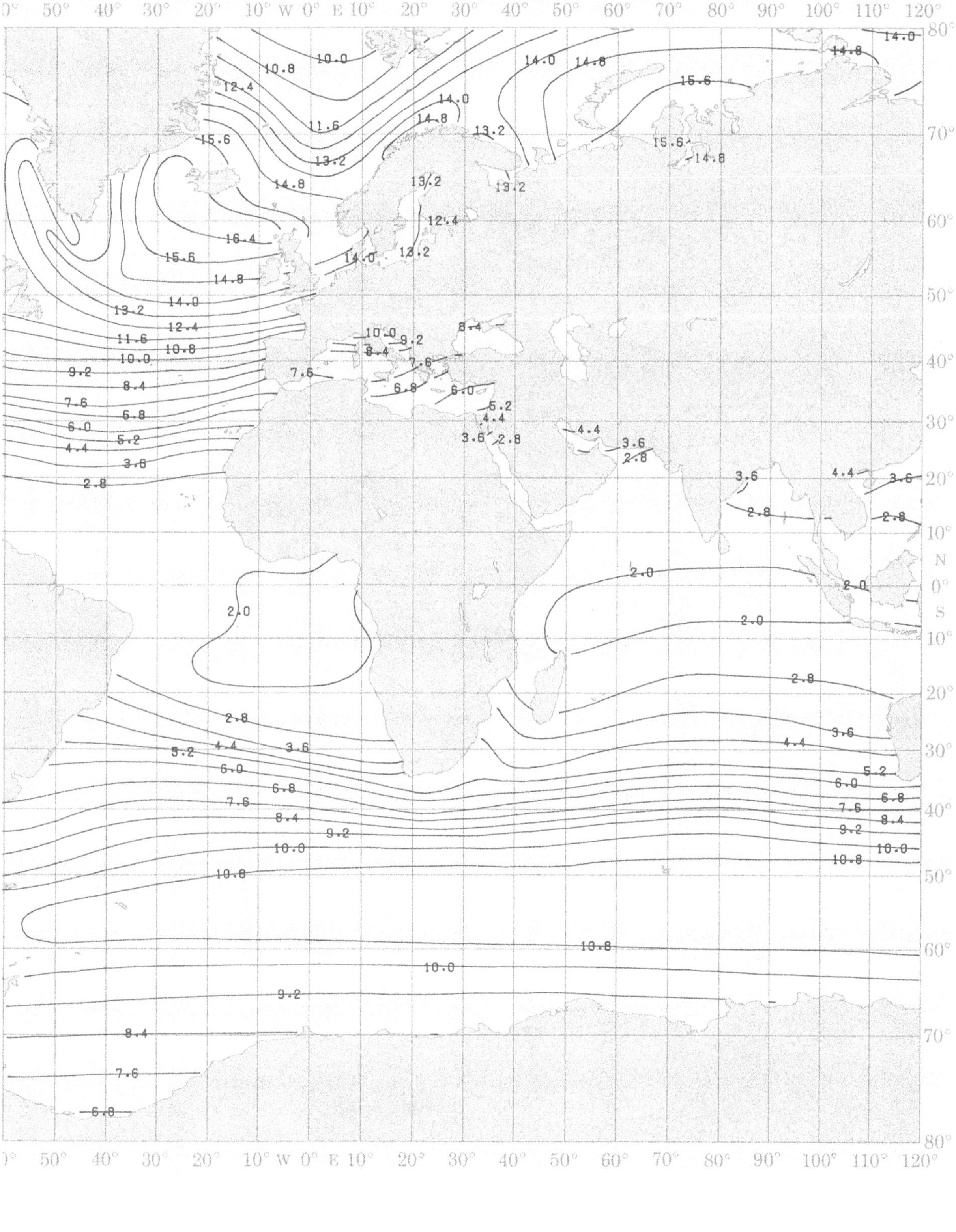

EN VIRESCIT GALILÆVS ALTER
Anagr.
EVANGELISTA TORRICELLIVS
Sereniſſimi M·Ducis Hetruriæ
Mathem.cus & Philosus
Obijt·Anno Dom MDCXLVII, Aet·XL

In a Class by Itself

Manual of Barometry, (WBAN), Vol. 1, U.S. Weather Bureau, 1963. A definitive 800-page reference book on all aspects of all types of barometers in use at the time, including altimetry applications. Special emphasis on barometer calibration procedures and reduction of station pressure to sea level values. The "WBAN" that appears in the title seems to be a Weather Bureau document number. (A Vol. 2 is described in this book, but may not have been published.) This monumental work does not have an author listed, but several professional publications from the era cite the book and list the author as L.P. Harrison, as is also stated in the Preface. This book with the same title, but without the WBAN, is also cited as *NAVWEPS 50-1D-510*, Bureau of Naval Weapons, Washington, D.C., 1963.

History

The History of the Barometer, W.E. Knowles Middleton, 1994, Baros Books, UK. The classic study. See also *A Brief History of the Barometer,* Journal of the Royal Astronomical Society of Canada, Vol. 38, p. 41, which is a 25-page summary of his book with bibliography.

FitzRoy and His Barometers, Philip R Collins, 2008, Baros Books, UK. Presents the history of this pioneer in the barometer world. The author shows and explains many instruments that are attributed to FitzRoy.

An Account of Dr. Robert Hook's Invention of the Marine Barometer, with its Description and Uses, E. Halley, Philosophical Transactions of the Royal Society of London, 269, 1701, p. 791.

Origins of the Marine Barometer, Anita McConnell, Annals of Science, Vol. 62, No. 1, 2005, p. 83-101.

A Discourse of the Rule of the Decrease of the Height of the Mercury in the Barometer, according as Places are elevated above the Surface of the Earth, with an Attempt to discover the true Reason of the Rising and Falling of the Mercury, upon Change of of (sic) Weather. Edm. Halley. Journal Philosophical Transactions (1683-1775), Volume 16 - 1686/1692

Aneroid Principles

Experiments on Aneroid Barometers at Kew Observatory, and their Discussion, C. Chree, Philosophical Transactions of the Royal Society of London. Series A (1896-1934), Vol. 191 -1898

The Aneroid Barometer, its Construction and Use, George W. Plympton, Third Edition, 1885, D. Van Nostrand, New York.

An Account of certain Experiments, on Aneroid Barometers, made at Kew Observatory, at the expense of the Meteorological Committee, B. Stewart, Proceedings of the Royal Philosophical Society, London, 1868, Vol. 16, p. 472

Naval Oceanography Command Barometer Calibration Program, NAVMETOCCOMINST 13950.3C, Commander, Naval Meteorology and Oceanography Command, Stennis Space Center, MS, 1986. See also for instructions on reading aneroid barometers: NAVMETOCCOMINST 3141.2 and NAVMETOCCOMINST 3144.1.

Meteorology

Modern Marine Weather, David Burch, 2008, Starpath Publications. Covers principles and practice, including weather map reading and the use of GRIB formatted forecasts.

Chapman Piloting, Seamanship, and Small Boat Handling, 65th ed., Elbert S. Maloney, Hearst Books, 2006. A one-book library for mariners, with a short but uniquely good section on weather and barometers.

Guide to Meteorological Instruments and Methods of Observation, WMO-No. 8, Seventh edition, 2008 (www.wmo.ch)

The Standard Atmosphere, Greeg, W.R. The Monthly Weather Review, May, 1920, p. 272-273; See also Report No. 147, National Advisory Committee for Aeronautics, December 17, 1921. First presentation and first adoption of the ISA.

Meteorological Observations and Essays, John Dalton, First edition, 1793, London, T. Ostel Publisher. Second edition, 1834, Manchester, Harrison and Crosfield Publisher.

Weather and Weather Instruments for the Amateur, P.R. Jameson, Fourth edition, 1923, Taylor Instruments Company. It was significant for its weather forecasting tips using a barometer. At that time, Taylor was one of the world's leading barometer manufacturers.

Characteristics of the hurricane storm surge, Weather Bureau, Technical Paper No. 48. Harris, D. Lee, 1963. U.S. Dept. of Commerce.

Electronic Barometers

Federal Meteorological Handbook No. 1— Surface Weather Observations and Reports, FCM-H1-2005, Office of the Federal Coordinator for Meteorological Services and Supporting Research, NOAA

World Meteorological Organization, *1992a: The WMO Automatic Digital Barometer Intercomparison* (J.P. van der Meulen). Instruments and Observing Methods Report No. 49, WMO/TD No. 474, Geneva.

Sources of Data and Maps

Ocean Prediction Center for marine maps: www.opc.ncep.noaa.gov

Hydrometeorological Prediction Center: www.hpc.ncep.noaa.gov

National Data Buoy Center for recent reports: www.ndbc.noaa.gov

National Climatic Data Center for archived data: www.ncdc.noaa.gov

UK and Europe: www.ffreithwen.co.uk/uk-weather

New Zealand: www.metservice.com

Australia: www.bom.gov.au

Metrology

Abridged Final Report of the Eleventh Session of the Commission for Instruments and Methods of Observation, 1994, WMO-No. 807

The Expression of Uncertainty and Confidence in Measurement, M3003, 2nd edition, January, 2007, United Kingdom Accreditation Service (UKAS)

Comments on "A Statistical Determination of the Random Observational Errors Present in Voluntary Observing Ships' Meteorological Reports" N. Bruce Ingleby, Journal of Atmospheric and Oceanic Technology, Vol. 18, June 2001, p. 1102.

Reducing Station Pressure to Sea Level

See *Manual of Barometry WBAN.* This is the main reference.

Problems with the Mean Sea Level Pressure Field over the Western United States, Matthias Mohr, Monthly Weather Review, Vol 132, p. 1952-1965, August, 2004. An overview of the process and discussion of the Plateau Correction.

An Example of Uncertainty in Sea Level Pressure Reduction, Patricia M. Pauley, Journal of the American Meteorological Society, Volume 13, Issue 3, September 1998.

Surface Pressure Analyses: Clearing the Confusion In the Presence of Differing Solutions, Brian Klimowski, Rapid City, SD, NWS, www.crh.noaa.gov/unr/?n=mslp

Mean Sea Level Pressure Reduction in Canada and the Correction for Plateau Effect and Local Lapse Rate Anomaly: Ferrel versus Bigelow, Christopher A. Hampel, American Meteorological Society's 13th Conference on Integrated Observing and Assimilation Systems for Atmosphere, Oceans, and Land Surface (IOAS-AOLS), Jan 10 - 15, 2009, paper P2-14. A very nice presentation of the parameterization of the Plateau Corrections across Canada. Online at http://ams.confex.com/ams/pdfpapers/148573.pdf

Altimetry

See *Manual of Barometry WBAN*. This is the main reference.

Air Navigation, HO Pub. 216, US Gov. Printing Office, 1955. Has in depth coverage of altimetry and pressure pattern navigation.

Dilution Of Precision Revisited, Dennis Milbert, Navigation: Journal of The Institute of Navigation. Vol. 55, No. 1, Spring 2008. Compares vertical and horizontal GPS accuracy.

Exploring the Ocean Basins with Satellite Altimeter Data by David T. Sandwell and Walter H. F. Smith. www.ngdc.noaa.gov/mgg/bathymetry/predicted/explore.HTML.

Geoid and its Geophysical Interpretations, Petr Vaníek, Nikolaos T. Christou, CRC Press, 1993. Includes explanations and examples of the perturbations of the level of the sea surface.

Miscellaneous

Storm Surge and Inverse Barometer Effect in New Zealand, www.niwascience.co.nz/services/free/sealevels/tararu. Daily plots showing total storm surge (deviation from predicted tides) throughout New Zealand and computed IBE to show how much of the surge is due to pressure.

Weather and Air Pollution as Triggers of Severe Headaches, Kenneth J. Mukamal, Gregory A. Wellenius, Helen H. Suh, and Murray A. Mittleman, Neurology, Vol 27, March, 2009, p. 922-927. Most of the news media presentations of this work do not include the details or how to interpret the statistical results.

Water Vapor in the Climate System, Special Report of the American Geophysical Union, December 1995, www.agu.org. A topic of GPS meterology.

How to Detect Low Frequency Acoustic Waves in the Atmosphere, Stephen P. Hansen, The Bell Jar, 1996, Vol. 5, No. 4, Autumn, 1996. Online at www.belljar.net/microbar.htm.

Air Pressure Waves From Mount St. Helens Eruptions, Jack W. Reed, Journal of Geophysical Research, Vol. 92, No. D10, p. 11,979-11,992, Oct. 20, 1987.

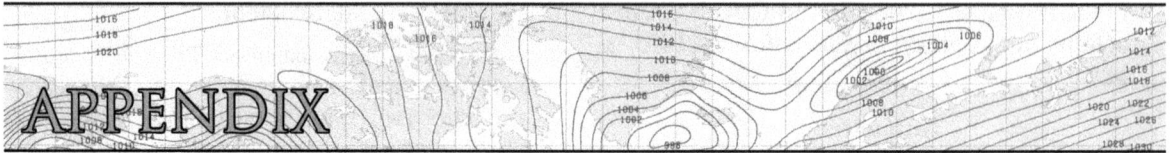

APPENDIX

A1. Pressure conversions (inches and millibars)

A2. Standard Atmosphere

A3. Reducing Station Pressure to Sea Level Pressure

A4. Using Spreadsheet Software for Calibration Analysis

A5. Forecasts using Pressure and Wind

A6. Density Altitude

A1. Inches of Mercury to Millibar Conversion Table

in	mb	in	mb	in	mb	in	mb	in	mb	in	mb	in	mb
28.40	961.8	28.81	975.7	29.22	989.5	29.63	1003.4	30.04	1017.3	30.45	1031.2	30.86	1045.1
28.41	962.1	28.82	976.0	29.23	989.9	29.64	1003.8	30.05	1017.7	30.46	1031.5	30.87	1045.4
28.42	962.5	28.83	976.3	29.24	990.2	29.65	1004.1	30.06	1018.0	30.47	1031.9	30.88	1045.8
28.43	962.8	28.84	976.7	29.25	990.6	29.66	1004.4	30.07	1018.3	30.48	1032.2	30.89	1046.1
28.44	963.1	28.85	977.0	29.26	990.9	29.67	1004.8	30.08	1018.7	30.49	1032.6	30.90	1046.4
28.45	963.5	28.86	977.4	29.27	991.2	29.68	1005.1	30.09	1019.0	30.50	1032.9	30.91	1046.8
28.46	963.8	28.87	977.7	29.28	991.6	29.69	1005.5	30.10	1019.3	30.51	1033.2	30.92	1047.1
28.47	964.1	28.88	978.0	29.29	991.9	29.70	1005.8	30.11	1019.7	30.52	1033.6	30.93	1047.5
28.48	964.5	28.89	978.4	29.30	992.3	29.71	1006.1	30.12	1020.0	30.53	1033.9	30.94	1047.8
28.49	964.8	28.90	978.7	29.31	992.6	29.72	1006.5	30.13	1020.4	30.54	1034.2	30.95	1048.1
28.50	965.2	28.91	979.0	29.32	992.9	29.73	1006.8	30.14	1020.7	30.55	1034.6	30.96	1048.5
28.51	965.5	28.92	979.4	29.33	993.3	29.74	1007.2	30.15	1021.0	30.56	1034.9	30.97	1048.8
28.52	965.8	28.93	979.7	29.34	993.6	29.75	1007.5	30.16	1021.4	30.57	1035.3	30.98	1049.1
28.53	966.2	28.94	980.1	29.35	993.9	29.76	1007.8	30.17	1021.7	30.58	1035.6	30.99	1049.5
28.54	966.5	28.95	980.4	29.36	994.3	29.77	1008.2	30.18	1022.1	30.59	1035.9	31.00	1049.8
28.55	966.9	28.96	980.7	29.37	994.6	29.78	1008.5	30.19	1022.4	30.60	1036.3	31.01	1050.2
28.56	967.2	28.97	981.1	29.38	995.0	29.79	1008.8	30.20	1022.7	30.61	1036.6	31.02	1050.5
28.57	967.5	28.98	981.4	29.39	995.3	29.80	1009.2	30.21	1023.1	30.62	1037.0	31.03	1050.8
28.58	967.9	28.99	981.8	29.40	995.6	29.81	1009.5	30.22	1023.4	30.63	1037.3	31.04	1051.2
28.59	968.2	29.00	982.1	29.41	996.0	29.82	1009.9	30.23	1023.7	30.64	1037.6	31.05	1051.5
28.60	968.5	29.01	982.4	29.42	996.3	29.83	1010.2	30.24	1024.1	30.65	1038.0	31.06	1051.9
28.61	968.9	29.02	982.8	29.43	996.7	29.84	1010.5	30.25	1024.4	30.66	1038.3	31.07	1052.2
28.62	969.2	29.03	983.1	29.44	997.0	29.85	1010.9	30.26	1024.8	30.67	1038.6	31.08	1052.5
28.63	969.6	29.04	983.4	29.45	997.3	29.86	1011.2	30.27	1025.1	30.68	1039.0	31.09	1052.9
28.64	969.9	29.05	983.8	29.46	997.7	29.87	1011.6	30.28	1025.4	30.69	1039.3	31.10	1053.2
28.65	970.2	29.06	984.1	29.47	998.0	29.88	1011.9	30.29	1025.8	30.70	1039.7	31.11	1053.5
28.66	970.6	29.07	984.5	29.48	998.3	29.89	1012.2	30.30	1026.1	30.71	1040.0	31.12	1053.9
28.67	970.9	29.08	984.8	29.49	998.7	29.90	1012.6	30.31	1026.5	30.72	1040.3	31.13	1054.2
28.68	971.3	29.09	985.1	29.50	999.0	29.91	1012.9	30.32	1026.8	30.73	1040.7	31.14	1054.6
28.69	971.6	29.10	985.5	29.51	999.4	29.92	1013.2	30.33	1027.1	30.74	1041.0	31.15	1054.9
28.70	971.9	29.11	985.8	29.52	999.7	29.93	1013.6	30.34	1027.5	30.75	1041.4	31.16	1055.2
28.71	972.3	29.12	986.2	29.53	1000.0	29.94	1013.9	30.35	1027.8	30.76	1041.7	31.17	1055.6
28.72	972.6	29.13	986.5	29.54	1000.4	29.95	1014.3	30.36	1028.2	30.77	1042.0	31.18	1055.9
28.73	973.0	29.14	986.8	29.55	1000.7	29.96	1014.6	30.37	1028.5	30.78	1042.4	31.19	1056.3
28.74	973.3	29.15	987.2	29.56	1001.1	29.97	1014.9	30.38	1028.8	30.79	1042.7	31.20	1056.6
28.75	973.6	29.16	987.5	29.57	1001.4	29.98	1015.3	30.39	1029.2	30.80	1043.1	31.21	1056.9
28.76	974.0	29.17	987.9	29.58	1001.7	29.99	1015.6	30.40	1029.5	30.81	1043.4	31.22	1057.3
28.77	974.3	29.18	988.2	29.59	1002.1	30.00	1016.0	30.41	1029.8	30.82	1043.7	31.23	1057.6
28.78	974.6	29.19	988.5	29.60	1002.4	30.01	1016.3	30.42	1030.2	30.83	1044.1	31.24	1058.0
28.79	975.0	29.20	988.9	29.61	1002.8	30.02	1016.6	30.43	1030.5	30.84	1044.4	31.25	1058.3
28.80	975.3	29.21	989.2	29.62	1003.1	30.03	1017.0	30.44	1030.9	30.85	1044.7	31.26	1058.6

A2a. Standard Atmosphere — Pressure and Temperature vs. Altitude

Feet	Meters	Pa/Po	Pa	Po-Pa	Ta F°	Ta C°	Feet	Meters	Pa/Po	Pa	Po-Pa	Ta F°	Ta C°
0	0	1.0000	1013.3	0.0	59.0	15.0	1200	366	0.9574	970.1	43.2	54.7	12.6
5	2	0.9998	1013.1	0.2	59.0	15.0	1250	381	0.9556	968.3	44.9	54.6	12.5
10	3	0.9996	1012.9	0.4	59.0	15.0	1300	396	0.9539	966.5	46.7	54.4	12.4
20	6	0.9993	1012.5	0.7	58.9	15.0	1350	411	0.9522	964.8	48.5	54.2	12.3
30	9	0.9989	1012.2	1.1	58.9	14.9	1400	427	0.9504	963.0	50.2	54.0	12.2
40	12	0.9986	1011.8	1.5	58.9	14.9	1450	442	0.9487	961.3	52.0	53.8	12.1
50	15	0.9982	1011.4	1.8	58.8	14.9	1500	457	0.9470	959.5	53.7	53.7	12.0
75	23	0.9973	1010.5	2.7	58.7	14.9	1600	488	0.9435	956.0	57.2	53.3	11.8
100	30	0.9964	1009.6	3.7	58.6	14.8	1700	518	0.9401	952.5	60.7	52.9	11.6
150	46	0.9946	1007.8	5.5	58.5	14.7	1800	549	0.9366	949.1	64.2	52.6	11.4
200	61	0.9928	1005.9	7.3	58.3	14.6	1900	579	0.9332	945.6	67.7	52.2	11.2
250	76	0.9910	1004.1	9.1	58.1	14.5	2000	610	0.9298	942.1	71.1	51.9	11.0
300	91	0.9892	1002.3	10.9	57.9	14.4	3000	914	0.8962	908.1	105.1	48.3	9.1
350	107	0.9874	1000.5	12.8	57.8	14.3	4000	1219	0.8637	875.1	138.1	44.8	7.1
400	122	0.9856	998.7	14.6	57.6	14.2	5000	1524	0.8320	843.1	170.2	41.2	5.1
450	137	0.9838	996.9	16.4	57.4	14.1	6000	1829	0.8014	812.0	201.3	37.6	3.1
500	152	0.9821	995.1	18.2	57.2	14.0	7000	2134	0.7716	781.9	231.4	34.1	1.1
550	168	0.9803	993.3	20.0	57.0	13.9	8000	2438	0.7428	752.6	260.6	30.5	-0.8
600	183	0.9785	991.5	21.8	56.9	13.8	9000	2743	0.7148	724.3	289.0	27.0	-2.8
650	198	0.9767	989.7	23.6	56.7	13.7	10000	3048	0.6877	696.8	316.4	23.4	-4.8
700	213	0.9750	987.9	25.4	56.5	13.6	11000	3353	0.6614	670.2	343.1	19.8	-6.8
750	229	0.9732	986.1	27.2	56.3	13.5	12000	3658	0.6360	644.4	368.8	16.3	-8.8
800	244	0.9714	984.3	29.0	56.2	13.4	13000	3962	0.6113	619.4	393.8	12.7	-10.7
850	259	0.9697	982.5	30.7	56.0	13.3	14000	4267	0.5875	595.2	418.0	9.2	-12.7
900	274	0.9679	980.7	32.5	55.8	13.2	15000	4572	0.5643	571.8	441.4	5.6	-14.7
950	290	0.9661	978.9	34.3	55.6	13.1	16000	4877	0.5420	549.2	464.1	2.0	-16.7
1000	305	0.9644	977.2	36.1	55.4	13.0	17000	5182	0.5203	527.2	486.0	-1.5	-18.7
1050	320	0.9626	975.4	37.9	55.3	12.9	18000	5486	0.4994	506.0	507.3	-5.1	-20.6
1100	335	0.9609	973.6	39.6	55.1	12.8	19000	5791	0.4791	485.5	527.8	-8.6	-22.6
1150	351	0.9591	971.8	41.4	54.9	12.7	20000	6096	0.4595	465.6	547.6	-12.2	-24.6

The standard atmosphere has a surface temperature of 59° F (15° C) and a lapse rate of minus 3.56°F/1000 ft (1.98°C/1000 ft). The standard surface pressure is 1013.25 mb and the pressure drops at a rate that can be computed from Pa = Po [1 - (6.87535*H/1,000,000)]^5.2561, where Pa is the pressure at altitude H (given in feet), and Po is the base or surface pressure, 1013.25 mb. The notation x^y means x raised to the power of y.

If you live at an elevation of 1100 feet, your pressure will read 39.6 mb lower than reported at sea level if your barometer is properly calibrated. If the barometer in your boat is 10 feet above sea level, your barometer reads 0.4 mb lower than it should if not corrected to sea level.

To record barometer offsets for calibration at some elevation (say 1,100 feet), record the time and date of your observation and your barometer reading (say 953.6 mb), along with the proper sea-level pressure at your location for that time obtained by interpolating Internet data (say it is 990.0 mb). Then compute the expected pressure at your elevation if the barometer were exact (Pa/Po x your reading), which in this example would be 0.9609 x 990.0 = 951.3 mb, so we see that our barometer reads too high by 953.6 - 951.3 = 2.3 mb at an instrument pressure of 953.6 mb.

A2b. Standard Atmosphere — Density and Boiling Points

Feet	Meters	Pressure in Hg	Density relative	Boiling Point °F	Air Temp F°	Feet	Meters	Pressure in Hg	Density relative	Boiling Point °F	Air Temp F°
0	0	29.92	1.000	212.0	59.0	1200	366	28.65	0.965	209.9	54.7
5	2	29.92	1.000	212.0	59.0	1250	381	28.59	0.964	209.8	54.6
10	3	29.91	1.000	212.0	59.0	1300	396	28.54	0.963	209.7	54.4
20	6	29.90	0.999	212.0	58.9	1350	411	28.49	0.961	209.6	54.2
30	9	29.89	0.999	212.0	58.9	1400	427	28.44	0.960	209.5	54.0
40	12	29.88	0.999	211.9	58.9	1450	442	28.39	0.958	209.4	53.8
50	15	29.87	0.999	211.9	58.8	1500	457	28.33	0.957	209.3	53.7
75	23	29.84	0.998	211.9	58.7	1600	488	28.23	0.954	209.1	53.3
100	30	29.81	0.997	211.8	58.6	1700	518	28.13	0.951	209.0	52.9
150	46	29.76	0.996	211.7	58.5	1800	549	28.02	0.948	208.8	52.6
200	61	29.70	0.994	211.7	58.3	1900	579	27.92	0.946	208.6	52.2
250	76	29.65	0.993	211.6	58.1	2000	610	27.82	0.943	208.4	51.9
300	91	29.60	0.991	211.5	57.9	3000	914	26.82	0.915	206.6	48.3
350	107	29.54	0.990	211.4	57.8	4000	1219	25.84	0.888	204.8	44.8
400	122	29.49	0.988	211.3	57.6	5000	1524	24.89	0.862	203.0	41.2
450	137	29.44	0.987	211.2	57.4	6000	1829	23.98	0.836	201.1	37.6
500	152	29.38	0.985	211.1	57.2	7000	2134	23.09	0.811	199.3	34.1
550	168	29.33	0.984	211.0	57.0	8000	2438	22.22	0.786	197.4	30.5
600	183	29.28	0.983	210.9	56.9	9000	2743	21.39	0.762	195.5	27.0
650	198	29.22	0.981	210.8	56.7	10000	3048	20.58	0.738	193.6	23.4
700	213	29.17	0.980	210.8	56.5	11000	3353	19.79	0.716	191.7	19.8
750	229	29.12	0.978	210.7	56.3	12000	3658	19.03	0.693	189.8	16.3
800	244	29.07	0.977	210.6	56.2	13000	3962	18.29	0.671	187.8	12.7
850	259	29.01	0.975	210.5	56.0	14000	4267	17.58	0.650	185.9	9.2
900	274	28.96	0.974	210.4	55.8	15000	4572	16.89	0.629	183.9	5.6
950	290	28.91	0.972	210.3	55.6	16000	4877	16.22	0.609	181.9	2.0
1000	305	28.85	0.971	210.2	55.4	17000	5182	15.57	0.589	179.9	-1.5
1050	320	28.80	0.970	210.1	55.3	18000	5486	14.94	0.570	177.9	-5.1
1100	335	28.75	0.968	210.0	55.1	19000	5791	14.34	0.551	175.8	-8.6
1150	351	28.70	0.967	210.0	54.9	20000	6096	13.75	0.533	173.8	-12.2

The International Standard air density at 15°C at 1013.25 mb and Relative Humidity = 0 is 1.225 kg/m^3.

The air density of moist air can be calculated from: saturated vapor pressure (in mb)

$SVP = 6.1121*exp^{[17.67*T/(T+243.5)]}$, where T = air temperature in °C, and the actual vapor pressure,

$VP = RH*SVP/100$, RH is the relative humidity. Next find the mixing ratio

$XM = 0.622*VP/(P-VP)$, where P is the pressure in mb.

Then from that find the air density,

$RHO = [P*(1+XM)]/[0.28703*(T+273.16)*(1+1.16078*XM)]$.

A3. Reducing Station Pressure to Sea-Level Pressure

Recalling that the vertical rate of pressure change is always thousands of times higher than the horizontal rate that creates the wind and weather we care about, it is easy to see that observed pressures at various elevations must be carefully normalized to sea level if we are to learn about the true pressure pattern at hand.

In this section we outline how meteorologists determine sea-level pressures from the reports they receive from varying elevations. We do not have call to do this ourselves very often, but the procedures are here if you care to. To be more precise, this is how meteorologists used to do it, based on procedures specified in detail in the Manual of Barometry (WBAN). These procedures give some insight into the physical factors that contribute to the reduction, but in practice today they use a much more empirical method, covered at the end of this section.

Step one is to clarify the concept of sea-level pressure at, for example, a high plateau located inland, far from the sea—or even far from anywhere whose elevation might be near sea level. This is certainly an abstract concept, but one that is needed to normalize the observations.

The procedure is to imagine a large hole in the ground at the elevated station that reaches down to sea level. Then the question reduces to estimating what the pressure would be at the bottom of this hole based on the pressure we read at the elevated station level, along with the temperature and dew point of the air at the station level.

We know the weight of the air from the station level on up to the top of the atmosphere. That is just the station pressure we observe. So the problem reduces to figuring out how much the fictitious air column weighs in the fictitious hole.

An easy way to approximate the answer is to assume the air in the hole behaves exactly like the International Standard Atmosphere (ISA). Then we can just go to Table A2 and look up the answer. For example, consider being at an elevation of 1,200 feet above sea level. From Table A2 we see that this elevation corresponds to a pressure drop of 43.2 mb in the standard atmosphere. So if our actual station pressure were 985.5 mb, we would estimate that the pressure at sea level was 985.5 + 43.2 = 1028.7 mb.

This approximation assumes the air in the hole has exactly the average properties of the standard atmosphere. This is unlikely to be true, and we could even know this ahead of time by comparing the station pressure and temperature with the standard atmosphere values at our elevation. We can improve on this ISA approximation significantly, but it takes some number crunching to do so.

The weight of the air in the hole depends on the density of the air, which in turn depends on the average temperature of the air column as well as the moisture content—the ISA assumes dry air (relative humidity = 0%). For a better estimate of the weight of the air column, we need a better estimate of the average temperature of the air column. A complicating factor is the amount of water vapor in the air. This not only changes the density of the air directly, it also affects how the temperature changes with increasing elevation.

The standard way to simplify these calculations is to define the "virtual temperature" (T_V) of moist air as the temperature that dry air must have in order to

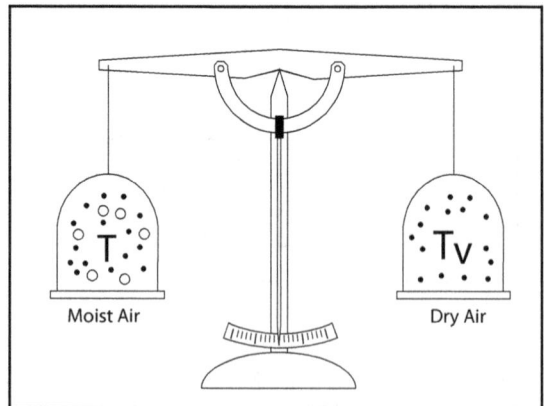

Figure A3-1. *The virtual temperature T_V of a moist air parcel is the temperature that dry air must have in order to achieve the same density and pressure as a sample of moist air. Since moist air is always lighter than dry air, Tv will always be somewhat higher than T. In this schematic, the two same volumes of air have the same mass and pressure. One is dry at temperature T_V; the other contains moisture at temperature T.*

produce the same pressure and density the moist air has. The definition is illustrated in Figure A3-1.

We can then study the properties of a column of moist air as if it were dry air by replacing the average temperature with an average T_v. The formula for Tv depends on the station temperature, pressure, and dew point. In principle, each equation in Chapter 9 on altimetry that contains a T, should have that T replaced with T_v for the most accurate results. We will calculate this T_v in a moment, but first a more basic practical matter.

We will need a measurement of the station pressure if we are to find the sea-level pressure. If you have actually measured the station pressure yourself, then you are done. That is the one you will use. But if you are testing this procedure of reducing station pressure to sea-level pressure by analyzing data from another location, you still need the station pressure at that location, but you will soon learn that information may not be available. With the exception mentioned at the end of this section, station pressures are rarely reported. What they do, instead, is automatically reduce the station pressures to sea-level pressures and report those. All airport reports, however, always compute the altimeter setting, discussed in Chapter 9. The reports are called "Metars," derived from a French phrase meaning weather reports from airports.

Altimeter setting, by definition, depends only on the station pressure and elevation of the station, so we can unfold the altimeter setting (AS) to get the station pressure (Ps) we need from the equation:

$$Ps = [AS^{0.1903} - (1.313 \times 10^{-5}) \times H]^{5.255},$$

where H is the station elevation in feet. This is the hypsometric equation with the temperature replaced with the ISA lapse rate. AS is given in inches of mercury, so Ps will be inches of mercury as well, but we can convert to mb as:

$$Ps \text{ (mb)} = 33.864 \times Ps \text{ (inches)}$$

The above two equations are not from the WBAN procedures, but taken directly from NWS computer code. I apologize for the mixed units necessary if we use the exact equations presented in both methods.

Once we have the station pressure, we can proceed with the WBAN procedure by computing the virtual temperature of the air. Start with finding the vapor pressure of the air (e) in mb from:

$$e = 6.11 \times 10^E$$

where e is in mb,

$$E = 7.5 \times T_d / (237.7 + T_d),$$

and T_d is the dew point of the station air in °C. Then we can find T_v in °K from:

$$T_v = (Ts + 273.15)/[1 - 0.379 \times (e/Ps)]$$

where e and Ps are in mb, and Ts is the station air temperature in °C. The factor of 0.379 is the ratio of molecular weights of water to air.

The Ts, as always, takes special care. It is the temperature of the air at the station elevation, but not at the time the station pressure was measured. This Ts should be the average of the temperature at the time of the pressure measurement and the temperature at the station 12 hours earlier. Add the two and divide by 2. It has been found over the years that this accounts for the small, but detectable diurnal variation of the pressure (Table 5.6-1). This whole process is an attempt to do the best at a difficult task, so every factor counts.

Once we have T_v at the station level, we need to figure the average T_v in the fictitious air column. At this point we fall back on the ISA for an estimate of how the temperature changes in the fictitious air column. To find the *mean* virtual temperature (T_{mv}) in °K use the ISA lapse rate to get:

$$T_{mv} = T_v + [273.15 + 0.0065 \times (H/2)].$$

Now we rewrite the hypsometric equation from Chapter 9 for the sea-level pressure P1 = Psl, P2 = Ps, with Z1=0 and Z2 = H = height of the station in meters as:

$$Psl = r \times Ps,$$

where

$$r = \exp[H / (29.28980 \times T_{mv})].$$

r is a fraction with no units, called the "pressure reduction ratio." H must be in meters and T_{mv} in °K. Recall °K = °C + 273.15°.

This can be thought of as the basic solution. As an example, check data from Table A2, such as H = 600 m, Ts = 11°C (in dry air T_v=Ts), with Ps = 942.1 mb. Then you should find that Psl = 1013.25 mb, since we used the ISA values. Change Tv to 2°C to get 1015.6 mb or use 20°C to get 1011.0 mb. If you assume the relative humidity of that 20°C air is 75%, then the dew point is 15.4°C, and this will yield T_v = 22.1°C, which in turn would imply Psl = 1010.5 mb. The humidity correction is more important in warm air than in cold.

This basic solution is the one generally used for stations below 50 meters elevation in the WBAN procedure. For higher stations two more corrections are made. First the height H is converted to a *geopotential height* (H_{gp}), because the weight of the air depends on gravity, and the strength of the gravitational force varies with latitude and with elevation. This is a very small effect, but it can adjust a high elevation by several meters, which could have an effect on the pressure that is larger than what the humidity does. Samples of geopotential corrections are given in Table A3-1. It is made up of two terms. The latitude factor increase H with increasing latitude, whereas the elevation factor decreases it with increasing elevation.

Finally there is what is called the "Plateau Correction" to the temperature, which can be a significant correction of up to 10°C or more to T_v, leading to large changes in Psl for high elevations in extreme temperatures. The correction was first proposed by William Ferrel in 1886, which is more evidence of his genius. His reasoning and reckoning still apply today, though there have been improvements to this overall process since then.

Ferrel noted that average summertime sea-level pressures deduced at high elevations were too low, and average wintertime sea-level pressures were too high, compared to averages from around the country determined at lower elevations. When deduced at high elevations, the summer-winter difference in average sea-level pressures was about 10 mb higher than from stations closer to sea level. In other words, he noted an effect that was obviously caused by the land within a process that was supposed to remove the effects of land. And so a correction was called for.

He concluded that the effective lapse rate must be different when the high land is present from what it would be if the land were removed. In short, the practice of using the ISA lapse rate for the fictitious air column was not right, and the seasonal average sea-level pressure differences gave him a way to estimate a correction.

He formulated his correction to be applied to the sea-level pressure itself as:

Correction (mb) = 0.064 (Ts-Tn) (H/1,000),

where H is elevation in feet, Ts is the station temperature, and Tn is the annual average temperature at the station, both in °C. Thus an air temperature that is 20°C higher than the average temperature at an elevation of 5,000 ft would add 6.4 mb to the sea-level pressures. This correction smooths out the seasonal differences seen in average sea-level pressures across the land.

By 1900 it was recognized that this correction could be improved by reformulating it in terms of adjustments to the lapse rate itself, yielding a more accurate mean virtual temperature. In modern times, each weather station over 50 meters high reporting sea-level pressures has its own Plateau Correction factor it uses to optimize the reduction to sea level. Samples are presented in Table A3-2 for sta-

Table A3-1 Selected Geopotential Heights, H_{gpm} (meters)*						
Elevation		Latitude				
feet	meters	0°	30°	45°	60°	75°
984	300	299.4	299.8	300.2	300.6	300.9
1968	600	598.7	599.5	600.3	601.1	601.7
3937	1200	1197.4	1198.9	1200.5	1202.1	1203.3
5905	1800	1795.9	1798.2	1800.6	1803.0	1804.7
7874	2400	2394.3	2397.4	2400.6	2403.8	2406.1
9842	3000	2992.6	2996.5	3000.5	3004.4	3007.3

* From: H_{gpm} = (g/9.8)xH - 0.0000001574xH^2
where g = 9.80616x(1 - 0.0026373 cos(2Lat) + 0.0000059 cos^2(2Lat)

tions above and below 1,000 ft elevation.

The Plateau Correction is called F(s) as a reminder that it depends on the station. It is applied to T_{mv} as:

$$T_{mv} \longrightarrow T_{mv} + F(s).$$

Ferrel had developed one of the first ways to decide if the "sea-level pressures" over elevated lands were correct. He also looked, as others did and still do, at neighboring stations that might be at lower elevations to compare their sea-level results to seek a uniform flow of the sea-level isobars.

Another evaluation used today is to plot out the sea level isobars predicted by the sum of all the station reports, and then compare the wind speeds and directions they predict with what is actually observed. In one sense, this is the ultimate test. We want the isobars so we can predict the wind, and if we do get isobars that predict the wind properly then we are doing a good job of measuring and deducing the isobars.

In modern meteorology there is still another crucial way to evaluate the reduction process and that is to compare the measured isobars with those pre-

dicted by any of several computerized atmospheric models. The models predict many properties of the atmosphere, at many levels of the atmosphere, not just at sea level. To the extent these other predicted properties agree with the observations, we want the predicted isobars to agree with observations as well.

If a model, for example, reproduced the isobars and other properties of the atmosphere over low lands very well, but over high lands or steep slopes the predicted isobars did not agree, but still other predicted properties of the atmosphere did agree, then we could consider that maybe the model is right and the way we are deducing the isobars in these difficult regions is not yet optimized. In short, the interplay between model predictions and deduced sea-level pressures is yet another way to evaluate the process, and one that is actively pursued at present.

Figure A3-2 (on the next page) shows samples of how the station pressure reduction constants might be evaluated with model computations to get the most useful set of sea level isobars.

Table A3-2 Sample Plateau Correction* F(s) in °F								
		Station Temperature °F						
		-20	0	20	40	60	80	100
Annual normal temperature °F		*For Elevations BELOW 1,000 feet*						
45		24.9	18.6	11.1	2.4	-7.6	-18.8	-31.1
50		26.9	20.7	13.4	4.7	-5.1	-16.2	-28.4
55		29.0	22.9	15.7	7.2	-2.5	-13.6	-25.7
60		31. 0	25.1	18.0	9.6	0.0	-10.9	-23.0
65		33.1	27.3	20.3	12.1	2.6	-8.2	-20.3
Station	*Elevation*	*For Elevations ABOVE 1,000 feet*						
Greenville, SC	*1,040 ft*	31.2	25.3	17.9	9.7	0.4	-10.5	-22.6
Las Vegas, NV	*2,180 ft*	31.0	25.1	18.0	9.8	0.2	-10.6	-22.6
Redmond, OR	*3,084 ft*	24.6	19.2	11.4	2.5	-7.8	-19.2	-31.6
Green River, UT	*4,087 ft*	23.3	16.7	9.8	2.2	-7.0	-18.4	-31.2
Fort Apache, AZ	*5,004 ft*	26.2	20.0	12.8	4.9	-4.5	-15.6	-22.8
Colorado Springs, CO	*6,072 ft*	18.4	10.4	2.2	-4.7	-11.5	-22.5	-35.5

* These corrections are listed for selected then-active stations in the Manual of Barometry WBAN. *Fort Apache (Whiteriver Airport) is no longer a Metar reporting station.)*

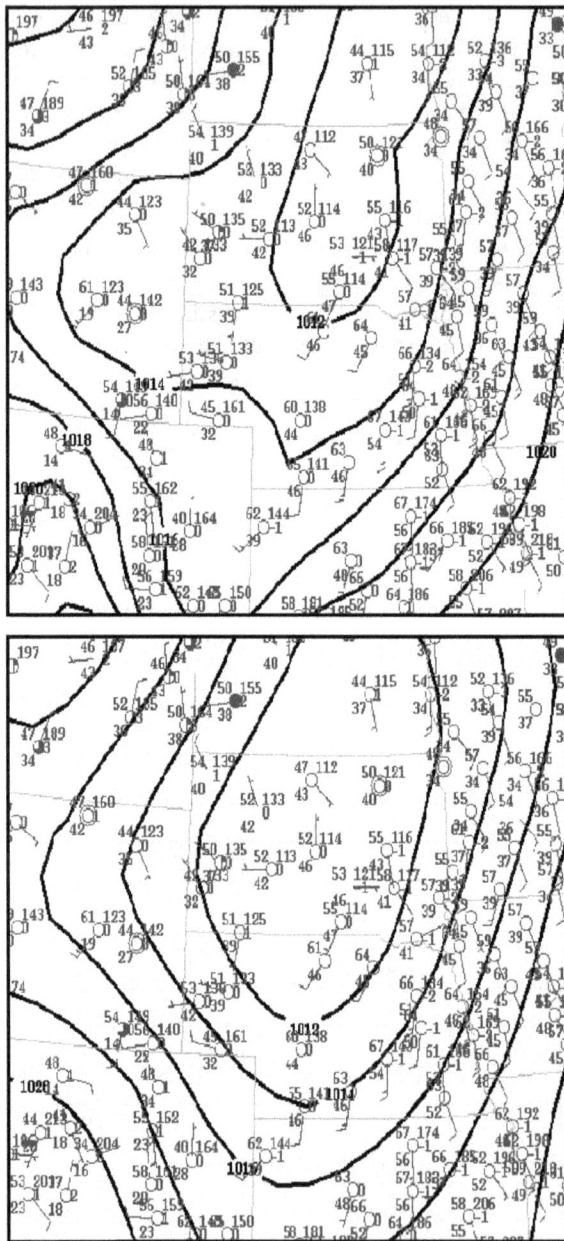

Figure A3-2. *Isobars on the top are the best fit to the actual station measurements shown on the map. The bottom shows isobar predictions from a computer model, which differ in several details. The extent the differences are due to reduction procedures is always under study. There are several competing models that might be used in this type of analysis to improve the reduction process. See www.crh.noaa.gov/unr/?n=mslp*

Sample Pressure Reduction

KCOS is Colorado Springs, CO, station elevation 6171 ft (1880.9 m), latitude = 38.8°N gave this Metar report: "101554Z AUTO 05005KT 10SM SCT020 OVC029 08/03 A3017 RMK AO2 SLP194 T00830028 TSNO. Observed 1554 UTC 10 May 2009, Temperature: 8.3°C (47°F), Dewpoint: 2.8°C (37°F) [RH = 68%], Pressure (altimeter): 30.17 inches Hg (1021.8 mb) [Sea-level pressure: 1019.4 mb]"

The question is, how did they get the reported sea-level pressure of 1019.4?

WBAN Procedure

Step (1). Find the reported station temperature from 12h earlier, which is: Observed 0354 UTC 10 May 2009, Temperature: 9.4°C (49°F), and from this figure the average station temperature. Ts = (9.4+8.3)/2 = 8.9°C = 48°F.

Step (2). From the altimeter setting (30.17) and elevation (6171 ft), find the station pressure Ps = 24.03" = 813.8 mb.

Step (3). From Ps (813.8 mb), Ts (8.9°C), and Td (2.8°C), find virtual temperature T_v = 9.8°C = 283.0°K

Step (4). From H = 1880.9 m (6171 ft) at Lat = 38.8 N and Table A3-1, find geopotential height Hgpm = 1880.5 m.

Step (5). From Hgpm (1880.5 m), T_v (9.8°C) find mean virtual temperature T_{mv} = 15.9°C = 289.1°K

Step (6). From Ts (8.9°C = 48°F) and interpolation of Table A3-2, find Plateau Correction F(s) = -7.4 F° = -7.4 x (5/9) = -4.1 C°. Note the correction is a temperature interval, not a temperature.

Step (7). From corrected T_{mv} (15.9 - 4.1 = 11.8°C) and H_{gpm} (1880.5m) find r = 1.2527, and using Ps = 813.8 we find Psl = 1019.4 mb.

This agrees with the Metar report, but the result is very sensitive to which values are rounded at which stage of the computation. Changes could lead to variations of ±0.2 mb. Multiple tests from various stations would have to be done to see how well this historic method compares to the modern method used in the U.S. NWS. Other nations use other procedures.

ASOS Procedure

Starting sometime around 1992, the NWS in collaboration with the Federal Aviation Administration and the Department of Defence initiated an Automated Surface Observations System (ASOS) to collect and distribute weather data around the country. The data are collected by high precision sensors and then evaluated and analyzed by software at the stations, which are then transmitted to the various agencies and made available to the public.

Atmospheric pressure measurements are of course a crucial part of the program. Each station includes multiple electronic pressure sensors, which are compared to each other continuously. From the measured pressure at known elevation, along with the temperature and dew point, the ASOS software computes: station pressure, pressure tendency, altimeter setting, sea-level pressure, density altitude, and pressure altitude.

The station pressure and altimeter setting are determined from the sensor pressures independently, but they are related as mentioned earlier. Since they are computed independently, you will find times when the equation given does not relate them exactly as they are published. You can find station pressures, altimeter settings, and sea-level pressures to practice with and compare at this link

http://www.wrh.noaa.gov/mesowest/getobext.
php?table=1&wfo=lox&sid=KCOS

by changing the last 4 letters to the Metar of interest. To find the closest Metar to your location you can use www.starpath.com/barometers, or go to the graphic map link at

http://www-frd.fsl.noaa.gov/mab/metar

and to find the specifications of the station (elevation, location, ID) go to

http://www.weather.gov/tg/siteloc.shtml.

The ASOS procedures have simplified the WBAN procedure significantly, and after crunching numbers with the latter procedure for some hours it is easy to appreciate the virtue of this approach. They no longer use mean virtual temperatures or plateau corrections, but instead simply define the sea level pressure as

$$Psl = Ps \times r + C,$$

where r is the pressure reduction ratio and C is the pressure reduction constant. A station will use either r or C, but not both. Typically stations below 100 ft would use C, in which case r = 1. C is then basically the ISA correction, perhaps adjusted to some extent for the location. It does not depend on temperature.

Higher stations use r values (C = 0) from a table of values stored in the local ASOS computer that are unique to that station. A sample for KCOS is shown in Table A3-3. Using this table, and Ts = 48 °F,

$$Psl = 813.8 \times 1.2526 = 1019.4 \text{ mb},$$

which is obviously easier to obtain than using the WBAN procedure—if we happen to know the official r factors. At least for now, these do not seem to be public information, so the WBAN method is the only guideline for making these reductions at arbitrary locations. Even with that, we must make some estimate of the Plateau Correction based on WBAN values.

Table A3-3 Pressure reduction factors for KCOS*							
Ts	r	Ts	r	Ts	r	Ts	r
-20	1.2792	10	1.2675	40	1.2558	70	1.2448
-19	1.2788	11	1.2671	41	1.2554	71	1.2445
-18	1.2784	12	1.2667	42	1.2550	72	1.2443
-17	1.2780	13	1.2664	43	1.2546	73	1.2440
-16	1.2776	14	1.2660	44	1.2542	74	1.2437
-15	1.2772	15	1.2656	45	1.2538	75	1.2435
-14	1.2768	16	1.2653	46	1.2534	76	1.2432
-13	1.2764	17	1.2649	47	1.2530	77	1.2429
-12	1.2760	18	1.2645	48	1.2526	78	1.2427
-11	1.2756	19	1.2642	49	1.2522	79	1.2424
-10	1.2752	20	1.2638	50	1.2518	80	1.2421
-9	1.2748	21	1.2634	51	1.2514	81	1.2419
-8	1.2744	22	1.2630	52	1.2510	82	1.2417

* Ts is the 12-h average temperature in °F at the surface. The full table runs from -40°F to 100°F. The elevation of the table data is listed as 6170 for location 38° 49'N, 104° 43'W. These values are unique to the Colorado Springs KCOS station.

A4. Using Spreadsheet Software for Calibration Analysis

A digital spreadsheet is just a page of columns of numbers with mathematical relations between them or derived from them. Popular PC spreadsheet programs include *Microsoft Excel* and *Open Office Calc* (a freeware product), among many others. For typical calibration applications, this process does not do anything we could not do by just writing the numbers in a notebook and computing the differences by hand, but if you do work with computers and have not used spreadsheets before, this is a good way to get started. It will save very much time and minimize mistakes in the calibration process, plus let you make graphic plots of the data that can be very informative.

Figure A4-1 shows a simple example. Beside the columns of times and dates, there are pressure observations from a home barometer and a column of the pressures at the same time from the NWS at a nearby station. The next column (E) can then be defined as the difference between D and C. It is important to define the correction as True minus Observed, so you end up with a correction you add to the Observed to get the True.

You can label the first row to be a header defining its contents, and you can move rows and columns around on the page and sort the data as you choose. In short, this is a very convenient way to accumulate and analyze your calibration measurements.

	A	B	C	D	E
1	Local Date	Local Time	Baro Reading	True Pressure	Correction
2	11/28/2008	1400.0	1015.0	1015.0	0.0
3	11/29/2008	1100.0	1018.5	1019.5	1.0
4	11/30/2008	1400.0	1017.0	1017.6	0.6
5	12/1/2008	1000.0	1008.4	1007.7	-0.7
6	12/1/2008	1700.0	1007.0	1005.7	-1.3
7	12/2/2008	1000.0	1010.0	1009.4	-0.6
8	12/2/2008	1200.0	1008.2	1007.0	-1.2
9	12/2/2008	1700.0	1005.3	1004.1	-1.2
10					
11					

Figure A4-1. *Sample calibration data entered into a spreadsheet program (Microsoft Excel). The contents of the E column are defined as the difference between the D column and the C column. Once a cell definition is made, it can be copied by dragging it onto the full column. The definition of the E4 cell shown here is listed in the fx line above. A similar spreadsheet program is available at no charge from www.openoffice.org.*

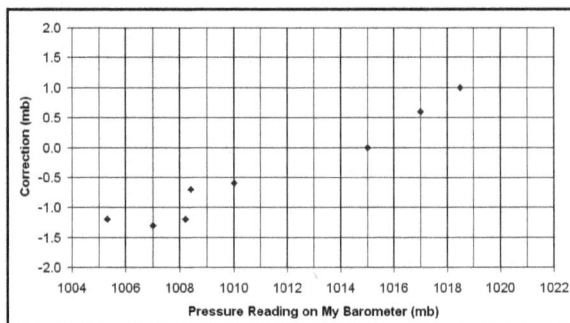

Figure A4-2. *Sample plot of a calibration curve made from a spreadsheet program. This one was made by selecting column E in Figure A4-1 and then clicking the chart icon. The scales can be customized to emphasize the data. Remember the horizontal scale must be your barometer reading (column C), not the true pressures. Once the chart is made, you can click any horizontal line to change the range of corrections shown, and likewise change the distribution of the vertical scale lines as well. Notice that the plot will put the data in the right sequence of increasing pressures, even though the measurements were recorded in a changing sequence.*

Appendix 5a. Weather Forecasting Table — Northern Hemisphere*		
BAROMETER AT SEA LEVEL	*WIND*	*CHARACTER OF WEATHER*
Rising		
1019 to 1023	Rising rapidly	SW to NW	Fair followed within 2 days by rain.
≤ 1016	Rising slowly	S to SW	Clearing within a few hours and fair for several days.
≤ 1009	Rising rapidly	Going to W	Clearing and colder
Steady		
≥ 1023	Steady	SW to NW	Continued fair with no decided temperature change.
1019 to 1023	Steady	SW to NW	Fair with slight temperature changes for 1 or 2 days.
Falling		
≥ 1023	Falling slowly	SW to NW	Slowly rising temperature and fair for 2 days.
≥ 1023	Falling slowly	E to NE	In summer with light winds, rain may not fall for several days. In winter, rain in 24 hours.
1019 to 1023	Falling slowly	S to SE	Rain within 24 hours.
1019 to 1023	Falling slowly	SE to NE	Rain in 12 to 18 hours.
1019 to 1023	Falling rapidly	S to SE	Wind increasing in force; rain within 12 to 24 hours.
1019 to 1023	Falling rapidly	SE to NE	Increasing wind and rain within 12 hours.
≥ 1019	Falling rapidly	E to NE	In summer, rain probably in 12 hours. In winter, rain or snow with increasing winds will often set in when the barometer begins to fall and the wind sets in from the NE
≤ 1016	Falling slowly	SE to NE	Rain will continue 1 or 2 days.
≤ 1016	Falling rapidly	SE to NE	Rain with high winds, followed within 36 hours by clearing and, in winter, colder temperatures.
≤ 1016	Falling rapidly	S to E	Severe storm imminent, followed within 24 hours by clearing and, in winter, colder temperatures.
≤ 1009	Falling rapidly	E to N	Severe NE gale and heavy rain; in winter, heavy snow followed by a cold wave.

Intended for midlatitudes of the Northern Hemisphere. Adapted and reorganized from U.S. Army Field Manual 55-501, Marine Crewman's Handbook, 1999.

Appendix 5b. Weather Forecasting Table — Southern Hemisphere*						
Rising Pressure				**Steady Pressure**		
Barometer	*Wind*	*Forecast*		*Barometer*	*Wind*	*Forecast*
> 1015	S, SW	Continued fair for 24 hours, slightly cooler		> 1015	S, SW	Continued fair for 48 hours
	W, NW	Continued fair for 12 hours			W, NW	Continued fair for 12 hours.
	N, NE	Fair weather			N, NE	Rain within 24-48 hours
	E, SE	Rain/showers at first, diminishing over next 18 hours, cooler; winds decreasing.			E, SE	Continued fair, cooler
				1010-1015	SW, W, NW	Fair for 1-2 days
1010-1015 (rapid rise)	SW, W, NW	Fair, followed by rain within 48 hours.			N	Rain within 18-24 hours
(normal rise)	SW	Fair for 48 hours, cooler by 3-5° C		1000-1010	SW	Continued (rainy) conditions
					W, NW	Fair for 12 hours
(normal rise)	W, NW	Fair for 48 hours, cooler by 2-4° C			N	Rain within 12-18 hours
(slow rise)	NW, N	Clearing within a few hours, then fair for days		1000-1015	NE	Rain within 12-18 hours, foggy in spring/early summer
(normal rise)	N, NE	Fair			E, SE, S	No change next 6-12 hours if a front has just passed, then rain/gales for 6-12 hours
	E, SE	Clear(ing) and cooler				
	S	Rain likely for 6-12 hours then clear(ing) and cooler		< 1000	S, SW	Continued (threatening?) weather, cooling by 3-5° C.
< 1000	S, SW	Clearing within a few hours, cooler by 3-6° C			W, NW	Continued (stormy) weather
	W, NW	Clearing within six hours			N, NE	Front coming with rain and a south to southwest wind change within six hours.
	N, NE	Clearing				
	E, SE	Clearing and cooler			E, SE	No change until pressure rises or falls

* For the midlatitudes of the Southern Hemisphere. Reproduced from "How to Read a Barometer" (metservice. com) by NZ MetService Weather Ambassador Bob McDavitt, author of the excellent book Mariner's Met Pack— Weather of the South West Pacific.

Appendix 5b. Weather Forecasting Table — Southern Hemisphere*

Falling Pressure			Falling Pressure (continued)		
Barometer	*Wind*	*Forecast*	*Barometer*	*Wind*	*Forecast*
> 1015	SW, W	Continued fair for 24 hours Slowly rising temperatures by 1-3° C.	1000-1010	SW	Fair for 12-24 hours
	NW	Fair for 6-12 hours, rising temperatures by 2-4° C		W	Continued fair for 12-15 hours, Then possible southerly
	N, NE	Rain within 18-24 hours, wind Increasing, temp rise by 1-3° C.		NW	Fair for 18-24 hours, front coming?
	SE, S	Rain within 24-48 hours		N, NE	Rain within 6-12 hours
1010-1015 (slow fall)	N, NE	Rain within 12-18 hours (or more rain) wind gradually increasing, perhaps foggy.		E	Wind increasing, rising minimum temperatures by 3-5° C.
(rapid fall)	N, NE	Strengthening winds, rain in 9-15 hours, or continued rain		SE, S	Rain within 12 hours but if front has just passed... and pressure is still falling. then rain and gales next 6-12 hours (in comma head).
(slow fall)	E	In summer, light winds, possibly DRY for several days. In winter, rain in 24 hours.	< 1000	SW, W	Fair for 6-9 hours with dry air, then possible southerly
(rapid fall)	E	In summer, rain probable within 12-24 hours. In winter, rain or snow, wind swinging southeasterly and then rising.		NW, N	Rain within six hours Winds reaching gale Minimum temps rising by 1-2° C
(slow fall)	SE	Rain within 12-18 hours, or continued rainy. Wind might increase.		NE, E	Rain within six hours
(rapid fall)	SE	Rain within 9-15 hours, wind increasing, followed within 36 hours by clearing. Conditions, then, if winter, frosty.		SE, S	Rain, or rain imminent. (snow in winter).

	Appendix 5C. Tips on Barometer Observations*
1	The rise of the mercury mostly indicates fair weather, but the falling of it unsettled weather, as sleet, rain, snow, hail, strong winds, and storms.
2	In sultry weather, when the mercury falls, lightning and thunder may be expected.
3	In the winter, the rising of the mercury indicates frost; however, should it fall 3 or 4-10ths of an inch (7 to 10 mb) during a frost, a thaw will certainly follow. But in continued frosty weather, should the mercury then rise, it will surely snow.
4	When soon after the falling of the mercury unsettled weather occurs, expect a short duration of it, when it proves fair shortly after the mercury has risen it will not be of long continuance.
5	In bad weather, when the mercury is in a rising state, continuing so for two or three days, a succession of fair weather may be expected.
6	In fair weather when the mercury is in a falling state, continuing so for the space of two or three days previous to rain, in such a case a great deal of falling (deteriorating) weather may be expected, accompanied probably with high winds.
7	Changeable weather, uncertain respecting its duration, is indicated by the unsettled state of the mercury.
8	During wet weather, when the mercury is in a rising state, an interval of fair weather may be expected soon to follow.
9	In very hot weather, the fall of the mercury indicates thunder.
10	The range of the barometer is greater in winter than in summer.
11	When the sun passes the meridian, the barometer, if in the act of falling, continues to fall, and the falling is accelerated.
12	When the sun passes the meridian, the barometer, if in the act of rising, falls, or becomes stationary, or rises more slowly.
13	When the sun passes the meridian, the barometer, which is stationary, falls, if it has not risen before, or after being stationary; in which case it usually becomes stationary during the sun's passage.
14	Northerly winds, almost invariably, raise the barometer, while southerly winds constantly depress it.
15	Great falls of the barometer are usually attended by a rise of temperature above the mean heat of the season; and a great rise of the barometer by a depression of temperature

* **Table Notes.** Selected and *adapted from* Ample Instructions for the Barometer and Thermometer, etc., *compiled by George Leoni, Instrument Maker, New York, 1841. These have been selected from a longer list of notes, and numbered here for the sake of reference—selected because they add some insights not mentioned or stressed elsewhere herein, or phrased in a different way. The word "mercury" and "barometer" are interchangeable in this reference. Again, there are no fixed rules that always work. These just give some idea of what might be expected.*

A6. Density Altitude

If the air temperature differs from that of the International Standard Atmosphere (ISA, Appendix 3) for your altitude, then the air density is higher or lower than expected. This graph is a way to figure the altitude that would normally have the density you have. The result depends on how much your air temperature differs from that expected in the ISA. For example: at 5,000 feet, you would expect an air temperature of 40°F (5°C), but if your actual air temperature were 70° F, the air density you have would be equivalent to that of about 6,800 ft.

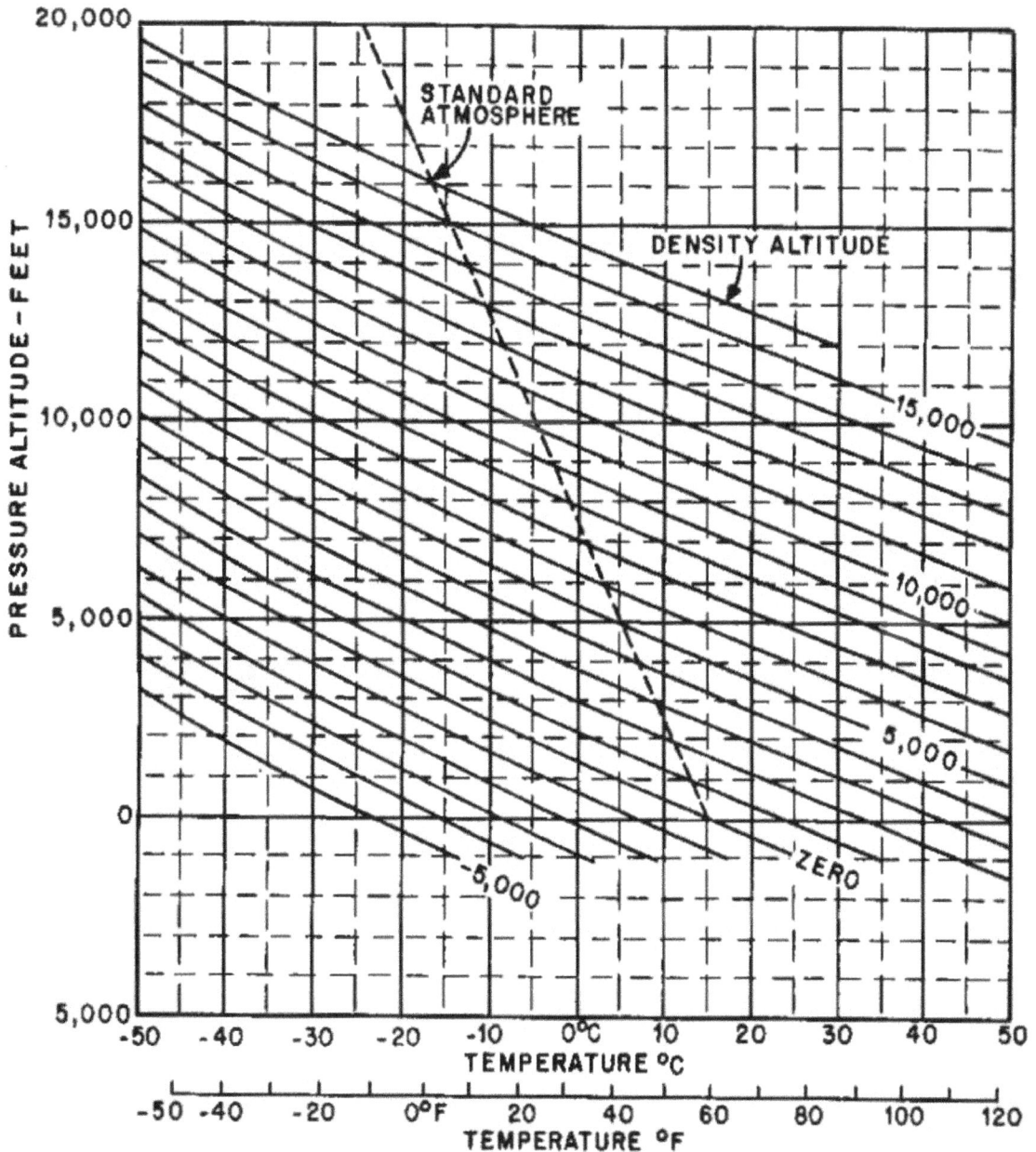

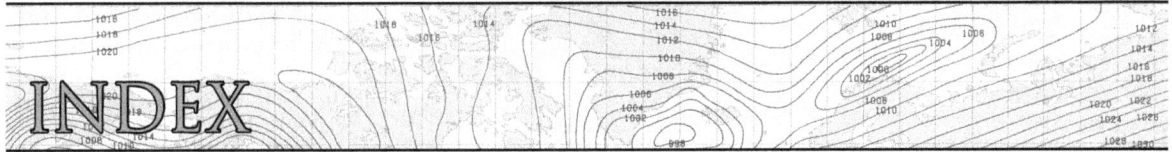

*Numbers in **bold** indicate pages with related tables or illustrations, or the term is mentioned in a caption.*

waves
    atmospheric, 21, 22
    effect on barometer reading, 136
    pressure waves, 123, 215
    ultrasonic, 62
WBAN. *See Manual of Barometry*
weather. *See* wind; rain; temperature;
    clouds; relative humidity; fore-
    casting; warning; *Modern Marine*
    Weather
weather maps. *See also* GRIB
    barometer indications, 94
    for calibration, 62, 72, 74, 78, 147
    history, 19-21
    isobar spacing, 23-24, 37, 74, 87
    850 mb, 152-153
    500 mb, 32, 105
    interpolate isobars, 78
    practical usage, 33-35
    pressure cross section, 18
    sources, 18, 67, 162
    symbols, 24, 27, 34
    surface analysis, 33-36, 78, 106-108, 162
    testing with barometer, 13, 103-107
    Unified Surface Analysis, 34, **36-37**
Weather Trainer (software), 73
weatherfax. *See* radiofacsimile
weather radio. *See* NOAA Weather Radio
westerlies, prevailing, 58, 161
Wheeler, Dave, 20
wind, surface. *See also* Buys Ballot Law
    barometer indications, 89, **90-91**,92-94, 230
    flow around Highs and Lows, **23-25**
    direction, 17, 19, 34, 87-89, 93-94, 103, 107
    map symbols, **24**
    shifts defined, **38**
    speed, 20, 87-89, 92, 107, 109, 114, 141, 223
    ship reports, **34**
    from isobars, 24, **87-88**
winds aloft 20, **90**
WMO (World Meteorological Organization), 13, 28, 50, 56, **64**, 66, 95-96, 125-127, 135, 162, 214
Wrinkles in Practical Navigation (Lecky), viii, 93

Y
Yanagi barometer, 129-130

Z
zulu time (i.e. 12z), 33. *See also* UTC; synoptic times

About the Author

David Burch is a recipient of the Institute of Navigation's Superior Achievement Award for outstanding performance as a practicing navigator. He has logged more than 70,000 miles at sea including twelve transoceanic yacht races, with several first place victories and a passage record for boats under 36 feet that lasted 16 years. He also navigated the only American entry in the storm-ridden 1993 Sydney to Hobart Race.

On the academic side, he is a past Fulbright Scholar with a PhD in Physics. He sailed as a research scientist on the NOAA Ship *Discoverer* in Alaska and Arctic waters. In the arena of weather analysis, he received a USCG citation for the successful prediction of the arrival date and location of a transoceanic kayaker who had been missing at sea for 51 days—an extensive exercise in evaluating archived, live, and forecasted data on wind, current, and sea state. In 2006 he provided the daily weather and navigation guidance to the first place finisher of the Transatlantic Rowing Race—the first rowers in recorded history to row across the North Atlantic and end up precisely at their intended destination (now in the *Guinness Book of World Records*).

He took an active part in discussions with the NWS and USCG in successfully defending the mariner's need to maintain the 96-hr forecast maps and more recently provided similar testimony for the successful defense of keeping the high seas HF broadcasts of both voice and radiofax weather data.

As the Founding Director of Starpath School of Navigation in Seattle and one of the lead instructors, he taught marine weather for more than 20 years. He continues to work on the development of online courses in marine weather and navigation at starpath.com.

Other books by David Burch

Radar for Mariners

Emergency Navigation

The Star Finder Book

Fundamentals of Kayak Navigation

Celestial Navigation

Inland and Coastal Navigation

Radar Workbook

Weather Workbook

Onboard Exercise Book

Practical Chart Problems

Modern Marine Weather

www.ingramcontent.com/pod-product-compliance
Lightning Source LLC
Chambersburg PA
CBHW080756300326
41914CB00055B/910